MW01133698

Social Work Ethics in a Changing Society

Social Work Ethics in a Changing Society

MICHAEL REISCH

University of Maryland – Baltimore

SAN DIEGO

Bassim Hamadeh, CEO and Publisher
Amy Smith, Senior Project Editor
Abbey Hastings, Production Editor
Jess Estrella, Senior Graphic Designer
Stephanie Kohl, Licensing Coordinator
Natalie Piccotti, Director of Marketing
Kassie Graves, Vice President of Editorial
Jamie Giganti, Director of Academic Publishing

Copyright © 2021 by Cognella, Inc. All rights reserved. No part of this publication may be reprinted, reproduced, transmitted, or utilized in any form or by any electronic, mechanical, or other means, now known or hereafter invented, including photocopying, microfilming, and recording, or in any information retrieval system without the written permission of Cognella, Inc. For inquiries regarding permissions, translations, foreign rights, audio rights, and any other forms of reproduction, please contact the Cognella Licensing Department at rights@cognella.com.

Trademark Notice: Product or corporate names may be trademarks or registered trademarks and are used only for identification and explanation without intent to infringe.

Cover image: Copyright © 2020 iStockphoto LP/Eoneren.
Interior design image: Copyright © 2013 Depositphotos/alliesinteract.

Printed in the United States of America

cognella® | CUSTOM
3970 Sorrento Valley Blvd., Ste. 500, San Diego, CA 92121

Brief Contents

Contents

Preface

Why Ethics Matters More than Ever

For several decades, the spread of neoliberal social policies and their underlying ideological rationale has dramatically altered social workers' relationship to the state, the market, the public and private sector organizations that develop and implement societal priorities, and the people and communities with whom social workers work. The emphasis on controlling individual behavior as a condition for the receipt of services and the "marketization" of those services by the agencies that deliver them has created new ethical dilemmas and challenges for practitioners in all fields. Social workers employed in "host institutions"—those dominated by other professions and disciplines, such as hospitals, schools, for-profit corporations, the criminal justice system, and the military—experience these challenges to an even greater degree, challenges further compounded recently by heightened awareness of racism in all areas of society. Other factors that have altered the landscape of social work practice include greater demographic and cultural diversity, increased political polarization, the growing influence of social media, and the expanded use of technology in practice. The tragic consequences of the Covid-19 pandemic have cast the importance of ethics into a harsher, more urgent light.

Although the revised National Association of Social Workers' (NASW) *Code of Ethics* (2018) and the *Global Social Work Statement of Ethical* Principles of the International Association of Schools of Social Work (IASSW, 2018) and the International Federation of Social Workers (IFSW, 2018) proclaim social justice and inclusion as fundamental tenets of the profession, disagreements over the meaning of these concepts persist. Hyperpartisanship in the political and cultural arenas, particularly among diverse racial and cultural groups, creates ambiguity about how to apply social justice principles to social work practice. Particularly in interdisciplinary and interprofessional organizations, this ambiguity adds another element of complexity to the challenge of determining what constitutes ethical practice.

Many long-standing underlying assumptions of social work practice, such as the relatively benign role of government, the homogeneity and voluntary nature of our clients and constituents, and our ability to respond to dramatic economic, cultural, and technological changes using traditional practice approaches, may no longer be valid. In addition, we can no longer conceptualize our practice solely in local or regional terms, or confine it to discrete, isolated fields. New issues, such as climate change, global health emergencies like the coronavirus pandemic, persistent civil conflicts, and the growing influence of social media, have exacerbated the effects of major demographic shifts and new cultural norms about gender, family, and work.

In combination, these issues have transformed intersectoral relationships in the social welfare field, altered the mission, goals, and culture of social service agencies, shifted the focus of social work practice, and transformed our professional vocabulary in unexpected ways. Changes in the state's role in social welfare provision and widening socioeconomic inequality have altered the nature of the worker-client relationship and produced new ethical challenges. As of this writing, it is unclear if the nation's response to the current pandemic will reverse these trends and revive our collective commitment to meeting human needs and respecting people's basic rights.

Overview of the Book

This book is an attempt to provide students, faculty, and practitioners with suggestions as to how to interpret long-standing ethical principles in this increasingly fractious and rapidly changing environment and how to use these principles as guides for practice in an uncertain future. It can serve as a text for semester-long courses on social work ethics, as a primary or supplemental text in practice courses at either the undergraduate (BSW) or graduate (MSW) level, or as a text in doctoral-level courses on the philosophy of social work and social welfare or in comparable courses in related disciplines.

The book has five innovative features. One is an analysis of the new challenges for social work values and ethics that significant social, political, cultural, and technological changes have produced in recent years. A second consists of guidelines for ethical practice based on a philosophic foundation, rooted in social justice principles. Third, it presents several frameworks to help readers resolve the dilemmas created by the ambiguous concepts and omissions found in contemporary ethical codes. Fourth, it uses global sources to provide a comparative perspective on the interpretation and application of social work values and ethics. Finally, it contains extensive case examples and reflection exercises, based in part on the author's practice experience, that illustrate ethical dilemmas in all areas of practice created or complicated by the emerging challenges of social and cultural diversity.

The book begins with a summary of key ethical concepts and principles and points out the distinctions among them. It then provides a brief history of social work ethics and analyzes their core assumptions in the context of new realities. It provides a few broad frameworks used to analyze ethical dilemmas and concludes by applying ethics to policy practice through the example of the 2010 Affordable Care Act.

Chapter 2 examines the question of why ethics are important for social work practice. It then traces the theoretical foundations of social work ethics, discusses some of the criticisms of the profession's approach to ethics, and presents several models of how to resolve ethical dilemmas. It concludes by assessing the strengths and limitations of the NASW *Code of Ethics*.

Chapter 3 addresses the conflict between personal and professional values, the reasons for this conflict, and the role of the NASW *Code* in resolving such conflicts. It analyzes the effects of this conflict on several challenging practice situations and discusses the implications for teaching the next generation of practitioners.

Chapter 4 explores the significance of prioritizing the client's interests in ethical practice. It addresses the challenge of determining the client's interest, the role of trust in ethical practice relationships, and the effects of technology on this issue. It introduces several topics that subsequent chapters will discuss in further detail: the ethic of care, the impact of multiple loyalties, and the relationship of social justice to social work ethics.

Chapter 5 provides tools to assist students and practitioners make ethical assessments and ethical decisions in practice. It analyzes the effects of new complicating factors on both processes and discusses how the NASW *Code of Ethics* can be helpful.

Chapters 6–11 provide in-depth content on critical ethical principles and issues in social work practice. These include confidentiality and the duty to warn (Chapter 6), self-determination and paternalism (Chapters 7 and 8), boundary issues and dual relationships (Chapter 9), obligations to third parties (Chapter 10), and the role of social justice and human rights in ethical practice (Chapter 11). Chapter 12 concludes the book with a discussion of future challenges for ethical practice in the social work field.

About the Author

Michael Reisch is Distinguished Professor Emeritus at the University of Maryland, School of Social Work. He has taught MSW- and PhD-level courses on "Social Work Values and Ethics," "Equality and Social Justice," and "Social Work Practice and Social Justice" at six major U.S. universities and several universities abroad. His books include *Macro Social Work Practice: Working for Change in a Multicultural Society*; *Social Policy and Social Justice: Meeting the Challenges of a Diverse Society*; *Social Work and Social Justice: Concepts, Challenges, and Strategies* (with Charles Garvin) and the *Routledge International Handbook of Social Justice*. His essays have appeared in such publications as *Rethinking Values and Ethics in Social Work*, *The Routledge Handbook of Critical Social Work*, *The Routledge Handbook of Social Work Theory*, *The Routledge Handbook of Critical Pedagogies for Social Work*, *Social Work and Health Care Ethics*, and *Ethics* (by Sarah Banks).

Reisch is a Fellow of the American Academy of Social Work and Social Welfare, and a recipient of the Council on Social Work Education's Significant Lifetime Achievement Award and the Career Achievement Award of the Association for Community Organization and Social Action. He has also received teaching, research, and service awards from the University of Maryland, the University of Pennsylvania, the University of Michigan, San Francisco State University, and the National Association of Social Workers, and been honored by several legislative bodies and nonprofit organizations.

Acknowledgments

I wrote this book during a challenging time in the United States and in my personal life. Despite or perhaps because of these challenges, the book provided me with the opportunity to reflect on my career, in particular why and how ethics and values have always played such an important role as guides to my practice, research, and teaching. It rekindled my appreciation for mentors and colleagues who instilled and exemplified these values and for the students who pushed me to clarify their meaning for their generation.

The comments of numerous reviewers of the initial manuscript greatly improved its quality and coherence. I am grateful for their generous assistance. Any errors, misstatements, or misjudgments that remain are entirely my responsibility. I want to thank the editorial staff of Cognella, who have consistently been helpful and supportive in the book's production, and especially Kassie Graves, editor par excellence, for her encouragement, guidance, patience, and astute suggestions. Finally, I want to thank my wife, Lily, who always understood why I was working before dawn in my study, even before I made a pot of coffee.

Values, Ethics, and Social Work Practice

Past, Present, and Future

Introduction

Social work frequently proclaims itself a value-based profession. For well over a century, social work's claim to professional status has rested on its commitment to high ethical standards in its work with vulnerable populations and on behalf of societal well-being. Today, our ability to apply these commitments to ethical practice has become more complex and confusing than ever. The current coronavirus pandemic and preexisting multifaceted problems created by climate change, increasing socioeconomic inequality, persistent racism and sexism, and the challenges of a demographically and culturally diverse society compel us to reexamine the assumptions underlying our core values, reaffirm our ethical principles, and clarify their meaning for our current and future work.

Chapter 1 begins to address these issues. The chapter consists of three parts. The first section clarifies the meaning of several key concepts: ideology, values, morals, and ethics. The chapter then presents a brief history of the development of social work ethics, from the 19th-century origins of the profession to the present. This section introduces some persistent ethical issues that will shape the landscape of practice in the future. The next section introduces several major frameworks we can use to analyze the variety of ethical dilemmas that arise in our practice. We will return to these frameworks throughout the book. The final section of the chapter illustrates how changes in public policies create ethical challenges in our daily practice.

ETHICAL DILEMMA 1.1   Crisis at the Border

Julia A. is a social worker assigned to a facility in Texas housing migrant children from Central America. Government agents separated them from their parents at the U.S.–Mexico border. A private organization contracted by the Department of Homeland Security operates the facility. Julia's job is to ensure that the children in her charge receive adequate health care and nutrition, and whatever supportive counselling she can provide. She is also responsible for trying to connect these children to their parents or other relatives in the United States.

Julia observes that the conditions in the facility are overcrowded and unsanitary. The children do not have enough nutritious food to eat. They lack blankets and toothbrushes and are required to sleep on the floor. Julia has expressed her concerns about these conditions to her supervisor, but her supervisor told her repeatedly that things will improve and that she should "just do her job." Her supervisor cautions her that her work contract includes a clause prohibiting her from communicating with outsiders without explicit permission.

Weeks pass and nothing changes. The health and mental health of the children continue to deteriorate. Julia fears that some of the children, particularly the youngest ones, will experience permanent trauma. Julia has a college friend who works for a local radio station and has contacts with sympathetic legislators. She thinks about calling or texting her friend about what she has observed at the facility. She worries, however, that her effort may be futile, as the facility has rebuffed previous attempts by journalists to enter. She also worries that if her supervisors learn what she is doing, she will lose her job, and she needs the job to help repay her sizable student loans and send money to her widowed mother.

Questions:
1. What are the *ethical issues*—as opposed to the practice issues—involved in this situation?
2. What would you advise Julia to do?
3. How would you decide?

This case, drawn from recent headlines, is a compelling example of the type of ethical dilemmas that social workers often face in our daily practice. These dilemmas involve resolving conflicts of duty (in this situation, to the children and Julia's employer), assessing the limits of confidentiality and whistleblowing, determining the role of self-interest and self-care in our practice, and defining the extent of our ethical imperative to work for social justice. This book will discuss these and other issues in more depth and detail.

First, to provide some background for these future discussions, we will summarize the meaning of several broad core concepts: ideology, values, morals, and ethics. We will also distinguish the subtle differences between an ethical conflict, an ethical dilemma, and an ethical challenge. In addition, we will define some basic ethical principles—autonomy, nonmaleficence, beneficence, justice, and veracity.

Key Ethical Concepts

Ideology

A persistent challenge in understanding and applying ethical principles to contemporary social work practice is confusion or ambiguity over the meaning of oft-used terms. One of these terms is the word *ideology*. In modern parlance, ideology often has a negative interpretation.

For example, the media frequently portray an ideological position as "extreme," in contrast with a more flexible position based on politically pragmatic consideration of "real-world" conditions.

Yet, in order to make sense of the myriad stimuli in our environment, everyone has a unified worldview (what Germans call a *weltanschauung*), even if we are often unaware of it. There is no such thing, therefore, as a nonideological position, however practical one's opinions may seem. At its simplest meaning, an ideology is a systematic, coordinated body of ideas about human life and culture that enables us to explain, categorize, and rationalize the various phenomena we observe and encounter in our daily lives and work. For example, our ideology influences whether we believe an individual's problems largely result from social conditions or behavioral choices. This perspective, in turn, shapes our ideas about how to respond to the wide range of human needs we encounter in practice.

Since the 19th century, leading Western thinkers have examined the origins and functions of ideology, with particular attention to its role in structuring or rationalizing social, political, and economic institutions, social relations, individual and group behavior, and cultural beliefs. Marx (1978) viewed ideology as a byproduct of an era's socioeconomic system. In his view, it formed what he termed the cultural "superstructure" that reflected a society's mystifications, fundamental assumptions, and interpretations of history, based on the interests of the dominant class. In sum, he regarded ideology as a response to historically specific conditions that ultimately acquires an identity of its own. For example, 19th century liberalism provided the ideological rationale for the structural conditions needed to create a market economy supported by representative government and the expansion of civil liberties. To a considerable extent, this ideology still has considerable influence, particularly in the United States.

The great French sociologist Emile Durkheim interpreted the origins and role of ideology through a similar but less materialist lens. Durkheim (1964, 1976) regarded ideology as an outgrowth of what he termed the "collective unconscious" of a group or class that is rooted in its desire to preserve the status quo. Note here that while Marx regarded ideology as—at least initially—a justification for change, Durkheim viewed it as a means to maintain long-standing conditions. He asserted that all ideologies included a unified belief system or worldview, a systematic, unconscious distortion of reality to conform to this worldview, and a particular purpose or set of goals. Think about Durkheim's interpretation. How does it appear in American politics and popular culture today?

Contemporary social workers have offered their own interpretations of the concept and its influence on practice. Lewis (1982) defined ideology as a *system of values* that we accept for ourselves and impose on others. In Gil's words (2013), ideologies have "interpreted, justified, and reinforced ways of life as they emerged and were reproduced and stabilized, regardless of differences in institutional orders. ... [T]hey ... reflect the interests of individuals and classes who supported a status

IMAGE 1.1. Karl Marx

IMAGE 1.2. Emile Durkheim

quo from which they benefited objectively and subjectively" (pp. 49–50). For example, some contemporary activists would argue that "white supremacy" is an ideology that shaped U.S. institutions throughout its history and persists today. Frederic Reamer, a leading scholar of social work ethics, acknowledges how ideological differences shape practice frameworks but does not explicitly connect the profession's dominant ideology to its primary values or the ethical principles derived from them (Reamer, 2018a).

FOR REFLECTION AND DISCUSSION

1. How would you define your personal ideology or worldview?
2. What are its principal characteristics or beliefs?
3. What are a few examples of how these beliefs influence your approach to life and to social work practice?

Values

As Lewis (1988) points out, our ideology determines the values we apply to our conduct in the world, as social beings and as social workers. Values, he asserted, "are generalized abstractions" that reflect what we believe is good and right. In combination, "they provide the building blocks for different ideologies" (Reisch, 2003, p. 122). Values emphasize what we *should* do, not merely what we consider interesting or desirable. They guide our moral judgements and shape our behavior and ways of thinking in our personal lives and professional practice. In sum, they are a constellation of preferences concerning both *what* merits doing and *how* to do it.

It is important to note here, particularly in our increasingly diverse society, that while ideologies and values are "in our mind," they are not mere abstract entities. They are, instead, largely unacknowledged expressions of our class or group self-interest, including our self-interest as professionals. Socioeconomic and political conditions and our individual and group histories shape our values and, in turn, shape our perceptions of these conditions. By influencing our view of these conditions, they ultimately determine whether we strive to maintain or attempt to transform them.

ETHICAL DILEMMA 1.2 Resolving Value Conflicts in Practice

Oliver T. is a young social worker employed by a multipurpose family service agency in a major city. One of his tasks is to review the data the agency uses to evaluate the effectiveness of its school dropout prevention program. The foundation that funds the program requires these data annually to determine if it should continue to provide the agency with the resources needed to sustain it.

In reviewing the data, Oliver notices that some of it is incomplete and that some of the information

reported is not entirely accurate. He brings these matters to the attention of his supervisor, Mr. F., who assures him that the agency will send the missing data to the foundation soon and that the discrepancies in the data are minor. Mr. F. also tells Oliver that providing a full accounting to the foundation would jeopardize the program's existence and that it is too important to the community to risk this possibility.

Oliver is torn. On the one hand, he is aware of the impact of the dropout prevention program and the agency on the community. If the agency loses funding, the community's youth, their families, and the community as a whole will suffer. On the other hand, although Oliver trusts his supervisor and enjoys his job, he knows that if he "signs off" on the report, he will be lying and risking potential damage to his career and the agency.

Questions:
1. What are the competing values in this situation?
2. Which values would you prioritize? What are your reasons?
3. What would you advise Oliver to do?
4. What might be the consequences of your choices?

Value Conflicts

Note the different values involved in Oliver's situation. These value conflicts in social work practice exist for several reasons. A fundamental reason is that, as the above case demonstrates, social workers confront multiple dimensions of values in practice on a daily basis. These include our personal values; the values of our profession; the values of our clients and constituents; and the values of our organization, community, and society. In many situations, these values are different, sometimes diametrically opposed. In other cases, even when these values complement each other it is literally impossible to satisfy all of them at the same time.

In the broader environment in which contemporary practice occurs, value differences often create persistent, seemingly intractable cultural and political conflicts around such issues as abortion, assisted suicide, transracial adoption, affirmative action, immigration, and LGBTQI rights. They also appear in ongoing debates over the respective roles of government and the private sector in social provision, the relationship between parents' rights and children's rights in the child welfare field, the connection between personal privacy and collective security, and the balance between individual freedom and social equity. These societal conflicts inevitably percolate down to our daily practice, frequently in unexpected ways.

Value conflicts in our society emerge from several sources. Increasing cultural and demographic diversity produces not only different interpretations of the world and different value priorities; it often creates obstacles to intergroup trust and understanding. The growing isolation of communities—compounded recently by the need for social distancing during the coronavirus pandemic, identity-based social insularity, and heightened political polarization—exacerbate the challenges created by long-standing religious and moral disputes. Ironically, even the different ways social groups define the concept of social justice itself reflect this conflict (Reisch, 2010a). Growing economic, physical, and social insecurity; real or perceived resource scarcity; omnipresent power differentials; and the increasing separation of our work and personal lives further complicate the ethical landscape of practice.

Some authors argue that the contradiction between social work's social justice mission and its professional aspirations creates a fundamental and unresolved value conflict. This conflict makes it more difficult to translate the values we express in our official rhetoric into practice and policy and increasingly makes our espoused goals and those of the organizations in which we practice incompatible. A leading British social work ethicist, Sarah Banks (2011), describes how in recent years "increasing managerialism and marketisation in the field of social work ... has [eroded] ... practice premised on values of social justice and human dignity" (p. 5). Particularly in policy advocacy, a conflict frequently emerges between our stated values and the realities of political compromise. Finally, during the past three decades the emphasis within the field on scientific objectivity, as exemplified by the focus on "evidence-based practice" and intervention research, can conflict with the subjective, partisan stance implied by the profession's code of ethics (Hudson, 2016; Haynes & Mickelson, 2011).

Morals

We often equate our value judgements with our personal morals, but values and morals are not identical. Morals are principles or habits with respect to right or wrong conduct. They provide rules and standards of behavior in our lives and, in some cases, in our practice. (For example, in the above case, Oliver had to decide whether to violate his personal moral code that included a prohibition on lying.) In a broader sense, morals can also be defined as generally accepted customs regarding our social conduct and what is considered "right living" in a community or society. Our cultural traditions, customs, and rituals reflect and reinforce a community's morals. A basic difference between morals and values is that we often base the former on religious beliefs—that is, reference to a higher, uncontestable external authority. This reliance on external validation for our beliefs sometimes creates ethical challenges for social workers when our personal values and morals conflict with our professional values and obligations, such as our duty to our clients or employers.

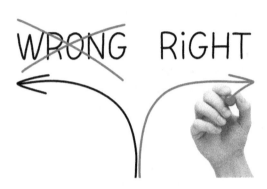

FIGURE 1.1. Morals

Feminist social workers, like Gray (2010), argue that an ethics of care (discussed in more detail later in this book) provides a more complete view of morality as a guide to practice. They also contend that the profession needs to determine whether this approach offers a better understanding of morality than traditional rule-based practices. Gray maintains that struggling with this difficult conceptual issue may help us resolve the complex practice problems we face in an increasingly hostile environment.

Ethics

Finally, this brings us to the fourth important concept—ethics. At their core, ethics are the behavioral dimension of values. They are rules of conduct that link our morals and values in a manner that is consistent with our overall worldview or ideology. For example, in social work practice, they create a fiduciary responsibility or duty that we owe our clients and constituents. They also lead to practice principles derived from our values and morals that form the basis of actions we take to achieve preferred ends (Lewis, 1987).

What often creates confusion for many students and practitioners is that we use the term *ethics* in a variety of other ways in our culture. Sometimes, we define it synonymously with what is customary in a group, community, or society (its mores). For example, ethics tell us how we should behave under certain atypical circumstances, such as a funeral. At other times, we conflate ethics with adherence to formal laws or policies, with professional codes of conduct or etiquette, or with religious rules or commandments, such as "Thou shalt not kill or steal."

In a broader sense, we can also regard ethics as a systematic framework or process that helps us examine the underlying assumptions of our practice and establish a consistent basis for resolving value differences or moral dilemmas (Engelhardt, 1981). This book will use the term in both its specific sense (a reflection of value-based behavior) and its wider sense (a process for resolving conflicts of values or goals).

In general, ethical concepts in social work practice fall into two distinct categories. One consists of specific principles or rules that create *prescriptions*—idealized "oughts" or "shoulds," such as prioritizing our clients' interests; the other comprises *proscriptions*—taboos or things one must never do, such as exploit a client's vulnerability to satisfy our personal needs or desires. In social work, the trust relationship that is critical for us to work effectively with clients and constituents forms the basis for establishing and maintaining our ethical responsibilities. Ethical guidelines also indicate how the profession or its authorized agents should sanction those who violate ethical norms, including what punishments or remedies we may appropriately apply to our colleagues and under what circumstances.

Banks (2016) makes another important distinction, between what she terms "everyday ethics" and "textbook ethics." The latter emphasizes the application of general ethical principles and strict rules to resolve ethical dilemmas through normative ethical frameworks. By contrast, the former focuses on practitioners as moral agents who develop solutions to the ethical problems they confront in a specific context.

It is equally important for us to understand what ethics are not. They are not a reflection of our personal feelings about what is right or wrong. Remember, in social work practice, ethics connote an obligation to our clients, constituents, colleagues, employer, and society as a whole, not just a means to express our preferences.

While religious ideals have influenced social work ethics since the emergence of the profession, our professional ethics do not directly correspond to any particular set of religious beliefs, or any source for that matter that derives its authority from a higher power. In an increasingly diverse society, this raises a difficult issue: Should our practice ethics apply to all people regardless of their religious or secular beliefs, personal identity, or individual behavioral choices? In other words, are ethics universal? Alternately, should a certain degree of cultural relativism shape our ethics?

Ethics are also not the same as what is legal or customary in a particular society. For example, North American slavery, South African apartheid, and the Nuremberg laws in Germany were all legal, but they were hardly ethical by any stretch of the imagination. Similarly, prejudicial or discriminatory behavior against immigrants, racial and religious minorities, or the LGBTQI population may have been (and may continue to be) socially acceptable in some communities, but it is not ethical. Finally, ethical practice and competent practice are not identical. Many highly competent persons in all fields, including social work, sometimes engage in ethical misconduct or tolerate ethical violations committed by their colleagues.

Ethical Issues, Dilemmas, and Conflicts

At this point, it is natural to ask: If social work values and goals are generally clear and our ethical conduct is directly related to these values and goals, why should it be so difficult to determine what constitutes ethical choices in our daily practice? There are several basic answers to this reasonable question.

One is that our ethical principles sometimes conflict with each other either due to the complications of a particular practice situation or ambiguity in the NASW *Code of Ethics* itself. Like a majority of the Ten Commandments, the *Code* generally dictates what we should not do (proscriptions), but less frequently provides guides as to what we should do (prescriptions), particularly in circumstances where the right course of action is unclear.

FIGURE 1.2. Ethical Conflicts

It may be useful at this point to clarify the subtle distinctions among several terms that will appear frequently in this book. An *ethical issue* occurs when a situation contains both right and wrong features, such as when the physical protection of a child requires their removal from parental custody. An *ethical dilemma* arises when we have to choose between two or more "good" or "bad" options and there are no certain guidelines as to how we should proceed. We often face examples of the former when deciding how to allocate limited resources or whether to "blow the whistle" on a colleague. An *ethical conflict*—a phrase often used interchangeably with an ethical dilemma—exists when external pressures, such as a lack of time or information, further complicate a difficult choice. Determining whether to provide emergency assistance to a child or an incapacitated adult without consulting their parents or family is an illustration of this predicament.

General examples of ethical dilemmas or conflicts in practice include the following:

- Truth-telling vs. the protection of an individual, group, or organization's interests or well-being
- "Doing good" for a client (paternalism) vs. support of their right to self-determination
- Allocating finite resources among equally needy populations or programs
- Reconciling our respective duties to our clients and our employer
- Complying with laws or rules that conflict with our professional values or duties
- Choosing between achieving just ends and using potentially unjust means
- Deciding whether to "blow the whistle" on a respected colleague or employer

Most of the cases in this book involve some form of ethical conflict or dilemma in which a social worker is compelled to choose between such options.

In addition, pragmatic conditions sometimes create ethical challenges for practitioners. There are occasions when the reasons one must act (or not act) are unclear due to a lack of sufficient information. At other times, we lack sufficient time to make a reasoned, ethical judgment. Finally, there are situations when our professional ethics conflict with our obligations to third parties, such as our employer or funder, or to legal authorities.

SUMMARY OF KEY CONCEPTS

Ideology	A unified worldview; a systematic, coordinated body of ideas about human life and culture that enables us to explain, categorize, and rationalize the various phenomena we observe and encounter in our daily lives and work.
Values	Generalized abstractions that reflect what we believe is good and right; a constellation of preferences concerning both what merits doing and how to do it.
Value Conflicts	Disputes over which fundamental personal, professional, or societal goals we should prioritize that emerge from demographic, cultural, political, and ideological differences.
Morals	Principles or habits with respect to right or wrong conduct. They provide rules and standards of behavior in our lives.
Ethics	The behavioral dimension of values: (1) rules of conduct that link our morals and values in a manner consistent with our overall worldview or ideology, leading to practice principles derived from our values and morals that form the basis of actions to achieve preferred ends, and (2) a systematic framework or process that helps us examine the underlying assumptions of our practice and establish a consistent basis for resolving value differences or moral dilemmas.
Ethical Conflict	A situation when external pressures, such as a lack of time or information, further complicate a difficult choice about which action to take.
Ethical Dilemma	A situation when we have to choose between two or more "good" or "bad" options and there are no certain guidelines as to how we should proceed.
Ethical Issue	A situation that contains both right and wrong features—that is, one in which the right action will inevitably produce undesirable consequences.

Some Key Ethical Principles

Ethical discourse frequently uses some terms that have different meaning from their general use. In order to understand the literature on social work ethics and articulate your own positions, it is helpful to become familiar with these terms.

Autonomy

The principle of autonomy is a core idea of Western ethics and political philosophy. It refers to the ability to self-govern, to lead life according to reasons, values, or desires that are genuinely one's own. The two philosophers most closely associated with this principle are Immanuel Kant and John Stuart Mill. Based on the Enlightenment belief that all individuals are capable of rational thought, Kant (1781/1999) argued that a person is autonomous when no external factors, such as peer pressure, religious beliefs, or coercion, influence their decisions. Mill expanded the definition of autonomy to reflect the sensibilities of the Romantic era in which he wrote. According to Mill (1859), a person is autonomous to the extent that they make decisions based solely on their own values and desires.

The principle of autonomy lies at the foundation of social work's affirmation of the right of each individual and community to self-determination, to make critical decisions about the course of their lives, and to shape their own destiny. As we will discuss in more detail in Chapters 7 and 8, persistent issues arise when it is unclear if a person's decision is truly autonomous and when it may be necessary to override that decision to preserve an individual's well-being or that of third parties. These issues are often at the heart of the ethical dilemmas we face in our practice.

Nonmaleficence

The principle of nonmaleficence states that there is an obligation not to inflict harm on others. It is closely associated with the maxim in the Hippocratic Oath all physicians take: First do no harm. At times, it means to inflict the least possible harm to achieve a beneficial outcome, to accept a lesser harm in order to prevent a greater harm, or to sacrifice a certain benefit in order to obtain a more desirable one.

Social workers frequently confront situations that involve what we refer to colloquially as "trade-offs." For example, we may have to deny certain services to individuals who repeatedly fail to follow a program's preconditions to receive a particular benefit in order to protect the integrity of the program, be fair to other participants, and produce a better result for the client. Alternately, due to externally imposed policies, a service recipient may have to participate in certain classes or accept a job in order to receive a needed resource. In individual or group counseling sessions, participants may have to "hear" and acknowledge painful truths about their lives or behaviors in order to be able to take positive steps to improve them.

Beneficence

Beneficence refers to the act of helping others, of "doing good." It states that practitioners and researchers should prioritize the well-being of service consumers or research participants. Whereas nonmaleficence prompts us not to harm others, beneficence creates an affirmative obligation to help others. A persistent issue in the social welfare field involves disputes over the limits on the scope of beneficence. In policy development, for example, considerable differences exist over the optimal size and scope of the nation's social safety net, who should be eligible to receive assistance and for how long, and what conditions the government may impose as a precondition for the receipt of aid. Recent policy disagreements about the provision of expanded unemployment insurance and emergency food assistance during the pandemic are vivid illustrations of these disputes. In practice, differences among colleagues often arise over how much "slack" we should give to noncompliant or resistant clients and the extent to which the right of a community to self-determination may limit the rights of others.

Justice

Justice is one of the oldest principles of religious and secular ethics. It refers to the quality of being morally righteous and promoting the equitable treatment of all persons. Philosophers identify four different types of justice. One is *commutative justice*, based on the principle of equal-

FIGURE 1.3. Justice

ity. It refers to the fundamental fairness all individuals owe to each other in both private and public transactions. It also means that we should treat people in equal conditions equally. For example, all individuals in need of health care should have equal access to and receipt of the same quality of care regardless of the reasons they need care. In addition, commutative justice concerns the fair application of punishment for civil or criminal violations. The statement in the ancient Code of Hammurabi—"an eye for an eye, a tooth for a tooth" [but *only* an eye for an eye and *only* a tooth for a tooth]—reflects this principle.

Legal justice refers to equal treatment before the law, as inscribed over the building that houses the U.S. Supreme Court, and the obligation of a government to provide all citizens with equal protection under the law and due process before the law, as stated in the 14th Amendment of the U.S. Constitution. The right to a fair trial before a jury of one's peers illustrates this concept. Conversely, legal justice also refers to the responsibility of citizens to obey the law and respect the rights of others. Major issues in the United States today include whether, in fact, we apply our laws equally to all people and who is entitled to equal justice under the law. For example, does legal justice apply equally to undocumented immigrants, minors, and repeat offenders?

In the policy arena, ongoing disagreements exist as to what constitutes an equitable allocation of resources, who is deserving of equitable treatment, and what resources we should distribute at all. These arguments inevitably spill over into our practice and the decisions organizations make about the structure of their finite budgets. These issues are essentially about the application of *distributive justice.*

Finally, we come to *social justice*, probably the most ambiguous and most disputed principle of justice. In the broadest definition, it refers to the establishment of fair relations between individuals and society. Yet, people of widely different worldviews and backgrounds assert that their goals are the only socially just outcomes (Reisch, 2002). Based on the establishment and preservation of fundamental universal human rights, during the past century it has come to mean equitable distribution of material and nonmaterial goods, social privileges and status, access to and opportunity for growth and personal expression, and full participation

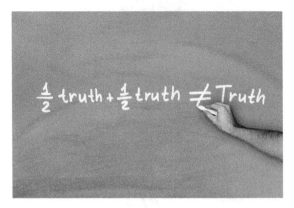

FIGURE 1.4. The Importance of the Truth

in critical decision-making. Social justice is an ethical imperative or core principle of social work as established in the National Association of Social Workers (NASW) and International Federation of Social Workers (IFSW) ethical codes. Chapter 11 contains a fuller discussion of this principle and its implications for ethical practice.

Veracity

Veracity refers to the truthfulness of a person in general, a statement or action by that person, or the accuracy of a particular assumption, idea, or concept that underlies our actions. Truth is a critical component of maintaining the trust that lies at the core of every relationship in social work practice. It is also the basis of support for a "science of social work" and evidence-based practice. There are occasions in our work, however, when we must decide whether to tell the truth or the whole truth, to whom we are obliged to tell the truth, and if it is ever ethical to lie. As discussed in future chapters, issues regarding truth-telling sometimes overlap with ethical issues regarding paternalism (e.g., should we withhold information from a dying patient?), whistleblowing, and conflicts of duty.

SUMMARY: KEY ETHICAL PRINCIPLES

Autonomy
The ability to self-govern, to lead life according to reasons, values, or desires that are genuinely one's own, without the influence of external pressures or authority. It is the basis of the concept of self-determination.

Nonmaleficence
The obligation not to inflict harm on others. Alternately, to inflict the least possible harm to achieve a beneficial outcome, to accept a lesser harm in order to prevent a greater harm, or to sacrifice a certain benefit in order to obtain a more desirable one.

Beneficence
The act of helping others, of "doing good," of prioritizing the well-being of others. The main difference between beneficence and nonmaleficence is that beneficence creates an affirmative obligation to help others whereas nonmaleficence prompts us not to harm others.

Justice	The quality of being morally righteous and promoting the equitable treatment of all persons. There are four general categories of justice. *Commutative justice* refers to the fundamental fairness all individuals owe to each other in both private and public transactions. It also means that we should treat people in equal conditions equally. *Legal justice* refers to equal treatment before the law (due process) and equal protection under the law. It also refers to the responsibility of people to obey the law and respect the rights of others. *Distributive justice* concerns the equitable allocation of material and nonmaterial resources. *Social justice* goes beyond an equitable distribution of material and nonmaterial goods to include equity of social privileges and status, equal access to and opportunity for growth and personal expression, and full participation in critical decision-making (i.e., just processes).
Veracity	The truthfulness of a person in general, a statement or action by that person, or the accuracy of a particular assumption, idea, or concept that underlies our actions.

A Brief History of Social Work Ethics

The ancestors of today's professional social workers entered what was initially called the field of "charities and corrections" motivated by a variety of impulses, including strong moral convictions. Inspired by a combination of religious and secular ideas, they frequently used principles derived from moral philosophy to justify their work on behalf of the poor and disadvantaged. In the late 19th and early 20th century, their ideas came from diverse sources. One was the Social Gospel Movement, whose proponents sought to apply the teachings of Jesus to contemporary problems. Another was American Pragmatism, particularly the work of John Dewey and William James (Berringer, 2019). At the same time, immigrants from Europe transmitted concepts derived from European social thought, such as evolutionary Marxism, radical syndicalism, and anarchism. Immigrants from Latin America and East Asia introduced non-Western cultural values, such as a community's collective responsibility for its members, or *mutualismo*. Finally, these

IMAGE 1.3. John Dewey

IMAGE 1.4. William James

immigrants and African Americans integrated the idea of self-help into their social welfare practices (Iglehart & Becerra, 2011; Reisch & Andrews, 2002).

Despite the growing diversity of the U.S. population, some leaders of the emerging social work field continued to reflect the class prejudices and racial, ethnic, and religious biases of their dominant cultural milieu. They supported restrictions on immigration and expressed concerns about the threat immigrants posed to American civilization. They used racial and ethnic stereotypes to describe their new clients, and considered certain groups, such as African Americans and Native Americans, incapable of assimilation into mainstream society (Reisch, 2013a). Even as they sought to "do good," many social workers did so largely out of noblesse oblige and a paternalistic belief in their moral superiority (Park & Kemp, 2006; Gaylin et al., 1978).

These contradictory impulses had a significant impact on early social work practice and the development of social work ethics. On the one hand, concerns about social justice provided the basis for sustained advocacy on behalf of low-income women and children, immigrants, and industrial workers (Stern & Axinn, 2017; Knight, 2005; Elshtain, 2002; Sklar, 1995; Wise, 1909). On the other hand, for the most part social workers did not express equal concern for the plight of racial and sexual minorities during this era (Iglehart & Becerra, 2011; Lasch-Quinn, 1993). Moral principles also helped social workers forge intellectual connections between their domestic priorities, their support for civil liberties, and their belief in the peaceful resolution of labor-management disputes and international conflicts (Addams, 1895, 1922; Wald, 1915; Kelley, 1905). These shared principles, however, did not motivate our professional ancestors to involve clients and constituents in the design, implementation, or evaluation of existing programs and services (Abramovitz, 2018; Iglehart & Becerra, 2011; Park & Kemp, 2006).

For decades, social workers, particularly but not exclusively in the Charity Organization Societies (COS), maintained paternalistic attitudes toward the poor, regarded racial and ethnic minority groups as incapable of self-determination, and coupled their sense of professional responsibility for the disadvantaged with assertion of professional control over their clients. Unlike social workers today, they did not regard the maintenance of clients' confidentiality as a paramount ethical principle, nor did they give primacy to their clients' interests over those of the elite institutions to which they were beholden for financial and political support (Margolin, 1997; Specht & Courtney, 1994; Sklar, 1990; Wenocur & Reisch, 1989). Ultimately, social workers needed to reconcile these conflicts in order to pursue professional status enhancement in the emerging, highly competitive market economy. They solved this problem by emphasizing the ethical foundations of their work and promoting the still prominent notion that social work was a "value-based profession" (Li, 2019; Wenocur & Reisch, 1989).

As the social work profession evolved and expanded during the 20th century, it elaborated on its foundational moral principles and organized them into formal codes of conduct. On several occasions, professional organizations updated these codes to address issues that the earliest social workers either did not consider or could not envision. Mary Richmond, a leader of the COS movement and the author of the landmark social work text *Social Diagnosis* (1917), wrote a code of ethics in 1920; subgroups within the profession drafted similar codes during this period. In 1947, the American Association of Social Workers (AASW) adopted a formal code; its successor, the National Association of Social Workers (NASW), published its first code in 1960 (Reamer, 2018a).

Thus, for more than a century, this dual effort—to balance diverse, often conflicting moral principles while attaining professional recognition from elite sponsors—led social workers to create ethical codes that emphasized such concepts as self-determination, confidentiality, and truth-telling, and, more recently, to establish six core values or "ethical imperatives" for practice. They are service, social justice, the dignity and worth of the individual, the importance and centrality of human relationships, integrity, and competence. The latest, more expansive codes of ethics and mission statements of the NASW (National Association of Social Workers, 2018), and the IFSW (International Federation of Social Workers, 2019) reflect similar concepts and tensions.

IMAGE 1.5. Mary Richmond

During the last half of the 20th century, concerns about the applicability of the NASW *Code* to the changing realities of practice spurred efforts to expand upon and specify some of its ambiguous provisions. These concerns also reflected several important transformations in the social and cultural environment. One, inspired by the new social movements of the 1960s and 1970s, involved the need for the profession to pay increased attention to issues of racial, gender, and cultural diversity (Reisch, 2019c; Reisch, 2018a). Another reflected the growing influence of biomedical ethics, symbolized during these years by the creation of three national-level commissions by the Ford and Carter administrations. A third was the resurgent interest in clinical practice in a wide range of settings, a development that led to what Schriver (1990) termed "the gentrification of social work"—the privileging of clinical or therapeutic forms of practice above other modalities. In the view of past and current critics within the field, this resulted in the profession abandoning its original mission of societal betterment (Brady et al., 2019; Reisch & Andrews, 2002; Specht & Courtenay, 1994).

More recently, in response to a variety of emerging changes inside and outside the profession, NASW revised its *Code* several more times. These environmental changes included the increasing complexity and scope of practice, new developments in the nation's cultural climate, the expanded use of technology, the spread of private practice, the growing influence of state licensing boards, and the emergence of social media as a tool of information and interpersonal communication (Sage et al., 2019; Young et al., 2018; Reamer, 2018a). Among the more noteworthy revisions in the NASW *Code* were the addition of new protected categories, clarification of the relationship between social workers' legal and ethical obligations, strengthening provisions protecting clients' rights to privacy and confidentiality, greater attention to the duties involved in conducting ethical research, and elaboration of the importance of maintaining professional boundaries (National Association of Social Workers, 2018).

Questioning Old Assumptions, Addressing New Realities

Nevertheless, despite the enormous changes in the practice environment that occurred during the past several decades, with a few notable exceptions most contemporary literature on social work ethics continues to make the same basic assumptions as our professional ancestors, including the following:

- *Government is a relatively benign institution that, in general, supports the mission and goals of social work practice.* Recent policy developments at the federal and state level in such diverse areas as immigration, reproductive rights, and food assistance call into question this assumption.
- *Our clients and constituents share common cultural values and norms and, even when they do not, they desire to assimilate eventually into the mainstream culture.* Ongoing disputes about the criminal justice system, the role of public education, and the very nature of social welfare appear to contradict this belief.
- *Social service agencies and practitioners have the capacity to respond to the various transformations underway in the nation's economy and culture without making major alterations in the ways in which we practice or conceptualize practice.* The challenges both public and nonprofit agencies face in addressing the consequences of increasing cultural and demographic diversity, socioeconomic inequality, the coronavirus pandemic, and persistent calls for fiscal austerity require us to develop new approaches to policies, programs, and services.
- *Our clients are primarily voluntary in nature. This is the basis for our ethical obligations to them.* Due to recent policy changes in the fields of child welfare, criminal justice, behavioral health, and cash assistance, more of our clients are involuntary. This creates new ethical challenges in our work with these individuals.
- *Our professional status requires the maintenance of current ethical guidelines.* If we are to preserve our commitment to social justice, we may have to rethink at least some aspects of our current rule-based frameworks to resolve emerging ethical conflicts.

FOR REFLECTION AND DISCUSSION

1. How do programs and practice in your agency reflect these assumptions?
2. In your judgment, which of these assumptions are still valid?
3. Which of them are questionable? For what reasons?
4. What are the ethical implications of practicing as if all these assumptions were still valid?
5. What are the ethical implications of failing to question them?

The problem with our unquestioning acceptance of these long-standing assumptions is that they do not sufficiently take into account the ethical implications of recent domestic and global phenomena. These include the emergence of a truly multicultural society in the United States and the development of a multipolar and interdependent world as demonstrated even prior to the current pandemic by such critical issues as climate change, global poverty, civil conflict, mass migration, and human trafficking. In the United States, the appearance of new cultural norms about family, gender, and sexuality; a more polarized political climate, fueled by social media and virulent identity-informed divisions; and increasing social inequality created by economic globalization, technological innovations, and deliberate policy choices have also fundamentally changed the practice environment. For example, they have altered the relationship between the nonprofit sector (historically, a primary location for social work practice in the United States) and the government with serious implications for the mission, goals, and focus of social work practice. They have affected the profession's vocabulary, theoretical frameworks, political posture, and the nature of the worker-client relationship. Inevitably, transformations of this magnitude and scope have serious implications for the ethical dimensions of practice (Reisch, 2019a).

Lastly, social work scholars in recent decades, particularly outside the United States, have raised new ethical concerns and urged the profession to address new value-laden questions (Hugman & Carter, 2016; Bell & Hafford-Letchfield, 2015; Banks, 2012). These include the ethical and legal implications of the expanding array of practice models used by social workers, including the ethics of practicing "virtually" (Mattison, 2018; Boddy & Dominelli, 2017; Reamer, 2013b). They also include the ethical limitations of applying scientific expertise and a narrow definition of "evidence" to the formulation of service interventions (Banks, 2016; Weinberg, 2016). Other concerns reflect the altered nature of professional boundaries in a rapidly changing domestic and global culture (Palk & Stein, 2020; Reamer, 2017; Strom-Gottfried, 2016), the application of ethical standards to practice involving the use of animals (Walker & Tumilty, 2019; Taylor et al., 2014), and the role of self-care in the NASW *Code of Ethics* itself (Willis & Molina, 2019). To prepare for our discussion of these and other issues in subsequent chapters, it is useful at this point to clarify the frameworks we can use to understand the components of ethical practice and how to apply them to the dilemmas we may face.

Frameworks for Analyzing an Ethical Dilemma

The social work literature has identified four main approaches to the resolution of ethical dilemmas. One approach maintains that clients' interests are always primary. Although this approach would appear to be consistent with the ethical guidelines in the NASW *Code*, there is often a problem determining what exactly constitutes a client's "best interest." The extensive interprofessional literature in the child welfare, health care, and aging services fields illustrates this challenge (George & Awal, 2019; Pringle & Thompson, 2019; Lowe, 2018).

A second approach recommends the use of a "prime directive" in which the values of a profession or an organization (or the policies it is obligated to follow) are imposed on the situation. From one perspective, this top-down approach appears to be consistent with social workers' ethical duty to employers and to obey the law. If followed, it would enable us to comply with shifting agency and policy guidelines. From another perspective, it is contrary to the profession's historical emphasis on client self-determination, its long-standing focus on client empowerment, and recent concerns about explicit and implicit biases in the theories underlying practice (Reisch, 2019d; Stepney, 2019; Timms, 2018; Weinberg, 2016; Jani & Reisch, 2011).

Most ethicists, however, including those in the social work field, primarily use two prominent approaches to the resolution of ethical dilemmas. One is some version of a *deontological* approach, a term derived from the Greek word for "first principles." This approach requires the construction of a hierarchical or lexical order of values that is then applied (consistently, one hopes) to every practice situation. Among modern Western philosophers, probably the most influential exposition of this approach was by John Rawls in his classic work, *A Theory of Justice* (1999).

In social work practice, the development and implementation of a value hierarchy could, for example, establish that a client's self-determination is a higher value than the protection of a client's well-being, or vice versa. This approach might be particularly useful for social workers in fields of practice where conflicts between a client's choices and well-being often occur, such as health or behavioral health care. It might not be sufficiently flexible, however, to address the increasingly complex situations that confront social workers in other practice settings, such as child welfare or elder care, particularly in a rapidly changing cultural environment.

The other common ethical framework uses a *teleological* (from the Greek for "final purposes") or consequentialist approach, the most famous of which is utilitarianism. Utilitarianism is a doctrine originally developed by British philosophers Jeremy Bentham and John Stuart Mill in the 19th century, and applied to contemporary issues by scholars such as Lazari-Radek and Singer (2017). In an era much like our own, when faced with the challenge of how to respond to increasing inequality, Bentham maintained that those actions to be preferred were those that maximize happiness and well-being at the individual level and promote the interests of the largest number of people at the societal level (1996). Mill's principle of utility stated simply that a just society maximizes social benefits while minimizing social harms (1971). Popular literature often summarizes these ideas, somewhat inaccurately, as "the greatest good for the greatest number." (What Bentham (1907), who was also a mathematician and engineer, actually wrote in describing his 'utilitarian calculus' was "the greatest net balance of satisfaction." This could imply that a great deal of happiness [e.g., wealth] for the few could outweigh a small amount of happiness for the many.)

A utilitarian approach requires us to construct an ethical scale that measures the potential consequences of the various possible choices we face when confronted with an ethical dilemma. Although this sounds complicated, especially for the "mathematically challenged," we do it all the time in our personal lives. Think about our decisions to form or end a relationship, buy a house, accept or leave a job, or enroll in a social work program.

There are several difficulties, however, with a utilitarian approach. One is determining how much respective "weight" to apply to the numerous consequences of each choice. For example, how should we balance the cost in time and money of pursuing a social work degree with the benefits we would accrue from future employment?

Another problem is determining the distinction between short-term and long-term consequences, such as the immediate satisfaction of a client's need for services versus its future impact on a client's ability to control their surroundings and become more self-sufficient. A third challenge is measuring the impact of alternate choices on third parties, including a client's family, community, or society as a whole. A fourth problem results from the impossibility of including in our calculations the unintended and unforeseen consequences that inevitably arise regardless of which choice we make. Finally, as discussed briefly above, many ethical dilemmas involve the need to make forced choices between competing "goods" that are difficult, even subjective, to quantify or of such a different nature that a comparison between them is impossible (Rawls, 1999).

FOR REFLECTION

1. Which of the above approaches most appeals to you?
2. What are the reasons for the appeal of this approach?
3. Which approach have you used most often in your personal and professional life?
4. What challenges have occurred in implementing it?

The first three of the following frameworks attempt to synthesize elements of a deontological and consequentialist approach. Both Reisch and Lowe (2000) and Reamer (2018a) propose a 7-step framework that synthesizes elements of a deontological and consequentialist approach. The former focuses on challenges faced by macro social work practitioners, while the latter is primarily for clinical social workers. Both, however, can be used in all practice situations.

REISCH & LOWE'S 7-STEP FRAMEWORK

1. Identify the ethical principles that apply to the situation.
2. Collect additional information needed to examine the ethical dilemma in question.
3. Identify the relevant ethical values and/or rules that apply to the ethical problem.
4. Identify any potential conflicts of interest and those likely to benefit from or be harmed by such conflicts.
5. Rank order the appropriate ethical rules in terms of their importance in this situation.
6. Determine the consequences of applying different ethical rules or ranking these rules differently.
7. Determine who needs to resolve the dilemma.

REAMER: THE ETHICS DECISION-MAKING FRAMEWORK

1. Identify the ethical issues, including the social work values and duties that conflict.
2. Identify the individuals, groups, and organizations likely affected by the ethical decision.
3. Tentatively identify all viable courses of action and the participants involved in each, along with the potential benefits and risks for each.
4. Thoroughly examine the reasons in favor of and against each course of action by consulting with codes of ethics, legal principles, ethical theories and guidelines, social work practice theories and principles, relevant laws, policies, and practice standards, and personal values.
5. Consult with colleagues and appropriate experts.
6. Make the decision and document the decision-making process.
7. Monitor, evaluate, and document the decision (p. 88).

A more complex framework, derived from biomedical ethics (Thomas, 1978), is adapted below.

THE ETHICS WORK-UP

Steps

1. Identify and state the facts of the situation and their likely consequences as best as you can.
2. Identify all related value factors (personal, professional, social, human) present for all actors (individuals, groups, organizations) involved in the situation.
3. Identify and specify the major value conflicts in the situation.
4. Set priorities for the values that you identified as in conflict in step 3. State the reasons that would support this priority setting in your view.
5. Identify and present the argument in support of the reasons advanced in step 4, by answering the following questions:

   – What underlying ethical norms support your view?

   – Why should we accept these norms as guides for conduct in this situation?

   – What do these norms imply for how we should arrange values in a priority order? (Revise the priorities established in step 4 if required to do so at this point. That is, step 5 requires one to make an argument showing why we should accept certain value priorities and what their implications are for how one should act in the situation.)

   – What are the policy implications if we applied your decision about this situation more generally (i.e., via laws, regulations, specific ethical canons, precedents, etc.)?

6. Critique the arguments given in steps 4 and 5. How could one challenge the value priorities developed in step 4 and defended in step 5? Do the implications identified in step 5, in fact, follow from the priorities developed in step 4 and defended in step 5? How could you defend your position developed in steps 4 and 5 from these critiques?

Writing from the perspective of nursing, Thompson and Thompson (1981) proposed the following framework. Its guidelines apply a predominantly consequentialist approach:

1. Assess the overall situation by identifying the problem(s) that exist, determine what decisions need to be made, distinguish between those aspects of the situation that require an ethical decision from those that can be resolved through empirical evidence, and list all the parties potentially affected by the decision.
2. Decide if you need additional information, and, if so, develop a strategy to obtain it.
3. Identify your personal values and beliefs regarding the ethical dilemma and the professional responsibilities established by the *Code of Ethics*.
4. Identify the value conflicts that exist in the situation.

5. Identify the range of action options and their potential implications.
6. Determine who should be the key decision-maker.
7. Critique your decisions.
8. Determine a course of action and implement it.
9. Evaluate the consequences of your decision for future use.

Figure 1.5 illustrates the common features all frameworks use to analyze ethical dilemmas.

Now, apply one of these frameworks to a specific (fictional) case.

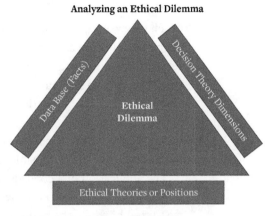

Analyzing an Ethical Dilemma

FIGURE 1.5. Analyzing an Ethical Dilemma

ETHICAL DILEMMA 1.3

The Case of Jean V.: Which Approach Would You Use?

You are a social worker in the child welfare unit of the local Department of Social Services. You are working with a client, Jean V., an unemployed single father raising his small daughter, Cosette, whom the Department is investigating on suspicion of child neglect. You believe that despite his struggles with abject poverty, Jean is a loving father. Yet, you have serious concerns about Cosette's well-being.

During your most recent appointment, Jean confessed to you that he stole some bread from a neighborhood bakery in order to feed his starving child. He also told you that the baker reported the crime to the police and identified him as the thief. As a result, a righteous and dogged police officer, Inspector J., is pursuing Jean. At the end of the appointment, Jean revealed that he plans to flee the city and asked for your assistance in finding a foster placement for his daughter until he can safely return.

The state has recently instituted harsh laws against theft and strict standards regarding parental suitability. It has also prohibited state agencies from serving an individual convicted of a felony or permitting felons to maintain custody of their children. Your supervisor has repeatedly made it clear that the agency would not tolerate a client's legal misconduct. In addition, as a social worker, you are legally obligated to report any condition or behavior that would justify the removal of a child from their family. A felony conviction clearly falls into this category.

You are aware of the severe punishment Jean will face if he is arrested, tried, and convicted. You are also aware that if he goes to prison, it is highly unlikely he will see his daughter again, at least not for a very long time. The child is somewhat emotionally fragile, particularly since the death of her mother, and you are concerned about the effects of long-term separation from her father. You are also concerned about the quality of foster care she will receive given the paucity of suitable home placements in the city and recent scandals about child abuse in foster families.

What would you do?

Questions:
1. What are the conflicting value and ethical issues in this situation?
2. What role should your personal values play in determining your course of action?
3. To whom do you owe an ethical duty in this situation? How would you prioritize your obligations to those parties?
4. Which of the above frameworks would you use to help you determine a course of action?
5. The NASW *Code of Ethics* establishes an ethical imperative to work for social justice. How would you reconcile your decision with the *Code*?

If we applied a deontological framework to the above situation, we would first determine which values we consider most important. Suppose, for example, we viewed the protection of people's well-being as our highest value. If so, we would decide to shield Jean from the law to serve the best interests of his dependent daughter, Cosette. On the other hand, if we believed that obedience to societal laws and rules was of the highest value, we would report Jean to the authorities because he clearly violated these laws. (This would also imply that you accepted the premise that convicted felons do not make suitable parents.) In this instance, we would be less concerned about the consequences of our decision than with maintaining certain principles. Ideally, we would apply this hierarchy of values consistently in our practice.

The application of a consequentialist framework to this case would require us to pose different questions. We would have to consider what is likely to happen to Jean and Cosette if we turned him into the police or, alternately, failed to report the matter. We would also need to take into account the possible short-term and long-term effects of either decision on third parties, including our employer, society as a whole, and our career. Doing so would require us to engage in the difficult fact-finding suggested by the frameworks presented above.

These steps illustrate what philosophers sometimes call the process of "act utilitarianism"—weighing the consequences of different choices in the context of a specific situation. Ideally, we would then reflect on the implications of our decision if we developed a rule we would subsequently apply in similar circumstances. Ethicists refer to this as "rule utilitarianism."

Applying Ethics to Policy Practice: The Affordable Care Act

Ethical dilemmas do not arise solely in our practice with individuals and families. Many situations in macro social work practice with communities and organizations and in policy advocacy present challenging ethical situations as well (see Reisch, 2018c; Meenaghan et al., 2013). Ongoing controversies about the 2010 Affordable Care Act (ACA) reflect these conflicts as do issues that have emerged during the coronavirus pandemic (Gellert, 2020; Krugman, 2019).

As the case of the ACA demonstrates, the implementation of complex social policies inevitably produces ethical and legal challenges for practitioners in the health care field (Keith, 2020; McCoy, 2018). The ACA, for example, increased funding for components of health care provision that reflect the priorities of the social work profession, such as preventive and primary care, wellness programs, interprofessional collaboration, and school- and community-based care. At the same time, the law's compulsory cost control measures compel health care providers to determine how to allocate resources and address the consequences of increasing disparities in access (Reamer, 2018b; Rivlin, 2013). These conflicting goals created ethical, moral, and ideological challenges that will become even more complex in the future as the U.S. population diversifies further and as the use of technology in health and behavioral health expands (Stoltzfus Jost, 2017; Vecchione, 2012; Visse et al., 2012).

Practice Implications

The rapidly changing and uncertain context of health policy will also create new ethical challenges in our practice. As stated above, conflicts have already emerged between the ACA's dual goals of containing costs and improving service access and quality. At the same time, the unprecedented consequences of the coronavirus pandemic have illuminated the structural flaws in the U.S. health care system (Seervai, 2020). How we respond in the future to these systemic issues will reflect our basic values and ethics.

In a broader sense, differences in the underlying values and assumptions of the medical and biopsychosocial models that underlie most social work practice are another source of ethical conflict (Jani & Reisch, 2011). At the same time, increased emphasis on interprofessional practice in health care and other institutional settings, such as criminal justice, education, and immigration, will exacerbate long-standing tensions over status hierarchies, assigned roles and responsibilities, and boundaries. How these tensions will appear in whatever constitutes the "new normal" once the current pandemic abates is already a subject of endless speculation (Naughton, 2020).

Because the implementation of most policies occurs through complex administrative systems, tensions will also arise between our ethical obligations to obey administrative regulations and our duty to support client self-determination and self-management (Reisch, 2012). As resources become increasingly scarce, we will experience increased pressure to balance institutional efficiency and effective practice, particularly with clients exhibiting multiple problems that do not lend themselves to quick solutions. Inevitably, the nation's hyperpartisan political climate will intensify the inherent conflict between the creation of universal access to health care and other vital services and the need to direct sufficient resources to correct persistent racial, ethnic, and gender inequities (Reisch, 2019d). Recently, the diverse responses of federal, state, and local officials to the consequences of the pandemic illustrate the implications of this conflict all too clearly.

Ethical dilemmas could also arise over what constitutes reasonable standards of care or best practices for specific populations or problems. The tension between the growing demand for fiscal and outcome accountability and the establishment of trust among clients who possess justifiable suspicions of authority will create additional challenges for already overburdened practitioners. Finally, the obligation to provide individuals and families with full disclosure of the costs and risks of treatment and the desire to encourage them to seek health care services as promptly as possible will produce further ethical challenges (Reamer, 2018b). The effects of the pandemic on the nation's most vulnerable communities demonstrates that that this challenge is no mere hypothetical.

The following case, based on actual events, illustrates how policy change affects the ethical dimensions of practice in what appears at first to be a simple situation.

ETHICAL DILEMMA 1.4   **The Retired Taxi Driver**

You are a social worker employed in a geriatric care unit of a local hospital. Several times during the past year, the hospital admitted Arnold S., a retired taxi driver, for a number of medical problems including end-stage renal disease, for which he receives kidney dialysis three times each week. Because of his complicated medical condition, he is on multiple medications that he frequently confuses or does not take. Arnold's partner and caretaker died a year ago. He has no other family and lives alone in a basement apartment. His frequent hospitalizations are a direct result of his inability to take his medications correctly and to care for himself properly, despite efforts to provide him with in-home care. The issue is not financial; the 2010 Affordable Care Act (ACA) now covers many of the services he requires (Gorin & Moniz, 2019).

The hospital is under increasing pressure to limit its in-patient population. Not only is such care more expensive, but under the ACA, the hospital's readmission rates and measures of patient outcomes affect its overall funding. The recent pandemic has strained the hospital's resources to the breaking point. There is considerable interest, therefore, in finding alternative ways to address Arnold's problems, although neither the ACA nor the NASW *Code of Ethics* provide specific ethical guidelines in this regard (Graber & O'Brien, 2019; McCoy, 2018; Vecchione, 2012).

During his last hospitalization, Arnold confides in you and several of your colleagues that he enjoys being in the hospital because it provides him with what he needs most: people who care for him and about him. You get the distinct impression that Arnold's failure to take his medications correctly may be, at least in part, deliberate in order to require readmission to the hospital.

Questions:

1. How would you respond to Mr. S.?
2. On what ethical principles would you base your response?
3. What are the conflicting ethical duties in this situation?
4. What approach would you use to decide a course of action?

This case encapsulates a classical ethical dilemma with an added twist arising from the stipulations of the ACA. One of the principal forms of paternalism in social work practice is physical interference with a client's intentions or actions, against their wishes, ostensibly for their own good. Paternalistic practice also violates people's right to self-determination, a fundamental ethical concept in social work. In the case of Mr. S., refusing to admit him to the hospital for treatment would be a form of coercive interference justified by both the need to comply with federal policy guidelines and the belief that such action would be in his best interest (Dworkin, 1972).

Health care professionals, including social workers, have rationalized the paternalistic treatment of clients under such circumstances in several ways. One standard rationale is that a patient or client lacks information that, if available, would lead them to consent to the interference. A related justification is that the client is incapable of understanding relevant information, either temporarily (due to age or condition) or permanently. Because forecasts predict there will soon be an increase in elderly clients like Mr. S., this situation is likely to become more common in the years ahead. Other justifications are based either on the client's consent to the paternalistic intervention prior to the interference or the belief that the client would likely consent after the interference when presented with all the facts. Neither of these conditions appears to be satisfied in the case of Mr. S.

Social workers have historically regarded the conflicting value, client self-determination, as a universal right that is particularly significant for those receiving help. From this perspective, self-determination is, therefore, both an end and a means—a precondition to the fulfillment of one's personal goals and the key to the maintenance of personal dignity and worth. The emphasis on self-determination also assumes people's ability to make their own decisions if given the opportunity.

NASW's revised *Code of Ethics* (1.01) reflects the primacy of self-determination as well as its limitations:

> Social workers' primary responsibility is to promote the well-being of clients. ... However, social workers' responsibility to the larger society or specific legal obligations

may on limited occasions supersede the loyalty owed clients, and clients should be so advised.

The next provision in the NASW *Code* (1.02) may be particularly applicable to Mr. S.'s situation:

> [Although] social workers respect and promote the right of clients to self-determination, [they] may limit clients' right to self-determination when, in the social worker's professional judgment, clients' actions or potential actions pose a serious, foreseeable, and imminent risk to themselves or others.

The unequal distribution of resources and power between workers and clients and between clients and powerful institutions (which government policy often reinforces) makes the resolution of this and similar ethical dilemmas even more complicated (Maurer et al., 2017). The involuntary or quasi-involuntary situation of many clients, such as Mr. S., and the conflict between a client's rights (in this case to care and social well-being) and society's need to control service costs further compound the ethical dimensions of this situation (Brown, 2018).

In this case, in order to support Mr. S's right to self-determination, you must also consider several related issues. First, you must take into account the extent of his competence and comprehension of his situation and the importance of preserving his trust, especially if it is likely he will need further care in the future. You must also guard against various risks. These range from a malpractice suit by the client, if the decision not to admit him to the hospital leads to a deterioration of his physical condition, to fiscal sanctions imposed on the hospital by the government. In addition, you must take into consideration the importance of preserving your professional integrity and the confidence of your supervisors. Lastly, particularly with clients who may be impaired, you must assess if the harmful consequences that are likely to occur without interference are irreversible and if an option exists that would preserve a wider range of freedom for Mr. S. only by restricting his liberty temporarily (Lowe, 2018; Kusmaul et al., 2017).

This relatively straightforward case, therefore, reflects several key points discussed in this chapter. First, it reveals the importance of clarifying our values and determining which values have priority in our practice. Second, it illustrates the need to consider the different effects of ethical decisions on various stakeholders in a given situation. Third, it underscores the importance of applying a consistent approach to the resolution of ethical conflicts. Finally, it demonstrates how the inextricable dynamic of policy and practice creates diverse and unexpected ethical challenges.

Summary

This chapter defined the core concepts that provide the foundation for ethical discourse, traced the historical development of ethics in the social work profession, discussed the types and sources of ethical dilemmas, and presented several frameworks for their possible resolution. Finally, it illustrated how ethical conflicts can emerge in all forms of practice and how policy change can produce new ethical challenges for social workers. Other chapters will explore the ethical dilemmas that arise in a variety of practice situations in depth. Chapter 2 examines in more detail the philosophical and theoretical bases of contemporary social work ethics.

Reflection Exercise I: How Does Your Agency Translate Its Values into Practice?

Levy (1973) identified three core dimensions of values that influence how social workers practice: our preferred conceptions *of people*, our preferred outcomes *for people*, and our preferred instrumentalities (ways) *for working with people*.

Think about the agency in which you work (or have worked) or where you have an internship. How does the agency reflect these dimensions of its values in its various practices?

Reflection Exercise II: Group Membership and Personal Morality

1. Are there universal ethics that apply to all people? Should there be?
2. If ethics are culturally relative, which ethical principles should vary according to people's cultures?
3. What are the potential consequences of ethical relativism?
4. What should be the roles of religious and secular ideologies in shaping our ethical conduct in practice?

Credits

Img. 1.1: Source: https://commons.wikimedia.org/wiki/File:Karl_Marx_crop.jpg.
Img. 1.2: Source: https://commons.wikimedia.org/wiki/File:%C3%89mile_Durkheim.jpg.
Fig. 1.1: Copyright © 2013 Depositphotos/ivelin.
Fig. 1.2: Copyright © 2011 Depositphotos/iqoncept.
Fig. 1.3: Copyright © by Olmec (cc by-sa 3.0) at https://commons.wikimedia.org/wiki/File:Wikipedia_scale_of_justice.png.
Fig. 1.4: Copyright © 2013 Depositphotos/AndreyPopov.
Img. 1.3: Source: https://commons.wikimedia.org/wiki/File:John_Dewey_cph.3a51565.jpg.
Img. 1.4: Source: https://commons.wikimedia.org/wiki/File:Wm_james.jpg.
Img. 1.5: Source: https://commons.wikimedia.org/wiki/File:Mary_Ellen_Richmond.png.

The Foundations of Social Work Ethics

Introduction

Over 40 years ago, the philosopher Daniel Maguire (1978) described the current state of our society with uncanny prescience:

> Ours is a naked and brittle condition in which no values seem secure. Businessmen defend as essential to their competitive positions practices which an older ethic reserved to liars and thieves. ... Politics has lost all remnants of innocence as political scandals reveal the depth and breadth of corruption in political and corporate life. ... The system of justice is no longer trusted. (p. 5)

Maguire's assessment of the barriers to the creation of a more just and caring society underscores the importance of understanding the ethical foundations of social work practice in order for us to apply our core principles effectively in an uncertain future.

This chapter covers several topics that reflect this critical issue. It begins with a discussion of why a concern about ethics is a central component of social work practice. The next sections provide background material on the theoretical foundation and some critiques of contemporary social work ethics. The following section expands on the content in Chapter 1 on approaches to ethical decision-making and includes two suggested value hierarchies as guides to ethical decision-making. The chapter concludes with an assessment of some emerging challenges to the ethical practice of social work and the strengths and limitations of the NASW *Code of Ethics* in addressing them.

ETHICAL DILEMMA 2.1	Why Should I Care About Ethics?

You are a first-year student whose internship is in a public child welfare agency. You have become aware that several workers in your unit do not report some incidents of suspected child neglect when they come to their attention. You share your observation with your field liaison who advises you not to say anything and to focus on what knowledge and skills you can acquire in your placement. She suggests there may be good reasons for the actions of more experienced child welfare workers. The more you reflect on the matter, however, the more you feel conflicted about this advice. It is keeping you awake at night.

Questions:
1. What are your concerns about this situation?
2. If one of your primary goals is to get a good social work education and, ultimately, a good job after graduation, why should you get involved in this matter?
3. What do you think should be the role of ethics in social work practice?

Why Do We Care About Ethics?

As this situation illustrates, something disturbs us if we adopt a purely self-serving approach to practice. Although we might be able to justify such an approach on pragmatic grounds, most of us would be bothered if we let the matter drop. Most likely, this is because we sense that more than our self-interest is at stake. There are fundamental ethical issues at play that are (or should be) of particular concern if we are to become a member of a value-based profession.

The focus of ethics, therefore, is not merely to distinguish between good and bad, right and wrong, but to establish the duties and obligations that result from these distinctions. Without an ethical framework, narrow self-interest might be the primary guide to our behavior, particularly in a society that celebrates individualism and competition and measures "success" largely in terms of the accumulation of material goods and the acquisition of power, status, and celebrity. Imagine living in a community or society in which people define doing the "right thing" as doing solely "what's best for me." (Some observers would argue that we already live in such a society.)

To prevent such an undesirable eventuality, all cultures developed a version of ethical thinking to establish what constitutes moral behavior in our interactions with others. Although ethical norms and values throughout the world originally emerged from religious roots, ethical discourse in the West since the Enlightenment of the 18th century has evolved beyond particular theocentric belief systems to incorporate both the use of reason and the consideration of nonrational factors such as our emotions.

As a result, for the past three centuries a combination of religious and secular views of ethics has shaped public policy and daily practice in the broadly defined social welfare field for the purpose of creating and maintaining social harmony, which generally implied the preservation of the social and political status quo. In addition, as the evolution of ethical discourse occurred for the most part in relatively homogeneous and hierarchical societies, the values of the dominant culture prevailed. During recent decades, however, the emergence of multicultural, heterogeneous societies and a multipolar world has made the definition and creation of an ethical society increasingly complicated.

Consequently, an underlying assumption of contemporary ethical discourse—that no one should impose a vision of the "good" on others—is now frequently at the heart of contentious debates over such issues as sexuality, gender identity, abortion, the right to die, and capital punishment. In this context, the development of what Engelhardt (1982a) termed a "peaceable community" presents two persistent ethical challenges that have important implications for social workers: how to respect people's autonomy in a culturally diverse environment, and how to establish a universally accepted view of morality, especially by reason alone. There is even a question today whether the latter goal is desirable.

These challenges create a particular problem for professionals who base their values on religious beliefs. This is because at its core "the concept of a public morality is ambiguous. It ... does not involve the imposition by force of any particular view of the good life upon unconsenting innocents. ... It recognizes the weaknesses of reasons unaided by claims of special revelation or unique historical experiences" (Engelhardt, 1982a, p. 68).

Despite, or perhaps because ethics is a uniquely human enterprise, it also confronts the distinctly human activity of questioning the purpose of existence itself and the implications of this questioning for our behavior in the world. It requires us to rely on more than our instincts, biological impulses, or reason alone. According to Maguire (1978), the role of ethics is "to provide a method for judging [contemporary] ... realities" (p. 7)—an essential aspect of being a person. As the ultimate goal of social work and social policy—ideally—is to enable people to be fully human, ethics is an essential component of all forms of our practice regardless of where or with whom this practice occurs.

We base our ethical conduct on our underlying values—our preferences regarding what actions constitute acceptable social behavior under particular circumstances. Levy (1976a) organized these values into four basic categories as the chart below reflects.

LEVY'S 4 BASIC VALUES

(1) *Instrumental values*	The means by which we achieve our goals
(2) *Intrinsic values*	Values that are independent of other things (e.g., the value of health)
(3) *Object values*	Values that involve our perceptions and exist independently of our knowledge (e.g., our preference for certain foods or colors)
(4) *Potential or future values*	Values that will define the type of society we strive to create

Professions like social work formalize these values into rules of conduct that shape our moral judgements, practice principles, and official standards. For example, the NASW *Code of Ethics* (2018) grounds its behavioral guidelines and practice principles in specific (although largely unstated) ethical theories. As discussed below, no universal acceptance of these theories or the actions they prescribe or proscribe exists. This is because many ethical issues and their underlying assumptions remain under contention.

Western philosophers have generally divided ethical discourse into normative and nonnormative categories. The former focuses on identifying moral standards and developing modes of thinking that will help us comprehend these standards. In its applied form, it can provide an action guide for resolving ethical dilemmas. The nonnormative category includes descriptive ethics and metaethics. Descriptive ethics focuses on the analysis of moral behavior and beliefs. Metaethics involves defining the central concepts of ethical discourse, such as "rights" and "duties" (Reamer, 2018a).

According to Reamer (1980), a central metaethical question is "How should we derive ethical principles for conduct?" The answer to this question relies on two very different approaches. One approach, termed *cognitivist*, asserts that principles are true or false; we can derive them through scientific inquiry or intuition. This approach influences the current emphasis on the "science of social work" (Brekke & Anastas, 2019).

A *noncognitivist* approach argues that moral principles reflect subjective preferences shaped by our environment, culture, and upbringing. This approach reflects concepts derived from social constructivism and postmodernism (Halvorsen, 2019; Hugman, 2019; Zizek, 2018; Kukla, 2013). At present, there is no consensus in the social work literature on which approach is preferred.

In the past, scholars argued that reason (science) or intuition (feelings) alone were insufficient to determine all ethical principles. Over 80 years ago, ethicists expressed concern about the impact of the assumptions of scientific thinking on ethical discourse because the pursuit of scientific objectivity negated the role of subjective values (Reamer, 1983a). Similar criticisms appeared in the 1970s and 1980s.

IMAGE 2.1. English Poor Laws

At that time, Grange (1974) maintained that a traditional, "evidence-based," and hypothesis-driven conception of science did not adequately encompass the full meaning of being. Maguire (1978) suggested that the application of "value-free science" also includes recognizing the need for greater moral responsibility. Lewis (1982) argued that what we often characterize as "intuition" actually reflects our reliance upon experience to forge an analogy to current circumstances. The debate over the meaning, utility, and ethical implications of scientific, "evidence-based practice" persists to this day, in part because of its uncritical and largely unexamined application of normative ethical principles (Gambrill, 2019; Khoury, 2019; Diaz & Drewery, 2016).

Forty years ago, Reamer (1980) asserted that the application of normative ethical principles creates three ongoing issues for practitioners: (1) developing and justifying the core values that will guide social work practice, (2) establishing what obligations exist and how extensive these duties are, and (3) formulating moral principles to guide policies and behavior in professional settings. Among the earliest secular examples of the influence of moral principles in Western social welfare were the English Poor Laws and the U.S. policies they subsequently influenced.

The connection between moral principles and social practices, however, went beyond the public sector. Although often overlooked in mainstream histories of social work, statements by leaders of voluntary charitable organizations in the late 19th and early 20th centuries reflected prejudicial values toward immigrants, racial and ethnic minorities, women, and low-income individuals similar to those articulated by government officials (Jani & Reisch, 2018; Reisch, 2013a; Iglehart & Becerra, 2011; Park & Kemp, 2006). Despite these biases, with the emergence of professions at the turn of the 20th century, concern over ethics expanded from the realm of philosophers and theologians to members of those occupations that possessed societal sanction to intervene in others' lives, such as nurses, teachers, physicians, and social workers.

In the United States, reforms during the Progressive Era (~1890–1918) and the New Deal (1930s) moderated these prejudicial attitudes to some extent, at least in the policy realm. Nevertheless, social workers largely ignored the importance of ethical concerns in practice until the 1950s, coinciding with a resurgent interest in professionalism (Reamer, 2018a; Wenocur & Reisch, 1989). Since its initial publication in 1961, the NASW *Code of Ethics* presented its ethical prescriptions as general principles based on the profession's statement of core values (i.e., its ethical imperatives) and outlined rules of conduct as guides for practice.

Today, an increasingly contentious environment heightens the need for us to pay attention to such long-standing ethical issues as confidentiality, truth-telling, the conflict between legal and ethical obligations, the limits of self-determination and paternalism, and the challenges of equitable resource dis-

IMAGE 2.2. Attitudes toward Poverty Shifted During the Great Depression

tribution, whistleblowing, and negotiating boundaries between workers and clients. In addition, increasing demographic and cultural diversity, technological advances, and the influence of social media have complicated the ethical picture further. In this complex climate, Banks (2008) concludes that social work ethics now refers specifically to "the study of the norms of right action, good qualities of character and values relating to the nature of the good life that are aspired to, espoused and enacted by social workers in the context of their work" (p. 1238).

FOR REFLECTION: THE FUNCTION OF ETHICAL CODES

1. What do you think are the primary purposes of ethical codes?
2. How do they affect how you practice social work?
3. What do you consider their primary advantages and disadvantages?

ETHICAL DILEMMA 2.2   How Do You Think About Ethics?

You are a social work student who is struggling to balance a full course load, a 3 day/week internship, a part-time job, and family responsibilities. At times, the stress seems overwhelming and you are worried you might have to drop out. You tell a neighbor, who graduated with an MSW from a different school some years ago, about your situation. She is sympathetic and offers to give you a few of her old term papers on subjects similar to those covered in your courses. There is a very small chance of discovery. You are tempted to accept her offer, although the ethics of the matter concern you.

Questions:
1. What would you do?
2. What ethical principles are at stake?
3. How would you reach a decision about this issue?
4. How would you justify the decision?

Theoretical Foundations of Social Work Ethics

The purpose of ethics is to determine what types of behavior are desirable, in general and under particular circumstances. Two millennia ago, Aristotle wrote that the goal of ethics is to achieve the highest good for individuals and the community as a whole (Aristotle, as cited in Hittinger, 1989). Ethics, therefore, "involves the systematic examination of moral life and conduct ... whether personal or professional" (Engelhardt, 1982, p. 69). The practice of ethical reasoning provides social workers with the tools we need to create and sustain our moral obligations to other people as human beings, not merely as "clients" (Evans & Hardy, 2017; Banks, 2016).

Modern Western ethical discourse evolved during a period dominated by market economies, the emergence of nation-states, and the predominance of liberal values. It has largely focused on two basic issues: (1) the critical role of individual freedom (although the definition of freedom has changed during the past 300 years) and (2) the challenges involved in establishing on a rational basis or by consensus what constitutes the foundation of a moral life (Lorenz, 2016a). In addition to determining what is right or wrong, dominant cultures have used ethics to uphold established societal customs and as the foundation for formal rules of professional or civic conduct, particularly in institutional settings, and religious commandments (Gray, 2019; Clifford, 2016). Despite the continuing influence of religious doctrines, modern Western secular thought has primarily based ethical principles on reason (Davson-Galle, 2016).

This approach assumes that the application of ethics helps reconcile fundamental social and political

IMAGE 2.3. Aristotle

differences without coercion or resort to violence. To achieve this desirable end, however, societies must reach consensus about what values (or goods) should have priority and obtain broad agreement that these values can be established and maintained only if everyone participates freely in their selection and application. Because of the diversity of values and goals in contemporary society and the different ways people make ethical decisions, we must also recognize that reason alone is insufficient to determine what these values are, how we should define them, what their underlying goals are, and how to implement these values in practice. As this book suggests, these are no simple tasks for social workers, in part because the core values of the profession are somewhat ambiguous, subject to frequent contestation, and rarely supported by logical arguments alone.

FIGURE 2.1. Core Values

Gerald Dworkin's (1988) division of moral theory into three categories helps explain the basis of current conflicts about ethical decision-making in our society and in social work. He suggests that there are three types of moral theory:

1. those that focus on ends to rationalize the means employed;
2. those based on rights, to be achieved regardless of the consequences involved in satisfying those rights; and
3. those that emphasize a duty to act in a certain way, either because it serves a worthy goal or is required to satisfy another's rights.

These approaches sometimes conflict, primarily because the interests of individuals and groups may conflict with those of other individuals and groups or the community at large. The resolution of these interests through reason alone, therefore, may be impossible in today's hyperpartisan and socially polarized environment. The anxiety produced by the recent pandemic and its economic consequences exacerbates this already difficult situation.

Hittinger (1989) suggests that throughout history people have used six approaches to ethical inquiry to resolve such differences. The oldest and most extensive approach he termed "divine command ethics." This approach relied on revelation and belief as its justification. In many parts of world, including regions of the United States, this approach still has extensive influence. For example, as discussed in Chapter 3, it creates particular challenges for social workers who adopt a "faith-based" approach to practice to reconcile their beliefs with the secular language of the NASW *Code of Ethics*. This approach also creates challenges for nonreligious practitioners who work for sectarian agencies or with people who have strong religious convictions.

The second and third approaches—"natural virtue ethics" and "natural law ethics"—emerged from the ancient Greeks and the Judeo-Christian tradition. The former, best exemplified by the writings of Aristotle (1999), emphasized the importance of moral education as a means of teaching shared communal values. Communitarian thought is its closest contemporary secular example (Etzioni, 2018b; Sandel, 2013). The latter approach appeared during the Enlightenment as a synthesis of natural philosophy and Western religious values. Although it references a divinity, its basic appeal is to reason rather than faith, as reflected in the language of the American Declaration of Independence.

This approach expanded somewhat on the earlier work of the British philosophers Thomas Hobbes (1651/2016) and John Locke (1689). In their writings, they argued for "natural rights ethics" that focused on individual rights and liberties instead of personal virtue and obligations to the community or the sovereign. This concept of ethics influenced both the United Nations *Universal Declaration of Human Rights* (1948) and the long-standing social work principle of self-determination.

IMAGE 2.4. Thomas Hobbes   IMAGE 2.5. John Locke

The German philosopher Immanuel Kant (1781/1999) took these ideas further and developed what Hittinger (1989) refers to as "rational duty ethics." Kant's approach places reason at its center, founded on two core principles. First, that actions based on reason alone should be the basis of universal laws expressed through a hierarchy of values (a deontological approach to ethics). Second, that one's actions should always treat other persons as ends, not means, because they are rational beings. In other words, Kant's "categorical imperative" states that respect for persons is not a value to be weighed with others but a precondition for ethical behavior, what modern philosophers refer to as a "side constraint." This rule-driven, primarily individually focused approach, reflected as well in the NASW *Code of Ethics*, emphasizes freedom and autonomy, and establishes expectations for how social workers should treat the people with whom we work (Banks, 2016; Gray, 2010).

IMAGE 2.6. Immanuel Kant

In the early and mid-19th century, Jeremy Bentham (1838–1843/1996) and John Stuart Mill (1861/1971) introduced an alternative approach to the resolution of ethical dilemmas—utilitarianism. They argued that morality is always situational and the rightness or wrongness of alternative courses of action can only be determined by weighing their consequences. For the past 200 years, this consequentialist approach has, with some modifications, dominated Western ethical discourse and shaped much of U.S. social policy (Chichilnisky et al., 2020; Smith et al., 2019).

During the past half century, however, critiques of both approaches have appeared. Critics of deontology have asserted that it is overly formal and rigid, that any hierarchy of values is inherently subjective and determined by one's culture, history, and social status, and that reliance on reason alone to assess the ethics of a given situation is insufficient. They also point out the potential conflicts between what is good for an individual and the preservation of their autonomy, as reflected in the tension between preserving a person's self-determination and enhancing their well-being through benevolent paternalistic impulses. An additional problem of a deontological approach, one that is particularly relevant for social workers concerned about empowerment and privilege, is determining who has the authority to establish value hierarchies or make ethical decisions, especially when working with persons in vulnerable conditions (DeMartino et al., 2017; Hugman, 2016).

Critics of utilitarian thinking have also identified several problems. First, they argue that the goal of utilitarianism—whether stated as "the greatest good for the greatest number" or the "greatest net balance of satisfaction"—may not benefit the entire community and can, through its emphasis on efficacy (e.g., cost-benefit analysis), rationalize the existence of enormous social inequalities (Subramanian, 2019; Sandel, 2013; Rawls, 2001). For example, think how we interpret data regarding the nation's Gross Domestic Product, or GDP. This indicator reflects the total value of goods and services produced in the United States, but it reveals nothing about the distribution of these goods. In fact, in recent decades increased inequality has emerged concurrently with GDP growth (Blau, 2019). This demonstrates in stark terms that the promotion of "the greatest good" could have negative consequences for a sizable portion of the population and may not be consistent with the attainment of the "common good." The stark racial and class differences in the impact of the recent pandemic painfully illustrate this problem.

A second problem with utilitarianism is the difficulty of predicting the consequences of any decision. What proponents of utilitarianism assess as "right" action may not produce any observable benefits. In addition, unintended consequences often appear both in the interpersonal sphere—think about the difficulty of predicting how an individual client might respond to a specific intervention—and in the macro arena where policy or program changes can produce unplanned and often undesirable effects or where unforeseen intervening variables might influence anticipated outcomes. Examples of the latter include the byproducts of China's "one child" policy on the care of the elderly, and the failure of health policy reforms in the United States, such as Medicare and Medicaid, to control rapidly rising health care costs. Lastly, the development of a "utilitarian calculus" requires us to compare different types of consequences, short-term versus long-term consequences, and the effects of our decisions on third parties, who may not have been factors in the original "equation."

In his highly influential work, *A Theory of Justice*, John Rawls (1999) attempted to synthesize concepts derived from rule utilitarianism with the Kantian notion of universal individual rights. He argued that the central problem with utilitarianism is that it defines what is "good" and "right" separately. It then determines that the "right" is merely the maximization of an independently and subjectively defined "good." As an alternative, he proposed two core principles: the priority of liberty and the maximin principle.

The first principle states that each person is entitled to the greatest possible personal liberty

IMAGE 2.7. Jeremy Bentham

IMAGE 2.8. John Stuart Mill

compatible with liberty for all. In U.S. jurisprudence, for example, the Constitution protects Americans' right to free speech, even hate speech, but in the immortal words of Justice Oliver Wendell Holmes Jr., it does not give us the right to yell "fire" in a crowded theater. Recent policy debates about the extent to which property owners can use their property regardless of the environmental consequences or whether individuals can refuse to comply with government regulations imposed to slow the course of the coronavirus pandemic demonstrate how the application of the principle of individual freedom has become increasingly complicated and contested.

Rawls's second principle is even more controversial. It states that social inequalities are justified solely if they serve the interests of the least advantaged. For example, according to Rawls it is acceptable for a surgeon to receive a higher salary than a hospital orderly provided the surgeon used their skills to assist those with fewer assets and opportunities. Although this principle forms the basis of modern justifications for the redistribution of resources and is, therefore, seemingly compatible with social work values, critics on both the right and left of the ideological spectrum have challenged its presumptions or its omissions.

Conservative philosophers like Robert Nozick (1974) disagreed with Rawls's second principle. He distinguished between inequalities that are "unfair" (i.e., produced by deliberate discrimination) and those that are "unfortunate" (the consequence of the unequal distribution of personal talents or initial life circumstances). Contemporary political counterparts, like the libertarian U.S. Senator Rand Paul (R-Kentucky), maintain that the application of Rawls's second principle would undermine human initiative by disregarding the importance of merit and give government an undue and deleterious role in the economy and society. For much of U.S. history, similar criticisms of redistributive principles have exercised considerable influence on the development of social policy and social services. They continue to do so today, even in the midst of the worst economic crisis since the Great Depression, as reflected in the resistance of some politicians to the extension of unemployment benefits.

Sympathetic critics of Rawls, such as Amartya Sen (2009) and Martha Nussbaum (2013), point out that his principles omit certain crucial factors. For example, they do not take into account the significance of nonmaterial resources in promoting human well-being, the treatment of marginalized populations such as persons with disabilities, or the use of undemocratic processes to determine which resources to distribute. In addition, by focusing largely on the ends of distribution, they overlook how ethical considerations also require the use of just means.

Recently, there has been a resurgence of interest in the ethics of virtue, which dates back to Aristotle, and asks us to examine our assumptions about the role of humans in society. Proponents of global action to address climate change and environmental justice often rely on some version of virtue ethics (Erickson, 2018; Philip & Reisch, 2015). In contrast to "principle ethics," which focuses on rights, rules and obligations, virtue ethics goes beyond formal duties "to include character traits and ideals that assist in the development of ethical decision-making. ... [They] address how an individual decides which principle to apply ... when two or more principles are in conflict" (Donovan & Regehr, 2010, p. 179). Some proponents of virtue ethics have tried to reconnect morals and religion; others have promoted greater interest in natural law theory or a shift in focus from individual rights to community well-being (Papouli, 2019).

Based on the earlier work of feminist scholars in the fields of psychology (Gilligan, 1993) and political science (Eisenstein, 1979), feminist theorists have challenged the male-dominated approach to Western ethical thought (Lindeman, 2019; Clement, 2018). They argue that contemporary societal (and social work) values and ethics reflect two ideals that sometimes conflict: an emphasis on responsibility, with roots in religious values, and a focus on rights emanating from the primacy of individual freedom in liberal thought. The former ideal, the basis of virtue ethics, stresses caring, mercy, relationships, responsibilities, a nonjudgmental approach to practice, and the inherent humanity of all people (Jaggar, 2018). The latter, masculine model develops universal principles, such as equality and justice, and focuses on legal rights (Gray, 2010). Feminist ethicists assert that mere compliance with rules or value-driven principles, while often important, is insufficient to create ethical practice. "Perhaps," they argue, "morality is not about conforming to rules, but more about being trained to see problematic situations in a moral way" (Phoca & Wright, 1999, p. 123, as quoted in Gray, 2010).

In the United States, a consequence of this persistent dichotomous approach to ethics is the relegation of care to the private sphere, where it has become largely women's province, and to women-dominated professions like social work, teaching, and nursing in the public sphere. From this perspective, the promotion of an ethics of care is an attempt to reconnect social work practice to its origins as a caregiving set of activities. This view of ethics reflects the notion that caring and nurturing are core human needs, as much as the possession of material necessities. Its emphases are compatible with Nussbaum's (2013) "capabilities perspective" on social justice and with the notion of "common human needs" expressed by social worker Charlotte Towle (1945) 75 years ago. Proponents assert that a widely shared ethic of compassion is required to generate political support for policies that address the entire spectrum of people's needs. Unfortunately, as recent events demonstrate all too often, this is sadly lacking in the United States today, even in the midst of a pandemic or the aftermath of a natural disaster.

Virtue ethics also emphasizes the importance of communication and dialogue between workers and clients to produce shared understanding but not necessarily agreement (Pawar et al., 2017, pp. 193-204). At the institutional level, it would require the creation of democratic, universally participatory procedures. Similar to the ideas of social work pioneer Bertha Capen Reynolds (1951) and recent empowerment theorists (Stepney, 2019; Lee & Hudson, 2017), it stresses the role of mutuality in the caring relationship. It also goes beyond a focus on individual personal connections to examine their political dimensions by pointing out how policies have devalued the role of care and caregivers. (Ironically, feminists' emphasis on virtue ethics as intrinsic to human nature and the connection they point out exists between virtue and individual and community well-being harks back to Aristotle's definition of justice—a definition that excluded most Athenians, including women.)

A reliance on the ethics of virtue, however, creates two potential problems. First, as historians of social welfare have pointed out, the desire to "do good" for others may undermine people's autonomy and self-determination (Gaylin et al., 1978). Benevolent intentions can rationalize paternalistic behavior or even physical or emotional coercion under the guise of promoting an individual's "best interests." Second, the resultant individualization of care can lead to arbitrary and subjective preferences by the caregiver because of implicit biases or organizational fiscal and political priorities. On the other hand, reliance on universal principles can result in the failure to respond to unique individual circumstances and produce rigid practice prescriptions, particularly in large organizations (Fabricant & Burghardt, 2015). To date, the NASW *Code* has attempted to synthesize these two approaches. It has had limited success, however, in clearly articulating the underlying theoretical basis of either approach.

Approaches to Ethical Inquiry

APPROACH	SOURCE	KEY EMPHASIS
Divine Command Ethics	Ancient religions	Ethics based on revelation
Natural Virtue Ethics	Aristotle	Role of moral education
Natural Law Ethics	Enlightenment	Appeal to reason
Natural Duty Ethics	Kant	Rule driven, hierarchy of values
Utilitarianism	Bentham & Mill	Situational nature of morality
Social Justice Ethics	Rawls	Priority of liberty & needs of the least advantaged
Virtue Ethics	20th-century feminism	Caring, mercy, relationships, character, responsibilities

Other Critiques of Social Work Ethics

Since the 1980s, the growing influence of postmodernism has further complicated views of social work ethics by proposing the replacement of modernist theories that emphasize methodological objectivity with an emphasis on relativism and subjectivism, particularly in the use of language (Garrett, 2018). Postmodernists criticize rule-based ethical conduct and stress the role of ambiguity and uncertainty (Gray, 2010). Influential founders of postmodern discourse like Foucault (1998) and Bauman (1993) emphasized the self as the source of values and morals. Similar to proponents of virtue ethics, they stressed the importance of communication between people (negotiation) rather than leaving the determination of the ethical norms of a situation to the more powerful party. Foucault's critique is particularly relevant to social work as it draws attention to the role that knowledge and power plays in social workers' relationship with clients and to the dangers involved in embracing a view of practice as "ethically neutral."

Hugman (2003), however, criticized postmodernism's relationship to social work on three grounds that remain relevant today. First, he argued that it erodes the role of evidence, which is a valuable tool to combat the present environment of "alternative facts." This erosion also threatens to subjugate ethics to technique and formal codes of conduct.

Second, although postmodernism revises the relationship between social workers and service users along the more egalitarian lines proposed by radical social workers, Hugman asserted that "if the only difference between the professional and the service user is social power as compared to … professional knowledge and skill, then it could even be argued that the ethical demands for responsibility actually increase." Hugman's third critique of postmodernism is that it weakens the ability of social workers to combat the neoliberal agenda, particularly the media's distortion of reality to serve the interests of neoliberalism (pp. 1031–1032).

Other authors have raised similar questions about contemporary perspectives on social work ethics. Thirty years ago, Holland and Kilpatrick (1991) asserted that when moral duties conflict, the profession's ethical discourse largely emphasizes a utilitarian, cost-benefit approach that attempts to maximize the "good" and assess practice behaviors in terms of how they achieve this goal. Under such circumstances, they maintained, our duties depend on our ability to use our power and resources with compassion and integrity. They argued further that determining whether to focus on means or ends in resolving an ethical dilemma requires more than knowledge or technique. These critical assertions continue to have merit today.

Weinberg (2010) took a complementary position. She suggested that an underlying problem for social work ethics is the contradiction between practice as a "liberatory activity" and the embeddedness of most practitioners in institutions whose purposes are to regulate people and maintain the status quo (See also Soss et al., 2011). In addition, she pointed out that the needs of social workers' clients often conflict with each other, creating another paradoxical and challenging ethical situation. A third contradiction she identified is between the infinite nature of human needs and the finite nature of resources (material and personal) available to address them. Virtually every social worker experiences this tension regularly, whatever their method or field of practice.

Weinberg concluded that in combination these contradictions have produced a view of ethical practice that prescribes certain behavior in one-to-one relationships but pays lip service to the structural components that influence the practice context. This approach also supports the prevailing "master narrative" of the profession and its underlying assumption that the current environment is essentially benign (McKenzie-Mohr & Lafrance, 2017; Jani & Reisch, 2011). In addition, it influences "how certain ethical beliefs and qualities of character are constructed and performed" in an uncritical manner (Banks, 2006, p. xv).

According to Weinberg (2010) and historians of social work history (Reisch & Andrews, 2002; Specht & Courtney, 1994; Wenocur & Reisch, 1989), the source of this current dilemma for ethical practice lies in the professionalizing impulse. For over a century, the pursuit and protection of our fragile occupational status in a highly competitive market economy has compelled social workers to focus our practice on individual behavior (an emphasis on self-determination), individual responsibility (a focus on human agency), and individual (clinical) intervention. "As a result, social work practitioners often see ethics as being primarily a personal rather than a communal responsibility, supported by codes that place the blame for inadequacies squarely on the shoulders of individuals as independent actors" (Weinberg, 2010, p. 36). In recent years, the imposition of prescriptive codes, licensing regulations, and professional disciplinary committees that increasingly emphasize risk management reinforces this construction (Reamer, 2015b).

Hugman (2003) suggests that the solution to these longstanding problems is to replace the prescriptive nature of ethical codes with a "discursive code" that contains the following elements:

- An emphasis on core principles and values
- An embrace of diversity in the broadest sense of the term
- An ability to struggle with the inevitable contradictions that arise in practice
- Embrace of a "morally active" stance rather than merely following ethical prescriptions
- Recognition of the contextual nature of practice (p. 1037)

FOR REFLECTION: VALUES AND MORAL NEUTRALITY

1. Are all values equally valid?
2. If not, which values should be universal? Which ones should be subject to diverse cultural perspectives?
3. Should social workers be morally and politically neutral?
4. What might be the consequences if we maintained moral and political neutrality?
5. What might be the consequences if we adopted a more partisan stance?

As the above discussion indicates, most ethical dilemmas do not involve clear "right versus wrong" situations; rather, they involve increasingly complex choices between two "goods" or two equally unpalatable options, often with insufficient information or time. Determining how you approach such situations is a critical aspect of professional development. The following is an example of this type of ethical dilemma.

ETHICAL DILEMMA 2.3

How Should I Resolve an Ethical Dilemma?

You are a social worker in a community hospital responsible for the discharge planning of elderly patients. The hospital scheduled two patients, Ms. Jones and Ms. Smith, for discharge this morning. Both women recently suffered mild strokes and now experience partial dementia. They do not have life-threatening illnesses but are no longer capable of self-care. You have called the two assisted living facilities in your community to find a place for them and learned that one of the facilities has a single opening.

Ms. Jones has limited means but has a large, loving family who live nearby. They are willing to care for her, but doing so would put a considerable strain on their finances and require major adjustments in their lifestyle and living arrangements for an indefinite period. There is the possibility Ms. Jones could obtain some financial assistance to cover the cost of assisted living, but determining her eligibility could take some time.

Ms. Smith has no children, and her few surviving cousins live 2,000 miles away. Her husband left her a substantial estate and she could afford either assisted living or in-home nursing care. She indicated to you, however, that she would feel uncomfortable if a "stranger" lived with her on a regular basis. You have to decide within a few hours which of the women you will try to place in the assisted living facility.

Questions:

1. What process would you use to make this decision? For what reasons?
2. What factors would you take into account?
3. Whatever approach you chose, would you apply this process to other ethical dilemmas? Why or why not?

This dilemma underscores several factors that complicate the process of ethical decision-making in practice. One is the lack of adequate time to make the decision or to discuss the implications with Ms. Jones and Ms. Smith and their families. Another is the absence of sufficient information—about the accommodations the Jones family would have to make if Ms. Jones lived with them, what support they might receive if they agreed to this option, and about the availability and quality of in-home care in the community. A third factor is the difficulty in assessing the potential consequences of either decision on Ms. Jones, Ms. Smith, and their respective families.

Resolving Ethical Dilemmas

"Ethics is the moral strength to do what we know is right, and not to do what we know is wrong" (Silas, n.d., p. 1). As the above case illustrates, the challenge, of course, is that determining what is right and wrong in complex practice situations is not always easy. We often have to choose between competing rights or competing wrongs with no clear rules to follow. This is why it is important to develop a consistent, coherent framework to resolve such dilemmas.

While ethics generally is concerned with human conduct and moral choice in the broadest sense, professional ethics focuses specifically on the conduct of practitioners and the organizations in which we work in a specific context. In today's complex environment, the resolution of the ethical dilemmas that inevitably arise in our practice requires cross-disciplinary knowledge and the skills acquired through practice experience. As advocates of an ethic of care assert, scientific evidence alone is insufficient. To practice ethically, therefore, we need to be "aware of the moral ideals of the profession, become more sensitive to client values, and increase [our] sense of ethical responsibility" (Joseph, 1991, p. 98). This implies that ethical decision-making is a reflective and reflexive process. Yet, most of the social work literature on ethics, including the NASW *Code of Ethics*, is largely descriptive and does not provide much guidance as to how to make hard choices (Hardy, 2019; Congress, 2017).

Clark (2012) maintained that the literature largely focuses on four approaches to ethical decision-making: those based on induction from published ethical codes, decision-making algorithms, formal tribunals, and agency practices. As an alternative, he proposed the use of a hermeneutic or interpretive process to reconcile the specifics of an ethical dilemma with the shifting moral imperatives of the profession and the wider society.

As discussed in Chapter 1, virtually all frameworks to resolve ethical dilemmas contain some similar elements, whether they deal with human problems or those of other species (Walker & Tumilty, 2019). With near unanimity, they possess the following components: determining the facts, collecting relevant historical and empirical knowledge of the issues, clarifying the ethical criteria used, and justifying the reasons for their selection. They also involve making our value choices explicit, prioritizing our values, and assessing the consequences of alternative courses of action. Josephson (2002) succinctly summarized these "5 steps to principled reasoning" as

1. Clarify
2. Evaluate
3. Decide
4. Implement
5. Monitor and Modify

In the absence of a clear, consistent decision-making framework, we are likely to confuse ethical issues with practice problems. Although these two types of challenges overlap, they require distinct forms of resolution as the following dilemma illustrates.

What Constitutes an *Ethical* Dilemma?

You are a social worker employed by a community center in a multiracial urban setting. One of your responsibilities is to help the center's teenagers with family and school issues and to counsel them about career choices. One of the young men with whom you have developed a good relationship, Roberto S., asks to speak with you one afternoon. He will graduate from high school in a few months and is trying to decide what to do.

His parents want him to enroll in the local community college and eventually get a 4-year college degree. They believe this is the best option for him to get a well-paying job in the future. Roberto is a B student. He could probably do well in college, but he wants to enlist in the Marines. He has a strong desire to serve his adopted country and points out that he could obtain a government scholarship for college after he completes his tour of duty. He asks you to speak with his parents to help persuade them to give him permission to enlist.

You fear that Roberto would put his life and his future at risk if he enlisted. You would strongly prefer that he go to college. You also have strong feelings about the role of the military in U.S. society. How would you respond to Roberto's request?

Questions:
1. What type of dilemma does this situation reflect?
2. What, if any, conflict of values or ethical principles exists?
3. What values or principles would guide you in determining your response to Roberto?

This situation illustrates that it is equally important to recognize what ethical decision-making is not. It does not determine the most effective means of intervention in a specific practice situation. To do that, you would have to consult with your supervisor about whether it was appropriate for you to meet with Roberto's parents and, if so, how to approach them.

According to Silas (n.d.), an ethical decision in such matters is not only what is enforceable, legal, expedient, and excusable. (In the above case, you would not be committing an ethical violation by sharing what Roberto told you in confidence with his parents. He asked you to do so.) Nevertheless, there is always the possibility that, whatever you decided, third parties, such as Roberto's parents, could misinterpret your best intentions. In some circumstances, people and organizations with power might deliberately or inadvertently circumvent, misinterpret, or subjectively apply policies and procedures in a manner that undercuts your attempt to be helpful and supportive to a client. Finally, in other circumstances, the law may reflect long-standing injustices while appeals to societal customs or traditions may inadvertently perpetuate unfair practices.

Sometimes it is useful for social workers to explore how other professions have addressed similar issues. For example, four decades ago in the *American Journal of Nursing*, Smith and Davis (1980) listed four basic steps practitioners can use to resolve ethical dilemmas:

1. Gather as much information about the situation as possible, keeping in mind the parties to the situation, the context, and the possible courses of action and their potential consequences.
2. Determine who should make the decision based on criteria beyond technical expertise.
3. Decide the criteria to be use to select an alternative, including the purpose of the action.
4. Assess the implications and consequences of the action chosen.

To follow these steps in the case of Roberto S., you would initially need to find out several things prior to making a decision as to how to respond to his request. First, how strongly do his parents feel about his enlistment in the Marines? Second, what are all his motives behind the desire to enlist in the Marines and not enroll in community college? Third, what is his relationship with his parents like? Fourth, how much time does Roberto have to make this important decision? Finally, what other options might be available to satisfy Roberto's interests?

You would then have to determine whether Roberto can make this decision unilaterally or whether he needs his parents' permission. Next, you would clarify what values and principles you would prioritize to help you decide how to act. Consulting with your supervisor would be advisable at this point. Finally, you would have to assess the implications of either decision.

This approach is similar to several of the models presented in Chapter 1. Reamer's model (2018a), for example, relies on Gewirth's principle of generic consistency from which he derives three implications based on Gewirth's "supreme moral principle." First, social work practice decisions must be voluntary and purposive. These decisions involve three categories of social "goods": (1) basic goods—those that provide the necessary preconditions for life; (2) nonsubtractive goods—those that are necessary for individuals to maintain their critical capacities; and (3) additive goods—those goods that would enhance their overall well-being. The "goods" in Roberto's case clearly fall into the third category.

Second, social workers have a duty to determine whether an intervention is required and, if so, who has the duty to initiate that intervention. If not, what is the ethical basis for nonintervention? In the above situation, you would have to decide if any intervention is appropriate or would be helpful under the circumstances and, if so, who would be the best (most authoritative, influential, and ethically appropriate) person to intervene. Third, all ethical decisions involve making choices about material and nonmaterial resource distribution. This would require reflecting on what resources are at stake for Roberto and his family if he enlists in the Marines or decides to attend community college.

Based on these general principles, Reamer (1983a) proposed the following hierarchy of values to guide ethical decision-making.

REAMER'S HIERARCHY OF VALUES

1. The right to basic well-being takes precedence over another individual's right to freedom.
2. The right to freedom takes precedence over the right to basic well-being.
3. The obligation to obey laws, rules, and regulations to which one has voluntarily and freely consented ordinarily overrides the right to engage voluntarily and freely in a manner which conflicts with these laws, rules, and regulations.
4. The right to well-being may override laws, rules, regulations, and arrangements of voluntary association in cases of conflict.
5. The obligation to prevent basic harms (e.g., starvation) and to promote public goods (e.g., housing) overrides the right to retain one's property.
6. Rules against basic harms to the necessary preconditions of action (e.g., life, health) take precedence over rules against harms such as lying or revealing confidential information. (Reamer, 1983a, p. 34)

Using a somewhat difference approach, Dolgoff, Harrington, and Loewenberg (2012) developed the following hierarchy of values:

DOLGOFF, HARRINGTON, AND LOEWENBERG'S VALUE HIERARCHY

1. Protection of human life
2. Equity: Treating all persons in the same circumstances the same way
3. Autonomy/freedom (self-determination)
4. Principle of least harm (like medicine)
5. Better quality of life for all
6. Privacy and confidentiality
7. Truthfulness and full disclosure (See also Harrington & Dolgoff, 2008)

QUESTIONS

1. What are the similarities and differences between these two hierarchies?
2. Which one do you prefer? For what reasons?
3. How would you construct your own hierarchy? What would it look like?

Current Challenges to Ethical Decision-Making

Social workers have confronted ethical dilemmas in practice since the emergence of the profession. It is no exaggeration, however, that the ethical challenges we face today are more complicated and serious than ever. We all experience these challenges whatever method of practice we use and in whatever field of practice we work. Ethical challenges exist in our efforts to defend the rights and benefits of individuals in all types of organizations and to promote change in the policy arena. They also appear in areas of practice, such as environmental justice, and around issues like the use of social media, which scarcely existed a few years ago (Erickson, 2018; Young et al., 2018; Boddy & Dominelli, 2017).

Throughout social work's history, our professional status aspirations shaped how we applied ethical theories and principles to practice. In recent decades, the emergence of issues such as climate change, demographic diversity, and technological advances have produced new challenges about the meaning and application of social work's core values. As discussed earlier in this chapter, critiques of long-standing approaches to ethics have further complicated matters for practitioners (Shaw, 2018; Banks, 2016).

One contemporary response to the increasingly complex ethical environment of practice is the proliferation and expansion of new and revised codes of ethics around the world. Ironically, research reveals that social workers rarely use these codes as guides to practice, nor do they consciously apply existing models of ethical decision-making. Although social work students

"We have an agreement in principle.
The question is, do we all have the same principles?"

FIGURE 2.2. Ethical Principles

are encouraged to think about ethical issues in their practice, they less frequently learn how to implement the values underlying these issues (Barsky, 2019).

In addition, addressing the theoretical and political challenges to the notion of universally valid ethical principles has become increasingly important in our interdependent world (Hugman, 2017). A particularly vexing issue today is how to combine our ethical imperative to pursue social justice with contextually specific practice in multicultural societies. In response to this dilemma, Banks (2008) suggests the development of "more conscious linkages between social work ethics and politics" (p. 1244). Weinberg (2010) proposes that social workers move "beyond the [emphasis] on ... one-to-one relationship[s]" (p. 40) and reconstruct an ethical foundation based on community solidarity and the repoliticization of practice, a call echoed by other scholars (Lane et al., 2018; Reisch & Jani, 2012). Recognition of the political and ethical choices in any practice decision is particularly critical in the current environment. It requires open dialogue between colleagues and service users regarding the values that shape both our desired ends and the means we use to achieve them (Rasell et al., 2019).

The Problem of Technism

Over 30 years ago, Hittinger (1989) suggested that two major obstacles exist to the implementation of ethical practice: *technism* (increased emphasis on technique and efficiency) and *relativism* (the prioritization of personal preferences over universal standards). The promotion of evidence-based practice (EBP) is the latest manifestation of the former. It has led to a reification of the distinction between knowledge (facts), which are reputedly objective, and values, largely regarded as subjective and unscientific (Gordon, 1965). This trend also produced an emphasis on prediction and control, as illustrated by the current focus on intervention research. If anything, these trends are even more influential today.

Yet, the focus on EBP largely ignores the issue of who determines the objects of study and control, the ends for which we use research, the means by which we conduct research, and the ideological dimensions of all scholarship. Whatever research method we employ to inform our practice, there is no escaping the reality that all types of research involve a subjective, value-driven endeavor that influences both its stated and unstated goals and the ways in which we apply research findings (Nothdurfter & Lorenz, 2010).

FIGURE 2.3. Identifying Universal Values and Ethics in a Multicultural World Is a Growing Challenge

In contrast, "the discipline of ethics … [deals explicitly] with the question of ends and purposes which by methodological exclusion are absent from scientific purview (Hittinger, 1989, p. 19). In recent decades, this tension between the profession's scientific and humanistic epistemologies and traditions has intensified as challenges emerged to basing clinical interventions solely on scientific evidence (Larsson, 2019; Mersky et al., 2019). This is particularly true in fields like child welfare, in which social workers are the primary professionals (Keddell & Stanley, 2019; Hardesty, 2015). As Reamer has long argued (1983a), scientific research cannot help social workers make situationally appropriate ethical decisions around such issues as confidentiality, truth-telling, whistleblowing, and the allocation of scarce resources.

In sum, the persistent belief in value-free science poses significant risks to our ability to exercise moral judgement (Maguire, 1978). The involvement of social workers, individually and collectively, in politics is, therefore, "necessary and moral" as "politics will [always] … be an area where conscience and power meet, where the ethical and coercive factors of human life will interpenetrate and work out their tentative and uneasy compromises" (p. 19). In today's environment, where glaring power imbalances exist on every level of society, the importance of ethics as an arena where we question the unquestioned cannot be overstated.

The Problem of Relativism

Relativism is also an outgrowth of the fact/value dichotomy, most recently influenced by the introduction of postmodern and multicultural perspectives into social work practice. One perhaps unintended consequence of these new perspectives is the notion that we are incapable of resolving most ethical disputes. If fully embraced, this could produce a form of ethical paralysis among practitioners that would certainly be of little benefit to the people with whom we work, the organizations in which we work, and our own sense of efficacy and integrity (Singh & Cowden, 2017).

The concept of ethical relativism also raises three fundamental questions for practice: What exactly is an ethical issue or moral dilemma? How do we identify one in today's morally and culturally ambiguous environment? If we identify one, how do we resolve it in the context of competing values and norms? The increased emphasis on technique based on "value-free evidence" also draws clearer distinctions between good practice and ethical practice. This occurs, for example, in "the tensions we sometimes experience between *empathy* and *ethical judgment*, between psychological understanding and ethical evaluation" (Rhodes, 1992, p. 41, emphasis in the original). In the current political and cultural environment, however, is a nonjudgmental posture possible or even desirable?

Thirty years ago, Fleck-Henderson (1991) pointed out that practitioners face three sorts of moral dilemmas: those produced by the assumptions that underlie our theories, policies, and practice decisions; those that emerge due to the conflicts in our professional values or obligations; and those that arise because of conflicts with clients' values. In today's culturally diverse context, the growing influence of relativism exacerbates these challenges because our dominant culture produces and reinforces implicit biases that cloud our ethical judgement. These biases influence whether we recognize the existence of a moral dilemma; whether we are conscious of how our moral judgement influences our assessment of a situation; whether we feel responsible for resolving a recognized moral dilemma; and whether we act based on our decisions.

In addition, the increasingly prescriptive nature of practice interventions, particularly with involuntary clients, compels us to recommit ourselves to our core values of social justice and empowerment (Reamer, 2018b; Lorenz, 2016b). It requires new alliances, more creative approaches to advocacy, and a revival of a political component to our practice. At a minimum, there is a need to rethink our long-standing ideas about professional objectivity and apolitical practice (Reisch & Jani, 2012).

Another obstacle to ethical practice today is the disappearance of what Rhodes referred to 35 years ago as "a community of shared values" of caring and compassion (Rhodes, 1985, p. 104). During the past several decades, the acceptance of neoliberalism as a rationale for the consequences of economic globalization has fundamentally transformed the meaning of care and societal responsibility. The heightened polarization of American society today is but one reflection of this development. As a result, the social work profession has struggled to balance our dual emphases on rights (reflected in the ethical imperative regarding social justice) and responsibility (reflected in the focus on the client's interests and self-determination). If these values cannot be reconciled, it raises the question of what type of society the profession wants to create (Reisch, 2013b).

Organizational Challenges

The gap between our ethical preferences and our ability to implement them in practice stems in large measure from external stresses on the agencies within which most social workers practice (Weinberg, 2010). These include resource cuts and more prescriptive government regulations. In turn, these stressors lead to restrictive organizational policies, greater emphasis on cost efficiency, excessive caseloads, and the trend toward the "industrialization" of social work (Fabricant & Burghardt, 2015). These developments have a significant effect on two fundamental, interrelated ethical issues in contemporary practice. One is the conflict between individual rights and community well-being or between internalized and externalized authority. The other is between individual responsibility and human agency and compliance with imposed authority through laws, norms, or customs (Banks, 2016).

These stresses also exacerbate an ongoing contradiction of social work practice between the promotion of individual well-being and the enforcement of institutionally imposed moral regulation. We rarely place the persistent effects of chronic resource scarcity and the impact of structural and institutional constraints on practice decisions, however, at the center of our ethical discourse. On the infrequent occasions when we introduce them into our ethical decision-making process, we reinterpret the structural causes of people's problems to adapt our clients to the individualized focus of most social work practice (Weinberg, 2010).

At the mezzo level of practice, organizations have long based ethical decisions on three factors: (1) the balance between administrative flexibility and control, (2) the tension between supporting staff and advancing the organization's goals, and (3) deciding whether to emphasize internal processes or prioritize outcomes (Holland & Kilpatrick, 1991). The current risk-averse trend in management practice in the social welfare field has significant consequences for each of these factors and the overall ability of social workers to practice ethically (Thompson & Wadley, 2018; Baines, 2017). One result of this trend, the fear of legal liability, produced the increasing use of rigid codes of conduct to regulate practitioners' behavior (Reamer, 2015c).

Concerns about "risk management" also promote an emphasis on the preservation of client's individual autonomy rather than the pursuit of social equity (Weinberg, 2010). Conflicts between professional values and agency rules further compound the challenges social workers face due to chronic fiscal austerity in the context of growing service demands. These tensions are a major cause of staff burnout and declining job satisfaction (Travis et al., 2016; Wilson, 2016). At the same time, the privatization of social services has made them less accessible to marginalized populations and created new ethical dilemmas for social workers, as the consequences of the recent pandemic underscore all too vividly.

Several additional factors, including the new managerialism, greater public demands for accountability, and the increased use of technology in practice exacerbate the moral conflicts we experience in our daily work. In particular, the growing trend toward managerialism creates obstacles for ethical practice by narrowing the sphere of professional autonomy and increasing the vulnerability of both workers and service users (Harlow, 2018; Lawler, 2018). Banks argues that increased managerialism, reflected in the "new public management" and the "marketization of social services" (Salamon, 1993), threatens the profession's commitment to advocate "for the powerless, ... resist ... injustice and refuse ... to treat people as objects" (Banks, 2011, p. 2). The spread of licensing and private practice exacerbates this trend (Slater, 2020; Reisch, 2019a; Grise-Owens et al., 2016).

In this new environment, social workers must also consider the effects of managerial and ethical decisions on our colleagues. Issues such as the pressure to maintain interpersonal civility and satisfy the expectations of our agency's organizational culture in a stressful climate, address increasingly complex demands in our daily practice, and resolve persistent ambiguities about the meaning of our core values such as social justice all influence our ethical behavior. Increased concern over such issues as bullying, emotional abuse, and sexual harassment in the workplace create additional pressure on us to act ethically. Given this growing pressure, the role of organizational leadership has acquired even greater importance. Organizational leaders, not just CEOs but agency thought and political leaders, must now make conscious, strategic efforts to set the right tone, promote dialogue, sanction inappropriate and unethical conduct, and establish mechanisms of accountability for all staff (O'Brien, 2014).

Legal Issues

As mentioned above, the threat of legal liability presents another growing challenge to ethical practice (Reamer, 2015b; Woodcock, 2011). Most ethical dilemmas in this area arise from one of the following situations:

- Conflict between two ethical principles;
- Conflict between two possible alternatives where the situation is fraught with uncertainty, especially in terms of the potential consequences of either action;
- Conflict between the demand for action and the need for reflection (time pressure), particularly in unprecedented situations;
- Conflict between two unsatisfactory alternatives; and
- Conflict between ethical principles and obligations as an employee (Smith & Davis, 1980, pp. 1463–1464).

Yet, differences also exist in the nature of legal rights themselves. Smith and Davis (1980) distinguished among the following types of legal rights:

- A *guaranteed right* provides permission to act, guarantees protection from interference and cannot be withdrawn under any circumstances.
- A *nonabsolute right* gives permission and protection but may be withdrawn under certain circumstances.
- A *legal privilege* grants permission to act but may or may not provide protection from interference. Both, however, may be withdrawn at any time.
- A *legal liberty* provides permission to act but no protection from interference.

There are also differences in ethical rights not established by law (Deck, 2016). In this regard, Smith and Davis (1980) distinguished conventional ethical rights, based on customs and traditions; ideal ethical rights; and conscientious ethical rights that neither convention nor ideal rules may recognize.

In the mid-1980s, Sieghart (1985) suggested that when ethics and laws come into conflict, social workers should reference human rights law and international covenants to maintain their values in the face of legal challenges. This emphasis on human rights emanates from the basic premises of professional morality: that "moral questions ... can only arise in the context of a relationship ... between a professional and his [sic] ... client" (p. 118). Yet, despite the growing emphasis today on human rights within Western social work (Androff, 2018; Wronka, 2016a), "collective rights [have been increasingly] replaced by individual obligations" (Weinberg, 2010, p. 37) in many areas of social work practice. This tendency reinforces our focus on individual autonomy in an environment of increased social, economic, and cultural anxiety. Our approaches to substance abuse, obesity, and parenting reflect this tension, as do the diverse responses to the current coronavirus pandemic.

Ongoing attacks on social welfare provisions in the media and political arena heighten these anxieties and undermine the trust relationship essential to effective practice in both micro and macro settings. Two interrelated issues further complicate the ethical environment of practice. One is the inevitability of global change on a massive scale due to economic, ecological, technological, and cultural developments beyond our immediate control or predictive capacity. The other is the profession's long-standing tendency to dichotomize practice with individuals and families and efforts to produce community or policy change. The latter also makes it more difficult for social workers to recognize how macro-level transformation affects daily practice and transforms practitioners into disempowered passive objects, not unlike the people with whom we work.

Challenges in the Nature of Practice

This rapid and unprecedented transformation of the practice environment creates new, more urgent ethical challenges for social workers. Due to space limitations and consideration of the reader's patience, the multiple components of this transformation are too numerous to illustrate in this chapter. A few examples will have to suffice. They involve changes in where we work, with whom we work, and how we work.

Where We Work

Isolated rural communities, for example, present unique ethical challenges for social workers, as they do for policy makers. In the United States, these communities disproportionately experience the effects of deindustrialization, opioid abuse, climate change, and increasing incidence of suicide. The implementation of ethical principles such as confidentiality, privacy, the prohibition on dual relationships, and conflicts of interest take on new dimensions in rural areas where the nexus of interpersonal contacts is more complex than in most urban and suburban settings (Edwards & Addae, 2015). The different environment requires social workers who work in rural areas to assess the implications of the ethical principles espoused by the NASW *Code* for their practice and analyze the extent to which they need to modify these principles in order to balance practice efficacy and ethical practice.

With Whom We Work

As discussed previously, our work with an increasing number of involuntary or multiple-issue clients often from culturally diverse backgrounds produces new ethical challenges in our practice. An ethical dilemma specific to schools of social work as an institution may result from their participation—through internships or joint research projects—in community programs that sometimes involve coercive practices or with agencies whose values diverge from the mission of the school or profession, such as private, for-profit organizations. Other ethical dilemmas for educational institutions may result from their overemphasis on technical skill acquisition in place of a focus on relationship building or from greater priority given to rationing resources than to social equity (Gustavsson & MacEachron, 2014). Decisions whether to include controversial topics in the social work literature in assigned readings, classroom discussions, or in faculty meetings may also give rise to ethical dilemmas (Marson & McKinney, 2019).

In addition, the aging and increased diversity of the U.S. population have produced or intensified a variety of ethical dilemmas for practitioners. There is growing concern, for example, about the ethical dilemmas created by elder abuse, an issue that frequently demonstrates the tension between preserving clients' self-determination and protecting them from harm (Donovan & Regehr, 2010). This issue is further complicated by the tendency of some practitioners to give higher priority to a client's autonomy than to their safety (p. 178) and by the lack of specificity in the NASW *Code* or most treatises on social work ethics as to how to handle such situations. The changing demographics of our society also highlights the need to reconsider the meaning of such ethical principles as confidentiality, truth-telling, and the allocation of scarce resources in circumstances that involve terminal illness or family conflict.

How We Practice

According to Reamer (2006), ethical dilemmas often occur due to a lack of practitioner competence, particularly when they employ nontraditional and unorthodox methods. He maintains
that the use of such modes of intervention increases the risk of ethics complaints, civil suits,
and criminal charges. To avoid such situations, Reamer recommends avoiding interventions
that clearly violate ethical guidelines and following the eight components of the procedural
standard of care. These are "(1) consulting colleagues; (2) obtaining proper informed consent;
(3) obtaining proper supervision; (4) reviewing relevant ethical standards; (5) reviewing
relevant regulations, laws, and policies; (6) reviewing relevant literature; (7) obtaining legal
consultation when necessary; and (8) documenting and evaluating decision-making steps"
(p. 194).

There are both similarities and differences in the application of such ethical guidelines to
practice with individuals and macro practice. One similarity is that most forms of social work
intervention require a partnership between the social worker and the social worker's clients
or constituents. Both forms of practice also require the application of critical consciousness
about the sources of people's issues and the use of critical thinking in developing strategies
to address them. In addition, in all forms of practice, ethical conduct is often situational
(Alinsky, 1971).

Common ethical conflicts also appear in all forms of practice. One conflict is between people's
right to self-determination and autonomy (what philosophers sometimes refer to as negative
freedom) and their right to the assistance required to protect their well-being and increase their
future prospects (positive freedom). Another conflict is between satisfying peoples' interests
as they define them and well-intentioned, but often paternalistic efforts to protect them from
harm. A third conflict exists between practice that focuses solely on an individual or group's
interests and practice that balances these interests with the "common good."

One important difference between macro practice and practice with individuals and families
is that in the former situation social workers may more often be a member of the same geographic community or community of identity as their constituents. Boundary issues between
workers and clients or constituents take on a different posture in these circumstances. A second
difference is that in macro practice social, community, or structural change, not individual
change, is a primary goal. A third difference reflects the distinction between people being
viewed as constituents (in macro practice) as compared to clients, who may be involuntary in
some circumstances or regard themselves as service "consumers" in others.

Strengths and Limitations of the NASW *Code of Ethics*

The revised NASW *Code of Ethics* (2018) attempts to address many of these rapid changes, particularly regarding the use of technology. It has also disseminated over three dozen changes in
practice standards related to the use of technology in both practice and educational contexts
(Gilliam, 2015). As discussed further in the chapter on confidentiality, the *Code* also contains
revised language regarding the duty to warn to include harm to "others" (instead of "another
identifiable person"). This stemmed from a 2016 Washington state case (*Volk v. DeMeerleer*)
that required a mental health professional to protect the foreseeable victims of DeMeerleer,

who later murdered a woman and her son and attempted to murder another of her children (Ferretto, 2018). These revisions strengthen the *Code*'s ability to provide social work students and new practitioners with guidelines for ethical practice.

Criticisms persist, however, over the *Code*'s "legalistic perspective [to ethical decision-making] that undervalues other important professional ethical sources" (Woodcock, 2011, p. 21). Unlike the resources available for the legal and medical professions that address ethical issues at a more sophisticated and specific level (Gillon, 1986), the NASW *Code* continues to omit content on how social workers should address legally risky or highly political situations (Lane & Pritzker, 2018b). It also lacks guidance on how we can adapt our universal ethical principles to circumstances that differ from the assumed "norm," such as the ethical dilemmas faced by rural social workers (Edwards & Addae, 2015) or those confronted by practitioners working with nonmajority cultures. To enhance our ability to resolve new and persistent ethical dilemmas, Woodcock proposes that social workers explore the similarities and differences between our approach to ethics and those of psychology, literature, economics, and the military.

Implications for Social Work Education

Because of these rapid transformations in the environment of practice, the place of ethics in social work education is even more vital today than it was several decades ago when Joseph and Conrad (1983) called for its resurgence (Reamer, 2019c). Unfortunately, in most programs ethics is still taught either as part of required courses or as an elective (Council on Social Work Education, 2019). This infusion model generally results in squeezing limited coverage of ethics content into the teaching of practice techniques. The failure to make ethical thinking a core component of the curriculum increases the possibility that ethical issues in our practice will receive insufficient attention at a time when they are more critical than ever. In the absence of additional educational content on ethics, the profession's foundations of altruism, compassion, human dignity, and social justice will come under increasing strain from the pressures of economic globalization, fiscal austerity, increasing demographic and cultural diversity (Payne & Askeland, 2016), and the effects of climate change and unpredictable pandemics.

Summary

This chapter began with a discussion of why ethics is and has always been a central concern of social workers. It provided a concise overview of the theoretical foundation of social work ethics, including recent theoretical developments and some of their critiques. In conjunction with the material in Chapter 1, it presented models of ethical decision-making and value hierarchies that subsequent chapters of the book will apply to specific cases. The chapter concluded with a discussion of current challenges to the application of social work ethics in our practice and education, and the strengths and shortcomings of the latest NASW *Code of Ethics*.

Future chapters will go into more detail about the application of specific ethical principles to practice. Before exploring these issues, Chapter 3 will examine the challenges involved in balancing our personal and professional values in practice.

Ethical Responsibilities in the NASW *Code of Ethics* (2018)

- Responsibilities to Clients
- Responsibilities to Colleagues
- Responsibilities in Practice Settings
- Responsibilities as Professionals
- Responsibilities to the Social Work Profession
- Responsibilities to the Broader Society

Key Ethical Principles in Practice with Individuals and Families

- Self-Determination: Respect for diversity, human agency
- Informed Consent: Purposes, costs, risks, alternatives, limits of action, partnership
- Client-Worker Boundaries
- Confidentiality and Truth-Telling and Their Limits

Ethical Issues Specific to Macro Social Work Practice

- Involuntary membership in social or political action/freedom to withdraw
- Informed consent (especially regarding risk)
- The limits of confidentiality
- Cultural differences (e.g., the meaning of group roles, styles, values and goals; community, leadership)
- Legal liability: Can community practitioners be guilty of malpractice?
- Means-Ends Dilemmas
- Allocation of Scarce Resources

Credits

Img. 2.1: Source: https://commons.wikimedia.org/wiki/File:Gustave_Dor%C3%A9_-_Poor_Children_of_London,_circa_1882-83.jpg.
Img. 2.2: Source: https://commons.wikimedia.org/wiki/File:Lange-MigrantMother02.jpg.
Img. 2.3: Copyright © 2014 Depositphotos/MidoSemsem.
Fig. 2.1: Copyright © 2014 Depositphotos/PixelsAway.
Img. 2.4: Source: https://commons.wikimedia.org/wiki/File:Thomas_Hobbes_(portrait).jpg.
Img. 2.5: Copyright © 2011 Depositphotos/georgios.
Img. 2.6: Source: https://commons.wikimedia.org/wiki/File:Immanuel_Kant_3.jpg.
Img. 2.7: Source: https://commons.wikimedia.org/wiki/File:Jeremy_Bentham_by_Henry_William_Pickersgill_detail.jpg.
Img. 2.8: Source: https://commons.wikimedia.org/wiki/File:John_Stuart_Mill_by_John_Watkins,_1865.jpg.
Fig. 2.2: Copyright © 2016 Depositphotos/andrewgenn.
Fig. 2.3: Copyright © 2013 Depositphotos/Tribaliumivanka.

Personal vs. Professional Values

Introduction

Social workers have struggled with the conflict between their personal and professional values and beliefs since the emergence of the field as a formal occupation in the late 19th century. Originally, this conflict stemmed from the vast class and cultural differences between the earliest social workers and the people with whom they worked and interacted. Many of our predecessors often had difficulty reconciling the profession's democratic goals and commitment to scientific objectivity with their longstanding class, ethnic, racial, and religious prejudices. As recent articles on unrecognized and unconscious bias in social work practice and education demonstrate, this issue persists even if it appears in different, more subtle forms (Weng & Gray, 2020; Brown et al., 2019; Kang & Garran, 2018; Dupper, 2017).

During the past half century, the emergence of identity-based social movements and acrimonious "culture wars" in the United States has added new dimensions to this long-standing challenge to our practice (Reisch 2020b; Hartman, 2019). Students, faculty, and practitioners contend almost daily with the tensions generated by the gap between their deeply held personal values and their allegiance to those of the profession. This chapter will discuss the sources of this conflict, its effects on our practice, and some possible ways to address it. Its topics include the origins of our personal values, the types of values that exist in our culture, the roots and evolution of social work values, the role of the NASW *Code of Ethics*, and the nature and sources of value conflicts in our practice. It will illustrate how these conflicts appear in such settings as social work with military personnel and veterans, practice with stigmatized and vulnerable populations, and work with clients or constituents who possess strong religious beliefs. Because understanding the distinction between personal and professional values is a critical component of students' socialization into the field, the concluding section will discuss in some detail the implications of these value conflicts for social work education.

ETHICAL DILEMMA 3.1   ## A Friendship at Risk

You are a social worker in a nonprofit, nonsectarian agency who is working on a collaborative health care project with another nonprofit organization affiliated with Catholic Charities. Your primary contact in the collaborative is a good friend from your MSW program. A major focus of the project is to enhance the quality of maternal and child health care in your community. One of the major areas of concern is the lack of quality reproductive and prenatal health services.

Although you and your colleague cooperate effectively and cordially in nearly all regards, you have reached an impasse over an aspect of this issue. Whatever her personal beliefs, your colleague's employer forbids her from contributing her time in any way to a program or service that violates long-established church doctrine on birth control and abortion. The chief program officer of a large foundation approached you recently about applying for a major grant that would, if approved, provide substantial resources for a range of health services the community desperately needs, including those that address family planning and women's reproductive health. Because of its limited staff, your agency needs the support of your colleague's organization to obtain this potential funding and utilize it effectively. The deadline to apply for the grant is within a month and it will take considerable time to pull it together. What do you do?

Questions:
1. What are the different values in conflict in this situation?
2. What process would you use to prioritize the values to guide your course of action?
3. How would you apply this process to other situations in which values come into conflict?

Origin of Our Personal Values

Our personal values emerge from our cultural background, the range of our life experiences, our interpretation of these experiences, and the immediate context of our personal and professional lives. They reflect what we know, think we know, do not know, and may not be able to know at all. These various influences contribute to the development of a "philosophy of life which dictates ... [our] actions and attitudes toward society in general, individuals within society, ... [and] toward selected groups ... [in] society" (Engelhardt, 1982a, p. 65).

FIGURE 3.1. The Range of Our Personal Values

As a result, our individual philosophy becomes a key component of our private and professional "self." The ethical decisions we make, therefore, reflect our "interpretation of the environment in which we were raised and the world in which we live" (Engelhardt, 1982b, p. 6). They evolve over time shaped by our society's customs, traditions, institutions, and laws. Because other individuals have had different life experiences and may interpret shared experiences differently, our ethical theories, values, and principles are always subject to dispute. The case above illustrates one way in which our different histories and current circumstances may create conflicts in our practice.

Values also reflect how we choose, prioritize, and act on our preferred outcomes for ourselves and for others. If you are uncertain as to whether something you believe is value based, ask yourself whether it is (1) prized; (2) freely and thoughtfully selected from among several alternatives; and (3) acted upon, repeated, and shared with others. If you answered "yes," it is value based.

EXERCISE: UNDERSTANDING OUR PERSONAL VALUES – PART I

Listed below are 16 values. Your task is to arrange them in order of their importance to you as guiding principles in your life. Study the list carefully and place a "1" next to the value that is most important for you, place a "2" next to the value that is second most important, and so forth, down to "16."

__ A materially comfortable life

__ Equality (universal personhood)

__ An exciting, stimulating, active life

__ Family security (caring for your loved ones)

__ Personal freedom (independence, free choice)

__ Happiness (being content with your life)

__ Inner harmony (freedom from inner conflict)

__ Mature love (physical and spiritual intimacy)

__ Physical security (protection from attack or harm)

__ Pleasure (an enjoyable, leisurely life)

__ Self-respect/self-esteem

__ A sense of accomplishment and making a lasting contribution

__ Social recognition (respect, admiration from others)

__ True friendship (close companionship)

__ Wisdom (a mature understanding of life)

__ A world of beauty (nature, the arts, music, etc.)

EXERCISE: UNDERSTANDING OUR PERSONAL VALUES – PART II

Place a check in front of those values that correspond to your own, and an "X" in front of those you personally reject. Then go back and rank order the three values that you hold most strongly by placing a "1" beside your preeminent value, a "2" by your second most strongly held value, and so forth. Rank order the three values that you reject most strongly in a similar way.

It is valuable to:

__ Get ahead	__ Help others
__ Be honest	__ Be tolerant
__ Participate in civic life	__ Explore new horizons
__ Work hard	__ Succeed in every endeavor
__ Be clean	__ Be self-reliant
__ Honor one's parents	__ Obey the law
__ Be loyal to one's country	__ Help other nations become democratic
__ Be free	__ Be partisan
__ Pursue happiness	__ Know your heritage
__ Accrue goods and wealth	__ Build things
__ Become educated	__ Save time
__ Be religious	__ Find a better way
__ Know the right people	__ Be proud of your community
__ Live in the right places	__ Adjust to prevailing social norms
__ Be productive	__ Stand up for one's beliefs and ideas

In addition to acting upon the values we most cherish, we also distinguish between terminal values and instrumental values. Terminal values refer to the goals and objectives of our actions in the world. Instrumental values refer to the ways we select to achieve these goals and objectives.

Terminal Values Include:

A comfortable life	Inner harmony
An exciting life	Mature love
A sense of accomplishment	Personal or national security
A world at peace	Pleasure
A world of beauty	Salvation
Equality	Self-respect/self-esteem
Family security	Social recognition
Freedom	True friendship
Happiness	Wisdom

Instrumental Values Include:

Ambition	Imagination
Broadmindedness	Independence
Capability/competence	Intellect
Cheerfulness	Logic
Cleanliness	Love/tenderness
Courage	Obedience
Forgiveness	Politeness
Altruism	Responsibility
Honesty	Self-control

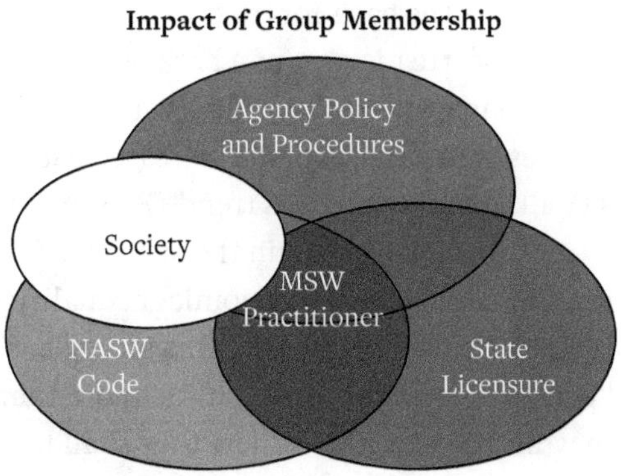

Throughout its history, the social work profession has emphasized the integration of values into practice and the knowledge upon which we base our practice. In addition to various Western secular philosophies, a major source of these values is the Judeo-Christian ethic (Canda et al., 2019). As U.S. society has become more diverse in recent decades, however, there is growing pressure to expand our ethical principles to include values derived from other faiths and other cultures. Rapid cultural changes, reflected in divisions over issues of life and death, sexuality, privacy, and privilege, inevitably produce challenges to long-standing

Impact of Group Membership

FIGURE 3.2. Factors That Shape Our Professional Values

values and raise concerns about their current and future suitability. In addition, the ambiguity of our rhetorical statements of values presents a persistent problem of translation, particularly in a society with diverse interpretations of such broadly framed concepts as social justice, personal and community well-being, freedom, and human dignity.

Nevertheless, social workers continue to look to our values to shape general practice goals and the means we select to achieve them. For many social workers, our work is a critical component of our personal identity in virtually all fields of practice, whether we are micro or macro practitioners. The dynamic transformation of societal values in recent years implies that our personal and professional values can never be fixed. Constant changes in customs, mores, and behavioral norms inevitably influence our core values and the ways we implement them in practice. This underscores the need to "strive for some consistency between the political values we profess and the personal lives we lead" (Lens, 2001, p. 361).

As self-proclaimed "value-based professionals," social workers assume that the presence of a forthright, rule-based code should form the basis of our ethical practice. The question remains, however, whether the values underlying this code merely serve as a rationale for the profession's existence and as broad guides to practice, or if we can actually use them to inform practice on a more specific, day-to-day level.

A persistent, value-laden issue for social workers emerges from the tension between our professional autonomy and the degree to which we must succumb to different forms of external control (Dustin, 2016). In return for the status social workers and the organizations in which we work obtain as professionals, we not only have to provide benefits to society, but we also have to demonstrate our qualifications (through acquisition of training from accredited schools) and meet a range of accountability standards through ongoing peer review, licensing regulations, and adherence to policy decisions. As recent developments reveal, the political climate can increase or reduce this tension depending upon which ideas about social welfare, human well-being, and the people with whom we work are ascendant.

Although our professional status rests in part on the scientific basis of our practice, our system of values (ideology) is the primary source of the public's trust that we need to forge effective relationships with the people with whom we work and to maintain the support of political and economic sponsors. In today's hyperpartisan environment, however, the acceptance of this ideology as the basis for trust has become increasingly difficult to establish and maintain. This erosion of trust is part of a broader decline in confidence in all societal institutions at a time when competition for resources and social anxiety about the future have intensified. Different sources of information, the increased use of social media, and demographic and cultural diversity all contribute to this trend (Reisch, 2020c).

A growing issue within the social work field is how to apply our values to struggles against racism, sexism, socioeconomic inequality, and other forms of invidious, structural discrimination. One component of this struggle is the recognition that the relationship between the "personal" and the "political" is more than a mere feminist slogan. It refers to "the process in which people discuss how they shall live" (Tobach, n.d., p. 7). In the current environment, social work's response to the rise of new social movements, such as Occupy Wall Street, Black Lives Matter, and #MeToo, has affected social work practice and education through an increased emphasis on consciousness raising, awareness of privilege, and greater attention to white supremacy, heterosexism, transphobia, and gender relations (Reisch, 2020b).

Social work values, however, are often distinct from societal priorities at a given moment, although "they are supposed to represent a standardized reflection of collective responsibility, implicit in the role of social work in society" (Levy, 1973, p. 36). Ideally, these values are independent, whether their foundation rests upon secular and religious ideologies, scientific evidence, or some combination of the two. Yet, there is considerable disagreement within the profession about the degree to which individual social workers can differ about the field's fundamental values or their interpretation in practice. This debate is not merely an abstract discussion, as social work's values ultimately shape with whom we work, how we work with them, and for what purpose (p. 38). In sum, values determine our conception of human need, our methods of helping, and the means we use to determine whether our help is effective (Fitzgerald, 2016; Green, 1999). In our increasingly diverse society, different interpretations of these values ultimately create controversy over how we should treat people in day-to-day practice.

The Role of the NASW *Code of Ethics*

Social work's organizing values define our primary functions and purposes but, despite its many useful principles, the NASW *Code of Ethics* cannot and does not provide much guidance as to how we should apply these values in every conceivable practice situation. In fact, studies have found that although most social workers are familiar with the *Code of Ethics*, this familiarity does not correspond with their adherence to the principles outlined in the *Code*. An additional complication arises when we practice "within systems [whose] priorities ... are in tension with social work values, such as prisons, criminal courts, and ... agencies charged with surveillance [or] social control" (Shdaimah & McGarry, 2018, p. 22). This is particularly true in courtroom situations where the relative power of the various actors (different professions, defendants, third parties) and the different definitions of "evidence" create significant conflicts. Working within so-called host institutions, therefore, places additional responsibility on social workers to use our professional discretion in the application of our basic values. Yet, our use of that discretion is increasingly constrained by the hierarchical arrangement of most agencies and by social policies, fiscal pressures, and accountability measures over which we have little control. These external forces place social work values under recurrent threat.

Consequently, we must be more than "street-level bureaucrats" (Alden, 2015; Lipsky, 2010) who interpret policies and procedures in our daily practice. We must become, in Hasenfeld's (2010) phrase, "moral entrepreneurs" who exercise a form of principled resistance to frequently impossible ethical circumstances. In interprofessional organizations, such as hospitals, interdisciplinary ethics committees can serve a useful purpose in resolving the various issues and different professional perspectives regarding contemporary ethical dilemmas that inevitably arise.

Conflicts of Values

ETHICAL DILEMMA 3.2   "Don't Tell Me How to Raise My Children"

Elaine S. is a social worker in a local public high school. One afternoon, an 18-year old-student, Maria R., comes to her office and breaks down in tears. After Maria composes herself, Elaine asks her why she is crying. Maria tells her that a classmate who she likes very much asked her to the senior prom. When she told her parents, her father absolutely forbade her to go. Maria tells Elaine that her father believes it is immoral for unmarried couples to dance together and that girls who go dancing are no better than prostitutes who will never find a worthy husband. She also confides that her father locks her in her room every night and refuses to allow her to go out, even with her girlfriends. Maria then reveals that she is so depressed at times that she has considered committing suicide. She begs Elaine to call her father and persuade him to change his mind.

After consulting with her supervisor, Elaine calls Mr. R. and expresses her concern for Maria's physical safety and emotional well-being. He tells Elaine that he loves his daughter very much and schedules an appointment. The meeting begins politely, if a bit awkwardly. After a short while, however, when Elaine tells Mr. R. that Maria is depressed because of his decision about the prom and how he locks her in her room at night, he becomes quite angry. "How dare you tell me how to raise my child," he shouts, and then abruptly leaves Elaine's office.

Questions:

1. What is the conflict of values in this situation?
2. Whose values are in conflict?
3. To what extent is it ethical for social workers to express their values—directly or indirectly—when working with people whose values may differ?
4. In a family dispute, is it ever ethical for a social worker to side with one of the parties?

A core feature of a profession is supposed to be moral impartiality. In the above situation, however, it appears that Maria's father interpreted Elaine's comments as an indirect way to side with his daughter against him. How might Elaine have expressed her concerns about Maria differently to reduce the possibility that Mr. R. would react as he did? Do you think she behaved in an unethical manner? If so, what ethical principles did she violate?

The value conflicts we experience as social workers emerge from several possible sources. One is the conflict that exists at times within our own values. A second is the conflict between our personal and professional values. A third, as in the above situation, are the conflicts between our professional or personal values and the values of the people with whom we work, the organizations in which we work, or the society as a whole. One of the ethical challenges for social workers today, therefore, is to take responsible individual and social action in an environment of considerable risk due to widening differences between professional values and social values. We often have to make difficult choices in ambiguous circumstances. These choices are, in effect, political choices (Warner, 2015; Reisch & Jani, 2012).

As professionals, however, we are required "to prevent ... [our] own value orientations from intruding upon the optimization of ... [our] professional values" (Levy, 1976b, p. 113). This is particularly important when our personal values conflict with those of clients and constituents. Our fiduciary duty to clients always comes first, even if it is difficult to decide which duty takes priority when the values of our clients differ from each other as in the case of the R. family. In Levy's words, "To be a professional practitioner is to give up some of one's autonomy and to relinquish some of one's rights as a freely functioning human being" (p. 113). This creates a particular challenge in an era where one's group identity has acquired increased importance. According to Levy, the central "issue to be resolved ... is not whether ... [we are] entitled to ... [our] personal values even when they run afoul of the professional values to which ... [we are] committed. ... But whether ... [we] are free as a member of a human service profession to give priority to ... [our] personal values over the values by which ... [we are] expected to be constrained because of ... [our] professional responsibility" (p. 119). Contrary to widespread belief, this does not mean we must abstain from taking sides when our fundamental values are in jeopardy. It means that we should "make choices in terms of the facts as they can best be established, and in terms of principles that remain consistent no matter to whom they are applied" (Frankel, 1969, p. 33).

In addition to political conflict in the broadest sense of the term, differences between our private beliefs and professional behavior often create a disjuncture in our practice and heighten our personal distress. In practice, our life experiences, socialization, education, and age influence our ethical judgments. The specific context of our work, including the organizational culture, our assigned roles, and the current political climate, also affects our decision-making (Beckett et al., 2017; Banks, 2016). Despite our desire to uphold our personal values and ethical principles, our professional status also determines how we identify and apply ethical concepts to practice. A further complication is that in certain circumstances our ethical duties may require us to go beyond our legal obligations (Barsky, 2019; Congress, 2017).

There are numerous examples in our practice in which these conflicts may occur. Social workers engaged in counseling with victims or perpetrators of domestic violence or sexual abuse may struggle to maintain a professional posture if they have experienced a similar trauma. A practitioner working in the child welfare field who grew up in foster care may experience ethical conflicts when faced with a decision about separating children from their parents. An advocate for people who are homeless or addicted to opioids may have trouble working with policy makers who are indifferent to their plight.

Particularly for individuals with strong religious beliefs, there is a constant challenge of balancing their private conscience with their professional responsibilities, especially in an increasingly heterogeneous society. It requires us not to impose a particular set of religious or cultural values on those with whom we work or on society as a whole. This imperative is reciprocal: society cannot impose its values upon unwitting others. The implication here is that respect for freedom is at the core of maintaining a pluralistic community.

This belief in the importance of mutual respect requires us to recognize that free choice is not an absolute—either for ourselves or for others. Preserving the core principle of self-determination creates a persistent vexing challenge for social workers who work with individuals who violate widely accepted moral standards. It also presents problems for those whose work involves controversial issues such as abortion, sexual behavior, and end-of-life decisions. One solution to these ongoing challenges is to develop and implement an ethical framework that accepts the existence of multiple moral positions and emphasizes the process by which they are reconciled rather than the attainment of a specific outcome (Engelhardt, 1982b).

REFLECTION EXERCISE: WHAT PERSONAL AND PROFESSIONAL PROBLEMS DO YOU FACE TODAY?

List what you consider the five most important problems you face today
- a. in your personal life, and
- b. in your work with others.
1. How do your personal beliefs influence how you think about these problems?
2. How do they influence your ethical behavior in practice?

Challenging Practice Situations

Ethical dilemmas in our practice arise when we must "choose between two options of near or equal value" (Olson, 2014, p. 183). Certain practice situations present unique challenges in this regard. The following section briefly discusses several arenas of practice in which these challenges occur for social workers: service in the military, practice with stigmatized populations, work with particularly vulnerable populations, and the use of religion or spirituality in practice.

FIGURE 3.3. The Challenge of Ethical Dilemmas in Our Practice

Ethical Social Work in the Military

Ironically, since World War I social workers have been working with the military, veterans, and related organizations such as the Red Cross in various capacities while colleagues have actively opposed war and militarism (Wooten, 2015; Olson, 2014; Reisch & Andrews, 2002). Particularly in a clinical setting, social workers in the military may have to choose between their obligations to service members (e.g., soldiers experiencing post-traumatic stress disorder, or PTSD) and their duty to serve the military mission. In addition, the core social work principles of social justice and self-determination are in opposition to the military credo of self-sacrifice for the military unit (Johnson et al., 2018; Simmons & Rycraft, 2010) and may be interpreted in widely varying ways by service personnel of different cultural backgrounds (Freeman & Shaler, 2016; Petrovich, 2012). These differences also create a particularly vexing ethical problem for the profession as long-time advocates for peace. How can we reconcile this core value with our responsibility to prepare service members to return to combat?

The ethical conflicts that arise in military social work are less acute and easier to negotiate in noncombat situations and in practice with veterans and their families. In the latter instance, this relative ease is because these individuals have already served and are experiencing socio-economic and psychological challenges that emerged, at least in part, from their tour of duty. The ethical conflicts with this population are more typical of those we experience in other practice settings. They range from the micro (e.g., confidentiality and boundary issues) to the mezzo (e.g., conflicts with authority figures), to the macro (e.g., whether it is ethical to serve in the military or work in the Veterans' Administration during a controversial war). A critical challenge in such circumstances is when to rely on our professional judgment, obey an ethical imperative, or follow orders issued by the chain of command.

Ethical Practice with Stigmatized Populations

Although many of the people with whom we work suffer from social stigma, exclusion, and marginalization, arguably the group that experiences the most stigma, particularly in today's environment, are sex offenders. Working with sex offenders creates ethical dilemmas for social workers beyond those generally associated with practice. The involuntary nature of most of these clients, the lack of resources in the agencies that serve them, and the generally inhospitable environment of such settings exacerbate these challenges (Rooney & Mirick, 2018). A core challenge in this area of practice is to provide effective treatment within a context of restrictive policies and frequently noncompliant clients. Another ethical issue for practitioners in this field is how to balance public safety and individual rights. To help reduce the stress of such challenges, researchers recommend that practitioners who work with these clients seek additional training and supervision, and practice self-care on a regular basis.

Ethical Practice with Particularly Vulnerable Populations

Two of the most vulnerable populations with whom we practice are children and older adults who are victims of various forms of abuse (Morris et al., 2018; Mills, 2017). According to Hardesty (2015), ethical dilemmas in frontline child welfare practice arise from the persistent tension between the agency's demand for an "objective" perspective and the practice principle of understanding the specific, sometimes culturally determined perspective of the families with whom we work. This tension between objectivity and "perspectivalism" exists "because objectivity asks the worker to make knowledge claims that are disembodied, disinterested, and divested of emotion, while perspectivalism asks precisely for embodiment, interest, and emotional engagement, [thus] the two concepts are fundamentally incompatible" (p. 462).

This dilemma illustrates broader epistemological and ethical debates that have appeared within the profession during the past several decades about the role of research, evidence, and knowledge as guides to practice (Fook, 2016; Reisch & Garvin, 2016). A recurrent issue, specific to child welfare workers, is determining which forms of knowledge are legitimate to apply in practice. Another is avoiding the combined pitfalls of *value neutrality*—the principle that directs us to keep our emotions and biases in check when dealing with certain situations—and the loss of professional discretion in the pursuit of practice efficiency. The former risk "is all the more troubling when frontline social services' gendered and racialized dimensions are taken into account" (Hardesty, 2015, p. 492). To address these challenges, Hardesty stresses the need for child welfare workers to "adopt a more rigorous and inclusive definition of evidence," critically assess the connection between knowledge and values, and challenge the assumption that current techniques are independent "of their cultural and political contexts" (p. 494). As in the child welfare field, concerns over the continuing risk of harm for suspected victims of elder abuse—especially in unresolved situations—create both an ethical dilemma and a personal struggle for practitioners, who fear they did not do enough to protect their clients (Bows & Penhale, 2018; Donovan & Regehr, 2010).

ETHICAL DILEMMA 3.3   "I Know What's Best for My Mother"

You are a social worker in a community center that provides day services for older adults through a grant from the local Area Agency on Aging. One of the women in the program, Helen B., has shown signs of increasing dementia. She is a widow who lives alone in a small apartment. Her only child, Maureen, is a single mother in her early 40s who has three children. She lives in a suburb over an hour away.

Helen has not come to the program for over a week. After trying to telephone her several times without success, you decide to make a home visit to check on her. While in her apartment, you notice an unmade bed with soiled linens, piles of dirty dishes in the kitchen, bags of unopened mail, and stacks of month-old newspapers in the hall. Helen is sitting in her bedclothes in a darkened room watching television. It appears that she has not eaten for a while.

You are alarmed, call Helen's daughter, and ask her to meet you as soon as possible. The next evening she arrives for the appointment after a long workday. You tell her what you found in her mother's apartment and suggest that Helen needs an assessment by a physician. You raise the possibility that Helen might require either regular in-home assistance or to move to an assisted living facility.

Maureen responds defensively. She tells you she can neither take her mother into her own home nor afford to pay for assisted living. You reply that you understand but that Helen may need full-time attention to safeguard her well-being. You offer to help Maureen find quality help for her mother as well as sources of financial assistance. Maureen becomes increasingly agitated. "Are you implying I don't care about my mother? I know what's best for her." She refuses your offer of help. "I'll take care of this myself," she says as she rises to leave your office.

Questions:

1. In what ways is this situation similar to or different from Ethical Dilemma 3.2?
2. What values are in conflict?
3. How does Helen's apparent vulnerability influence your view of the ethics involved?

The Use of Religion and Spirituality in Practice

The use of prayer in practice represents another potential area of ethical controversy (Oxhandler & Giardina, 2017). It differs from the rationale behind incorporating spirituality into one's practice because, in the latter situation, it is widely acknowledged by the profession that religious beliefs are particularly important to many of the people with whom we work in our multicultural society (Skipper et al., 2018; Hatch et al., 2017). Sheridan's research (2010) cautions both against the overuse of prayer as a practice intervention without obtaining client permission and the under use of prayer when it may be culturally relevant and helpful. She identifies two core ethical issues in these circumstances: (1) "Is it ever ethical to pray for 'particular outcomes' for clients and, if not, what kind of prayer is appropriate?" And (2) "When is it necessary … to seek permission from clients to engage in private prayer for them, and how should this be accomplished?" (p. 117). Given the power imbalance between social workers and clients in virtually all practice settings, heightened sensitivity to these issues is particularly important, especially when working with vulnerable populations, such as older adults, particularly those for whom religious beliefs are central to their lives. Hodge and colleagues (2010) identified three ethical principles to guide practice in such situations: "(1) respect for client autonomy [by avoiding the imposition of spiritual beliefs different from clients or ignoring their beliefs entirely]; (2) sufficient competency in the client's spiritual tradition; and (3) practicing within the boundaries of professional competency" (p. 3). As in all practice, the emphasis should be on prioritizing the client's interests.

Despite this helpful advice, in the current context there may be no way to find a middle ground between certain religiously based value positions, such as those around sexual orientation or abortion. In such circumstances, our goal should be to establish the basis for a meaningful interpersonal or intergroup dialogue, not to side with one set of values or the other (Zuniga et al., 2016). This reflects Engelhardt's (1982a) earlier conception of ethics as a process through we can create a "peaceful community."

ETHICAL DILEMMA 3.4   "Please Pray with Me"

You are a social worker in a local hospital. One of your patients, JoAnne G., has stage 3 ovarian cancer. The doctors have recommended she enter a lengthy therapy regimen in a nearby medical center that has produced dramatic results in clinical trials. Through your contacts in the medical center, you have made tentative arrangements for JoAnne's transfer to this facility.

JoAnne is married and has four children. She is a person of deep religious faith and is active in her church. She is not concerned about herself but worries how her husband and children will manage without her when she is gone. She decides that she wants to forego treatment and will rely on God's grace to help her and her family in this difficult time. You believe she is making a bad decision that will endanger her life and place an undue burden on her family. You try unsuccessfully to get her to reconsider. You believe in science and do not have strong religious convictions. Before JoAnne leaves the hospital, she asks you to join her in praying for her safety and the well-being of her family.

Questions:
1. What would you do?
2. Is it ethical to pray with JoAnne if you do not share her beliefs and think she is making the wrong decision?
3. If you refused, how would you explain it to her?
4. On what basis would you make your decision?
5. What would you do if JoAnne had decided to undergo the therapy regimen and asked you to pray with her for its success?
6. Would you apply the rationale for these decisions to similar situations?

Think about how you would apply the recommendations of Sheridan (2010) and Hodge et al. (2010) to this situation. If you agreed to pray with JoAnne, you would clearly not be imposing your values on her or ignoring her religious beliefs; in fact, she has asked you to accept hers by praying for a particular outcome with her. Yet, as you have strong feelings about the choice she has made, you must consider whether it would be unethical or hypocritical to join her in the specific prayer she requests. In addition, as JoAnne's spiritual tradition is quite different from yours, do you have sufficient competence in this tradition to participate with her in a sincere and honest manner?

Implications for Social Work Education

Concern about teaching ethics in the United States dates back at least as far as John Dewey, who had a strong influence on social work leaders during the early 20th century like Jane Addams (Berringer, 2019). Dewey was "mainly concerned that [content on ethics] should be assimilated into the totality of educational experience and not treated as a special object of instruction" (Bereiter, 1978, p. 20). Through his influence, in the 1920s social work educators began to incorporate ethical content into their programs in a more focused way as part of a broader effort to establish the field's professional credentials (Austin, 1997).

Traditionally, ethical teaching in social work has addressed three central issues: (1) identifying the source of our values; (2) determining when to apply these values in a given situation; and (3) reconciling differences between our personal values and those of the profession and the wider society. For social workers, the latter has often involved balancing individualistic and collectivist (or communitarian) value orientations.

Several factors have contributed to growing attention to the importance of content on social work ethics in BSW and MSW programs. These include the perception of declining moral standards, particularly among the nation's political leaders, increased societal violence, and a declining faith in institutions. The teaching of ethical content, however, whether in the classroom or field instruction, requires careful preparation. It is not easy to translate abstract concepts, such as social justice, into meaningful practice principles and behaviors. In today's climate, the heightened sensitivity and vulnerability of many students makes it increasingly difficult to help them resolve personal value conflicts and recognize the necessity of compromise in practice situations. Another challenge involves enabling students to identify the cultural bases of their values and the potential conflicts between these values and those of the people with whom they work. Addressing this latter challenge is particularly important in today's environment because social work and the social and behavioral science upon which we base our practice and education can never be value free.

Due to these challenges, teaching content on social work ethics today must go beyond educating students about the variety of ethical theories. It has to prepare students to develop critical thinking skills, moral reasoning, broad worldview, and practice wisdom (Congress, 2017) that will enable them to apply these concepts to concrete situations in an increasingly complex, diverse, and technologically driven society and organizational context (Joiner, 2019; Strom-Gottfried, 2019; Hugman, 2013). Ethics education in social work should also challenge students' implicit assumptions and biases (Pugh, 2017; Hancock, 2012; Wahler, 2012) and enable them to avoid serious ethical violations by developing their personal code of ethics consistent with professional standards (Gambrill, 2017; Smith, 2012). In addition, ethics education must take into account the influence of the internationalization of social work education on the composition of student bodies, the location of field placements, and the different assumptions of our colleagues and service users (Lorenzetti et al., 2019; Jönsson & Flem, 2017; Valutis, 2012; Duffy & Hayes, 2012). Lastly, ethics education should also incorporate content about the specific dilemmas social workers confront when engaged in advocacy (Gilster et al., 2020; Hoefer, 2019) or practice with particularly vulnerable clients, such as those who are suicidal (HuAlmeida et al., 2017).

Through the development of a critical framework, students will be better able to understand the strengths and limitations of the NASW *Code of Ethics* and become aware of the different interpretations of core concepts such as social justice within the profession itself (Dotolo Lindhorst et al., 2018; Bhuyan et al., 2017; Reisch & Garvin, 2016; Olson et al., 2013). They will also be better able to recognize how their personal values and practice environments affect their ethical decisions (Edwards & Addae, 2015). In the present climate of increased cultural sensitivity and cultural relativism, a question emerges as to whether we can continue to teach ethics and values from a universal perspective, even if we generally consider certain values, such as "do no harm," an absolute value. A persistent challenge for educators, therefore, is reaching agreement on what specific values to teach and the extent to which deviations from the profession's ideological mainstream can be tolerated (Lerner, 2020).

Conservative criticisms of the profession's mandate to teach content related to "social justice" and "oppression" based on the imperatives in the NASW *Code* further complicate this pedagogical issue. Media critics like Will (2007) argue that this mandate represents the imposition of ideological orthodoxy and constitutes a form of indoctrination that discriminates against students whose values diverge from the professional mainstream. Some social work educators have echoed these charges (Lerner, 2020; Toft & Calhoun, 2020; Thyer, 2010; Fram & Miller-Cribbs, 2008; Hodge, 2006). Do you agree? Have you ever felt pressure to conform in either classroom instruction or your internship?

This controversy raises a basic question for educators—whether the educational process changes students' values or whether their values were already different from the mainstream prior to their entry in professional programs (Logan et al., 2017; Theobald et al., 2017; Sanders & Hoffman, 2010). Forty years ago, a study found that younger students were more likely to experience a value change due to their education (Judah, 1979). Earlier studies, however, revealed that few differences existed in "the values expressed by beginning and graduating women students" (Hayes & Varley, 1965, p. 41). They also suggested that a student's gender might influence the values that lead them to enter the profession and how they respond to their educational experience. Among women, religion and social class were primary factors that shaped different value orientations. These differences were even more pronounced among men, although men overall were less motivated by religious beliefs. In addition, some health care educators argued several decades ago "there is no evidence that teaching ethics changes behavior" (Pellegrino, 1989, p. 490).

Recent studies by Jani and colleagues (2016) and Osteen (2011), however, produced more nuanced findings. Their research found that while nearly all students enter the field of social work out of a desire to help others, this desire stems from three different sources: religious or spiritual beliefs, practical necessity (acquisition of a professional credential), and past personal experience. As a result, exposure to ethical content in social work education had three different effects on students: confirmation of preexisting values, encouragement to incorporate social work values into their personal values, and recognition of value incongruity. Some students deal with the latter through selective acceptance of certain social work values, others by attempting to forge a compromise position, and still others by externalizing the conflict. The educational outcomes of different programs also vary widely (Sanders & Hoffman, 2010).

Given these diverse findings, social work educators have not reached a consensus over which ethical principles to teach and how to educate students to distinguish right from wrong in practice settings. To address this challenge, Morley and colleagues (2019) suggest that the teaching of ethics in the classroom should emphasize the acquisition of

- Judeo-Christian

- Islamic

- Buddhist

- Native American

FIGURE 3.4. Religious Influences on Our Values

skills in ethical analysis and the ability to recognize an ethical issue rather than focusing on rule-based behavior alone. Students can then apply this analytical ability in field education through critically reflective practice (Theobald et al., 2017).

It is equally important for students to recognize early in their education that their efforts to "do good" may take different forms for diverse clients and may create conflicts between their benevolent impulses and the goal of respecting cultural differences. These conflicts can occur in three ways. One is the conflict between Western social workers' presumptions about the existence of universal human rights and the ethical imperative to respect cultural variety. A second is between practitioners' inability to understand fully the worldviews of people from different backgrounds, despite their efforts to attain "cultural competence," and the profession's mission to help all people regardless of their background. The third is between social workers' ethical obligation to practice without bias and prejudice and the existence of personal, implicit biases, particularly those that we neither recognize nor acknowledge (Goldberg, 2000).

The emphasis in contemporary social work education on multiculturalism, privilege, and oppression, and a renewed focus on the primacy (and meaning) of social justice further complicates this picture. The Council on Social Work Education (2015) requires schools to measure students' concrete educational "outcomes" by demonstrating competence in the application of these abstract values to their course assignments and internships. They must also demonstrate the ability to resolve conflicts between their personal and professional values, although there are few valid metrics for doing so.

There is also increasing concern that "the personal value bases of MSW students … are both divergent and convergent in relationship to the values of the profession" (Osteen, 2011, p. 424). This and other more recent findings suggest that social work educators may be making questionable assumptions about the values students possess when they enter professional programs (Begun et al., 2017) and may also have similarly erroneous assumptions about their colleagues (Toft & Calhoun, 2020). These ambiguities are at the heart of ongoing debates regarding the extent to which the profession should tolerate diverse opinions about basic values in educational or practice settings (Lerner, 2020).

In addition to external environmental stressors, studies have also found that students often experience three problems when asked to incorporate social work values into their practice: (1) learning how to be nonjudgmental, (2) dealing with the difficulty of living up to their espoused values, and (3) acknowledging that they dislike certain people with whom they work. Because of these problems, social work educators have to help students accept that it is impossible to avoid making value judgments. It requires students to become more self-aware and better able to distinguish their private values from the professional values they have pledged to uphold.

As students struggle with these challenges, they frequently blame themselves when they cannot live up to the high standards they set or when circumstances beyond their control compel them to compromise. They feel frustrated by their inability to reconcile their ethical commitments with the difficulties in fulfilling these commitments imposed by environmental barriers. In the classroom, tensions also exist between the integration of the profession's values and the creation of a "safe environment" in which students can learn. This is particularly difficult when no consensus exists about the meaning of these values or what commitment to them implies. Under these circumstances, there is the constant risk that ambiguous definitions of fundamental values will make it more difficult to assess students' professional behavior, particularly in their internships. Sometimes, students direct their frustration about the challenges they face at teachers, field instructors, classmates, or administrators. This often intensifies preexisting conflicts in the school and exacerbates other long-standing educational issues (Glassman, 2016; Royse et al, 2016).

The purpose of teaching social work ethics throughout the curriculum, instead of limiting its instruction to a unit in a required course or an elective, is to underscore the centrality of the profession's values through a balanced presentation and enable students to develop their critical faculties. Another important component of infusing ethical content in all courses is the role modeling that occurs through the careful selection and development of professional mentors (Brown et al., 2019; Katz et al., 2019; Lewis, 2003c). It is also helpful to connect students with individuals in the community who can convey to them the potential effects of their professional decisions on others' lives (Lorenzetti et al., 2019; Duffy & Hayes, 2012). In the final analysis, these features of social work education appear to matter more than how faculty teach ethical content (DiFranks, 2008).

ETHICAL DILEMMA 3.5   "My Family Needs Me Now"

You are a social worker in the student services office of a large school of social work. A 2nd-year MSW student, Charles J., makes an appointment to tell you that he is dropping out of the program, two months before his graduation. You are shocked because Charles is one of the best students in the school, a leader in the student government organization, and someone widely admired and respected by his classmates and teachers. Admitted on a scholarship after completing his BA from a small private college in the Southwest, he clearly possesses all the qualities needed to be an excellent social worker and a leader in the field.

Charles explains that his father is critically ill and no longer able to work. As the oldest child in his large family, he is now responsible for its economic survival and has to provide emotional support and guidance to his younger siblings. You inform Charles that he could take a one-year leave of absence to help his family and return the following year to complete his studies. You feel that if he drops out, not only will his prospects suffer, he will be unable to contribute as much to his community or society as a whole. Charles thanks you for your kind words, but declines your offer of help. "My family needs me now," he says. "That is more important than my own success."

Questions:
1. What values are in conflict here—for you and between you and Charles?
2. How would you reconcile the conflict between your personal and professional values and between your values and those Charles prioritizes?
3. To what extent would you resolve similar values conflicts in the same way?
4. How is the value conflict in this situation similar to or different from the value conflicts described in the other ethical dilemmas in this chapter?

Two Final Issues

Despite increased attention to issues of diversity, inclusion, and multiculturalism in social work education, schools of social work often overlook the unique challenges that students (and faculty) of different racial, class, and gender backgrounds undergo in professional programs.

- NASW Policy Statements
- Abortion/Contraception
- LGBTQI Rights
- Assisted Suicide
- ACA
- War
- Immigrant Rights
- Relocation Services
- Interracial Adoption

Conflicts Between Personal, Agency & Professional Values

FIGURE 3.5. Conflict-Ridden Issues in Our Practice

Through exposure to new ideas and their initial socialization to a professional subculture, they risk the loss of some critical features of their personal and group identity (Craig et al., 2017). Their vocabulary and value priorities may change dramatically through the influence of mentors and peers. Their new identity may create conflicts with their families and their former friends and acquaintances, especially for individuals who are the first members of their family to obtain professional status. Unlike race, ethnicity, and gender, which are more or less "fixed identities," social class is more subject to change, identity confusion, and masking (Karpman & Miller, 2020).

This conflict of identities sometimes affects social work faculty as well. A quarter century ago, a professor from a working-class background framed this identity dilemma succinctly and painfully: "The only way I can be intellectual is dishonestly. Being intellectual is not part of my nature. ... Graduate school hadn't really changed the way I think; it had only made me, although obviously not too convincingly, appear to think a certain way" (Dews & Law, 1995, p. 332). As someone who grew up in a working-class family and lived in public housing through college, I often had similar feelings as a graduate student and junior faculty member. In some ways, these emotions have persisted throughout my career.

Another issue that schools of social work need to confront is the contradiction between the profession's social justice rhetoric and our interest in organizational stability and survival. The latter is the basis of our longstanding assumption that the primary means of effecting social change is through established institutions. In an era of increased social discontent in which social media enhance the voice and power of numerous social movements and, in contrast, often disseminate disinformation to foment social discord, is this "insider strategy" still viable? Is it consistent with the profession's stated mission? Unless educators and practitioners can bridge the gap between social work's stated ideals and its actions in the real world, our commitment to these values will acquire an increasingly hollow ring.

Summary

This chapter discussed the oft-conflicting relationship between our personal and professional values. It addressed the various philosophical, historical, and circumstantial influences that shape the formation and evolution of our values, and those of the social work profession, and how we struggle to reconcile them in our practice. It also discussed the role of the NASW *Code of Ethics* in helping to resolve these conflicts. Throughout the chapter, there are examples of how these conflicts appear in practice with certain populations and in specific practice situations. The chapter concluded with the implications of this issue for social work education.

Beginning with Chapter 4, the book will focus on the meaning and practice implications of social work's core ethical and value concepts. Chapter 4 examines the connection between our interpretation of the "client's interest" and how we translate this concept into practice.

Reflection Exercise I: Identifying Your Personal Values

1. What are your major personal values?
2. How do they coincide or conflict with the professional values of social work?
3. How do your beliefs and personal morality shape the values that guide your practice?
4. What are/should be the roles of religion and secular ideologies in shaping our practice?
5. What conflicts do they create?
6. How does your group membership create conflicts between your personal and professional values?
7. Are all values equally valid?

Reflection Exercise II: Translating NASW's Core Values into Practice

The preface to the NASW *Code of Ethics* proposes six core values that constitute the profession's "ethical imperatives":

- Service
- Social Justice
- Dignity and Worth of the Person
- Importance of Human Relationships
- Integrity
- Competence

1. How do you interpret these imperatives?
2. How would you translate them into your practice?

Reflection Exercise III: What Are Your Agency's Value Priorities?

Think about the values that inform the mission and goals of your agency of employment or internship.

1. What values does the organization prioritize?
2. How does it translate these values into practice?
3. How does the organization balance "charitable" and "justice" perspectives?
4. How do these values reflect its conception of "need" and "help"?
5. How does practice in the organization reflect the diverse values of the people with whom it works and of the staff of the organization?

Credits

Fig. 3.1: Copyright © 2015 Depositphotos/gustavofrazao.
Fig. 3.3: Copyright © 2012 Depositphotos/herminutomo.
Fig. 3.4a: Copyright © 2014 Depositphotos/egal.
Fig. 3.5a: Copyright © 2015 Depositphotos/siraanamwong.

The Client's Interest

Introduction

The NASW *Code of Ethics* (2018) begins with the following statement:

> Social workers' primary responsibility is to promote the well-being of clients. ...
> However, social workers' responsibility to the larger society or specific legal obli-
> gations may on limited occasions supersede the loyalty owed clients, and clients
> should be so advised. (1.01)

This statement makes two assertions that, if read carefully, might confuse students and
even experienced practitioners. On the one hand, it affirms the ethical obligation of all social
workers, in all fields of practice, to put the needs of our clients first—above our personal or
professional needs, or that of our employers. It then, however, qualifies this duty by stating
that under certain circumstances other obligations may take precedence.

Taken as a whole, the statement raises several fundamental questions with which all social
workers contend on a regular basis. First, how do we assess what is in a person's interest and
what constitutes a person, group, or community's well-being? Second, how do we determine
who is the client? Third, what means are ethically permissible to promote that desired end?
Fourth, what are the limited occasions when other duties—multiple loyalties—supersede our
obligation to those with whom we work? Who decides when those occasions exist? Finally, what
do we do when there is a conflict between the diverse interests of our clients or constituents or
when the interests of two or more of our clients or constituents conflict?

This chapter covers several of these interrelated topics. First, it discusses how we determine
what is in the client's interest and how we decide who is the client in a particular situation.
Next, it explores the effect that technology has on assessing and addressing a client's interest and the role trust plays in defining people's interests. It presents an alternative ethical
approach—the "ethics of care"—to traditional interpretations of our ethical obligations. Next,
it discusses the challenges created when we have multiple loyalties in a given situation. The
chapter concludes by applying the profession's core concept of social justice to the challenge
of serving clients' diverse interests. Several ethical dilemmas and reflection exercises in
the chapter will help develop your critical thinking about these challenging issues.

"What Is the Client's Interest?
(Based on a true story)

Amy L. is a social worker employed by a social service agency that operates a summer camp for disadvantaged urban youth. Two of the youth in the unit for which she is responsible are brothers—Sammy (12) and Jose (11). Sammy is, by all accounts, a terrific young man—intelligent, sensitive, and a positive leader among his peers, with a great deal of potential. He is also devoted to his young brother. Jose is also intelligent, but he is a very troubled youth, who is defiant of authority and frequently provokes fights with other boys. Both brothers, however, seem to enjoy the camp experience, particularly Sammy. Amy and the other staff have become particularly fond of him.

Amy has spoken with Jose on numerous occasions (and by telephone with his parents and a caseworker at the referring agency) about his behavior. She tells him he must stop fighting or the camp will have to send him home. None of her efforts has been effective. After consultation with the referring agency, Jose's parents, and her supervisor, Amy decides to recommend that the camp send Jose home. Jose's parents, his caseworker at home, and Amy's supervisor, Barry M., concur with this decision.

When Sammy learns that his brother is going home, he asks to meet with Amy. In the meeting, he states unequivocally that if his brother is going home, he is too. Amy think this is not in Sammy's best interest because of all the benefits the camp has provided to him so far and all the growth he has demonstrated—growth that she believes will help him succeed in school when he returns home. There is also the possibility of her agency helping Sammy obtain a scholarship to a college preparatory program in his community if he finishes the camp session. His parents are excited about this potential opportunity; they could not afford it without financial assistance.

Sammy tells Amy that back home his brother will keep getting into fights in the neighborhood and in school, and that he has to protect him. Amy is concerned that Sammy could get hurt defending his brother or get into trouble with juvenile authorities. Her agency has the authority to keep Sammy in the camp for the rest of the summer with his parents' approval, but she cannot decide what to do.

Questions:

1. Who are the clients in this situation?
2. What are their interests in this situation?
3. Which client's interests should take priority? For what reasons?
4. How would you decide what to do?
5. What principles would you extract from your decision-making process that you would apply to other circumstances? Is this situation so unique that it stands alone?

As in other ethical dilemmas discussed in this book, the central question in the above case is "What should I/we do?" Yet, we cannot resolve this situation solely by seeking guidance from abstract principles. We must also pay attention to the context and all its mundane details. One way to look at this situation is to determine if it constitutes an ethical issue, an ethical problem, or an ethical dilemma. An ethical issue is a situation with an ethical component that does not require us to make a decision. This is clearly not the case in the situation above. An ethical problem requires a decision but the course of action is clear. This would be true if there was a legal requirement or organizational mandate to pursue a specific course of action.

On the other hand, the case of Sammy and Jose involves a difficult choice between 2 unappealing options, neither of which is clear to the person responsible for making the decision. This dilemma appears in both clinical and macro practice (Reamer, 2019b; Lane & Pritzker, 2018b). Part of the challenge in resolving this dilemma is determining who are the clients, what their interests are, and which clients and which interests should take priority. Simply applying a hierarchical set of principles or weighing the different consequences of the available choices would be insufficient. Making this type of decision is a critical part of ethical practice and is the focus of this chapter.

Determining the Client's Interest

The primacy of clients' interests in social work practice reflects the profession's "bedrock" ethical belief that all people have value, regardless of their demographic or socioeconomic status (Barsky, 2019; Bent-Goodley, 2017). As the nation has become increasingly diverse and society's sensitivity to the implications of this diversity has commensurately increased, our understanding of how this diversity influences clients' interests has expanded with multiple consequences for our resolution of the ethical dilemmas that inevitably arise in practice.

The definition of a client's interest usually reflects one of several factors. In the case of voluntary clients, the preferences or priorities individuals state explicitly or implicitly in their choice of a particular service or program or social worker (as in private practice) are the key determinants. In the case of involuntary clients—for example, in the child welfare or criminal justice system—the state decides what is in the client's interest. In both situations, the fiscal, political, cultural, and administrative interests of the agency and community; the worker's expertise, prior experience, practice framework, and personal preferences; and the generalizations drawn from recent research all influence what constitutes the client's interest.

Some circumstances, however, are ambiguous. Social policies or private sector (e.g., foundation) funding preferences may prescribe, prefer, or proscribe certain forms of intervention. These will influence what options clients possess and to what extent they can express their interests to shape the nature of the service transaction (Horne, 2018).

FOR REFLECTION
1. What are some restrictions you have observed on placing the client's interest first in clinical practice? How can we recognize them?
2. How do we determine if/when other interests should take priority? What criteria should we apply?
3. Which "other interests" may be more important? For example:
   - The interests of other clients (e.g., in a family)
   - The interests of other clients in your agency
   - The interests of the agency itself (as a whole)
   - The interests of third parties in the community or society as a whole
   - Your personal interests (e.g., your reputation)
   - The reputation or status of your organization
4. What ethical dilemmas have you encountered that involve determining the client's interest?
5. What factors influenced how you responded to these interests?

To complicate matters further, the helping process is dynamic; even when initially clarified it is likely that a client's interests will change as a consequence of altered life circumstances, shifting organizational resources, and the effects of the change process itself. Recognizing and adapting to these evolving interests requires the collaborative effort of worker and client through ongoing negotiation (Reisch & Garvin, 2016; Finn, 2016). Ethical practice, therefore, occurs in a dialectical rather than linear fashion. "It is likely to be complex, involve differences of perceptions, and ... be influenced by agency requirements that condition the availability of service" (Lewis, 1980, published in Reisch, 2003, p. 17). Ideally, the worker must give priority to those interests that reflect a synthesis of client needs and desires and worker judgment, one that both find acceptable. As social workers, we can attain this synthesis only through honest dialogue, conditioned on trust, cultural humility, and patience.

Identifying and prioritizing clients' needs and desires is no simple task. One challenge is to determine which types of needs should be paramount in a society whose members have vastly different historical and contextual experiences. The need hierarchy developed by Abraham Maslow may not be universally accepted. At different times in a person's life course the hierarchy may change in ways that a social worker may have difficulty understanding. For example, in 1968 when African American sanitation workers in Memphis, Tennessee, protested their unequal treatment, they carried signs that stated simply "I am a Man." Yes, they desired higher wages and better working conditions, but they also wanted their employers (and society) to treat them with respect.

Another challenge for social workers is the difficulty of distinguishing between valid cultural differences between themselves and the people with whom they work, and implicit bias. If a primary value of the profession, as stated in the NASW *Code of Ethics*, is respect for human diversity, how is this value reconciled with support for basic, universal human rights? When they conflict, as in situations where clients exhibit racist, sexist, or homophobic beliefs—for whatever reason—what is the ethical course of action? (Dominelli, 2017; Miller & Garran, 2017).

Unfortunately, the NASW *Code of Ethics* provides only limited assistance in resolving these issues. As quoted at the beginning of this chapter, its first article states: "Social workers' primary responsibility is to promote the well-being of clients." Yet, it goes on to qualify this assertion: "However, social workers' responsibility to the larger society or specific legal obligations *may on limited occasions supersede* the loyalty owed clients, and clients should be so advised" (emphasis added)." How do we determine when other conditions exist which may supersede our loyalty to clients? The *Code*, therefore, while declaring that our primary responsibility is to our clients, acknowledges the existence of other responsibilities, as later chapters will discuss, but does not rank them in importance. At times, preference given to these other responsibilities—for example, to the wider community, to the law, or to one's employer—will justify the denial of a particular client's interest or the selection of one set of interests over another as the following case illustrates.

ETHICAL DILEMMA 4.2   Who Are the Clients?

You have been working with a multiracial community organization in your city about issues of neighborhood safety for the past 2 years. You have demonstrated your commitment to the community in several ways— by the close relationships you have established with many community members, by the long hours you have devoted to your work, and by your decision 18 months ago to move into the neighborhood. As a result, you have become a trusted advisor to the community organization with which you are working on key strategic issues. The board of the organization has become an effective instrument of the community and has operated on the principle of collective solidarity—that is, once the board makes a decision after extended discussion, its members commit to supporting it publicly. You are an ex officio member of the board.

Despite the best efforts of the organization, violent crime has continued to increase in the community, and community residents are increasingly frightened and angry. They are particularly angry about the failure of the city government and the police to take effective action, although the organization's leaders have met several times with city officials. Another major concern is the racial disproportionality in the number of arrests, "stop and frisks," and incidents of police misconduct that occur. These ongoing problems have had a deleterious effect on other programs that nonprofit agencies have attempted to establish in the community, in such areas as public health and behavioral health care, financial counseling, job training, and after-school tutoring.

At last night's board meeting, the organization's board unanimously voted to propose to the membership (which consists of hundreds of community residents) that the organization establish Community Anti-Crime Patrols staffed by a representative sample of neighborhood volunteers. These patrols would cruise the neighborhood, particularly during after-school and evening hours when crime is most prevalent, make citizens' arrests of individuals suspected of involvement in illegal activities, and involve the police only if they observed a crime in progress. The board also voted that these volunteers carry legally acquired firearms. The board is confident that the membership will endorse these proposals at its meeting next week. It has asked you to assist the board in mobilizing support for the proposals before and during the membership meeting.

As a community resident, you share the concerns of the board about crime, violence, and police misconduct in the neighborhood. Yet, you and some other residents, mindful of incidents like the shooting of Trayvon Martin, are also concerned about impact on community safety of armed "vigilante-style" patrols. You have a strong commitment to nonviolent solutions to social issues and an equally strong commitment to the community and the community organization's leadership. You fear the possibility of accelerated, if unintended, violence in the community if the Anti-Crime Patrols are established. You also fear that the organization will lose credibility if this occurs. On the other hand, you are concerned that if you fail to endorse the board's proposal, you will jeopardize the trust you have developed with its members.

Questions:
1. Who are the clients in this situation?
2. What are their interests?
3. How would you determine whose interests should take priority?
4. Which ethical principles would guide your decision?
5. What are the potential consequences of your decision?

As this case reveals, it is often difficult to identify who is the client, particularly in macro practice, and whose interests are of greatest importance. There are circumstances, however, when we are not obligated to place a client's interest first. In clinical practice, if a client acts irresponsibly by repeatedly failing to come to appointments without adequate explanation, refuses to follow mutually established behavioral goals, such as taking medication, or makes excessive demands on a worker's time, the worker can ignore the ethical imperative to give primacy to the client's interest. In macro practice, if the client's interest involves the marginalization of a subset of the community, such as people experiencing homelessness, violates a core social work principle, or—as in the above situation—places other community members at potential risk, we are under no duty to prioritize that interest.

The limits of a worker's competence can also supersede the ethical obligation to act in the client's interest. This latter issue raises an important question for the profession: "How ... do we determine what is an appropriate consideration of clients' interests, when there is a differential in workers' abilities to arrive at definitions of interest, an assumption implicit in the [educational] levels of preparation of the worker?" (Lewis, 1980, published in Reisch, 2003, p. 19). Unfortunately, in an era of fiscal austerity and increasing cultural conflict and misunderstanding, other factors may override this critical consideration.

ETHICAL DILEMMA 4.3   **The Limits of a Client's Interest**

A few years ago, the media reported that a Danish zoo had euthanized a healthy 2-year-old male giraffe because of concerns that the preservation and reproduction of his DNA would weaken the overall gene pool of giraffes kept in captivity by a consortium of zoos that follow certain ethical and biological guidelines. News of this event created a global outcry on the internet. Although it concerns a nonhuman animal, this incident illustrates the dilemmas involved in determining what is the "client's interest," who is the client, and what limits exist.

Questions:

1. What are the components of "the client's interest" in this case? What analogies could you draw that would apply to practice with humans?

2. How do we determine what they are, especially for minors or people with impairments?
3. What do we do if/when clients' interests conflict with each other (e.g., a family situation)?
4. What do we do if/when these interests conflict with the interests of other clients?
5. What do we do if/when these interests conflict with the interests of third parties or society as a whole? How would we determine what these interests are in a diverse society?
6. How does the current coronavirus pandemic contain echoes of this incident?

The Effects of Technology

Defining the client's interest is both easier and more challenging today due to the introduction of technology in service provision such as teletherapy, a method that has become particularly useful during the recent pandemic (Zhou et al., 2020). Increasingly, the use of digital technology has transformed traditional modes of social work practice and altered the basic nature of the worker-client relationship. While technology can help reduce stigma, language barriers, and unequal access to assistance, it also creates new ethical dilemmas and practice issues. For example, greater anonymity may make it more difficult to assess what is really going on with a service user because we lack the ability to pick up visual cues and other subtle advantages of a face-to-face relationship. This is particularly difficult with minors, who may provide false information in order to receive services or have difficulty expressing themselves to adult practitioners. A separate problem exists in online work with groups (Doel, 2019), where there is a greater risk of a group member exploiting the vulnerability of one's peers for personal reasons (Harris & Birnbaum, 2015).

One of the most pressing ethical problems that technology creates is the increased possibility of boundary violations and the emergence of dual relationships. (See Chapter 9 for further discussion of boundary issues.) In light of these new challenges, "clinical social workers must consider whether [their] use of digital technology and distance counseling alters the fundamental nature of the therapeutic relationship" (Reamer, 2015a, p. 121). These changes also make it more difficult to determine exactly what is the "client's interest" in a given situation.

The importance of reconsidering the meaning of informed consent is another particular challenge in the digital age. Reamer suggests that "social workers are expected to assess clients' ability to reason and make informed choices about their receipt of distance counseling services," but this "can be especially challenging when social workers interact with clients only electronically, do not meet with them in person, and may have difficulty confirming their identity and age" (Reamer, 2015a, p. 124).

FOR REFLECTION

1. In using technology in practice, what steps are necessary to create the trust that is essential for effective, socially just, and ethical service?
2. In your practice, how has technology been useful in creating trust with clients? In what ways, if any, has technology created ethical problems? How have you attempted to resolve them?

Trust and the Client's Interest

Imagine a personal or professional relationship in which the participants did not trust each other. They would have to guess each other's motives and goals; they might easily interpret comments in precisely the opposite way intended. Fear, suspicion, and apprehension would inevitably tarnish the relationship. The individuals would lack understanding, mutuality, respect, and affection for each other. It would be far more difficult for them to identify and resolve any problems of communication that emerged.

Unfortunately, during the past several decades, deliberate state policies have made it more likely that our relationships with the people with whom we work, and even with our colleagues, resemble this imagined undesirable reality due to an increase in involuntary clients, ongoing resource scarcity, and the growth of prescribed interventions (Beckett et al., 2017). Our society's persistent inability to rectify long-standing inequalities based on race, gender, social class, and sexual orientation exacerbates this situation. A half century ago, Lewis (1972, published in Reisch, 2003) characterized this situation as an absence of justice and proposed a set of practice principles to rebuild the trust essential to the establishment of constructive helping and human relationships:

1. Social workers should provide equal access to available services with particular efforts made to ensure access for the most vulnerable.
2. When involuntary participation in a service is required for the protection of a person or third parties, social workers should do whatever is possible to protect the rights and self-determination of that person.

3. Agencies should not threaten clients with the withdrawal of services or benefits for failure to comply with mandated participation nor should they distribute resources inequitably to particular individuals or categories of individuals.

4. To the extent possible, programs should offer alternatives in the services provided, and where no alternatives exist, no prior conditions for the receipt of services should exist.

5. Service users should have the opportunity to participate in the determination of the course of their service and to assess whether the agency is implementing its services fairly.

6. Social workers should try to expand the available options for service users and take into account suggestions made by service users. Where restrictions exist, social workers should attempt to eliminate or reduce them.

7. Social workers should inform service users about all the programs for which they might be eligible in order for them to determine what might be in their interest.

FIGURE 4.1. Trust Is an Essential Part of All Social Work Practice

FOR REFLECTION

1. What do you think are the major components of a trusting relationship—in your personal life and in social work practice?

2. In practice, to what extent does this trust involve the demonstration of "caring" and rethinking the traditional boundary between worker and client? What ways to express care are appropriate in practice?

3. How can we establish and maintain trust in an environment of scarce resources in our work with involuntary clients or when our clients or constituents are from different cultures?

4. What is the difference between "caring for" and "caring about" people?

5. What expressions of caring or compassion are appropriate in constructing and maintaining a professional relationship? What criteria should we use to make this determination?

6. How do we apply these criteria to different circumstances—for example, clinical vs. macro?

7. How can we blend our caring and helping functions? What is the role of research in this regard?

An Alternative Approach: The Ethic of Care

In the past decade, numerous scholars in various disciplines have suggested a new approach to the determination of a client's interest, the "ethic of care" (Clement, 2018). Unlike traditional rights-based theories of ethical practice, "the ethic of care emphasizes the importance of context, interdependence, relationships, and responsibilities to ... others" (Koggel & Orme, 2010, p. 109). Based primarily on feminist theory and feminist social and behavioral science, this ethic seeks to break down divisions between theory and practice and between knowledge and values (Larrabee, 2016). It explicitly recognizes the political dimensions of all practice and "the relevance of care ethics to policy analysis and activism" by redefining the locus of social welfare from the state and its agents to "all relations and interventions that contribute to the well-being, health, safety and security of individuals, communities and nations" (Koggel & Orme, 2010, p. 111). Consequently, it inevitably focuses on issues of race, gender, class, and power and the role of institutions, not merely individual actors, in implementing means of care through clear identification of "the purpose of care, a recognition of power relations, and the need for pluralistic, particular tailoring of care to meet individuals' needs" (p. 113). Proponents of this approach believe it is applicable to all levels of practice, across a wide range of issues, and in contexts ranging from local to global (Hay, 2019).

In determining the role of care in social work, we must be conscious of the contradiction between the expressed caring values of the profession and the lack of care increasingly reflected in contemporary societal policies and practices. The unequal distribution of health and behavioral health services is a prime example. Despite the growing need for ongoing caring solutions among marginalized populations, the commitment of resources to this care has diminished in recent years, and the nation has yet to develop effective preventive measures to reduce the demand for this care. The recent pandemic illustrates the devastating consequences of this deficiency of care, particularly on low-income persons, people of color, and the aged.

The question thus reemerges, as Morris (1977) posed it over 40 years ago, is the role of social work to "care for" people or to "care about" their well-being? Think about the distinction between these approaches for a moment. You will recognize the differences between these types of caring and how they would lead to different action imperatives. To fulfill our obligation to care *for* people, we need to identify who needs care, what type of care they need, and how best to provide it. For example, think of work with a family experiencing multiple issues, as individuals and as a group, in the aftermath of the unexpected death of a family member.

Alternatively, to address the well-being of people we *care about*, in addition to working with them as individuals we need to advocate for social policies that would ameliorate the effects of the complex forces that undermine their well-being and propose structural changes that would prevent the issues that affect them from recurring. For example, if a child living in substandard housing developed asthma, we would need to assist the child's family in obtaining the health services they need and advocate for policies that would ameliorate such inadequate shelter conditions and stop them from emerging in the future. Both approaches require "a sensitive understanding of interpersonal relationships" (Morris, 1977, p. 359), greater attention to our ultimate purposes as social workers, and less attention to the maintenance of our tenuous professional status.

The application of an ethic of care, therefore, can advance the profession's interest in promoting social justice. It augments our focus on structural inequalities with an emphasis on "confronting oppressive narratives ... within society" (Dybicz, 2012, p. 278). To some extent, it brings social workers back to our roots in promoting the formation of reciprocal, collaborative relationships with the people with whom we work (Dotolo, Lindhorst et al., 2018; Munn-Giddings & Borkman, 2017).

FIGURE 4.2. Caring Is a Core Value of Social Work

Knowledge Development and the Ethic of Care

Scholars and practitioners have long recognized that to achieve successful outcomes, all social work involves the application of knowledge and the development of effective interpersonal relationships. The NASW *Code of Ethics* states this clearly in its preamble. During the past three decades, social workers have increasingly emphasized the use of knowledge (evidence) as the primary basis for effective interventions in both micro and macro practice (O'Hare, 2020; Drisko & Grady, 2019; McBeath, 2016). Eileen Gambrill (2011), a long-time advocate for evidence-based practice (EBP), argues that EBP helps practitioners address the uncertainties and ethical obligations that arise in practice through the *informed application* of research-generated knowledge. This implies that social workers need to use considerable discretion to ensure the accurate implementation of new ideas derived from current scholarship. At the same time, however, the concurrent focus on a somewhat abstract human rights-based approach to social work has combined with the uncritical adoption of EBP to blur the essential role of relationship in practice (Mapp et al., 2019).

Yet, "the ability to form a genuine connection with the clients one serves, to communicate that one cares about their well-being and values them as a person, continues to play a prominent role in the helping process" (Dybicz, 2012, p. 271). In this light, several alternative approaches to practice have proposed a different type of helping relationship in which genuine friendship plays a key role, albeit in different ways. These include the strengths perspective (Simmons et al., 2016), narrative therapy (Charon, 2017), resilience theory (van Breda, 2018), solution-based therapy (Gillingham, 2018), applications of the dialogical approach originally developed by Freire (1970; Ross, 2019; Yan, 2016), and post-modernism (Witkin & Irving, 2016). Each approach, however, presents its own set of ethical challenges (Loue, 2018, pp. 62–81).

One argument in favor of an ethic of care is that it can help counteract the dehumanizing effects of viewing people as categories rather than as unique individuals, an unfortunate and perhaps unintended consequence of the focus on evidence-based intervention research. This would be a particularly important, if challenging step in our increasingly identity-focused culture. It also elevates the importance of people's expertise about their own lives and circumstances and allows them to interpret their experiences in their own voice. This reduces the power imbalance that inevitably occurs in a professional helping relationship (Greene, 2017). Finally, it provides a counter-narrative that redefines the helping process away from a "problem-centered," expertise-driven model (Lewis, 1984b, published in Reisch, 2003) toward one that emphasizes the role of critical consciousness and mutuality (McGirr & Sullivan, 2017; Barak, 2016).

Critics of this approach point out that the emphasis on friendship risks the possibility of dual relationships that can produce negative consequences for the social worker, the client (or constituent), and the organization. The expanded use of digital technology as a medium of practice may exacerbate this problem. Yet, the alternative—the preservation of professional dominance and assumed hierarchies of knowledge—may create insurmountable barriers to effective, social justice-oriented practice in our diverse society (Reisch & Garvin, 2016).

Multiple Loyalties and the Client's Interest

In order to resolve dilemmas of multiple loyalties that may impede our ability to determine or act on behalf of a client's interest, practitioners must answer 2 fundamental ethical questions: (1) To whom do I/we owe a duty? (2) What is the nature of that duty? The possibility of unintended consequences arising from whatever decisions we make further complicates our attempt to answer these questions. We also have to assess the tradeoffs between the positive and negative effects of immediate (short-term) and potential future (long-term) outcomes, and take into account the possible effects of our decisions on third parties, some of whom we might not be able to identify initially.

As discussed above, the difficulty of determining who is the client complicates the resolution of this dilemma, as does the possibility of clients having ambiguous or multiple needs and desires. In addition, individuals from different cultural backgrounds may express their needs and desires in ways that differ from the cultural mainstream. They may also be reluctant to express these wishes openly due to cultural norms, lack of trust, or fear of reprisal.

There are 2 possible approaches to the second question (the nature of one's duty to clients). The first is "doing what the client wants." This approach has potential problems—for example, if the client's wishes conflict with the wishes of others, violate existing laws or social norms, or place impossible demands on the social worker's time or agency resources. A second possible approach, following Rawls (1999), is to prioritize the interest of the most vulnerable. The challenge here is determining what constitutes vulnerability, what types of vulnerability should take priority, and who has the authority to make this determination (Reimer & Thompson, 2019). We also have to decide if we should take into account the effects of our decision on the future vulnerability of individuals or communities.

Dworkin (1977) suggested that we could assess our professional obligations in such circumstances in three distinct ways. One way would be to focus on the goals of whatever actions we decide to take. Utilitarianism is the best-known approach of this nature.

A second, deontological approach would be to emphasize the rights that are at stake in the situation, both in terms of the outcomes desired and the process by which we select them. For example, we could stress a person's right to freedom, the right to adequate tangible or intangible resources, or the right to be a full participant in the decision-making process.

A third approach places priority on the fulfillment of a duty to the people with whom we work. Although this duty-based approach appears to be most compatible with the principles outlined in the NASW *Code of Ethics* and most social work literature, community and organizational practice present unique challenges in this regard (Evans & Hardy, 2017; McBeath, 2016; Hyde, 2011), as the following case demonstrates.

ETHICAL DILEMMA 4.4 *How* Do You Determine the Client's Interest?

You are a school social worker working in an impoverished inner-city neighborhood. The school and the surrounding district suffer from chronic underfunding by the city and the state. Teachers are overworked and underpaid, the physical facilities of the schools are in terrible condition, and the students' textbooks are considerably outdated. In response to these conditions, you joined a coalition organized by the teachers' union and neighborhood parents to advocate for more funding for the schools and a better contract for the teachers, which will expire soon.

After weeks of union negotiations with the school board, however, labor and management have been unable to settle the dispute. Sources tell you that the school superintendent and the Board of Education doubt the teachers will strike if contract talks break down. Nevertheless, the Board has threatened to fire any staff, including social workers, if they support a potential strike. In defense of its position, a Board spokesperson contended that if social workers supported the strike they would damage the students and violate the NASW *Code of Ethics*.

Upon your arrival at the school one morning, a teacher with whom you have been friendly tells you that the union voted overwhelmingly last night to strike effective in 2 days. Recently, similar strikes by teachers in several states have led to increased funding

for schools. She asks you to support the strike by refusing to cross a picket line and persuading your colleagues and the parents with whom you have been working to endorse the strike. You are sympathetic to the union's position and its overall goals but are aware that a lengthy strike will affect students' education and put your job at risk.

Questions:
1. What are the various interests at stake in this situation? To whose interests do you owe a duty?
2. If you think you have multiple, but conflicting duties in this situation, how would you prioritize them?
3. What action would best serve their interests?
4. What process would you use to make that decision?
5. What factors would you take into account? What social work values and ethical principles would influence your decision? How would you prioritize these values?
6. What might be the short- and long-term consequences of your decision?
7. Under what circumstances would you generalize the process used to make your decision?

Social Justice and the Client's Interest

Although rarely stated explicitly, determining the client's interest is also an issue of social justice. When we assess the circumstances of a particular situation, identify the key actors, and select a course of action, we are implicitly making a judgment about what actions or personal qualities deserve a reward or our attention and are compatible with our professed commitment to social justice. The judgments we make reflect societal values deeply embedded in our culture. They influence our decision whether to reward a person's "success" (good qualities), punish their "failures," or both. Unconscious bias may also affect this determination. In short, when we determine the client's interest, we are judging who deserves aid and under what circumstances, and whether the benefits generated by this desert should be individually or group based.

For the most part, Western approaches to this question of social justice fall into three broad categories. One, based on utilitarianism, would determine the client's interest by calculating which course of action would maximize the welfare of the "client," regardless of whom we identify as the client. A second, deontological approach would prioritize the implementation of a selected value, such as individual freedom. A third approach, drawn from communitarian concepts, would focus on what decision would maximize virtue and increase the well-being of the community as a whole (Etzioni, 2018b; Sandel, 2010). Let's look briefly at how we might apply these three approaches to the case presented at the beginning of the chapter.

Applying Social Justice to Practice

If we applied the first approach to the matter of Sammy and Jose, our initial decision would involve identifying the client whose interests we must protect. Is it Sammy, Jose, their parents, the agency, other campers, or Amy, the social worker? Each party has a different set of interests, only some of which overlap. Sammy has an interest in fulfilling his filial obligation to protect his younger brother and, although he does not state this openly, he probably has an interest in maintaining the benefits the camp provides and may provide for his future. Jose has not stated his interests directly, but he clearly is seeking attention and, in the judgment of several respected professionals with whom Amy consulted (with the concurrence of his parents), the camp cannot satisfy his ultimate interests, whatever they are. He also has an unspoken interest in self-protection and, apparently, only his brother's presence can meet that interest under current circumstances.

Sammy's parents want the best for both their sons, but what constitutes the "best" is very different for Sammy and Jose. The agency wants to provide the best possible service for all of its campers and does not want to risk its reputation or incur legal liability if harm comes to one or more of them. The social worker is concerned about her professional reputation and has an indirect interest in helping Sammy succeed and protecting Jose's well-being.

In effect, deciding whose interests take priority involves making an implicit decision about which interests are most important. It also involves assessing the consequences to all affected parties of prioritizing a particular individual's interests. For example, one could reasonably assume that sending Jose home without Sammy would put Jose at risk and probably undermine the camp's efforts to provide the maximum possible benefits to Sammy. On the other hand, sending both campers home might help protect Jose, but for how long and at what cost to Sammy's physical safety and future prospects, and to their parents?

If we took the approach that emphasizes the application of a particular value, we would have to select the value we regard as most important in this situation. For example, is it freedom of choice, protection from physical harm, or the maximization of an individual's life chances? If the preservation of free choice is our highest priority, whose choice should take precedence—Sammy (who is, after all, a minor) or his parents? If harm reduction is a priority, should we be equally concerned about the risk of harm to Jose, Sammy, or unknown third parties? Should we focus on the short-term risk or worry about the future? If the latter, whose future? If maximizing opportunity is the highest value in this situation, opportunity for whom and in what form?

Finally, if we adopted a communitarian approach in our attempt to reach an ethical resolution of this situation, how would we define the community and determine what constitutes its well-being? Should we focus on the community's short-term well-being (i.e., other campers and staff), which might involve the reduction of physical conflict and its effects? Or should we focus on the community's future well-being, which might include the potential positive impact that Sammy could make on his community and society as a whole?

Summary

This chapter addressed a fundamental question for all social work practice: determining how to identify and respond to the client's interest. The chapter identified the similarities and differences between micro and macro practice involved in resolving these issues. It discussed the implications of technology for this issue—a topic covered in subsequent chapters as well—and the importance of establishing trust and resolving multiple loyalties as preconditions for ethical practice in this regard. It presented an emerging approach to ethical practice—the ethic of care—and briefly discussed its implications for ethical practice. The chapter concluded by linking the challenges involved in determining the client's interest with the overriding goal of achieving social justice. The next chapter will expand on these matters by examining the dual challenges of ethical assessment and ethical decision-making.

Reflection Exercise: Defining the Client's Interest in Macro Practice

1. In working with a diverse, multiracial community-based organization, to whom do you owe a duty to help? In other words, who is the client and how can you determine the client's interest?
2. What is the reciprocal obligation, if any, of clients and constituents to the organization with whom they are working?
3. How can the organization balance a focus on individual and community empowerment with efforts to meet the immediate needs of community residents?
4. How can the organization develop support services that do not reinforce the dominant deficit or individual responsibility model as the source of people's problems?
5. Given resource and time constraints, how can the organization involve community members in defining their needs, proposing helping strategies, and evaluating the effectiveness of these interventions?

Credits

Fig. 4.1: Copyright © 2013 Depositphotos/victoreus.
Fig. 4.2: Copyright © 2015 Depositphotos/belahoche.

Making Ethical Assessments and Ethical Decisions

Introduction

Social workers make assessments in all modes and fields of practice. We assess a variety of factors, including a person, family, or community's history and culture, the environmental context of a problem or issue, the strengths or assets of our clients and constituents, the suitability of certain models of intervention to the particular situation, and the resources available to address it. What is always present but often overlooked is the ethical component of these assessments.

This chapter builds on the content in Chapters 2–4 and examines the issues involved in making ethical assessments and the ethical decisions based on these assessments. It presents a few approaches to these processes and includes several cases to illustrate the ethical dilemmas involved. It then discusses some recent complications in conducting ethical assessments and making ethical decisions, and concludes with an examination of how the NASW *Code of Ethics* is and is not a helpful guide to these processes.

ETHICAL DILEMMA 5.1   ### What to Do About Mr. K?

Mr. K. is an 84-year-old white man who lives alone in an urban neighborhood in an apartment building designed specifically for the elderly. Although his cognition is excellent, he repeatedly falls and injures himself. His last injury resulted in a serious hip fracture that confined him to a wheelchair and a bed. He has in-home services, which he reluctantly accepts, but which he complicates by directing verbal abuse toward the aides, all of whom are Black women from the West Indies.

Mr. K. has two children, a daughter who lives overseas and visits only 1–2 times each year, and a son who lives nearby but has limited time to help Mr. K. because of work and family obligations. Other than his son, Mr. K. has no relatives or surviving friends who could assist him. A long-time neighbor, who had been very helpful in the past, is now disabled herself.

The staff at the agency providing in-home services for Mr. K. has determined that he is at excessive risk if he continues to live alone. It recommends that he seek placement in an assisted living facility. Mr. K. strongly opposes this recommendation and insists he can manage on his own with the current support he receives. His medical prognosis, however, is not encouraging. The doctor treating him does not anticipate he will completely recover from his most recent fall and is certain that, without constant supervision, Mr. K. will incur additional injuries, with decreasing probability of recovery. He agrees with the agency's recommendation that only full-time supervision in an institution would be adequate to ensure Mr. K.'s well-being.

Mr. K.'s son has been seeing you for counseling. In the course of a session, he consults with you about the appropriate course of action to take. What would you recommend and for what reasons?

Questions:
1. Who are the key actors in this situation? What role should they play in the decision-making process? Who should ultimately make the decision?
2. How do ethical considerations influence the choice of decision-makers?
3. What ethical criteria should you use to make the decision?
4. To what extent should Mr. K.'s consent be required?
5. How would Mr. K.'s racial bias toward the in-home aides influence your decision?

Making Ethical Assessments

As this case illustrates, an ethical assessment usually involves choosing between competing goods and competing rights. The frequent ambiguities that accompany many practice situations create uncertainties that complicate these choices. Sometimes, for example, challenges to ethical assessment occur when a client's interest and those of their family are at odds. At other times, a lack of knowledge makes an informed decision more difficult. Ironically, however, "where ethical issues are involved, the additional clarification that facts provide may increase one's doubts" (Lewis, 1984a, p. 82; also published in Reisch, 2003).

Ethical issues in such circumstances also arise when a "client ... express[es] a preference for a future free of supervised restraint even if this increases risks of physical injury" (p. 83). Lewis maintained that, as a result, "an assessment ought not be so constructed as to deny a function to guiding imperatives, reducing [the available] choices to [the] situational preferences of individual actors" (p. 85). The choice of any approach to assessment, therefore, is never value free.

Social workers conduct assessments in all fields and every method of practice. In practice with individuals and families, assessment is the first step in the development of an effective and ethical intervention strategy (Reisch & Garvin, 2016). In community practice, assessment of a community's strengths and assets is a prerequisite for developing a plan of action (Reisch, 2018c). Administrators engage in various forms of organizational assessment, such as strategic planning, to resolve short-term and long-term agency problems, develop or evaluate programs, and consider how to initiate structural changes. The same is true in the formulation of a successful advocacy campaign (Healy & Sofer, 2019; Hoefer, 2019b). Most social work literature, however, focuses on the efficacy of such assessments and overlooks their ethical dimensions.

Making an ethical assessment requires us to integrate a number of elements that exist in every professional relationship, whether with individuals, families, or communities. As discussed in Chapter 2, we must first become fully aware of our personal values, life history, and current life context. It is important to understand how our culture, race, ethnicity, religion, gender, sexual orientation, age, ability status, and geographic region shape our worldview and our perceptions of others and their circumstances (Eltaiba, 2019; Congress, 2017).

At the same time, we must also acknowledge how our professional values and background influence our view of each practice encounter. This requires us to reflect on our education and work experience, particularly our experience working with people similar to those with whom we are currently involved in a professional relationship, and with issues similar to those with which we are dealing (even if the people who confronted these issues were quite different from our current clients or constituents). An important component here is the acquisition of a clear understanding of the explicit and implicit requirements of the NASW *Code of Ethics*, as well as an awareness of its limitations, gaps, ambiguities, contradictions, and shortcomings.

In addition, as discussed in Chapter 4, we have to recognize the potential existence of goal conflicts between us and our clients, between us and our organization (or the society as a whole), or between our clients and the organization that is providing them with services or benefits. A common example of the first instance occurs when social workers in the child welfare field have to decide whether to remove a child from their parents' custody. Conflicts between practitioners and their employers may arise when the social justice goals of the former clash with the fiscal priorities of the latter. Individuals receiving public welfare benefits, such as Temporary Assistance to Needy Families (TANF, often referred to as "welfare"), may regard their goals as physical and economic survival, while the agency with which they work may emphasize their attainment of self-sufficiency.

In conducting an ethical assessment, we also have to be able to identify an ethical issue or dilemma when it exists and to distinguish between practice issues that inevitably arise and ethical issues, which are far less common. Similarly, we have to differentiate between ethical and legal issues in order to determine when legal requirements compel us to violate ethical norms of conduct and when our ethical commitments supersede our legal obligations.

Two other components of ethical assessment are our professional judgment, based (ideally) on a familiarity with current research, and critical reflection on both our previous practice experiences and the present situation. Unfortunately, there is little empirical research on the topic of ethical decision-making to provide practitioners with evidence-based guidance on this challenging process (Trnka et al., 2019). Doyle, Miller, and Mirza (2009) found that "both personal and professional factors are related to ethical decision-making and predict the degree to which ethical decisions are discrepant" (p. 3). Hardy (2019) supports these research findings and notes that one's cultural beliefs, ethnicity, and gender have influenced social workers' ethical decision-making throughout the profession's history. Other factors, such as one's educational background, formal training in ethics, and commitment to professional values, are also significant indicators of one's approach to the ethical decision-making process. These findings have implications for how social work programs teach the next generation of practitioners (Barsky, 2019).

Because assessment of a practice situation ultimately determines the process by which you and the people with whom you are working will attempt to address (and hopefully solve) a problem or issue, it is important to be clear about the situational context at the outset. Think about who are the critical actors—those who must be involved in implementing whatever strategy the assessment produces and those directly or indirectly affected by the results of this assessment. It is equally important to consider what potential actions might ensue from different assessments, what is the intention or purpose of each possible action, and what the probable consequences of each option might be. Finally, it is important to take into account the environmental context in which the assessment occurs. Are there individual, organizational, community, or societal factors that might limit how you are viewing the situation and the options available to address it? What is the likelihood that an assessment would reduce or increase the possibility of an ethical issue emerging? For example, have those with the authority to make a critical assessment explored all possible outcomes? Have implicit biases about the client influenced their assessment in any way? To what extent have decision-makers considered the client's views of the issue?

FIGURE 5.1. Making an Ethical Assessment Is a Critical First Step in Practice

---

ETHICAL DILEMMA 5.2   ## Resolving a Complex Community Situation

You are a social worker in a multiservice agency in Southwest Detroit/Dearborn. It is the most diverse area in Southeast Michigan, with a population consisting of African Americans, Arab Americans, low-income Whites largely from Appalachia, and both long-term residents and recent arrivals from Central America and Mexico. In cooperation with an energetic state legislator, you have been able to obtain funds to build a new, expanded social service and recreational center that the community desperately needs. With the funds

provided by a planning grant from the state, you are responsible for assessing the community's perspective on what features the new center should possess.

Through informal conversations with leaders of various community groups, you have discovered they have different priorities regarding how to use the prospective center's resources. Because recent fires have destroyed or severely damaged neighborhood churches, both African American and Latinx community leaders want the center to be available for church services and programs with a religious orientation, such as Bible study classes. (Neither state nor private funds would explicitly prohibit this.) Other community members are either skeptical or resistant to this idea. In addition, spokespersons for the Arab American community, which is primarily Muslim and represents over one-third of the total population, insist that the new center have gender-segregated recreational facilities, particularly its gym and swimming pool. Other groups oppose this proposal, and it may not be possible to implement it given the limited budget.

The ad hoc planning committee asked you to develop an assessment strategy that takes into account these diverse perspectives and is consistent with the agency's social work values.

Questions:

1. What assessment process would you use to produce a plan whose recommendations might satisfy the diverse constituencies in the community to the greatest possible extent?
2. What ethical principles would guide your process?
3. How would you address the consequences if your recommendations do not satisfy every group?

Steps in Ethical Assessment

Lewis (1984a) proposed that practitioners should use the following approach to assess the ethics of situations like those described in this chapter to help them determine a course of action:

1. Apply a consequentialist analysis (if ... then) to the hypothetical courses of action.
2. Using a formalist (deontological) analysis, identify the underlying ethical imperative used to justify possible alternatives.
3. If both approaches yield a similar conclusion, implement the action suggested.
4. If the analyses produce different results, apply the option indicated by the consequentialist approach provided it does not directly contradict the imperative underlying the formalist analysis.
5. If the two analyses are in direct contradiction, use the formalist analysis and take steps to remove the factors that lead to this contradiction.
6. If the consequentialist analysis is weak or ambiguous, apply the formalist analysis in as limited a fashion as possible. At the same time, try to strengthen the variable required to develop an enhanced consequentialist analysis.
7. If one can implement neither analysis because of insufficient information, understanding, or experience, reconsider whether it is possible to utilize either step 4 or 5. (pp. 90–91)

How would apply this approach to the following case?

ETHICAL DILEMMA 5.3   Developing an Ethical
                                  Advocacy Strategy

You are an organizer for a local group, People for Adequate Welfare (PAW), a coalition of welfare recipients and their supporters in the community and state legislature. The organization operates in a democratic manner with all decisions approved by the membership or their designees on the steering committee.

After several years of little to no progress, this year the coalition has obtained considerable legislative support, although the 25% grant increase PAW proposed is more than most legislators will approve. The session is in its final stages and lawmakers are scrambling to reach agreement on the state budget before the state's constitutional deadline.

Less than 12 hours prior to the deadline, the chief of staff of the state senate majority leader calls you with the news that the budget will include a 15% increase in the welfare grant, provided that PAW and its legislative allies sign off and cease further protests and demonstrations. She needs your answer in a few hours.

PAW's steering committee has no meeting scheduled; its members are either working or dealing with family concerns and are difficult to reach.

Questions:
1. How would you apply Lewis's approach to make an ethical assessment of the situation in time to respond to the impending legislative deadline?
2. What ethical principles would you employ to determine your decision?
3. Under what other circumstances would you apply these principles?

Making Ethical Decisions

After assessing a given situation, social workers have to decide whether an action or intervention is required and, if so, what course of action to follow. In addition to a strategic analysis of the circumstances and context, we have to take into account the ethical and value dimensions of our decision. This process occurs whether this decision is in a clinical, community, or organizational practice setting. Whether we are developing a therapeutic intervention, planning a social action, developing an advocacy strategy, designing a program or service, or resolving a difficult fiscal or personnel problem, the process by which we make such decisions is fraught with potential ethical issues.

For example, an initial, often overlooked question is *who* should make the decision? Sometimes the answer is easy; in hierarchical organizations, agency by-laws or clear lines of responsibility and accountability (what the military refers to as the "chain of command") determine who possesses the requisite authority. In many social service organizations, however, particularly in the nonprofit sector, the situation is more ambiguous. An additional challenge is ensuring that the person or persons making the decision have the ability to fulfill their role and responsibility effectively and ethically. For example, if an agency executive lacks the resources required to implement a programmatic decision reached in consultation with community members, the failure to produce promised results may lead to long-lasting distrust among the various stakeholders. Similarly, if a clinical social worker cannot obtain a benefit their client needs after committing themselves to do so, it could undermine the relationship between them.

As the chart at left illustrates, there are multiple stakeholders and factors involved in the resolution of each ethical decision. One set of stakeholders includes the person or persons directly affected by the decision (e.g., a client and the client's family).

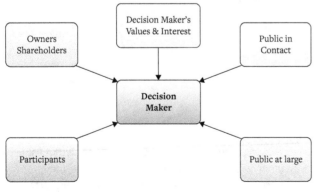

FIGURE 5.2. Stakeholders in Ethical Decision-Making

A second consists of colleagues who may participate indirectly in the decision-making process, such as in a "host institution" like a hospital or school. A third potential group of stakeholders consists of residents of the surrounding community in which similar ethical dilemmas might arise in the future. In certain circumstances, a decision may have repercussions, at least indirectly, for the public image of the social work profession, or for society as a whole. Lastly, of course, the social worker and those who may experience the emotional impact the dilemma creates are also key stakeholders.

Models of Ethical Decision-Making

In the mid and late 1980s, Joseph (1985, 1988) proposed three models to describe the process of ethical decision-making by social workers in health care settings that, they argued, were equally applicable to other fields of practice. These models are (1) the position model, (2) the expert model, and (3) the equality model.

Joseph found that the dominant model, especially in health care settings, was the position model. In this top-down model, occupational or organizational status determined the locus of decision-making. She concluded that this model produced the greatest conflict among the participants in the decision-making process, the least exchange of information, and the fewest opportunities for dissent or intragroup participation (Joseph, 1988).

By contrast, the equality model "produced the greatest degree of satisfaction" and maximized the involvement of patients and their families in ethical decision-making. "It was associated with high information exchange, high participation, and low role conflict" (Joseph, 1988, p. 10). The difference between the outcomes these models produce underscores the need to pay increased attention to the role of constructive dialogue and mutual respect in a group's decision-making process (Varghese, 2020; Ross & Parks, 2018). Adhering to these principles can also help minimize the conflicts that most often occur in interprofessional practice in which different professional cultures exist side by side (Bronstein, 2003).

As a preferred alternative, Joseph (1988) proposed a three-pronged collaborative model that focuses on making the ethical dilemma explicit; bringing value differences to the surface; and providing a guide for ethical choices. Similar to other models described in this book, it involves a multistep process for ethical decision-making:

1. Understand and describe the practice situation and the specific ethical issue clearly.
2. Collect background information on the perspectives of different stakeholders regarding the ethical issue.
3. Identify and prioritize the core values underlying the issue.
4. Articulate options for actions and provide a justification for each alternative.
5. Review and analyze the data collected and select an alternative. (Joseph, 1988, pp. 12–13)

More recently, Úriz and colleagues (2017) and Kaplan, Bryan, and Sanders (2017) reached similar conclusions in their analyses of current models of ethical decision-making but drew different implications from their findings. Úriz et al. divided the existing methods of decision-making used in social work into two groups: those that relied on the development of a hierarchy of ethical principles (a deontological approach) and those that applied a more comprehensive, multifaceted approach that took into account the context and consequences of a situation. They concluded "whichever methodology is chosen ... what is important is for it to be followed by a process of profound ethical reflection, a deliberative, reasoned, justified and well-argued process," the cultivation of moral character, and recognition of the inevitability of uncertain outcomes (p. 51).

Kaplan and colleagues similarly criticized an exclusive reliance on the use of a values perspective as the starting point in ethical decision-making. Instead, they propose an emphasis on the avoidance of harm, much like the Hippocratic Oath in medicine. They suggest that focusing on what we *ought not do* can produce "the conceptual and analytic clarity needed to address moral problems and foster a more meaningful collaborative approach with other disciplines in working through these problems" (Kaplan, et al, 2017, p. 1).

ETHICAL DILEMMA 5.4   ## Making Ethical Decisions in a Crisis

You are a social worker in a public elementary school. One of the students, Billy, with whom you have been working in an after-school program, tells you that he has a terrible toothache. You bring him to the school nurse, who examines Billy and sees that he has an enormous abscess that appears ready to burst. She takes his temperature, which is 103 degrees. The nurse suggests that he receive immediate treatment to avoid serious and potentially life-threatening consequences.

You try to call Billy's mother several times but cannot reach her. You run to the office of the school principal and ask him if the school's van driver could rush Billy to the nearest emergency room. The principal tells you that the van is unavailable because it is taking students on a long-planned field trip. You have a car and could drive Billy to the hospital, but you do not have his mother's permission to do so and lack the authority to request out-of-school health treatment for him. The principal forbids you to use your car to take Billy to the hospital without parental consent

and suggests you wait until you can reach his mother. He reminds you that if anything happened to you or Billy while you drove him to the hospital, you would be liable for the damages, would be subject to a malpractice suit, and would face disciplinary proceedings by the school administration.

Billy comes to you again in tears. He tells you that he is trying to be brave, but the pain is getting worse and he feels dizzy. You notice that he feels even warmer than before.

Questions:
1. What would you do?
2. What ethical principles would influence your decision?
3. What process would you use to make a decision?
4. Would you employ the same principles and process to other situations in which a social worker had to make a decision quickly in a crisis?

In resolving an issue like this, it is equally important to identify for whom you are making the decision and who has the authority to make the decision. It is also important to determine if selecting particular decision-makers would deprive an individual or community of its right to self-determination. In addition, it is important to consider if the decision-making process risks being paternalistic or perceived as paternalistic. It is also important to consider the role of third parties, such as Billy's mother, and the consequences for them that might result from your decision.

To make an ethical decision in such circumstances, we also need to consider a number of other questions. Will the decision-making process we employ undermine the ability of those affected by the decision outcome to make future decisions? If the individuals principally affected by a decision cede the authority for decision-making to others, what degree of consent do they need to provide? How should they convey this consent? What limits, if any, bound the authority of decision-makers in such circumstances? In the above case, it would be important to determine if Billy's mother had given the school permission to act *in loco parentis*. If so, under what conditions? Does the potential harm Billy could suffer from a failure to act on his behalf override any of these ethical considerations?

Finally, social workers must address several other issues. What criteria should we use to determine the selection of decision-makers? For example, should we base this decision on a person's technical expertise, position in the organization, prior experience with similar issues, or relationship with the affected parties? Would we apply the criteria we employ to all similar situations in the future, or are they specific to a particular situation? What, if any, moral principles are enhanced or negated by the proposed course of action?

In sum, all forms of social work require ethical decisions. In fields like health care, the decision-making process is currently receiving greater attention because of fiscal scarcity in an atmosphere of increasing need due to the pandemic. Even in normal times, routine processes such as discharge planning require decisions that involve matters of confidentiality, patients' autonomy, and the allocation of scarce resources. The assumptions underlying all ethical decision-making models that Blumenfeld and Lowe (1987) proposed over three decades ago, therefore, are still useful today:

1. Social workers possess the necessary skills to make decisions ethically;
2. Social workers have a commitment to helping people make informed choices.
3. Decision-making processes work best in the context of collaborative relationships.
4. Most decisions should occur within a prescribed timeframe to be effective and ethical. (p. 49)

Finally, most of the assessments and strategic decisions we make understandably focus on an immediate problem or issue. As Harry Hopkins, a leading social worker during the Great Depression of the 1930s famously testified to Congress: "People don't eat in the long-term, they eat every day." Nevertheless, in making ethical assessments or decisions, social workers must see the "big picture" and not focus exclusively on the immediate issue (Congress, 2017). If we do not take this broader view, we might fail to take into account significant aspects of the situation to the ultimate detriment of our clients or constituents (Bernacchi, 2017).

FIGURE 5.3. The Need to Make Ethical Decisions Can Arise at Any Phase of Social Work Practice

New Complications

The increasing complexity of the practice environment creates new hurdles to overcome in our efforts to make ethical assessments. As Reamer (1986) accurately predicted 35 years ago, the advent of digital technology, combined with recent medical advances, has increased the frequency that social workers face assessment and decision-making issues that involve the creation, enhancement, and termination of life. Consequently, in our current digital age, ethical decision-making has become far more complicated. It now involves issues of "practitioner competence, client privacy and confidentiality, informed consent, conflicts of interest, boundaries and dual relationships" (Reamer, 2013a, p. 163). As a result, the possibility of making an ethical mistake in the assessment or decision-making process, by omission or commission, has increased exponentially.

Certain practice situations, such as those involving elder abuse, are particularly challenging due to the ambiguous circumstances that often exist (Loue, 2018, pp. 207–231). This is due to the persistent lack of clear ethical and legal guidelines and the importance of balancing a client's safety with their right to self-determination (Heisler, 2019). In such situations, Donovan and Regehr (2010) recommend that social workers rely on virtue ethics as a complement to traditional principle ethics. While the latter focuses on rights, rules, and obligations, virtue ethics assume "that professional ethics encompass more than moral actions ... [and] include character traits and ideals [such as honesty, compassion, and respect] that can help us make ethical decisions" (p. 179). Particularly in ambiguous practice situations that sit at the nexus of clinical, legal, and ethical considerations, social workers need to be well versed in the implications of these three components of ethical decision-making (Teaster & Anextberger, 2019).

Another issue arises in our work with involuntary clients or those who, for whatever reasons and in various ways, resist the interventions we recommend. In this regard, Walton (2018) poses two important questions social workers need to consider in their decision-making. Should we deny services to clients who fail to follow through on agreed-upon courses of action? If so, is it ethical to make such decisions unilaterally?

To avoid unfortunate consequences in such situations, Walton suggests that agencies establish clear policies about the obligations clients incur when participating in a service program. They should communicate these policies in several ways at the outset of the service transaction and reinforce them when necessary. These recommendations demonstrate how the involvement of multiple stakeholders in the development, transmission, and implementation of organizational policies is critical to avoiding actions of dubious ethics that could lead to potentially deleterious consequences for clients and the agency's reputation.

To prevent such harms and develop an effective framework for ethical assessment and decision-making, social workers and clients should engage in a constructive dialogue about their respective ethical principles (Rollins, 2019; Marc et al., 2019). This suggestion implies that while we need to develop consistent guidelines in order to adapt to different practice situations, we must avoid basing our ethical decisions or the process by which we reach them solely on our personal preferences, emotions, or externally-derived statistics. We also need to recognize that clients generally approach difficult life decisions using one of three ethical styles.

For example, we need to provide individuals who prefer a "legalistic orientation" with definite rules they can apply to the decision-making process. Otherwise, complex or ambiguous circumstances may immobilize them. To avoid this possibility, we need to help clients recognize the emotional components of their decisions and empower them to make choices that reflect a more flexible perspective on perceived "rules."

Those whom Goldmeier (1984) referred to as "anti-nominally oriented persons" have overly flexible principles. These individuals react solely to the existential moment in order to arrive at a decision. In such situations, Goldmeier recommended we should attempt to assist them in seeing the broader context of their problem.

Persons with a "normative orientation" seek to base their decisions "in a system of ethics which, they hope, conforms optimally to personally compatible norms" (p. 46). Like Reamer (2013b), Goldmeier suggested that we use a framework for applying moral principles, such as Gewirth's Principle of Generic Consistency (1978), to develop and maintain an ethically normative decision-making style. Although we do not have to make this principle explicit to those with whom we work, it should serve as a guide to our practice.

Loewenberg and Dolgoff (1988) raised other important questions about these issues: "When is it justified to shift the ethical decision obligation to another person (not the social worker)? To whom should it be shifted … [and for what reasons]?" (p. 112). In their view, ethical decision-making also requires "accurate knowledge of the current societal value stance" (p. 113). This does not mean that social workers should acquiescence to these values, particularly if they come into conflict with our ethical principles, but we must take them "in consideration when assessing a problem situation" (p. 113). A persistent issue, especially in today's contentious environment, is how far we need to go in "considering" the dominant values of society when their application may be harmful to our clients.

As discussed in Chapter 3, in making ethical assessments and decisions we also need to clarify our personal values and make them sufficiently unambiguous and specific in order for them to serve as guides to ethical behavior. Given increasing external pressures, when we assess the potential consequences of a decision, we need to balance considerations of efficiency—how we use time and resources—with effectiveness—our ability to help people achieve desired goals.

Further complicating this process is the changing societal definition of a right. Because of these changes, we need to balance society's interest, exercised through benign or coercive mechanisms of social control, with the establishment and maintenance of a successful helping relationship. For example, in a behavioral health program, what role should an involuntary client play in the development of an intervention plan? Does a person who has violated societal norms or broken the law forfeit the right to define what they need and what type of help they will receive?

The Role of the NASW *Code of Ethics*

To the disappointment of students and practitioners who desire straightforward answers to complicated ethical questions, the NASW *Code of Ethics* "does not provide universal prescriptions for behavior, nor does it specify a hierarchy of values, ethical principles, or standards" (Doyle et al., 2009, p. 4). Although the latest revisions to the *Code* demonstrate some responsiveness to recent cultural and technological changes, its assumptions still reflect "'mainstream' cultural values and moral traditions [that] might … exclude culturally determined ethical standards of people from other backgrounds" (p. 5). Instead, the *Code of Ethics* provides a set of guidelines that emphasize rational ethical decision-making based on certain foundational values without acknowledging the source of these values.

This creates a challenge for making ethical assessments and decisions in an increasingly diverse practice environment. "In addition to managing competing professional values, social workers must also manage the influence of their own personal value systems while simultaneously considering their clients' values" (Doyle et al., 2009, p. 5). For these and other reasons, including self-diagnosed skill deficits, some social workers, particularly those with less practice experience, may be unable to identify the ethical issues that exist when making an assessment or be uncomfortable making ethical decisions under any circumstances.

Two decades ago, Freud and Krug (2002a) pointed out how the lack of clear guidelines in the NASW *Code*, as well as its inconsistencies and contradictions, may exacerbate the inherent challenges of ethical decision-making, particularly when parties to the decision have conflicting goals. They argued that the *Code* vacillates between absolute interdictions, circumstantial flexibility, and exhortations to broad standards of decency, and distinguishes between standards that are "enforceable" and those that are "aspirational" (p. 477). To a considerable extent, despite recent revisions, these criticisms remain valid.

Presaging contemporary proponents of an ethic of care, Freud and Krug (2002a) argued that social workers should supplement this rational model of ethical decision-making "with their emotions and intuition as shaped by our culture and our profession" (p. 474). They identified "three central elements" this perspective could add to ethical decision-making: "(1) increased attention to our moral intuitions and emotions; (2) institutionalized opportunities for dialogue about ethical concerns; and (3) open acknowledgement of, and respect for, moral diversity within a shared body of basic values" (p. 481). Yet, as Doyle and her colleagues pointed out, in today's multicultural society these recommendations fail to address the implications of how diverse cultural norms and values influence our emotions and intuitions, and those of our colleagues, clients, and constituents.

Analyzing the context in which ethical assessments and ethical decisions occur, therefore, is of particular importance. The complex combination of ethical, legal, and practice issues we regularly address also requires us to adapt to different situations by emphasizing different approaches based on the context. This need for flexibility underscores the importance of critical reflection and cultural awareness in our practice. A final challenge in this regard is the need for us to confront and try to overcome our frequent lack of power in many practice settings. This lack of power complicates our ability to resolve unethical situations and is often a source of considerable distress and job dissatisfaction.

Summary

This chapter discussed the challenges involved in making ethical assessments and the factors that complicate the process of ethical decision-making. These include the particular circumstances of the people with whom we work and the diverse values they bring to the practice relationship, external legal, political, and fiscal pressures, the culture of the organization in which our practice occurs, and the frequent ambiguity of desired outcomes. It also discussed the ways in which the NASW *Code of Ethics* is helpful and not helpful to these processes. The next chapter will address an issue of growing concern in our digital age: the application of the long-standing principle of confidentiality.

Reflection Exercise: Making an Ethical Assessment

1. Think about a recent assessment you conducted in your work in which there were ethical issues. What were the ethical issues involved?
2. How did you identify and resolve these issues?
3. How did your response to these issues affect your overall assessment of the situation?

Credits

Fig. 5.1 : Copyright © 2017 Depositphotos/Allexxandar.
Fig. 5.3: Copyright © 2015 Depositphotos/trueffelpix.

Confidentiality and the Duty to Warn

Introduction

If you had a serious emotional problem and finally overcame your initial resistance to seek help, would you feel comfortable speaking with a clinical social worker who shared intimate details of your life that you revealed in counseling sessions? Even in an era in which people share lots of personal information on social media, it is unlikely you would. The trust that is essential to a constructive relationship between a client and a helping professional would be threatened, perhaps permanently shattered. This trust is even more important when a person is in a position of financial, legal, physical, or emotional vulnerability. The importance of creating and sustaining this trust is the foundation for the ethical principle of confidentiality. The NASW *Code of Ethics* (2018) makes this clear in one of its first standards: "Social workers should protect the confidentiality of *all* information obtained in the course of professional service, except for *compelling professional reasons*" (1.07(c), emphasis added).

This chapter focuses on this core principle. It discusses the reasons why confidentiality is so important in our practice, the evolution of the concept in social work, how legal decisions have limited its application, the distinctions between privacy, confidentiality, and privileged communication, the importance of informed consent, and the meaning of a "duty to warn."

| ETHICAL DILEMMA 6.1 | The Limits of Confidentiality |

You are a social worker employed by the XYZ Behavioral Health Agency. The ABC Corporation has contracted with your agency to provide counselling services to its employees. You have been working with Richard A., a supervisor at the ABC Corporation, who has been seeing you because of marital difficulties and moderate depression. Richard is the sole wage earner in his family and will be eligible for his retirement pension in two years.

In the course of your counseling sessions, Richard confides that he has been abusing alcohol for the past year to help him cope with his marital difficulties. He tells you that he has often drunk alcohol on his lunch and coffee breaks but has taken precautions to hide his drinking from his supervisees and superiors. To date, his employers have not discovered his behavior. His personal performance evaluations and those of the unit for which he is responsible have continued to be above average.

The ABC Corporation has a "zero tolerance" policy regarding drugs and alcohol. In the past, it has dismissed employees who have violated this policy, whatever the quality of their work or the length of their tenure at the corporation. If Richard's employers discovered that he was drinking on the job, they could summarily dismiss him. (The corporation has an "at will" policy regarding employee termination.) If he loses his job, his household income and his pension

will be in jeopardy. Richard asks that you not reveal to anyone that he has been drinking.

Questions:
1. What would you do in this situation?
2. Which ethical duties are in actual or potential conflict in this situation?
3. What ethical principles would guide your decision?
4. What decision-making process would you use to choose a course of action?
5. To what extent would you generalize the basis of your decision to other, similar cases?

This case illustrates how the principle of confidentiality, so clear on the surface, can become complicated in practice. Reamer writes (2001): "Under what circumstances are social workers obligated to override a client's wishes and share confidential information?" (p. 490). Would you apply Reamer's deontological dictum—"Rules against basic harms to the necessary preconditions of action (e.g., life, health) take precedence over rules against harms such as lying or revealing confidential information"—to this situation? Would you make your decision based on the potential consequences to Richard, his family, and his employer of maintaining or revealing Richard's confidence? How would you decide which approach to use?

The Importance of Confidentiality in Social Work Practice

Confidentiality has long been a core ethical principle of social work and other major helping professions for several reasons (Wilson, 1980). First, it enables clients to exercise self-determination by enhancing their ability to decide what information to share or not share with a service provider. Second, it is critical to the establishment and preservation of trust between clients and workers—an essential component of a sustainable, effective helping relationship, especially in situations where clients are particularly vulnerable or reluctant to seek assistance (BrintzenhofeSzoc & Gilbert, 2017).

Third, it protects clients and all those within the client system against legal jeopardy, particularly those from vulnerable populations or in vulnerable circumstances. Fourth, it protects practitioners and their employers against potential legal risks they could incur if they disclose confidential information, particularly information that has harmful consequences for a client (Barsky, 2018). Finally, it preserves our integrity as social workers—for example, by preventing us from engaging in deceptive behavior (Koh & Reamer, 2020; Løvseth, 2017).

Alan Gewirth (2001) lists five core elements of confidentiality that social workers need to consider as guides to their practice. The first is the person who shares the confidence. What is this person's background and the specific context in which they share the confidence? To what extent does the person who shares the confidence increase their vulnerability by sharing this confidence? Would we heighten the person's vulnerability if we did not share the confidence?

The second element is the type of information the client shares in confidence. In what ways does sharing this information contribute constructively to addressing their needs or issues? Would breaking confidentiality risk depriving the client or others who depend on the client with essential goods or services? Would breaking confidentiality threaten the physical safety of the client or others? Would the failure to divulge confidentiality place others at risk of harm? All three of these potential outcomes are possible in Richard's situation. Gewirth asserts that the latter concern is a central issue of confidentiality.

The third element, where applicable, is the person or persons (third parties) about whom the client provides confidential information. How relevant is this information to the resolution of the client's initial (presenting) issues or those that subsequently emerge in the course of counseling? In macro practice situations, if the third party is an organization or the representative of an organization, what effects might the disclosure of confidential information have on the organization's reputation, fiscal situation, external relations, or effectiveness?

The fourth element is the recipient of the confidence. What is the nature of this person's relationship to the individual sharing the confidence? What obligations does the recipient have to third parties, including other individuals, organizations, or the community as a whole? Which of these obligations is ethical or moral, and which of them are legal? How does one balance the fulfillment of these obligations, particularly when they conflict or are mutually exclusive? In social work practice, these obligations might be considerably different if the recipient were the client's therapist, a colleague, or a member of the same advocacy coalition.

Finally, social workers must consider the reason for considering the information confidential. Is the confidence critical to the maintenance of the fiduciary (trust-based) relationship with the client? Would sharing the information jeopardize the future resolution of a person's problems or issues, or put the person at legal risk? In macro practice, would revealing the confidence undermine the execution of an organizing or advocacy strategy, or interfere with a critical collaborative interorganizational relationship where ethical dilemmas frequently arise?

FIGURE 6.1. Confidentiality Is Central to Social Work Practice

The Changing Meaning of Confidentiality

As these questions suggest, social workers cannot apply the core principle of confidentiality identically in all practice scenarios. In determining whether to maintain or reveal confidential information, or what information is confidential, practitioners must consider the background and context of a situation, including the ever-changing dynamic between worker and client, and between the worker-client dyad and the external environment, including relevant third parties.

Reamer (2018a) lists a dozen components that shape the context in which social workers apply the principle of confidentiality. The first is the client's right to privacy. In clinical practice, this right establishes the essential foundation for individuals, couples, and families to share personal information they would otherwise not reveal. In macro practice, it forms the basis for major policy decisions in such areas as reproductive rights (see *Roe v. Wade*) and the integrity of free elections (the secret ballot).

The second and third components are closely related. One is the importance of clients exercising informed consent before releasing confidential information to others. Clients need to be aware of under what circumstances a social worker may release this information. As discussed below, sometimes this is due to legal obligations, such as the protection of third parties. At other times, it is necessary in order for the client to receive essential services or to facilitate the coordination of the services provided to them. The requirement of informed consent is equally applicable in digital communication, online counseling (Mattison, 2018), and social research (Ferreira & Serpa, 2018). It is particularly important to word informed consent agreements clearly and explain them carefully when working or conducting research with young persons (McInroy, 2017), individuals with impairments (Prusaczyk et al., 2017), the elderly, and people who may have a limited understanding of English (Saldov & Kakai, 2016). Informed consent agreements not only protect the individuals who sign them, they also protect practitioners, researchers, and their employers from potential malpractice suits (Reamer, 2019b; Loue, 2018, pp. 57–79).

The principle of informed consent is the basis of well-established legislation, such as the 1996 Health Insurance Portability and Accountability Act (HIPAA), which guides practice in the health and behavioral health fields. (See further discussion of HIPAA below.) It also serves to protect the trust relationship at the core of social work practice, although its application to macro social work practice is somewhat more ambiguous and challenging (Tice et al., 2019; Folayan et al., 2018).

To understand the concept of informed consent, social workers also need to be aware of the difference in this regard between friendships and professional relationships. Although the betrayal of a confidence may jeopardize a friendship, the consequences are most likely to be emotional even if they are not long lasting. By contrast, the betrayal of a confidence in social work practice may affect a person's legal status, their ability to obtain vital benefits or services, and their ability to maintain a constructive working relationship with their social worker.

A related component of the principle of confidentiality involves the need to protect clients and third parties from harm. As discussed below, this not only concerns the duty to warn third parties (in situations of potential physical risk) but also the ethical responsibility to avoid inflicting emotional harm on others whenever possible. This component is particularly important to consider because of the high probability that unforeseen and often unintended consequences will occur if social workers share confidential information without permission or authorization.

The next cluster of components Reamer lists reflect external pressures on the disclosure of confidential information. They include the requirement or need to disclose this information either for legal reasons, to obtain a critical resource for clients (e.g., to third party payers), or to protect third parties from harm. Another pressure might involve disclosure to the media—for example, to support an advocacy campaign on behalf of a vulnerable community or subset of the population, or to correct false information spread among the public.

As discussed elsewhere in this book, the proliferation of electronic devices, such as cell phones, and the increasing impact of social media on our society and culture create other challenges regarding the meaning and maintenance of confidentiality. For example, if a client has already posted confidential information on a Facebook page or through a Twitter or Instagram account, to what extent does a social worker's obligation to maintain confidentiality still exist? Changes in clients' attitudes, particularly among young adults accustomed to posting intimate personal information online, complicate this issue further (Reamer, 2017).

Two decades ago, a study by Millstein (2000) revealed that respondents "are no longer confident that their clients expect their conversations with practitioners to be confidential" (p. 278). To a considerable extent, the widespread use of social media in recent years has further eroded this expectation. Two other components that Reamer (2015a) addresses—the protection of clients' records and their transfer and disposal—pose particular problems in this regard, especially in a digital age when hacking of internet transmissions and online trolling of parties have become increasingly common.

Then, there are practice situations that create unique challenges for practitioners. One common situation in clinical practice involves work with couples and families. For example, in marital counseling, under what circumstances should a social worker disclose information that one partner shared to the other, such as about an incidence of infidelity? A similar issue arises in family therapy, particularly when minor children reveal some information to the social worker in confidence about risky sexual activity or substance abuse that they wish to withhold from their parents. What principles should determine when to maintain or break these confidences?

Different challenges regarding confidentiality occur in practice with groups and communities. Effective clinical groups often require members to divulge confidential information—for example, about substance abuse or domestic violence (Carlson et al., 2019; Shenoy & Appel, 2017). Establishing and enforcing rules about the maintenance of confidential information outside the group are critical aspects of group work practice, despite their obvious difficulties. Another issue might arise if a domestic violence victim joins an online social media group for survivors to complement their therapeutic relationship, which may also be online. Revealing confidential information in the former venue could put them at risk of further abuse (Dolinsky & Helbig, 2015). Although the use of teletherapy can increase accessibility and help clients maintain anonymity and comfort, the social work literature has only begun to examine the ethical and security implications of these new practice horizons (Barsky, 2017; Boddy & Dominelli, 2017; Reamer, 2017; Harris & Birnbaum, 2015).

FIGURE 6.2. The Impact of Teletherapy on Confidentiality

In community practice and policy advocacy, confidentiality is equally important, although the circumstances in which this ethical issue arises are somewhat different (Tice et al., 2019). For example, in an advocacy campaign, the premature disclosure of strategic decisions can jeopardize social or political action efforts that depend on the element of surprise. In community change projects, building trust with local leaders often depends on maintaining confidentiality about the critical assessments of other community members or groups they may share (Izlar, 2019). Issues of confidentiality also arise in administrative or management settings, such as in the adjudication of a charge of sexual harassment or in delicate negotiations with a potential agency collaborator (De Graaf, 2019; Börjeson, 2018; Unguru, 2018).

Finally, social workers need to consider several other issues in assessing the role of confidentiality in a given situation. One is the importance of protecting the well-being and reputation of particularly vulnerable populations, such as prisoners; another is the protection of the reputations of the deceased. The former reflects a major ethical principle of social work enshrined in the NASW *Code of Ethics*–a commitment to social justice for marginalized populations. The latter illustrates our professional obligation to the people with whom we work, even after their death. For example, is it ever ethically permissible "to break a client's confidentiality to provide solace to a grieving [relative or friend]"? (Wallace et al., 2017, p. 327).

Another issue that is particularly relevant to faculty, including field instructors, and students is the protection of confidentiality during classroom instruction, supervisory relationships in internships, and professional development workshops. Millstein (2000) identified a number of risky situations in which social workers, social work educators, and students must exercise special care. These include presenting cases in classes, staff meetings, or at conferences; when collaborating with other professionals; and when working with insurers, particularly regarding at-risk populations, clients from different cultural backgrounds or age cohorts, or clients with unique problems. These conditions still apply today in an era where the empowerment of clients has become particularly important (Lunt, 2016). Although the NASW *Code of Ethics* (2018) is somewhat ambiguous, it clearly states that, in each of these examples, "social workers should disclose the least amount of confidential information necessary to achieve the desired purpose ... for which the disclosure is made" (1.07(c)).

This leads us to a discussion of the limits that exist in the application of the principle of confidentiality. The most prominent of these limitations involves the duty to warn.

The Limits of Confidentiality

Both the NASW *Code of Ethics*, which Woodcock (2011) rightly describes "as a highly and appropriately law-oriented document," (p. 22), and various legal restrictions (see below) place a number of limits on the application of the concept of confidentiality in practice. It is important to emphasize that these limits exist to protect third parties from abuse or from harming themselves or others (Barsky, 2018; Unguru, 2018). They also serve to protect or benefit a client by maintaining the client's autonomy (Barsky & Northern, 2017) and deterring latent paternalistic tendencies among practitioners or their employing organizations. (See Chapter 8 for further discussion of paternalism.)

In addition, limits on confidentiality exist because of legal requirements, such as the need to respond to a subpoena or court order. Under certain circumstances, we may override confidentiality to provide important information to colleagues who may be assisting us with a particular client, to benefit a family member, or to help a minor. Ironically, there are times when maintaining confidentiality could be harmful to the maintenance of a helping relationship, such as withholding vital client information from a colleague in another agency who is working with us to assist an individual with complicated multiple problems.

As stated earlier, a key element here is the importance of obtaining informed consent—that is, communicating with clients at the outset of the helping relationship those circumstances when you may be compelled to violate their confidentiality and for what reasons. As O'Neill (1989) stated in his discussion of the ethical issues involved in community practice,

> we work for the well-being of groups too broad to give informed consent to our interventions; we act in collaboration with others, but collaborative action does not free us from professional obligations; we reconnoiter, but reconnaissance does not provide us with perfect information; we may advise while others act, but we cannot walk away from the consequences of their actions. (p. 339)

Legal Restrictions on Confidentiality

During the past two decades, social workers have become increasingly concerned about "risk management" (Reamer, 2015b) and about the relationship between ethical behavior and legal liability. In this regard, a number of important pieces of legislation affect the application and limits of confidentiality and the right to privacy in social work practice. These include federal guidelines regarding the disclosure of alcohol and drug abuse records for employees, minors, and students; the 1974 Family Educational Rights and Privacy Act (FERPA); and the 1996 Health Insurance Portability and Accountability Act (HIPAA).

FERPA is a federal law that protects the privacy of students' educational records. Parents or eligible students may request that a school correct records that they believe are inaccurate or misleading. This legislation covers social workers employed in schools or who have contracts to provide services to schools or school districts. The application of FERPA requirements is particularly important in situations where a student may have received an inaccurate diagnosis of a learning disability or behavioral problem, where a student is without a permanent address due to homelessness, or where authorities suspect, without convincing evidence, that a minor student committed a criminal offense.

HIPAA is a federal law that established national standards to protect patients' information from disclosure to third parties without their consent or knowledge. It emerged roughly concurrently with the rise of managed care in the health care field and the growing role of insurance providers in determining the parameters of practice. A consequence of the latter is the increased risk of compromising clients' confidentiality when they or their providers submit claims to third-party payers (Groshong & Phillips, 2015).

A major goal of HIPAA, therefore, is to create a balance between protecting people's privacy and allowing the flow of vital information required to provide high quality health care. Social workers employed in health and behavioral health settings are legally obliged to comply with this legislation. This compliance includes, but is not limited to, informing clients of privacy practices during the first session and creating procedures to maintain the confidentiality of clients' records, especially when we store or communicate these records electronically. Unfortunately, many clinical social workers are still unaware of the risks involved if they fail to comply with these laws. In sum, both FERPA and HIPAA demonstrate "the inevitable tension between the client's right to privacy in professional relationships and society's need to obtain certain information" (Groshong & Phillips, 2015, p. 142).

Another ethical concern for practitioners arises due to significant differences in state laws about the right to "privileged" communication and other related issues, such as the mandated reporting of child abuse and elder abuse. All 50 states have passed legislation mandating the reporting of child abuse—to comply with the 1974 Child Abuse Prevention and Treatment Act, although many practitioners fail to report such incidences because of concerns about the competence of the child protection system (Faller, 2017). This raises the important issue of when a social worker's professional judgment can override a legal mandate.

States differ, however, as to whether reporting elder abuse is mandatory or voluntary; whether reporting requirements apply to all elders or only those who are incapacitated or incompetent; and whether practitioners have the authority to conduct investigations and intervene, particularly in religious communities (Band-Winterstein, 2018; Rosen et al., 2017). State laws also differ in their regulation of such practice innovations as video conferencing (Shore et al., 2018). These variations underscore the need for social workers to know the reporting laws in the jurisdictions in which we work.

The Duty to Warn

In addition to this important federal and state legislation, two landmark judicial decisions, 20 years apart, significantly revised how social workers apply the principle of confidentiality and how the government defines privileged communication and privacy: *Tarasoff vs. Board of Regents of the University of California* (1974, 1976) and *Jaffee vs. Redmond* (1996). Privileged communication refers to an interaction between two parties in which the law recognizes a private, protected relationship. In such circumstances, whatever the two parties communicate to each other, either in person or in writing, remains confidential, and the law cannot force their disclosure.

This privilege exists because of the value society places on the maintenance of privacy in confidential relationships. The most common illustration is attorney-client privilege, based on the right of individuals to protect themselves against self-incrimination, as stated in the Fifth Amendment of the U.S. Constitution. Other examples include communications between spouses, clergy and congregants, physicians and patients, and therapists and clients. For the most part, only state legislation or court decisions can establish which communications have legally privileged status.

The concept of privacy, which is the basis of the principle of confidentiality, is somewhat different. It refers to a professional's promise (based upon professional ethics) to reveal nothing about a client without their consent. As discussed above, it is a core concept because of the fiduciary relationship that exists between social workers and clients, especially those who may be in physically, emotionally, or legally vulnerable circumstances. Under certain conditions, however, social workers may breach confidentiality "when disclosure is necessary to prevent *serious foreseeable and imminent harm to a client or other identifiable person*" (National Association of Social Workers, 2018, 1.07(c), emphasis added). The two important legal cases referred to above have had a significant impact on social workers' application of this fundamental principle.

The first case, *Tarasoff vs. Board of Regents of the University of California* (1974, 1976), involved a student, Prosenjit Poddar, who had been previously involved in a relationship with another student, Tatiana Tarasoff, at the University of California, Berkeley. Poddar informed a psychologist employed by the university counseling center that he intended to kill an unnamed woman, later identified as Ms. Tarasoff. Although the psychologist did not directly warn Ms. Tarasoff or her family, the psychologist notified the police who subsequently interviewed Poddar. They warned him to stay away from Tarasoff but took no other action. Soon thereafter, Poddar murdered Tarasoff; her family sued the campus police and the university health service for negligence.

In its decision, the California court imposed an *affirmative duty* on mental health professionals to warn a potential victim of the potential danger posed by a violent patient (*Tarasoff v. Regents of the University of California*, 1976). In a second decision (*Tarasoff II*), "the court changed the duty to warn into the duty to protect intended victims from the violent acts of the therapist's patient" (Kopels & Kagle, 1993, p. 102). This expanded the initial ruling and created an additional affirmative duty for therapists.

A subsequent ruling went still further. It held that mental health professionals, including social workers engaged in clinical practice, had a *duty to warn* appropriate persons when they became aware that a client *might* present a risk of harm to a *specific* person or persons (*Thompson v. County of Alameda*, 1980). In 1985, the state of California passed legislation that enshrined this judgment into law. These decisions constituted a radical change to existing laws as "under the common law, a person is under no duty to control the conduct of another nor to warn those endangered by that conduct" (Kopels & Kagle, 1993, p. 102). Today, most states have laws that either require or permit mental health professionals, including social workers, to disclose information about clients who have the potential to become violent or pose an imminent threat to other persons.

The second case, *Jaffee v. Redmond* (1996), focused specifically on the issue of clinical social worker-client privilege. In this case, an Illinois police officer, Mary Lu Redmond, responding to an apparent assault, shot and killed Ricky Allen, the alleged assailant. As the representative of Allen's estate, Jaffee sued Redmond for using excessive force. During discovery prior to the trial, Jaffee discovered that Redmond had sought counseling from a licensed clinical social worker and attempted to obtain the social worker's notes to assist in the cross-examination of Redmond at the trial. Redmond claimed the psychotherapist-patient privilege protected these notes.

The trial judge rejected this argument, and the jury awarded Allen's estate over a half million dollars in damages. On appeal, the Seventh Circuit Court of Appeals vacated the trial court's decision and affirmed the privilege that Redmond claimed. Jaffee appealed to the Supreme Court, which, in a 7–2 decision, upheld the ruling of the appeals court that the privilege Redmond claimed exists, was absolute, and applies to social workers engaged in clinical practice (*Jaffee v. Redmond*, 1996).

These cases raised a number of important issues. The *Tarasoff* cases underscored the importance of deciding what constitutes a "serious risk of harm" and determining *to whom* social workers owe a duty to warn. For example, does the duty relate solely to the identified potential victim or does it apply to third parties who may also be at risk? (Legislators have determined that practitioners must notify the police if the identified victim is a public figure.) In addition, how can practitioners discern if a risk is "foreseeable or "imminent"?

In this regard, researchers have unfortunately found that "clinicians are likely ... to be wrong in their predictions more than half the time" (Kopels & Kagle, 1993, p. 113). Given this high level of inaccurate forecasting, how do we identify a "foreseeable and identifiable victim"? What constitutes a "reasonable effort to protect" a potential victim? In addition, would the *Tarasoff* precedent establish a duty to protect individuals who express suicidal ideation (Lloyd-Hazlett et al., 2018)? Does the category of potential victims include the clients?

In response to these legal and ethical ambiguities, within 15 years after *Tarasoff*, 17 states "had enacted statutes to limit the liability of helping professionals for the violent acts of their patients" (Kopels & Kagle, 1993, p. 109). Most of these laws also provided therapists with immunity if they revealed clients' confidences in fulfilling their duty to warn. The presence of clarifying legislation, however, did not eliminate the need for practitioners to make special efforts to protect themselves against liability in the areas of assessment, documentation, and intervention.

The *Jaffee* case, while expanding the concept of privileged communication to social workers, also left certain issues undecided (Sun & Wasser, 2017). These include the extent of its application to non-federal cases (Alexander, 1997) and definitional questions such as what constitutes privileged communication (i.e., what is or is not included). Other issues relates to the circumstances when other priorities can overturn this privilege and who decides when those circumstances exist (Hills, 2020).

Studies conducted since these decisions revealed that many social workers remain confused about their implications for the maintenance of confidentiality. To clarify some of the ambiguities that, in combination, these decisions created, some states have passed laws that attempt to specify under what circumstances the duty to warn applies. By the late 1990s, all 50 states and the District of Columbia gave clinical social workers legal protection from the release of confidential information about clients, but in some states this protection is not absolute (Barsky, 2018; BrintzenhofeSzoc & Gilbert, 2017; Landi, 2017). The state of Maryland, for example, now includes the following in its legal code:

> In general, a cause of action or disciplinary action may not arise against any mental health provider or administrator for failing to predict, warn of, or take precautions to provide protection from a patient's violent behavior unless the mental health provider or administrator knew of the patient's propensity for violence and the patient indicated ... by speech, conduct, or writing, of the patient's intention to inflict imminent physical injury upon a specified victim or group of victims. ... The duty described under this section is deemed to have been discharged if the mental health provider makes reasonable and timely efforts to:
>
> 1. Seek civil commitment of the patient;
> 2. Formulate a diagnostic impression and establish and undertake a documented treatment plan calculated to eliminate the possibility that the patient will carry out the threat; or

3. Inform the appropriate law enforcement agency, and, if feasible, the specified victim or victims of:
   - The nature of the threat,
   - The identity of the patient making the threat, and
   - The identity of the specified victim or victims.

No cause of action or disciplinary action may arise under any patient confidentiality act against a mental health provider or administrator for confidences disclosed or not disclosed in good faith to third parties in an effort to discharge a duty arising under this section according to the provisions [described above]. (Maryland Family Law Code Ann., 2013, 5-609)

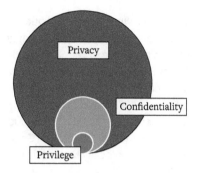

FIGURE 6.3. The Relationship Between Privacy, Confidentiality, and Privileged Communication

Thus, as the graphic right illustrates and the following cases reveal, what appears at first glance to be a straightforward ethical principle is actually considerably more complicated.

ETHICAL DILEMMA 6.2

What Constitutes *Foreseeable* Harm?

You are a school social worker at Abraham Lincoln High School. You have been seeing John D., a 15-year-old youth, for over a year. The school's principal referred John to you because of his behavioral difficulties and poor academic performance.

In the course of your work with him, you learn that John likes to play violent video games. Last week, he confided in you that he has recently fantasized about acting out some of the scenes in those games at school. He also tells you that his father is an NRA member who legally owns a semiautomatic rifle and pistol, which he stores in a closet in the basement.

During the past two decades, parents, school authorities, students, and some politicians have been increasingly concerned about violence in school settings, particularly since the events in Aurora, Colorado, Newtown, Connecticut, and Parkland, Florida. In addition to establishing a "zero-tolerance" policy regarding fighting and the possession of weapons of any sort

(including pocket knives, corkscrews, etc.), school and law enforcement officials have asked all staff to notify the principal when they suspect a student may be likely to instigate a violent incident. At her monthly meeting with staff, the principal, Ms. S., asks if anyone has any information about possible future violence in the school.

Questions:
1. Would you reveal your conversation with John to Ms. S.?
2. What is your ethical responsibility to John? To the other students and their families? To the school and its staff?
3. To what extent do the affirmative duties established by the *Tarasoff* case apply to this situation?
4. What ethical principles would guide your decision?

Whom Does Confidentiality Protect?
(This is a true story. The names are
unchanged because the San Francisco Examiner reported
this story. Cf. Matier & Ross, August 4, 1991.)

In 1991, Milledge Anderson, who had skipped out on his Pennsylvania parole after serving 12 years for aggravated rape, appeared in the office of the San Francisco Department of Social Services. There was a warrant for his arrest. On April 25, 1991, when Pennsylvania authorities alerted the San Francisco Police Department that Anderson might be in the city, they added that he might try to obtain welfare benefits (General Assistance, or GA, the state or locally funded program for single, childless adults).

A few days later, Inspector Tom Parisi and his partner in the Fugitive Detail Program went to the general assistance welfare office on Harrison Street. They told officials that Anderson was wanted and asked if he had any upcoming appointments. Officials at the office would not provide them with any information unless they presented a subpoena.

The warning by the Pennsylvania police was true. Anderson had already applied for $315/month in general assistance and had a second appointment scheduled in May 1991. Meanwhile, Lavinia Meadows, a caseworker assigned to the case, received a tip from a social work colleague that Anderson might be wanted. She ran a routine background check and discovered that he was, indeed, a fugitive.

Meadows called the parole office in Philadelphia, who told her that Anderson was "extremely dangerous" and that he had already assaulted a social worker in Pennsylvania. The parole officer, Ken Paul, also told Meadows she should call the police right away because "if you didn't get him he was going to do something. ... He's not normal. He just goes off."

Meadows told her supervisor, Russ Miller, who called his superior, Dorothy Enisman, for advice. Enisman told Miller to alert the department's security guards for possible trouble but explicitly instructed Miller and Meadows not to call the police. Miller followed her orders, but Meadows did not.

When Anderson showed up for his appointment on May 28, Meadows stalled him, saying some papers were missing. While Anderson waited, she called the police. They arrived, arrested Anderson, and later shipped him back to the Pennsylvania State Penitentiary in Graterford, Pennsylvania.

For her role in assisting in the arrest of a wanted felon, the department brought Meadows up on charges that could result in a five-day suspension. Her offense: insubordination and violating Anderson's right to confidentiality. Meadows fought the suspension with the support of her union, SEIU Local 535. At a departmental hearing on July 15, her attorney, Stewart Weinberg, argued that Meadows did not give police any information from Anderson's confidential file and, therefore, she broke no law or ethical duty. "He didn't say [to her] 'I'm a fugitive wanted in Pennsylvania.' She found that out as a result of a background check, and then became aware that she had a very dangerous person on her hands," Weinberg said. He also argued that Anderson's mere presence in California was a crime and that Meadows was legally obligated to call the police.

Inspector Gary Delagnes, Vice President of the Police Officers Association, agreed: "I would certainly think that the woman did the right thing. If it is the stance of the Department of Social Services that the confidentiality of a convicted rapist supersedes the best interest of the public, then I think they've got a pretty fouled-up philosophy over there."

The Department of Social Services saw the situation differently. Department officials stated that state law (Welfare Code 10850.3) permits social workers to release "specified" information on applicants "only upon a written request" from police. The Department's General Manager, Julia Lopez, said that the verbal request of Inspector Parisi was not sufficient and that the officers should have known that. Lopez further stated that surrendering information without a written request is a misdemeanor.

Meadows' attorney countered that the law only applies to how police obtain information and has nothing to do with Meadows. He asked, "Suppose Anderson started beating up on someone in front of Meadows. Could she not report that crime to the police? The woman is on the side of the angels. I can't believe how hypocritical they [DSS officials] are being in this case."

Lopez disagreed. "The fact of the matter," she said, "is that we both [the police and DSS] have responsibilities and obligations. … We want to help but we have to do it in a way that meets legal requirements." Regardless, Lopez asserted, Meadows was insubordinate for disobeying a direct order by calling the police. While she sympathized with Meadows, Lopez said, "She made a personal choice, and when you make a personal choice, you sometimes have to pay for the consequences of your actions."

Questions:

1. Did Ms. Meadows violate Mr. Anderson's right to confidentiality?
2. If she did, was her violation of his confidentiality justified? If so, for what reasons?
3. To what extent was the nature of his prior offense (aggravated rape) and his depiction by the Pennsylvania parole officer a justification for Meadows' action? If he was, for example, a convicted forger, would her action be equally justified?
4. Would the situation be different if Anderson came to Meadows for counselling instead of public benefits?
5. To whom did Meadows owe a primary duty in this case?
6. The department charged Meadows with insubordination. What circumstances, if any, justify the refusal to obey a direct order from a superior?

ETHICAL DILEMMA 6.4   **Harm to Whom?**

Jane D. is a social worker in a local behavioral health clinic. She has been working with a young man, Dylan R., referred to her agency by a high school counselor because of his tendency to start fights and engage in aggressive behavior with classmates, particularly but not exclusively with students of color. During the course of one of their sessions, Dylan confides that he has been researching white supremacist websites, and expresses fear and anger about the demographic changes sweeping the country and his community. At a subsequent session, he tells Jane that he has purchased several weapons and ammunition (which is legal in his state) and is considering taking unspecified action to call attention to the demographic "threat" facing the United States.

Jane has developed a trusting relationship with Dylan, as demonstrated by his comfort in taking her into his confidence. She believes that this trust will enable her to identify the sources of his beliefs and aggressive behavior and, ultimately, bring them under control. Consequently, she does not report his statements to school authorities or the police.

Several weeks later, Dylan enters a local African American church and murders nine of its congregants. In their investigation of the incident, the police learn that Dylan was Jane's client. They question her, and she tells them some, but not all, of what transpired in their sessions, withholding other information on the grounds of confidentiality.

An uproar ensues in the media and the professional community. In cooperation with Jane's agency, the local chapter of NASW begins an inquiry into her handling of the situation. Her agency puts her on leave pending the outcome. Some prominent individuals in the community call for Jane's arrest because she failed to notify the authorities and, they argue, prevent the tragedy.

In consultation with her attorney, Jane argues that the principle of confidentiality justified her silence about Dylan's comments in their sessions. She further asserts that the *Tarasoff* decision does not apply in this case because Dylan's threats were neither specific nor imminent.

Questions:

1. Which argument do you find more compelling? For what reasons?
2. How did you arrive at your decision?
3. What ethical principles can you derive from your decision?
4. What are the implications if you generalized these principles to other similar circumstances?

Summary

This chapter discussed the importance of confidentiality, an ethical principle that lies at the heart of all social work practice. Although the NASW *Code of Ethics* stresses the centrality of confidentiality, both the *Code* and policy developments at the national and state level have established limits on its application. Like all professional codes of conduct, the *Code* cannot address all practice situations that might arise, particularly in today's culturally fluid and rapidly changing environment. This underscores the importance of social workers being familiar with the relevant laws in their state and adopting a critical perspective in order to maintain the profession's core values.

Yet, there are other issues regarding confidentiality that neither the *Code* nor public policy addresses. For example, does the current definition of confidentiality maintain the status quo in social work—that is, does it serve as a means to affirm professional dominance by placing primary responsibility for determining when it applies on the social worker or on legal requirements established by external authorities to whom social workers must report? As Gewirth (2001) suggests, should social workers deprive clients of the protection of confidentiality if they do not behave in a way the social worker defines as morally acceptable? What duty of confidentiality does a social worker possess if an online client, such as an adolescent, lies about their age or identity to obtain counselling?

In addition, does a "one-size-fits-all" model of confidentiality work effectively in today's dynamic practice environment? Does the emphasis on client confidentiality reinforce "the status quo of an individual-based construction of social problems?" (Millstein, 2000, p. 271). This raises the overarching question of whether we need to redefine the concept of confidentiality beyond its origins in the physician-patient model. A related issue is whether clients' expectations regarding confidentiality have changed due to a combination of new social conditions, technological developments, and cultural shifts, as illustrated by the widespread use of e-mail, texting, video conferencing, and social media. Although the NASW *Code* has recognized the increasing importance of these issues, it still provides limited guidance in this largely unexplored territory of practice (Kimball & Kim, 2013).

Other complex issues yet to be resolved include how we should respond if our colleagues, co-workers, or clients violate the principle of confidentiality. In addition, what are the practice implications if workers and clients do not define confidentiality in the same way, particularly if they come from different cultural backgrounds? Finally, given the increasingly litigious nature of our society, what is the appropriate balance between professional judgment and legal mandates in resolving issues of confidentiality? For example, do clients implicitly waive the right to confidentiality if they file a malpractice suit against a social worker, based on the legal right of defendants to confront their accuser (Reamer, 2019b; Wheeler & Bertram, 2019; Loue, 2017; Landi, 2017)?

These questions underscore the need for additional training regarding the application of confidentiality in an environment increasingly characterized by collaborative relations, managed care, and accountability requirements created by legislation and court rulings. The next chapter discusses another core ethical principle of social work practice: self-determination. Similar to this chapter's discussion of confidentiality, it explores the issue of whether this principle is absolute or also subject to certain limitations.

Reflection Exercise: Determining The Limits of Confidentiality

In each of the following practice situations, the issue of confidentiality creates a dilemma for the practitioner. Think about what you would do if *you* were the practitioner. Would you breach confidentiality? On what principles would you base your decision? How would you apply these principles and justify the consequences of your decision? To what extent would you generalize these principles to other circumstances? How are these situations similar and different?

1. You work for a nonprofit organization that assists formerly incarcerated individuals with reentry issues into the community. You have been seeing a client, Joe J., who was released from prison 6 months ago after serving a 5-year term for armed robbery. Joe is married and has three minor children. You have developed a good rapport with him. In your last session, he confides in you that he is increasingly frustrated about his inability to find legitimate employment and has decided to buy a gun from someone he knows in his neighborhood and rob a local liquor or convenience store. He said it was the only way he knew how to support his family.

2. You have been seeing a couple, Mr. and Ms. S., in marriage counseling for a year. Shortly after your last session, Mr. S. asked if he could speak with you privately. In your conversation, he confides in you that he recently tested positive for the HIV virus. He says he is getting treatment and asks you not to tell his wife.

3. You are a social worker in a local high school. One of the seniors, Carol K., comes to your office one afternoon and immediately starts crying. After a few minutes, she tells you that she didn't get accepted by any of the top colleges to which she applied and that this morning her boyfriend broke up with her just a week before the prom. She tells you that she is so upset she is considering suicide and confides that in the past she has cut herself on several occasions when she was particularly depressed.

4. You are a family therapist working weekly with the Hendersons and their teenage son, Roger (16), and daughter, Melissa (14). Mr. Henderson is the local minister of an evangelical church. Roger calls you at the office before your next scheduled session with the family and tells you that he is gay. He doesn't want his parents to know because he is convinced that if he came out they would throw him out of the house and he would be homeless. During your sessions with the Hendersons, they have often said Roger is "acting strangely lately" and that his behavior is a source of family conflict.

Credits

Fig. 6.1: Copyright © 2013 Depositphotos/Colour.
Fig. 6.2: Copyright © 2020 Depositphotos/SiberianArt.

The Limits of Self-Determination

Introduction

The concept of self-determination has long been central to the practice of social work. Support for peoples' self-determination is a key component of affirming their individuality and humanity, one of the stated ethical imperatives of the profession. It also acknowledges their expertise regarding the forces that shape their lives, history, and current experience. The NASW *Code of Ethics* (2018) is forthright in this regard: "Social workers respect and promote the right of clients to self-determination and assist clients in their efforts to identify and clarify their goals" (1.02).

Yet, the issue of how extensive the concept of self-determination is remains unresolved. The NASW *Code* acknowledges this issue in the same standard: "Social workers may limit clients' right to self-determination when, *in the social worker's professional judgment*, clients' action or potential actions pose a *serious, foreseeable, and imminent risk to themselves or others*" (1.02, emphasis added).

This chapter discusses the roots and evolution of the concept and its application to social work practice. It explores the limits of individual and community self-determination and the circumstances that might require the application of these limits. It concludes with an examination of several specific challenges to demonstrate the importance of critical reflection on this core concept and the issues it raises in our practice.

ETHICAL DILEMMA 7.1   **Self-Determination vs. Client's Well-Being**

You are a social worker in the behavioral health unit of a community hospital. You have been seeing Scott F. for counseling to address his long history of alcohol abuse. At a staff meeting, you learn from colleagues that Scott is not attending the required group sessions in the hospital's program regularly or taking the medications prescribed to treat his diagnosis of Type II diabetes. When you confront Scott about these issues, he informs you that he resumed drinking last month to cope with the recent suicide of his wife Zelda and his subsequent inability to overcome chronic writer's block. You remind him of his obligation to comply with the rules of the hospital's program to which he voluntarily consented and express concern about the effects on his health if he continues to drink and does not take prescribed medications. Scott responds that he has lost the will to live and does not really care what happens to him. You are thinking about whether you should intervene in some way and what would be an ethical course of action.

Questions:
1. To what extent does Scott's right to self-determination override your obligation to work in his best interest? Should you continue to see him and allow him to participate in the hospital's alcohol abuse program?
2. How does his refusal to comply with his medication or treatment regimen affect Scott's right to self-determination?
3. Scott is taking a place in the hospital's treatment program that another person might use more effectively. How does this factor into your decision?
4. Who should ultimately make the decision about Scott's participation in the treatment program?
5. If you had to make the decision, what criteria would you use?

This case illustrates the difficulty of taking an absolutist position on the principle of self-determination and the different conclusions one might reach from applying a deontological or consequentialist approach to an analysis of such situations. If you opted for a deontological approach, which values would you assign the higher priority: Scott's right to exercise his self-determination or your obligation to protect his well-being and that of other individuals who might benefit from the hospital's program? On what principles would you construct this hierarchy? If, on the other hand, you adopted a consequentialist approach, what consequences would you weigh in formulating a "utilitarian calculus?" How would you measure their relative importance?

Self-Determination as a Right

The concept of self-determination emerged in the West during the 18th-century Enlightenment as a corollary of the recognition that all people had the ability to reason. Philosophers of the period argued that as every person possessed the capacity for rational thought, societal institutions were required to respect their individual autonomy, what we now refer to as their human agency, and their right to make decisions about the course of their lives. In one sense, the roots of this concept go back even farther to the emergence of secular humanism during the Renaissance and the transformation in the West from a God-centered to an anthrocentric view of the cosmos.

The Western emphases on individual rights, individual responsibility, and personal autonomy, embodied in the language of the U.S. Declaration of Independence and the Bill of Rights in the U.S. Constitution, complement this underlying belief in the universal capacity to reason. Despite the nation's recurrent failure to apply these rights fully to racial and sexual minorities and women they remain—at least in theory—fundamental principles of American society. Autonomy, in the sense these rights implied, means the ability to be one's own master, to do only what we consent to do, and to accept no externally imposed obligations except those freely undertaken. In the 21st century, both radical leftists and libertarians support certain aspects of these "inalienable rights." Some link the concept to the fulfillment of our humanity ("positive freedom"); others tie it closely to the individual's right to be left alone from government interference under nearly all circumstances ("negative freedom").

As discussed in Chapters 1 and 4, this emphasis on individual autonomy has often created significant obstacles to the creation of social policies in response to historic injustices or address collective needs, such as protection from a pandemic or the consequences of climate change. It also creates challenges in those practice situations in which individuals, for a variety of reasons, are incapable of exercising autonomy. (See Chapter 8 for a discussion of the concept of paternalism.) This is a particularly vexing issue in an increasingly interdependent and hyperconnected world in which global trade networks are an essential feature of modern life, computer-generated algorithms control the flow of information we receive on our cell phones, and public health and ecological crises do not recognize national boundaries. It ultimately raises an uncomfortable question: Is self-determination in today's environment an illusion, a legacy of the past that has shrinking contemporary relevance and may even be an obstacle to a just and sustainable society?

Self-Determination and the Social Work Profession

The concept of self-determination in social work practice emerged from these central components of the Western philosophical and political tradition and the gradual, grudging acceptance in the West of the revolutionary principle that *all people* have the capacity to reason. As recent events demonstrate, however, opposition to universal equality persists, often subtly rationalized by implying that members of marginalized groups have less intellectual or moral capacity or culturally acquired deficits. A persistent dilemma for social workers is how to base our practice on the belief that all people are capable of making rational judgments about their life situation and life course within a political and cultural milieu that frequently undermines this assumption (Horne, 2018).

Citing Biestek (1951), Levy (1983) argued "the right of self-determination [is] a self-directed responsibility" that enables individuals to define and achieve their life goals as they define them (p. 907). Although on occasion this right is constrained "by the rights of others, the capacity of clients to make choices, legal limitations, [and] societal norms" (Levy, 1983, p. 907), it provides the basis for legal and civil rights and privileges and for the primacy of other core social work values, such as confidentiality (Levy, 1973). Towle (1957) disagreed with this interpretation to some extent. She maintained that self-determination is more than a right; it is a fundamental human need that is the basis for human dignity and worth.

Unlike these social work scholars and philosophers of the 18th-century Enlightenment and their 19th-century successors who regarded self-determination as a "natural right," some contemporary social workers have argued that self-determination or absolute autonomy does not exist in the state of nature and is, in fact, merely a social construct, or even an illusion. They assert this is because the unrestricted application of self-determination inevitably creates a conflict between a person's self-determination and their welfare, and, on occasion, a conflict between their individual interest and that of society as a whole. To resolve this conflict, proponents of this perspective assert that social workers generally agree that "the idea of humans as rational social beings who must adjust within a community [in order to belong] ... places relative limits [on the principle] of self-determination" (Freedberg, 1989, p. 33).

These issues, debated for over a half century within the profession, are equally relevant for social work practice today. Yet, despite their differences, all of these scholars agreed that only compelling, substantiated reasons justify a preference for societal interests above those of the individual. The NASW *Code of Ethics*, on the other hand, if taken literally, leaves the resolution of this conflict entirely to the professional's judgment. The ambiguity this creates overlooks the possibility that a social worker's worldview and implicit biases may affect their judgment in such situations. In addition, in our increasingly diverse society, the forms in which people express their self-determination vary widely, as reflected by their personal and political priorities and the symbolic cultural artifacts that express them, including their religious faith. In response, some social work scholars maintain that we need to rethink our conception of self-determination to take people's religious beliefs into account (Wolfer et al., 2018).

Efforts in the profession to resolve different interpretations of self-determination led to the prominent place of the concept in mainstream social work practice that emerged nearly a century ago (Richmond, 1922). Radical social workers, such as Bertha Capen Reynolds, however, soon pointed out the "basic contradiction" in this synthesis between "a truly democratic relationship between social worker and client, based on the values of self-determination and individualism," and the role social workers played as "agents of a society in which the client is disenfranchised" (Freedberg, 1989, p. 34). Similar to recent critics of the application of the concept of "empowerment" (McLaughlin, 2016), Reynolds argued that self-determination was not a "right" social workers "gave" to their clients but one that they inherently possessed. Like today's proponents of worker-client mutuality to overcome the disempowering consequences of the external environment, Reynolds (1951) suggested that the worker-client relationship be viewed as an egalitarian alliance, not a hierarchy in which workers had the most control.

Support for clients' self-determination, therefore, not only acknowledges their unique qualities, it affirms their expertise about their past and present circumstances and their agency in making critical decisions about their lives. Consequently, although it is important to inform our practice with scientific evidence, the knowledge generated by research is insufficient if we do not concurrently recognize the multiple strengths and capacities our clients and constituents possess. Dybicz (2012) makes a strong argument for this recognition: "To solely apply one's scientific expertise to a helping situation would be a soulless form of practice. This is why social work so strongly embraces values such as ... self-determination" (p. 275). This perspective establishes self-determination as a main component in the development of helping strategies rather than placing it in a secondary, reactive role. According to Dybicz, it helps create a form of practice based on "democracy, reciprocity, collaboration, and equality" (p. 279)—and practice relationships founded on mutuality and dialogue.

Yet, social workers still struggle with the issue of whether and when we should limit the application of self-determination (Horne, 2018; Salazar et al., 2018; Timms, 2018). In part, this issue remains unresolved because "the unequal distribution of problems and resources for both the social worker and client ... severely limits capacities for client self-determination" (Freedberg, 1989, p. 34). In many practice situations, but particularly those involving the increasing proportion of clients who are involuntary, state-sponsored policies administered by social service agencies often reflect more interest in compelling clients to conform to preconceived

FIGURE 7.1. Self-Determination Is a Basic Human Right and a Core Principle of Social Work Practice

behavioral norms than in their right to exercise personal autonomy (Soss et al., 2011). The implication for ethical practice in this environment is that social workers cannot enhance their clients' self-determination solely on an individual by individual basis. Although we are often compelled by our ethical obligations and practical necessity to follow agency rules and policies, if we share the profession's commitment to social justice we must also address the economic and political realities that constrain people's opportunities, choices, resources, power, and access to vital services and information (Witt et al., 2019).

Recognizing these realities, many social workers have historically regarded clients' self-determination as a universal right, one that is particularly significant given the power imbalance between those giving and receiving help. From this perspective, self-determination is more than a desired condition; it is a precondition of practice, especially in our work with people whose vulnerability compels them to seek help. As stated in earlier chapters, this vulnerability creates a fiduciary responsibility for social workers that is the basis of all competent and ethical practice. Levy (1983, 1976a) argued that because of this responsibility there is no rationale to deny clients any rights that they would have if they had not sought, or been required to seek, a service or benefit.

Despite his benevolent intentions, Levy's assertion gives rise to a few concerns. First, probably because of the date of publication, his writings fail to acknowledge the implications of the dramatic increase in the number of involuntary clients, a disproportionate percentage of whom are from one or more marginalized populations. As stated earlier, a related complication regarding the application of self-determination is the frequently unequal distribution of resources and power that exists between workers and clients and between clients and powerful institutions and policymakers, upon whom social service agencies rely for financial and political support and legitimacy (Chandler et al., 2017; Karvinen-Niinikoski et al., 2017). In combination, the involuntary or quasi-involuntary status of many clients and the conflict between their rights to care and well-being and society's need to control service costs and impose certain behavioral standards contributes another element of complexity to the dilemma (Mossialos & Le Grand, 2019; Brown, 2018; Rooney & Mirick, 2018).

This phenomenon raises the difficult question whether involuntary clients have the same right to self-determination as those who initiate the helping process on their own (Smith, 2020; Chovanec, 2017; Barsky, 2014). For example, would a homeless person sacrifice their right to self-determination if admitted to a shelter? Does a recipient of a public benefit, such as TANF, Medicaid, or SNAP (food stamps), surrender their ability to determine their life choices? Should an individual convicted for a drug-related offense acquiesce to the deprivation of their right to express their views on the best course of treatment?

In such cases, in addition to considering whether the client's right to self-determination is sacrosanct, we must consider a number of other issues. First, we must assess the extent of the client's competence and comprehension of their situation (Wehmeyer & Shogren, 2016). At the same time, we must keep in mind the importance of preserving the client's trust, especially if it is likely they will need further care in the future (Gill et al., 2019; Francoeur et al., 2016).

Second, Levy's argument focuses solely on the application of self-determination to individual clients. He scarcely addresses the issue of how we should apply the concept in family practice when the goals of family members conflict. Nor does he contend with the challenge of interpreting the meaning of self-determination in community practice, where different groups within the community may have contradictory goals and the meaning of self-determination in such circumstances is ambiguous. (See Ethical Dilemma 7.3 below.)

In social work ethics, therefore, self-determination is both an end and a means—a precondition to the fulfillment of people's personal goals, and the key to the maintenance of their personal dignity and worth. The profession's emphasis on self-determination assumes people's capability to make decisions if given sufficient opportunity and necessary information. This assumption raises additional ethical issues that Chapter 8 will cover on the topic of paternalism.

Another consideration is how to protect social workers and their employing organizations against possible legal, financial, and reputational risks, such as a malpractice suit by clients or their families, fiscal sanctions imposed by the government, loss of accreditation, or bad publicity in the media if they violate a client's right to self-determination. An overarching issue in all such situations is the importance of preserving our professional integrity and, indirectly, that of the profession as a whole. Conversely, particularly with clients who may be impaired, we must assess if the harmful consequences that are likely to occur if we do not interfere with a person's exercise of their self-determination are irreversible. In addition, we must consider if the only way to preserve a wider range of freedom for our clients or constituents is by restricting it temporarily (Christie, 2018; Metzger, 2017; Raithby & Willis, 2017; Sexton, 2012).

Self-determination is also an important concept in social work advocacy, whether on behalf of an individual client (case advocacy) or constituents affected similarly by a social, economic, or political issue (class advocacy). To practice ethically, advocates must consult with those with whom they are working to define the issues to be addressed and what constitutes their "best interests" in selecting the goals, strategies, and tactics of an advocacy campaign. They must also respect people's differences in the assessment of complex political situations based on their diverse historical experiences and worldviews. Ethical advocacy also requires obtaining clients' or constituents' informed consent before employing specific strategies and tactics, and ensuring that the potential risks involved are clearly explained (Sutton & Carlson, 2019; Witt et al., 2019; Ezell, 2013).

Self-Determination in the NASW *Code of Ethics*

The ethical standards in the NASW *Code of Ethics* (2018) regarding self-determination stress both its critical importance and its limitations in practice. For example, in Standard 1.01, the *Code* states: "Social workers' primary responsibility is to promote the well-being of clients." As clients' autonomy is a major component of their well-being, this clearly implies that preserving a client's self-determination is in their best interest. It is also consistent with a strengths and assets-based approach to practice and the assumption that clients are the best source of knowledge about their needs and desires (Lunt et al., 2020; Logan, 2018; Arbeiter & Toros, 2017; Bernard & Thomas, 2016). Yet, the *Code* then modifies this seemingly clear position: "However, social workers' responsibility to the larger society or specific legal obligations may on limited occasion supersede the loyalty owed clients, and clients should be so advised."

The ambiguity of this statement could create considerable confusion among students and practitioners, particularly those with limited experience dealing with ethical conflicts. It gives rise to several critical questions: (1) What is the nature of our responsibility to the larger society when such conflicts emerge, and under what circumstances does it supersede our fiduciary responsibility to our clients and constituents? (2) To which specific legal obligations does the *Code* refer? (3) When should these legal obligations take priority over our commitment to clients? (4) From a practice-oriented perspective, what might be the effects on the worker-client relationship if we inform clients at the outset that loyalties to third parties or external institutions might take priority over our loyalty to them?

The next section of the *Code* does little to clarify these ambiguities. It begins by restating our commitment to clients: "Social workers respect and promote the right of clients to self-determination and assist clients in their efforts to identify and clarify their goals." It then goes on to qualify this position: "Social workers may limit clients' right to self-determination when, *in the social workers' professional judgment*, clients' actions or *potential actions* pose a serious, *foreseeable*, and *imminent* risk to themselves or others" (emphasis added).

As discussed in Chapter 6, the intention behind the qualifying provisions in the second sentence is a specific response to situations like those adjudicated in the *Tarasoff* case. Yet, if generalized beyond this specific case, there are several potential problems and at least one contradiction within these qualifiers. First, the critical role given to social workers' professional judgment appears to maintain the traditional worker-client hierarchy even as the *Code* seeks to emphasize the primacy of clients' right to declare their interests and ability to exercise agency (i.e., control) over the fulfillment of their interests and goals. It would also seem to contradict the profession's historical emphasis on empowerment (Simon, 1994).

The language in the *Code* also implies that social workers have the ability to predict the future, determine how clients might act under unforeseen and unknowable circumstances, assess the effects of those actions, and forecast the potential consequences of their actions on unanticipated third parties. Given the complexity of the issues many clients experience and the diverse environments in which most people live, the assumption that social workers, particularly those with limited experience, possess this predictive capacity is, at a minimum, subject to debate. In addition, the challenges involved in understanding how people from different cultures might respond to similar situations further undermines the presumption that social workers "know best" how clients might act and with what results.

The Limits of Self-Determination

As the NASW *Code of Ethics* states, but social workers often do not openly acknowledge, self-determination like confidentiality is, therefore, not an absolute right. The *Code* clearly establishes the "ethical responsibility to balance a client's right to self-determination with the protection of vulnerable populations from harm" (Donovan & Regehr, 2010, p. 178; see also Cheak-Zamora et al., 2019; Turan et al., 2019; Powers et al., 2018; McCallion & Ferretti, 2017). Most of the social work literature, however, continues to create considerable confusion about this core issue by framing it in this manner: we may violate a client's right to self-determination only if a clear justification exists. Determining whether such a justification exists, therefore, is at the heart of many ethical dilemmas. Yet, who has the authority or competence to assess whether a client has the capacity to make individual decisions? This assessment becomes even more complicated when the client is a group or community, particularly if it is from a different background than the social worker, and when the application of self-determination comes in conflict with existing laws or political realities.

The increasing diversity of cultural and political views in our society makes it even more difficult to apply the principle of self-determination in an undifferentiated manner. For example, under what circumstances do laws or policies take priority over the principle of self-determination? What if we determine that a law—such as one that compels social workers to deny services to undocumented immigrants or that forces women to seek reproductive health care far from their communities—is unjust and that obedience to that law not only impedes a person's self-determination, it violates our ethical imperative to pursue social justice? A related issue is what role community or societal norms, customs, and morals should play, particularly in an environment of increasing demographic and cultural complexity.

On the mezzo level of practice, a number of difficult issues also exist. What weight should we give to the rules, resource distribution patterns, and restrictions created by our agency of employment in order to comply with social policies developed outside of its control? At what point does allegiance to our organization become uncritical acquiescence to external authority, especially if it restricts clients' ability to self-determine? How can we assess the impact on third parties of clients' actions based on their exercise of self-determination? Which consequences, foreseen or unintended, are of sufficient importance to justify restrictions on people's self-determination? Consequences for whom? A key factor in resolving such issues is that we must match any limitations we place on people's self-determination by the importance of other interests. The following cases illustrate some of these salient issues and their different manifestations in practice with individuals and communities.

ETHICAL DILEMMA 7.2   "We Want a Family"

You are a social worker in a nonprofit, multiservice community center in a major metropolitan area. One of your responsibilities is facilitation of a group of adolescents, ages 15–19, who have received a diagnosis of moderate developmental disability or Down's syndrome. The group focuses on life skills development, preparation for employment, and socialization into adulthood.

Two group members, Brian S. and Mary J., met shortly after the center created the program. During the past several years they have become romantically involved, much to the dismay of their parents. Last evening, Brian's and Mary's parents came to your office visibly upset. Over the previous weekend, Brian and Mary announced that as soon as they reached their 18th birthdays (which would occur within a few months) they wanted to marry and eventually have a family. Their parents asked for your assistance in dissuading them from getting married. Neither family is wealthy; both families are concerned that Brian and Mary will not be able to support themselves, let alone raise or financially support children. Brian's parents are also worried because, according to medical tests, there is a 50% chance that his children could inherit the genetic condition that caused his disability.

Questions:
1. To what extent should Brian and Mary's condition affect their right to self-determination?
2. What rights do their parents or society have in this situation?
3. What ethical approach and ethical principles would you use to decide your course of action?
4. What are the implications of your decision for your view of the limits of the principle of self-determination?

ETHICAL DILEMMA 7.3   What are the Limits of a Community's Self-Determination?

Mount Pleasant is a well-established, multiracial neighborhood within a large city, whose racial and class composition has changed significantly during the past decade. While Mount Pleasant used to be predominantly White and middle income, it is now considerably more racially, ethnically, and economically diverse. Two-thirds of the residents are people of color, one-third of them are recent immigrants, largely from Central America, Southeast Asia, and the Middle East. Most of the residents are working class or lower-middle class. Unemployment is higher than the regional average, but the influx of immigrants has bolstered the commercial life of the community.

You are a social worker employed in the neighborhood by a nonprofit community center established over a century ago as a settlement house. You moved into the neighborhood several years ago and have developed a large number of close personal and professional relationships in the course of your work. You attend community meetings and events regularly and have become a trusted informal advisor to community leaders.

After a long national search, Amazon has selected Mount Pleasant as a finalist for one of its new headquarters. In return for tax incentives provided by the city and state, Amazon pledged to create thousands of jobs and to make a concerted effort to enhance the physical condition of the neighborhood. Two community groups in Mount Pleasant, however, have taken different positions on the possibility of Amazon moving into the neighborhood.

One group, the Residents Alliance of Mount Pleasant to Unite People (RAMP-UP) opposes Amazon's proposal for two compelling reasons. First, they argue that the government should use the billions in tax incentives offered to Amazon to improve local schools, health care facilities, housing, and public transportation. Second, based on the experience of other similar communities across the United States, Amazon's location in Mount Pleasant will lead to gentrification and rising housing costs that will price many residents out of the neighborhood.

The other group, Community United for a Resurgent Economy (CURE), supports Amazon's proposal. They argue that the promised jobs will produce an economic revival in Mount Pleasant that will generate sufficient revenue to support vital improvements in services and infrastructure. They also cite Amazon's pledge to take steps to enhance the community's appearance and dismiss the fears about gentrification RAMP-UP expresses.

The demographics of the two groups further complicate efforts to resolve the disagreement. RAMP-UP's membership primarily consists of long-time Mount Pleasant residents, largely African American and elderly Whites. By contrast, most of CURE's membership consists of new immigrants and younger White professionals.

Because the leaders of both groups respect and trust you, they have asked you to facilitate a meeting at which the two groups will attempt to resolve their differences. In addition to the practice challenges involved in this situation, there are also ethical issues that the questions below address.

Questions:

1. How does the principle of self-determination apply to this situation?
2. Does the self-determination of one group take priority over the other? If so, for what reasons? How would you determine if such a priority exists?
3. What ethical principles—not practical steps—would you apply to resolve this dilemma?
4. What model of ethical decision-making would you use? For what reasons?
5. In what ways is this dilemma similar to or different from the dilemmas described in Ethical Dilemmas 7.1 and 7.2?

Self-Determination in Practice

Social workers confront a number of issues in resolving the dilemmas outlined above. To summarize, one major concern—discussed in more detail in Chapter 8—is the conflict between personal or group autonomy and the application of paternalistic measures taken in people's best interest. Another issue is how to balance clients' and constituents' interests and rights with the obligations we incur in our professional role (to our organizations, society, the profession, and ourselves) to use limited resources efficiently and responsibly and in compliance with existing laws and agency policies. A third issue is how to respond ethically to the unequal distribution of resources, power, and status that exists between workers and clients or constituents, and occasionally among clients and constituents, that affects virtually all aspects of social work practice.

As mentioned above, a fourth issue is the increasingly involuntary nature of many clients, the growing desperation that drives many people to seek services, and the seemingly intractable problems that many marginalized communities confront. Recognition of these realities raises several uncomfortable issues with ethical overtones. In many fields of social work, are we engaged in a form of social control, even if our intentions are benign? Does our practice primarily focus today on achieving externally imposed goals rather than the goals of our clients and constituents? How do we reconcile the actual and potential conflicts that exist between the satisfaction of clients' rights and needs and the fulfillment of societal obligations, particularly in complex, often ambiguous situations such as those described above?

Specific Challenges

Our work in certain fields of social work practice or with particular populations poses unique challenges to the application of the principle of self-determination as the following examples illustrate.

Work with Children and Youth

Children and adolescents are a segment of the population that presents especially difficult challenges regarding the application of self-determination (Powers et al., 2018; Arbeiter & Toros, 2017). Preserving the self-determination of young people is particularly important because it demonstrates that we care about them as human beings. It helps to counteract the presence in their lives of a seemingly intractable power imbalance between even the best-intentioned social workers and the most sophisticated and socially aware youthful clients or constituents. Workers who embrace the importance of self-determination regard "the distinction between children and adults as oppressive" in assessing people's competence and their consequent right to express their autonomy (Barnes, 2012, p. 1288). They assert that the establishment of a caring relationship that safeguards youths' right to self-determination might also help reduce the inequality that exists in most of these worker-client interactions, avoid instances of benign paternalism, and produce more desirable outcomes.

Nevertheless, applying the concept of self-determination in our practice with adolescents is not without certain vexing problems. These exist, in part, because of conflicting views of the status of young persons in our society. On the one hand, we allow 18 year olds to vote, enlist in the military, marry without parental permission, drive automobiles, work for wages, and obtain reproductive health care, including abortions. We applaud their growing involvement in political and social action, and have even contemplated reducing the voting age to 16. On the other hand, we do not allow minors to purchase cigarettes or alcohol, or have consensual sexual relations if they are under the age of 18. In addition, many (but not all) states treat minors who have committed crimes differently from adults. We justify the latter by relying on research that found adolescents' brains (and their power to reason) do not fully mature until their mid-20s.

You may well ask at this point: What do these contradictions have to do with the place of self-determination in social work practice with youth? If we believe that adolescents have the capacity to make reasoned judgments in some circumstances (e.g., vote, drive a car, get married) but not others (e.g., drink alcohol in moderation, decide whether to engage in non-coerced sexual activity, or commit a crime with premeditation), what guidelines should we follow in assessing the limits of self-determination in our work with this population?

Think about: Under what circumstances would you apply an expansive definition of self-determination in your work with youth? Under what circumstances would apply a more restrictive definition?

Practice with Involuntary Clients

Many clients are compelled by a court order or agency decision to receive designated services. They are part of a growing proportion of our clients who do not fit the earlier profile of individuals who choose to enter a service relationship (Rooney & Mirick, 2018; Chovanec, 2017). In response to this development, Barsky raises a difficult issue, one that has become particularly relevant as a consequence of recent policy changes: "Given the primacy of self-determination, how ... can [social workers] ethically justify working with clients who are mandated to social work services?" (Barsky, 2014, p. 1).

The NASW *Code* does not provide much guidance in such matters. It has only one standard in regard to self-determination that references involuntary clients: "In instances when clients are receiving services involuntarily, social workers should provide information about the nature and extent of services and about the extent of clients' right to refuse service" (1.03(d)). Yet, the client's right to refuse service in these circumstances is determined by external authorities, as are the consequences if they do so. This dynamic reinforces the powerlessness of these clients and makes it difficult for them to resist the various forms of coercion to which they may be subjected (Smith, 2020). These coercive measures range from compulsory work requirements to participation in mandatory religious programs in order to receive even inadequate benefits or services (Shannon, 2017; Edin & Shaefer, 2016; Soss et al., 2011).

Think about: Under what circumstances would you support a client's right to exercise self-determination by refusing to participate in a mandated service activity? How would you justify this decision?

Self-Determination and Self-Harm

As Ethical Dilemma 7.1 reflects, a perplexing issue arises when we consider whether a client's self-determination extends so far as to give them the right to engage in self-harming behavior without interference. It also raises the question of who decides what acts are self-harming or unjustified under the circumstances. Reamer (2001) argued two decades ago that "most social workers ... believe that, generally speaking, competent adult clients have a right to assume risk, and even to fail, so long as they do not pose a serious threat to others" (p. 494). He makes an exception, however, for self-harming behavior such as suicide.

Levy (1983), however, posed a provocative question regarding this issue 2 decades earlier: If suicide "is an option a client might be privileged to exercise if not engaged in a social worker-client relationship ... should it not be available to a person who is so engaged?" (p. 917). If you were the social worker in Ethical Dilemma 7.1, which argument—Reamer's or Levy's—would you find most persuasive?

A related issue is whether clients who engage in socially irresponsible behavior or extreme risk-taking forfeit their right to self-determination (Auyong et al., 2018; Osho et al., 2016). This issue requires us to consider the following questions: What constitutes "irresponsible behavior" or unecessary risk? What standards should we apply? Who makes this determination? The history of the United States and the social work profession in making such determinations is fraught with racial, gender, and class prejudice as numerous scholars have pointed out (Abramovitz, 2018; Brown, 2017; Dominelli, 2017; Reisch, 2013a; Iglehart & Becerra, 2011; Park & Kemp, 2006). The effects of the Covid-19 pandemic have added new ethical dimensions to this issue, particularly in practice with older adults or individuals facing severe economic plight (Bailey & West, 2020; Bhatia, 2020; Gunnell et al., 2020; Wand et al., 2020).

The Impact of Technology

The expanded use of technology in the delivery of social services creates new challenges for social workers who wish to support clients' right to self-determination. These include inequalities in clients' access to the technology, problems with anonymity, and increased concerns about risk management (Reamer, 2013a, 2015b). In addition, the ability of clients to disguise or alter their identity while communicating online raises the issue of whether clients incur a reciprocal obligation (i.e., to be honest) in order for social workers to respect their self-determination, particularly in settings such as online group counseling (Harris & Birnbaum, 2015).

A specific example that creates a new challenge to clients' self-determination is the increased use of digital medication regimens. Dotolo, Petros, and Berridge (2018) argue that "absent strict legal orders, people have the right to manage their medications without oversight or covert pressures" (p. 371). The use of digital medication, however, "may subvert [their] autonomy ... to make choices about medication regimens and inhibit privacy about mindful nonadherence" (p. 371). They assert that it is one of several practice innovations in the behavioral health field that risks "a graduate erosion of self-determination and personal freedom by erring on the side of risk aversion and paternalism ... [and] compounds the injustices that ... people with mental illnesses [experience]" (pp. 371–372). Think about how you would apply these arguments to the situation presented in Ethical Dilemma 7.1. (See Chapter 8 for further discussion of similar issues.)

Discharge Planning and End-of-Life Care

Two other prominent areas of social work practice in which self-determination is an increasingly important concern are discharge planning, such as for home health care, and end-of-life care, particularly in hospice settings (Lloyd & Sullivan, 2018; Nedjat-Haiem et al., 2017; Wallace et al., 2017). Although social workers have been aware of these problems for some time, both the rapid aging of the U.S. population and recent policy developments, such as the ACA, have made their resolution more urgent. Despite this awareness, social workers are often constrained in such situations from discussing sensitive matters with clients because of state laws prohibiting euthanasia and assisted suicide. End-of-life decisions become further complicated by the desire to balance patients' dying wishes and need for pain management, families' right to self-determination, the absence of patient competence, relatives' failure to grasp the gravity of a patient's condition, and the frequent lack of advanced directives. Ethical dilemmas also arise as to whether to accede to a client or family's wishes regarding the location and timing of death (Wallace et al., 2017). The tragic consequences of the Covid-19 pandemic have added new ethical dimensions to this issue as many victims of the virus are unable to communicate their dying wishes or see their family at the end of their lives (Ekberg et al., 2020; Meyfroidt et al., 2020; Schrag, Hershman et al., 2020).

Summary

This chapter has explored the principle of self-determination in social work practice with particular attention to what, if any, limits exist on its application. It also discussed a question of increasingly contemporary relevance: Is the concept of self-determination universally applicable or should we apply different ethical norms in our practice with culturally diverse populations?

If the former, what exceptions, if any, are permissible or desirable? Another issue is whether the principle of self-determination, framed historically largely in terms of our obligation to individuals, applies equally to groups, families, or communities. A related issue is how to apply this principle when differences exist within a family, group, or community with which we are working. Finally, in assessing how to balance a person or group's right to self-determination with the interests of third parties and society, to what extent are we engaged in a "zero sum game"? That is, must we decide to favor one party or the other, or is some compromise ethical position possible?

The next chapter discusses an issue that is closely related to social work's core principle of self-determination: the nature of paternalism in social work practice and policy.

Reflection Exercise: What Does Self-Determination Mean to You?

1. Why do you think self-determination is a critical component of social work practice?
2. What, if any limits, would you place on the application of the concept? What principles would influence your decision in this regard?
3. To what extent would you apply the concept to members of a group or community? In what ways does the concept have a different meaning and different implications at the macro level?

Credit

Fig. 7.1: Copyright © 2014 Depositphotos/vaeenma.

Paternalism and Social Work Practice

Introduction

In his classic formulation of the hierarchy of human needs, Abraham Maslow (1943) included the desire for freedom and independence among "esteem needs." He considered these needs higher on the list of human motivation than basic physiological needs and the need for safety and security. In our practice, the application of Maslow's hierarchy often reveals an inherent conflict between helping people and maintaining their autonomy. This conflict lies at the heart of ethical issues concerning the role of paternalism in social work practice.

The goals of human dignity and universal respect are central values of the social work profession. These are also the major goals of social justice movements throughout history. Past examples in the United States include the antislavery movement, the campaign for women's suffrage, and organizing efforts on behalf of workers' rights. During the 20th and 21st centuries, movements on behalf of civil rights, marriage equality, gender equity, and environmental justice have expressed similar themes.

Although social workers have often allied with these movements, our daily practice may reflect a conflict between benevolent paternalistic impulses and respect for cultural differences. This conflict appears in interpersonal practice, in collaborative work with culturally diverse teams, and in the development and implementation of social policies (Lu et al., 2018; Hondius, 2017). It creates a barrier to the fulfillment of our ethical commitment to serve all people without discrimination and to practice with cultural humility and competence.

This chapter covers this controversial topic and discusses its implications for policy and practice. It begins with a brief history of the evolution of the concept of paternalism and its role in the development of the social work profession. It summarizes the different critiques of paternalism that have emerged since the mid-19th century and their implications for contemporary practice. It discusses the various justifications and rationales for paternalistic behavior in both clinical and macro social work practice, and it illustrates the complexity of this issue through the presentation of several ethical dilemmas.

"I Want to Die"
(Based on a true story)

On September 3, 1983, Elizabeth Bouvia, a 26-year-old BSW graduate of San Diego State University, admitted herself into the psychiatric ward of Riverside General Hospital. Confined to a wheelchair, Ms. Bouvia suffered from a severe case of cerebral palsy and degenerative arthritis that caused her great pain and left her able to control only the muscles of her head and right hand. In addition, Bouvia was alienated from her family and husband, and had been entertaining thoughts of suicide. She requested hospital authorities to allow her to starve to death painlessly. When they refused and ordered her to be force-fed, Bouvia contacted the American Civil Liberties Union, which assigned her a lawyer.

Through her attorney, Bouvia argued that she had the constitutional right, based on the right to privacy and the ethical concept of self-determination, to end a life of intolerable dependence on others for even her feeding and sanitary care. Bouvia did not expressly demand to stop eating; rather, she asked that the hospital allow her to exercise her right to self-determination by rejecting the intrusive care of others, a necessity whenever she wanted to eat. She also wanted the hospital to give her pain medication for her arthritis and did not want the hospital to discharge her from public care, as she had no money to pay her own doctors and nurses. (The film *Whose Life Is It Anyway?* presents a fictionalized depiction of some aspects of this issue.)

Attorneys for Riverside County, Bouvia's estranged husband, and two Southern California groups representing persons with disabilities opposed her request for an injunction to prevent Riverside General Hospital from discharging her, force-feeding her, or denying her pain-killing drugs. The attorneys representing her husband and the hospital argued that Bouvia suffered from temporary depression due to marital problems, failure to bear a child, difficulties obtaining financial support, and inability to find employment after earning her social work degree. Attorneys for the groups representing persons with disabilities argued that her voluntary starvation would profoundly discourage other persons struggling with their disabilities and lead some of them to commit suicide.

During the trial, California Superior Court Judge John H. Hews denied Bouvia's request to allow the hospital to help her starve to death painlessly. The judge ruled that her decision to starve to death was made "after careful and mature deliberation" and motivated by the "nature and extent of her physical disabilities" rather than because of any recent misfortunes. However, he ruled that although she had the right to commit suicide, which is legal in California, she could not ask society in the person of the hospital staff to assist her because she was not a terminally ill patient. Both sides in the case agreed that she had a life expectancy of at least 15 to 20 more years (Mathews, 1983).

Following this ruling, Bouvia indicated that she would drink liquid protein and maintain her current weight (which was about 95 pounds) until her appeals were exhausted. In response, Judge Hews said that if she eventually tries to fast at the hospital, there would be "no other reasonable option" than for the medical staff to force-feed her.

After the court's decision, a bitter dispute broke out among physicians regarding the case. Bouvia tried to resist the force-feeding by biting through the feeding tube. Four attendants would then hold her down while other staff inserted the tubing into her nose and pumped liquids into her stomach. Some physicians called this response battery and torture, while others claimed that the hospital was right to err on the side of continued life.

Bouvia appealed the lower court ruling and lost. Now, in addition to the force-feeding, she was hooked up to a morphine drip to ease the pain of her arthritis. Eventually, she appealed again and this time the court ruled in her favor that the force-feeding constituted battery.

After the final court case, Bouvia decided that she would live. In 1998, she appeared on the television program *60 Minutes*, on which she said that she was still in pain and had felt great pressure to continue living. She expressed the hope that she would soon die of natural causes. As of this writing, however, she is still alive.

Questions:

1. Was Ms. Bouvia's choice of death a rational choice and a proper expression of her autonomy? If so, under what circumstances is such a choice rational? How is it different from the choices Scott F. made in Ethical Dilemma 7.1?

2. If you think Ms. Bouvia was in full control of her faculties, does she have the right to refuse treatment that, if refused, would result in their death? If so, under what circumstances does this right exist?

3. Who has the authority to determine if a person is competent to make such a decision? What should be the roles of professionals or the person's family in this decision? By what means should a person's competency be determined?

4. If you were a social worker on the hospital staff assigned to Ms. Bouvia, what ethical dilemmas would this case create for you? How would you respond to them?

5. As her social worker, to what extent would you feel ethically obligated to respect her right to self-determination? Would the obligation to protect her from self-harm take precedence?

6. To what extent does the impact of Ms. Bouvia's decision on third parties matter? Who are the third parties in this case and what rights, if any, do they possess? What ethical obligations do social workers have to them?

7. In what ways does the situation change when the use of societal resources or the law is involved?

Now, think about how you would answer the questions in this somewhat similar case.

ETHICAL DILEMMA 8.2

Her Parents Wanted Her to Live
(Based upon another true story)

From 1990–2005, Terri Schiavo was in an irreversible, persistent vegetative state as a result of a cardiac arrest that deprived her brain of oxygen and left her comatose. For 2 years, doctors tried a variety of therapeutic treatments in vain attempts to revive her. In 1998, Schiavo's husband and legal guardian, Michael, petitioned the Sixth Circuit Court of Florida to remove her feeding tube pursuant to Florida law. He argued that she would not have wanted prolonged artificial life support without the prospect of recovery. Schiavo's parents disputed her husband's assertions and challenged Schiavo's medical diagnosis, arguing in favor of continuing artificial nutrition and hydration.

In April 2001, the court ruled that Schiavo would not have wished to continue life-prolonging measures and ordered the removal of her feeding tube; a few days later, however, staff in the hospital reinserted it. For years, Schiavo's parents continued to challenge the original ruling in court and the case attracted enormous attention in the national media and state and federal political circles up to the level of President George W. Bush. The president even returned to Washington to sign legislation ordering the case transferred to the federal court system, where it went through several appeals up to the Supreme Court, which on four occasions refused to grant certiorari.

In February 2005, nearly 4 years after the initial ruling, an appeals court again ordered the removal of the feeding tube. In March, hospital staff removed the feeding tube and Ms. Schiavo died two weeks later. All told, the Schiavo case involved 14 appeals and numerous legal filings in Florida; five suits in federal court; extensive media coverage; and the political intervention of the Florida state legislature, Florida Governor Jeb Bush, the U.S. Congress, and President George W. Bush. It became a cause célèbre in the pro-life movement and the right-to-die movement, and among disability rights groups.

Questions:
1. In what ways is this case similar to or different from the case of Elizabeth Bouvia? From that of Scott F.?

2. If you were a social worker in the hospital or hospice where Ms. Schiavo was a patient, what ethical principles would influence your perspective?

3. How did the concepts of self-determination and paternalism come into conflict in this situation?

4. What rights do third parties have in these situations? To what extent should they be respected?

FIGURE 8.1. What Is Paternalism?

The Evolution of Paternalism

Richard Sennett (1981) discusses three stages in the evolution of the concept of paternalism. The first stage occurred in patriarchal societies in which all people were blood relatives, and males were the linchpins of families and the source of all formal authority. Most ancient civilizations reflected these qualities, and this social structure persists in many countries today (Daly, 1978).

The second stage in the evolution of paternalism involved the formation of what Sennett termed a "patrimonial society." This was a more complex form of social organization in which property, political power, and social status passed between generations through male relatives, but people did not conceive of their relationships exclusively in terms of family. This type of society existed in the feudal period and the modern industrial era throughout the world and continues to exist in many nations and regions.

According to Sennett, the final, contemporary stage of social development in this regard is paternalism. He argues it is not necessary for patrimony to exist in paternalistic societies. However, males continue to dominate nearly all major institutions, ostensibly for protective purposes. In the United States, the gender imbalance in the military, police, firefighting, politics, and corporate boardrooms reflects this phenomenon. In effect, this is male domination without the requirement of family bonds, a formal social contract, or set of official rules, although frequently rationalized on religious or dubious quasi-scientific grounds. As men played and continue to play a major role in creating most contemporary social welfare institutions and establishing their formal policies and informal cultural norms, we could argue that U.S. social work today represents a paternalistic system in many ways, even if the majority of practitioners are female.

As discussed briefly in Chapter 7, Western views of ethics emphasize two principles that increasingly conflict in practice—autonomy and beneficence (Cohen, 2019; White, 2017). The desire to maintain autonomy influences clients' choice of services and their ability to make maximal use of the services and benefits agencies provide (Juhila et al., 2020). Clients who engage in self-destructive behavior are particularly susceptible to this tendency (Strickland & Stoops, 2018; Braye et al., 2017).

Beneficence, on the other hand, refers to our efforts to act in the best interests of others (Martela & Riekki, 2018). According to Engelhardt (1986), there is a danger in interpreting the latter based on Western standards (e.g., the "Golden Rule") "because of the divergent understandings of what should count as actually doing the good" (p. 75). He suggested an alternative interpretation of beneficence—"do unto others *their* good," that may be more suitable in our diverse society and interdependent world (p. 76, emphasis added). This alternative interpretation may be especially useful in our work with marginalized individuals (LaSala & Goldblatt

Hyatt, 2019) and in the midst of health care crises such as the Covid-19 pandemic that have disproportionate effects on already vulnerable populations (Muskens et al., 2019; Ngene et al., 2019; Guichon et al., 2016). The persistent conflict between autonomy and beneficence underscores the importance of ongoing examination of the ethical components of our practice and research (Caras & Sandue, 2018; Koepsell, 2017, pp. 61–71; Barsky, 2010) and our overall commitment to social justice (Clement, 2018).

Critiques of Paternalism

In his classic treatise, *On Liberty* (1859), John Stuart Mill first articulated a philosophical critique of paternalism. His view is compatible with that of contemporary libertarians and goes beyond the principles expressed in the NASW *Code of Ethics*. Mill wrote

> the only purpose for which power can be rightfully exercised over any member of a civilized community [*note the qualification*], against his [*sic*] will, is to prevent harm to others. His own good, either physical or moral, is not a sufficient warrant. ... Over himself, over his own body and mind, the individual is sovereign. (pp. 21–22)

Over a century later, the philosopher Gerald Dworkin (1972) expanded on Mill's definition. He characterized paternalism as "interference with a person's liberty of action justified by reasons referring exclusively to the welfare, good, happiness, needs, interests, or values of the person being coerced" (pp. 64–65). In some ways, the NASW *Code of Ethics* reflects similar sentiments. There are, however, a few subtle but significant differences between these philosophical perspectives and the NASW *Code*. The latter is somewhat more ambiguous in its interpretation of what constitutes an individual's good or self-interest. As social work is an applied profession, this ambiguity creates ethical challenges for practitioners in all fields, as reflected subtly but significantly in many social policies and all forms of social work practice.

> **FOR REFLECTION: HAVE YOU EVER BEHAVED IN A PATERNALISTIC MANNER?**
> 1. Think about an incident in your personal life when someone acted toward you in a paternalistic manner. What do you think were that person's motives? How did it make you feel? How did you respond? What happened?
> 2. Now, think about an incident in your practice when you had to decide what constitutes a person's "good" or best interest. How did you do this? What factors did you take into account? What were the results of your decision?

Applying Dworkin to the social work field, Reamer (2001) defined paternalism "as interference with a client's right to self-determination for his or her own good" (p. 494). In the areas of child welfare or family practice, for example, paternalism may involve the disclosure of confidential information against the client's wishes in order to save the client's life, protect the well-being of others, or facilitate the acquisition of necessary services. In such matters, "the conflict is between the client's self-determination and the client's welfare" (Levy, 1983, p. 905). It is often also a matter of preserving a person's dignity and worth. Levy points out "there is a tendency among social workers to justify intrusions on client self-determination on the basis of limitations of capacity or rationality ... and ... what social workers regard as contravening or superseding values or interests—those of community and society, ... or even of agency" (p. 915).

In this light, we can view critiques of paternalistic behavior as support for what Berlin (1969) referred to as "negative liberty": the "right not to be coerced or interfered with and the absence of restraint" (Reamer, 1983b, p. 255). In addition, paternalistic behavior sometimes involves withholding information from clients or constituents or misleading them about available courses of action. According to Reamer, "the concept of paternalism is narrower than the concept of self-determination," because the former "does not entail any consideration of third parties" (p. 256). [*The author disagrees with this assertion because decisions made in a paternalistic manner often have implications for a person's family—in the case of individual clients—or for future beneficiaries of a social policy or program that may affect their ability to exercise their self-determination.*]

Sources of Paternalism in Social Work Practice

The tendency toward paternalism in social work practice arises from several diverse sources. At its core, the chronic tension between the profession's social justice mission and status aspirations sometimes produces a gap between our rhetoric and daily practice. We have yet to resolve the conflict between promoting the interests of those with whom we work and acquiring from elites the sanction and financial resources we need to achieve this worthy goal.

One consequence of this lack of resolution is the focus of the NASW *Code* on practice with individuals, a form of social work that is more consistent with the values of the dominant culture, particularly in today's neoliberal climate. This has often led to a relatively narrow interpretation of the concept of paternalism. The frequent conflict between our professional values and those of the powerful host institutions in which many social workers work exacerbates this tension. Particularly in health care and legal settings, whose professional cultures are more hierarchical, the possibility of paternalistic behavior increases. In addition, in both organizational and policy practice, the pressure to compromise often undermines our efforts to protect the self-determination of our clients and constituents. Lastly, the preference for "objective," scientific knowledge as a guide for practice frequently undermines a more egalitarian view of clients' ability to "name their world" (Freire, 1971).

Paternalism in Social Policy

During the half century between the end of the Civil War and U.S. entry into World War I, rapid industrialization and urbanization and the arrival of millions of immigrants from Europe, Asia, and Latin America combined to produce a dramatic increase in poverty, particularly among women and children, and spurred the emergence of the earliest modern social policies. Championed by both conservative and progressive social work pioneers, these policies often reflected a "maternalist" perspective—based on the belief that the fate of the nation depended on fostering the well-being of its mothers and future mothers and their children (Weil, 2020; Chappell, 2018; Mathieu, 2016; Yingling, 2016). In addition to the irony of promoting the interests of women at a time when they still could not vote, these policies bore many other characteristics of the paternalism Mill had opposed. They also embodied the growing belief that the unprecedented consequences of rapid social change required the state to assume the role of "parent" (Gaylin et al., 1978).

For example, the policies developed during the Progressive Era (~1890–1918) initially focused on pensions for Civil War widows. They soon expanded to include widows of the thousands of workers killed annually by industrial accidents. Shortly before World War I, states began passing Mother's Pension legislation (Reese et al., 2018) to provide financial assistance to widows or abandoned women. By the 1930s, nearly all states had adopted similar legislation (Reese et al., 2017). These policies were the antecedents of Title IV of the 1935 Social Security Act and subsequent welfare reforms in the United States. Their underlying philosophy continues to shape similar policies in Latin America, Australia, and East Asia (De la Cruz, 2020; Ramm, 2020).

Other policies during this period reflected a similar orientation. They included laws that abolished child labor, created the juvenile court, built kindergartens and urban playgrounds, expanded and made mandatory public education, and enacted a wide range of public health and sanitary measures. Through the establishment of the Children's Bureau, the government conducted research on the needs of children and their caretakers for the first time (Prochner & Nawrotzki, 2019). The capstone policy of this era was the Sheppard-Towner Act, that provided federal funding for maternal and child health programs, primarily in rural areas, during the 1920s. Over the 20th century, as the United States expanded its patchwork state-funded "social safety net," these trends continued, particularly in the child welfare field (McGuire, 2018).

As a result, numerous examples of paternalism in contemporary social policies persist. One is the distribution of vouchers (for food, rent, or school tuition) in lieu of cash benefits. A subset of this form of paternalism is the prohibition on the use of the Supplemental Nutritional Assistance Program (SNAP, formerly food stamps) benefits for such items as prepared food, soft drinks, or cleaning supplies. (See Figure 8.2.) Besides the unspoken economic consequences of these restrictions, they reflect an underlying paternalistic assumption: that the state knows better how a (low-income) person, most often a woman, should spend their resources. More broadly, these policies also imply that the recipients of such benefits either may not know what is in their best interests or be trusted to apportion resources appropriately.

Another form of "benign paternalism" in social policy involves mandatory worker contributions to retirement (through Social Security and Medicare payroll taxes) and the obligation in the original Affordable Care Act to purchase health insurance. (Congress repealed the tax penalty attached to this provision in December 2017.) The imposition of mandatory work requirements to receive Temporary Assistance to Needy Families (TANF, aka welfare) and SNAP also reflects paternalism, as does the requirement that TANF recipients go through

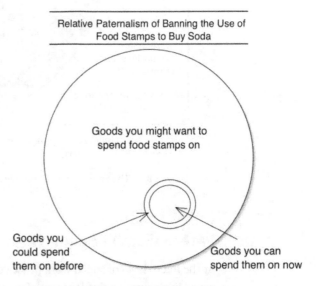

FIGURE 8.2. Paternalism in Social Policy—Regulations Regarding Food Stamps (SNAP)

programs that extol the virtues of marriage. Soss, Fording, and Schram (2011) described recent policies in the areas of welfare, criminal justice, and public housing as a combination of "neoliberal paternalism" and institutional racism. From this perspective, their overriding purpose is not beneficence but to deprive people of their autonomy by enforcing a disciplinary regime against low-income persons, controlling women's sexuality, and further marginalizing people of color and immigrants (Briggs, 2018; Kane, 2018; Sadowski-Smith, 2018; Foster, 2017).

Although rationalized by the need to control costs, policies that dictate which medical procedures public or private health insurance will cover represent another form of paternalism, as do policies concerning the availability and affordability of certain medications. For example, men may obtain drugs such as Viagra or Cialis to address erectile dysfunction with a physician's prescription and without state prohibition on their sale (Ayalon & Gewirtz-Meydan, 2019). A number of states, however, have banned or made it difficult for women to acquire RU-486, the "morning after" birth control pill (Iles, 2020; Mayans & Vaca, 2018).

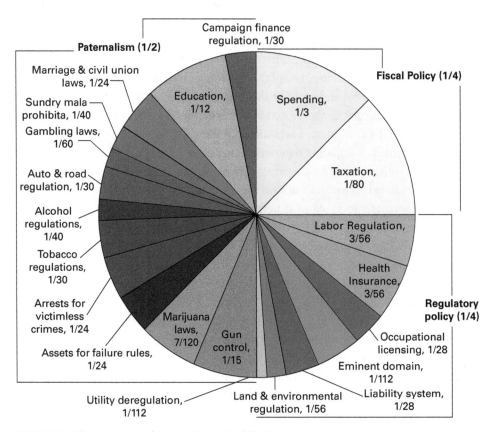

FIGURE 8.3. The Spectrum of Paternalism in Social Policy

Paternalism in Social Work Practice

At the micro level of social work practice, social policies, administrative regulations, and agency procedures create a similar form of paternalism. For example, they sanction the controlling role that case managers play in designing clients' health, behavioral health, or social service plans based on the assumption they are acting in their best interests. One could also argue that state laws licensing social workers and other professionals constitute another form of paternalism because they remove decision-making about from whom to seek services from the people who need them.

According to Reamer (2018a), paternalism generally takes three forms in day-to-day social work practice. One is through the deliberate withholding of information from clients or family members, ostensibly for their own good. This practice most frequently occurs in health care settings around such issues as a diagnosis of terminal cancer. In the macro practice area, it takes the form of failing to disclose to constituents strategic or tactical details in an advocacy or social action campaign or not sharing "bad news" about a recent setback in a social change effort out of fear of discouraging constituents from continuing their involvement.

A second form of paternalism involves lying to clients or providing them with misinformation for their "own good." This sometimes occurs in therapeutic situations with families in which a social worker might not tell a child the truth about their parents' feelings for them (or vice versa). In the macro sphere, this could involve distorting the realities of a social change campaign in order to keep a coalition intact, not revealing to community leaders how community members or allies feel about each other, or failing to tell agency staff about an impending funding crisis that might affect their jobs.

A third form of paternalism is, perhaps, the most egregious. It involves physical or legal interference with a person's intentions or actions, against their will, on the grounds it is for their own good. Examples include coerced medical treatment such as described in Ethical Dilemma 8.1, involuntary commitment to a mental health institution, forced relocation to a shelter for homeless persons, or preventing migrant children from reuniting with family sponsors based on the rationale they risk spreading the coronavirus.

Recognizing paternalism in the macro area is a bit more complicated because social, community, organizational, or institutional change, not individual change is the primary goal of practice. The people with whom macro social workers engage are constituents, not clients (except when serving as organizational consultants or lobbyists). Yet, the treatment of communities (in the broadest sense of that word) in a paternalistic manner can leave them more open to betrayal and manipulation.

Effective and ethical macro practice interventions, therefore, require partnerships to an even greater degree than work with individuals or families. They require social workers and constituents to develop a heightened awareness about the power dynamics within their relationship. This may become complicated further if the social worker is a member of the community, the affected population (in an advocacy effort), or an employee of the organization (in the case of organizational change). The resolution of ethical conflicts that may arise in any of these circumstances requires an assessment of its unique features and the specific context in which they occur.

In community practice, Ben Seattle (2011) distinguished between a "paternalistic community" and a "self-organizing community." In the former, a central authority may restrict communications between community residents and the organizations that represent them and thereby restrict the actions residents might take. By contrast, individuals in a "self-organizing community" can communicate freely among themselves and take steps to coordinate the strategies and tactics of various subgroups. Such communities are also capable of resolving internal disputes through democratic means without resort to the overriding influence or power of an external authority as often occurs in community development projects (Mendes, 2019).

A similar dichotomy exists in administrative practice between organizations run in a hierarchical manner by autocratic leaders who "know what's best," and transformational organizations that promote democratic forms of decision-making, seek to empower staff, and prevent employee burnout (Reisch, 2018c; Ugurluoglu et al., 2018). Paternalistic administrators can also affect agency practice in a variety of ways, from how they respond to the needs of marginalized populations, such as people living in poverty and individuals with disabilities, to how effective they are in promoting better work-life balance for their staff (Engel & Wolfe, 2017; Butz, 2016; Rajan-Rankin, 2016).

A Few Difficult Practice Examples

Godwin (2020) discusses one of the most difficult ethical decisions confronting social workers in the health care field—the extent of treatment provided to infants with severe congenital physical or mental disabilities. Should we base such decisions on a universal principle—that is, all life is precious? Or should we consider the family's and community's resources as part of our assessment of the child's overall future quality of life? If the latter, how do we avoid making a paternalistic judgment? This is a particular problem in societies like the United States, where increasing class and racial inequalities exist and there is increasing concern about the rising cost of health care.

A related challenge exists in the care of elderly individuals or those with terminal illnesses. Over three decades ago, Hopps (1987) pointed out that in our worship of technological innovation in the health care field, "our society has yet to learn how to accept aging gracefully or to integrate the disabilities that are associated with old age and even death with ongoing life" (p. 179). Here, individuals' loss of control over their life circumstances—a particularly acute issue in a society that worships personal autonomy—complicates the tension between preserving a patient's self-determination and acting in what we perceive to be their self-interest, particularly with individuals with dementia or a terminal illness (Donnelly et al., 2019; Aldrich, 2017; Glover & Branine, 2017). The disproportionate incidence of mortality among the aged during the recent Covid-19 pandemic highlights the significance of this issue.

In addition to the challenges racial and cultural diversity creates for these issues, increasing linguistic diversity further complicates their resolution. Studies have shown that people make different moral decisions depending on the language they use (Winskel & Bhatt, 2019; Wong & Ng, 2018; Ingmire, 2014). These findings raise serious questions about the communication gap that exists between workers and clients who speak different languages and about the less-recognized difficulty of translating complex terms from one language to another. The latter is a particular problem in health and behavioral health settings because of different cultural interpretations of physical and psychological conditions (Salvatore, 2017; Jani, 2010).

Another emerging issue in the behavioral health field is whether it is ethical for agencies to deny services to noncompliant clients. Walton (2018) argues that many programs that treat addicts, for example, engage in this practice too loosely. These paternalistic actions not only prevent people from obtaining an essential service, with potentially life-threatening consequences, they prioritize the judgment of the social worker or agency about critical decisions over those of their clients. To avoid such paternalistic practices in health and behavioral health settings, Dotolo and her colleagues (2018) propose greater public scrutiny of such decisions.

Practice with individuals with disabilities, particularly developmental disabilities, also produces ethical dilemmas for social workers, especially around such issues as their right to sexual autonomy and their exercise of civil liberties (Foley, 2017; Cooper, 2016; Gill & Schlund-Vials, 2016). In this area of practice, we face the challenge of striking a "balance between rights and responsibilities and the interpretations of a person's wishes and feelings" (Wilkins, 2012, p. 97). In such circumstances, we have an ethical obligation to inform clients of all their rights and all information relevant to their situation, not merely those that reinforce our preferred course of action. As in many other ethically challenging situations, the development of trust between workers and clients is a prerequisite for an effective resolution.

Justifications for Paternalism in Practice with Individuals and Families

Social workers and administrators in their employing agencies justify paternalistic behavior in a variety of ways. Some justifications are valid—for example, when we make decisions on behalf of very young children or adults who are totally incapacitated. Not all of these interventions are condescending, at least not explicitly. Other situations that arise in our work with adolescents, uneducated adults, or individuals with a diagnosed mental illness are more ambiguous. An ongoing challenge in our practice is determining, on the one hand, when benevolent paternalistic actions are valid and, on the other hand, when we have the authority to overrule paternalistic organizational policies applied without sufficient consideration of the unique circumstances of individual clients.

A common justification for engaging in paternalistic behavior is that clients (or constituents) lack critical information that, if available, would lead them to consent to others (experts) making decisions on their behalf—that is, voluntarily ceding their right to self-determination. The core issues to resolve here are why clients lack this information, how to provide it to them, and whether it is feasible to provide it in a timely fashion and a manner they can easily comprehend. Particularly in health, behavioral health, and legal settings, where information is often complex and expressed in deliberately obscure and exclusionary ways, social workers can play a crucial role in translating complicated information into more digestible formats.

A second, related justification for paternalistic behavior is that clients or constituents are incapable of comprehending relevant information, either temporarily or permanently, due to their age, educational level, or physical or psychological condition. There are obvious situations when this assessment is correct and in the best interests of an individual. Examples include young children, adults with dementia or lack of consciousness, and individuals who are clearly developmentally disabled or severely mentally ill. In such circumstances, it is imperative that we determine to what extent such individuals can understand at least some aspects of relevant information. We should also assess whether other individuals (such as family members or friends) can assist us in communicating and "translating" key information to our clients, and identify the persons who have the authority to act on our clients' behalf if necessary.

A third rationale for paternalism in clinical practice is that clients consented to the paternalistic intervention prior to its occurrence—for example, by signing an informed consent form—or are likely, based on our *prior* knowledge of their wishes, to have consented *after* the interference took place. In the former case, social workers should ensure that we educate individuals who sign such forms or their surrogates about their implications. Under no circumstances should we pressure them into signing under the rubric that "time is of the essence" or that such forms are "mere routine." In the latter instance, we need to be careful not to make assumptions about a person's wishes or project our own desired outcomes onto them. In too many cases, there is the risk that we will base these assumptions on patronizing attitudes about a client's capacity to make reasoned judgments because of the person's demographic or cultural characteristics.

To avoid such misjudgments in circumstances that may justify a paternalistic intervention, we need to consider the following questions: (1) Is the potentially paternalistic action consistent with what we already know about the client's permanent goals and preferences (e.g., has the client already expressed them clearly in the past)? (2) Is the client's incapacity or incompetence only temporary? Can we wait to act or make a decision until the client's condition improves? (3) Does the client lack relevant information that in the normal course of events the client will come to possess? Can we wait to act until the client receives and comprehends this information? (4) What conventions for behavior exist in our agency that may supersede our individual judgment? Finally, (5) Do we intend to apply a deontological framework in resolving this dilemma (e.g., self-determination is an absolute, top priority value)? Alternately, if we apply a consequentialist approach, is there a favorable ratio of benefits to costs in taking a paternalistic action?

In attempting to resolve these difficult issues, we usually need additional information. For example, we need to assess the client's attributes, such as individual competence, as demonstrated by their past ability to make sound decisions. We need to learn whether they have previously, and knowingly, given their consent for us or our colleagues to act on their behalf. We also need to assess the specific circumstances of the situation and the future implications of our decision. For example, are the harmful consequences of a paternalistic intervention likely to be irreversible? Will they affect third parties or the broader community who have not been involved in the decision-making process? What options exist that would preserve a client's wider range of freedom (self-determination) in the future even if we act temporarily to restrict that freedom? Finally, is the imperative to act immediately so compelling that it overrides any other ethical or practical considerations?

Justifications for Paternalism in Macro Social Work Practice and Policy

As discussed earlier in this chapter, macro social work practice and social policy development and implementation also exhibit paternalistic tendencies, often under the guise of "doing good" (Butz, 2016; Gaylin et al., 1978). A considerable number of contemporary fiscal and regulatory policies have explicit paternalistic overtones; many have become so much a part of the national "landscape" that we do not recognize their underlying paternalism. Policymakers usually rationalize such actions in one of several ways. One rationale is to protect the public health, national security, or individuals' health and safety. A recent example is the requirement that individuals wear masks and maintain social distance during the coronavirus pandemic.

Based on this rationale, during the 20th century the government adopted laws to protect the purity of food and medications, and to ensure the safety of a wide range of consumer goods, particularly those used by children, such as toys. Although there is persistent support for the concept of individual liberty among Americans, few people want to return to the days before the Food and Drug Administration (FDA) or Consumer Protection Agency tested products for their safety or question the need for such protections. Most people today support the ban on cigarette smoking in restaurants and offices, and strict laws that prohibit driving under the influence. Despite the media attention given to recent protests against "stay at home" orders during the pandemic, polls show that an overwhelming majority of Americans continue to support them. In some people's eyes, however, laws that regulate tobacco or alcohol use, restrict the sale of mega-size sugared soft drinks or food cooked with trans-fats, or require automobile passengers to wear seat belts may cross the line and deprive individuals of the right to make independent decisions about their health and diet.

A second rationale for paternalistic behavior in the macro sphere is to care for vulnerable populations, such as children, the elderly, and individuals with disabilities or mental impairments, or to protect people from harming themselves. Policies in this category include laws that prohibit the use of inflammatory materials in children's clothing and those that require child safety caps on medications, car seats for small children, and vaccinations against contagious diseases such as measles and polio. Few people contest most of these measures. There are still disagreements, however, about how far the government can go to protect individual well-being or the common good.

For example, some parents have objected to laws that require measles vaccinations for their children on the grounds the vaccine may cause autism, despite considerable scientific evidence that no such connection exists. Recent disinformation spread on the internet that promotes conspiracy theories about the origins of the coronavirus and the motives behind government's protective regulations during the pandemic and its efforts to produce a vaccine (Roose, 2020) demonstrates the politicization of what is essentially a public health issue. In a different vein, while laws that protect women, children, and the aged from physical or emotional violence are widely approved, those that deny women the right to make their own decisions about their reproductive health based on their age or gender are not.

The following case illustrates an issue that for some individuals may reflect paternalistic behavior on the part of the state and for others represents a sensible law designed to protect individuals from harm and society from unnecessary expense.

ETHICAL DILEMMA 8.3   "The Helmet Law"

You are a policy analyst and ethicist for the state legislature in a state that does not have mandatory helmet laws for motorcyclists. The state's Department of Health is increasingly concerned over the cost of treatment for motorcyclists who incur serious head traumas resulting from accidents in which they did not wear a helmet. The department has urged the legislature to draft a bill mandating that cyclists wear helmets when operating a motorcycle on a public road. A legislative committee drafted a bill along these lines; it is currently under consideration in both houses of the legislature.

In legislative hearings about this issue, representatives of cycling clubs, libertarian organizations, and the association of motorcycle dealerships testified against the bill. The president of the state cycling club claimed that helmets actually decrease riders' safety because they diminish their peripheral vision and impede their hearing. The spokesperson for the dealerships association argued that the bill would be economically disadvantageous for his association's members and lead to greater air pollution as motorcycles consume far less fuel than autos. Several libertarians maintained that the bill was an unnecessary infringement on cyclists' personal freedom. They asserted that as all cyclists were at least 18, they were legally adults who can make their own decisions about their health and safety.

In response to this testimony and apparent divisions in the legislature, a legislator introduced an amendment to the original bill. It would permit cyclists to receive a waiver of the helmet requirement provided they signed a release exempting both the state and private insurers from paying for their medical bills or lost income should they incur a head injury while riding on a motorcycle without a helmet. The committee chair and co-sponsor of the bill requested your advice as to whether to accept the amendment.

Questions:
1. What would you advise?
2. What are the ethical issues in this situation?
3. What is the ethical basis for your recommendation?

This case illustrates the conflict between preserving individuals' autonomy and protecting their well-being when they make a decision about the risks they are willing to take while engaging in an otherwise lawful activity. It raises the question of whether society's efforts to protect individuals from harm supersedes individuals' right to take knowing risks while engaging in otherwise lawful behavior. In addition, is it fair for the state to permit motorcyclists to exercise their autonomy on the condition they relinquish their right to future assistance if they need it? Given the power imbalance that exists between individuals and the state, is the state's offer a form of coercion? From a deontological perspective, how would the respective parties to the negotiation order the competing values? From a consequentialist perspective, which consequences do these parties believe should have greater weight in determining the outcome of the legislative process?

FIGURE 8.4. Paternalism Reflects Power Imbalances and Is a Form of Social Control

Ironically, a third rationale for state-sponsored paternalism is that it is sometimes necessary to preserve people's liberty. Governments usually frame these policies in one of two ways. Increasingly, they use "national security" to justify policies or practices that, at a minimum, create a minor inconvenience, such as removing our shoes at airport security checks or having our briefcases searched upon entering public buildings.

There are fierce disagreements, however, about some paternalistic policies. One is the provision in the 2001 Patriot Act that allowed the government to monitor patrons' book choices at public libraries. Another is the preventive detention of individuals whom officials identified as potential terrorists solely by their use of the internet. A third example is the inclusion of individuals on "no fly" lists based on their religion or ethnicity. Other controversial policies implemented with a similar justification include the "stop and frisk" tactics disproportionately employed by urban police against African American and Latino young men and, most recently, tracking people's movements through their cell phone use to help control the spread of the coronavirus. The following case illustrates a potential ethical dilemma in social work practice created by policies of this nature.

ETHICAL DILEMMA 8.4

Paternalism in the National Interest
(Based on actual or potential events.)

In early 2020, in response to the growing coronavirus epidemic, the Trump administration issued an executive order banning all travel to and from China or from any nation where the outbreak had not been contained. The president justified his decision based on the government's obligation to protect the public health of individuals and national security. Organizations from the American Civil Liberties Union (ACLU) to the Chamber of Commerce immediately protested, with objections ranging from concerns about civil liberties violations to damage to the nation's economy.

Your involvement in the matter is on a more micro level. You work for a nonprofit agency that serves recent immigrants and refugees. A number of your clients have elderly family members in China with whom they have attempted to reunite for several years. After a long wait, these relatives recently received permission from the government to immigrate to the United States. In response, they sold their homes and most of their belongings. If they had to remain abroad indefinitely, they would inevitably live a life of poverty because their relatives in the United States lack

the resources to provide them with ongoing financial support. On the other hand, several of your clients contracted the Covid-19 virus recently and one of them died. You have two young children and aging parents and fear that your community has not yet contained the epidemic. A group of these clients asked you to assist them in getting approval for their family members to immigrate.

Questions:
1. What would you do? What would be the ethical basis of your decision?
2. In situations like this, how can society or its agents, such as social workers, balance the needs of individuals and their families with those of the common good?
3. Who should make these decisions? What ethical principles should guide them?
4. Under what circumstances can the state act in a parental role (i.e., paternalistically)?
5. What are the implications if you generalized these principles to other similar cases?

This case illustrates another situation that tests the limits of autonomy and the state's ability to protect its citizens. It also demonstrates the different conclusions we might reach if we applied a deontological or a consequentialist approach. If we used the former approach, which values would we prioritize and for what reasons? If the latter, which consequences would we consider the most important and for whom? How would we measure their respective importance? For example, does the protection of the community's well-being against potential harm outweigh the desire to avoid the probable future destitution of the relatives left in China?

A fourth rationale for paternalistic policies is to achieve one of several desirable social goals, such as safeguarding the environment, promoting economic prosperity, and encouraging good morals and proper behavior. There are good, debatable, and questionable examples of each of these motivations. Past policies, such as the Comstock laws prohibiting the sale or mailing of "obscene" materials, the 18th Amendment that established Prohibition, laws banning the sale of contraceptives, current laws regulating gambling, and laws criminalizing the use of certain substances or certain forms of sexual behavior, even among consenting adults, continue to exist today.

Other recent controversial examples include laws that restrict access to, but do not outright prohibit, women's ability to obtain a legal abortion or reproductive health care. Laws that require individuals to use the restrooms designated for persons of their assigned sex at birth also fall into this category. Tax policies that give certain advantages to married couples or to families with children, the rating system applied to films by the motion picture industry, and proposals to restrict or remove certain content on Facebook, Instagram, or Twitter reflect more subtle paternalistic assumptions on the part of the state or private corporations.

Lastly, another seemingly contradictory rationale for paternalistic policies and customs is that they actually enhance some individuals' lives by eliminating the need for them to make difficult decisions for which they lacked the capacity. Past examples include policies that forbade women from owning property or businesses in their own name or signing contracts, the introduction of required curricula in schools, and—in the most egregious example—policies that rationalized slavery, racial segregation and the denial of voting rights to people of color and women. Over the past century, sweeping cultural and social changes have increased awareness of the paternalism embedded in public policies such as these or in long-standing cultural traditions and norms that reinforce them. In the United States, laws barring women or African Americans from owning property, signing contracts, or entering certain occupations are now obsolete, although these populations remain underrepresented in major economic, political, and cultural institutions. Expectations regarding appropriate social and sexual behavior have significantly changed recently as a consequence of #MeToo, Black Lives Matter, and related social movement activism.

To summarize, in determining when paternalism in practice and policy may be justified, we need to consider the following questions:

1. Can we engage in purely helpful paternalistic acts that do not interfere, constrain, or permanently restrict a person or group's ability to make decisions on their own behalf?
2. What do we consider acceptable and unacceptable grounds (rationales) for paternalistic interventions and under what circumstances would we rely on them?
3. In our work with dependent, vulnerable, and marginalized populations, to whom is justice served if we act in a paternalistic manner?
4. How does the use of informed consent enable institutions to engage in paternalistic interventions? What steps could we take to reduce the possibility of this occurring?
5. To what extent should we consider cultural, class, gender, religious, or age differences in determining whether to justify a paternalistic intervention?
6. What criteria should we use to determine what constitutes paternalism in addressing such specific issues as suicide, voluntary euthanasia, prostitution, or drug use?

Summary

This chapter has discussed the ethical conflicts that exist due to paternalistic behavior in both practice and policy settings. These conflicts fall into three interrelated categories. First, there is the conflict between individuals' right to autonomy (a form of negative freedom or liberty) and to self-determination versus their right to obtain the assistance or support they need to protect or enhance their well-being and increase their ability to self-determine and self-actualize in the future (positive freedom or enhancement of their individual agency). One way to frame this conflict is between a person's legal rights and moral rights. Another is to conceive of it as a conflict between individual and social rights.

A second category reflects the tension between fulfilling clients' interests, needs, and goals as they define them versus our desire and professional responsibility to protect them from harm by "doing good." A final area of conflict concerns the balance between focusing our practice solely on an individual's own good versus attempting to balance an individual's good with the common or societal good (Etzioni, 2019). This has been a constant struggle in U.S. society, as reflected recently in protests against state-sponsored restrictions during the coronavirus pandemic (Fernandez & Montgomery, 2020; Woodard, 2017).

In combination with Chapter 7, this chapter also discussed situations when paternalism might be justified. These include actions designed to protect the public's health, individual health and safety, the physical environment, or national security. They also include policies or practices intended to protect vulnerable populations from harm (such as laws regarding child abuse) or self-harm, and to care for special populations, such as the aged, individuals with severe physical disabilities, or those with severe mental or intellectual impairments. In each of these areas, the ethical challenge is determining under what circumstances and to what extent paternalistic practices may be applied.

Eriksson and Englander (2017) assert that greater emphasis on empathy with clients may help social workers overcome their tendency toward paternalism and facilitate the resolution of these dilemmas. As discussed in Chapter 2, they and other social work scholars maintain that a practice based on an ethics of care, rather than an ethics of rules, will enable social workers to recognize the client's context and situation more clearly and produce more effective worker-client relationships (Pease et al., 2017). Although these are thoughtful recommendations, they inevitably raise other complicated ethical issues, such as those to be discussed in Chapter 9—the challenges presented by boundary issues and dual relationships in our practice.

Reflection Exercise: Identifying Paternalism in Public Policy

Which of the following policies would you regard as paternalistic and for what reasons:

- Laws protecting children from child abuse, including laws banning spanking
- Laws against sexual harassment in the workplace
- Laws against suicide or voluntary euthanasia
- Legislation restricting the sale of cigarettes or e-cigarettes to minors
- Laws banning the sale or use of certain drugs, such as marijuana
- Laws banning the sale of alcohol to persons below a certain age, prohibiting its sale on Sunday, or restricting where it can be sold or consumed
- Laws or regulations controlling individuals' decisions regarding end-of-life care
- Laws banning the sale of trans-fat or super-sized soft drinks
- Zoning laws restricting the concentration of fast food restaurants in low income neighborhoods
- Zoning laws requiring owners of beachfront property to allow public access to the ocean
- Speed limits on highways or city streets
- Laws requiring the use of seat belts, or helmets for bicyclists or motorcyclists
- Laws requiring people to "social distance" or close businesses during public health emergencies
- Laws regulating who may marry, at what age, and to how many persons
- Laws prohibiting the use of "inflammatory" speech or requiring "trigger warnings" on television, in the movies, or in campus lectures

Credits

Fig. 8.1: Copyright © 2018 Depositphotos/sangoiri.
Fig. 8.2: Source: https://modeledbehavior.wordpress.com/2010/10/08/soda-food-stamps-and-paternalism/.
Fig. 8.3: Copyright © Jim Riley and Geoff Riley.
Fig. 8.4: Copyright © 2019 Depositphotos/Iconscout.

Boundary Issues and Dual Relationships in Social Work Practice

Introduction

Social work is a profession in which relationships are a paramount concern. Every method and field of practice involves the establishment, maintenance, and effective use of personal connections—with clients, constituents, colleagues, community allies, employers, and even adversaries. Sometimes, our work, particularly with vulnerable individuals and families, places us in highly emotional situations in which the strategic use of our relationships with them is a critical factor. In addition, as human beings, we cannot avoid the effects that the dire circumstances of the people with whom we work have on our feelings and behavior. Yet, social work is also a profession guided by strong core values and a commitment to ethical practice. That is why we must be especially careful to ensure that we balance our humanity with sound judgment and never substitute our own needs and desires for those of our clients (Brownlee et al., 2019; Congress, 2017).

This chapter addresses these sensitive, often confusing, and rapidly evolving issues in our practice. It covers the range of boundary issues and dual relationships that exist in our work, the effects of cultural diversity on our response to these issues when they arise, and how the increased use of social media and digital counseling has complicated these issues. It discusses some challenges to the rigid application of traditional guidelines regarding professional boundaries and several concerns about dual relationships that have appeared in recent years. The chapter concludes with a brief section on the implications of this issue for social work education.

ETHICAL DILEMMA 9.1   A Boundary Issue

You are a social worker in a family service agency. One day at work, as you retrieve a client's folder from the cabinet in which it was stored, you notice a file with the same name as the partner of one of your new friends.

You check the file and find that the phone number listed matched your friend's home number. You return the file without reading further, but you now know that your friend's partner is a client of the organization where you work. Your new friend does not know where you work as it never came up in a conversation. You face the dilemma of whether to tell your friend what you discovered or to wait until she asks about your work. If she does, and you answer honestly, then she might have to decide whether to tell her that her partner is a client of your agency. It is also possible that your friend does not know that her partner is receiving services or for what reasons. If your friend acknowledges that her partner is a client at the organization,

a related aspect of this dilemma is whether you should admit that you had seen her partner's file. Another potential scenario concerns what you should do if you encounter your new friend's partner while at work before the subject comes up in conversation.

Questions:

1. How would you characterize the ethical dilemma in this situation? What ethical principles are at stake?
2. How would you handle the situation? What process would you use to make your decision?
3. What ethical principles would you use to justify your decision?

The Range of Boundary Issues and Dual Relationships

As this relatively simple case illustrates, boundary issues have become increasingly complicated in social work practice, even when they occur accidentally. They no longer include such obvious transgressions as engaging in an intimate physical and emotional relationship with a client, former client, or family member of a client. In general, four types of ethical boundary issues may occur in our practice: those with our clients, our colleagues, our agencies of employment, and with the larger community (Reamer, 2019a, Zur, 2017).

For example, a potential boundary issue exists when a professional relationship with a client or constituent becomes a friendship. This gives rise to questions students frequently pose: is it an ethical violation if they meet a client or constituent in a nonprofessional setting such as a coffee house or if they accept an invitation to a client's wedding or funeral? A question arises as to whether proscriptions on such relationships apply equally to social workers who are not engaged in clinical practice. For example, do the same proscriptions apply in our relationships with members of a community organization or advocacy coalition with which we are working? How rigid does the boundary between our clients and constituents have to be in order to maintain an effective professional relationship?

Certain practice situations, such as those involving work in health care systems with people who are dying or grieving the loss of a loved one, may also blur traditional boundaries between social workers and clients (Fronek & Kendall, 2017). It can sometimes be difficult to determine where the boundary lies between treating clients with empathy and humanity, and behavior that creates emotional confusion in clients that could undermine practice goals. In such circumstances, an issue arises as to how social workers "can honor [their] genuine care and concern … for clients while still maintaining a professional relationship" (Wallace et al., 2017, p. 336).

Social workers can diminish the risks of such boundary transgressions in several ways. First, we need to affirm that the primary purpose of our practice is to enhance people's well-being. Our needs and desires, however compelling, should never take priority in our professional work.

Maintaining appropriate boundaries with clients and constituents, therefore, is an important component of fulfilling our obligations to them and meeting our practice goals.

Second, we need to engage in self-care, including the cultivation of relationships outside of our work, so that we are not tempted to use clients to fill a social or psychological void. This is particularly true during the current pandemic when many of us are socially isolated. Third, when we are unsure about the proper lines to draw in a professional relationship, we should consult with colleagues and supervisors who are more experienced and thus have probably addressed similar issues in the past.

Inevitably, the range of practice situations in which we work also creates the possibility for dual relationships to emerge, including some that are mandated (Younggren & Gottlieb, 2016). These include supervision, in which a mentor often plays a multifaceted role in a supervisee's life (Falender, 2016), the facilitation of self-help or support groups in which self-disclosure is not only common, it is expected (Haber & Deaton, 2019), and practice in corrections (Ward & Ward, 2016). Other practice environments where dual relationships often arise are work with adolescents or young adults, in which bonding is often necessary to establish trust (Corey et al., 2016), social work in rural areas where overlapping relationships are frequently unavoidable (Luse, 2018; Barnett, 2017a), practice in the military (Johnson & Johnson, 2017), and practice in faith-based communities (Sanders, 2017). In the macro arena, practitioners engaged in community-based advocacy (Ezell, 2013) and those who work in small, nonhierarchical non-profits (Hessle, 2016) may also have to balance the dual relationships that evolve. Some practice models, such as those proposed by proponents of an ethic of care (Hay, 2019) or a radical social work perspective (Bussey et al., 2020; Clark & Jaffe, 2018; Ferguson et al., 2018), encourage the establishment of more egalitarian worker-client relationships.

Virtually all relationships in social work, therefore, have the potential to create conflicts of interest, as they often do in all professional activities and in the course of our lives. Many of these conflicts are relatively insignificant and can be managed ethically and effectively (Guthmann et al., 2019). A different type of ethical issue exists, however, when these conflicts involve personal pecuniary (financial) interests or issues of status, prestige, power, and reputation. A social worker who uses or is tempted to use a professional relationship for a dual purpose, such as promoting a private practice or an alternative career, or even going into business with a former client, is clearly committing an ethical violation. Such violations could also involve promoting the interests of one's family, organization, profession, or group membership. Finally, they could reflect conflicts between maintaining the primacy of the client's interests (as discussed in Chapter 4) and the interests of society as a whole, or the "common good." Although most such conflicts juxtapose a choice between moral and immoral alternatives, others are less clear because of the particular and sometimes unusual contingencies of a situation that produced the conflict.

FIGURE 9.1. Maintaining Appropriate Boundaries Is an Increasingly Important Ethical Issue

Nearly two decades ago, Freud and Krug (2002b) asserted that "the [NASW] *Code*'s framing of the dual relations standard neglects other practice contexts and social work functions ... that have historically defined the social work profession" (p. 486). For example, as discussed throughout this book, relationships with constituents or co-workers in macro social work practice settings often reflect more ambiguity in their ethical dimensions. Boundary issues, however, exist in all forms of macro practice, although the social work literature and the revised NASW *Code of Ethics* continue to discuss these issues primarily as they apply to clinical interventions, as Freud and Krug suggested. Consequently, neither the *Code*, the policies of most agencies, nor recent scholarship address the various and somewhat unique boundary dilemmas that arise in the usual course of community or organizational practice (Hyde, 2012).

These omissions overlook the different type of relationships macro practitioners, especially community organizers and advocates, establish with the people with whom they work. Hardina (2004) points out that "friendships with members of the constituency group often are essential to the organizing effort, especially when the organizer needs to acquire knowledge about the culture and lifestyle of community members" (p. 597). Developing these relationships is a critical part of developing trust, especially when working with community residents of a different demographic background. Although Hardina expands the list of prohibitive relationships for organizers to include board members, employers, and targets (individual decision-makers), she questions whether the strict prohibition on sexual relationships and friendships is feasible if the community is one's client (p. 598). In policy advocacy, a different type of conflict of interest may emerge in practitioners' efforts to determine how to balance "what is in their client's best interest, both in the long and the short run and ... society's best interest" (Ezell, 2013, p. 42).

Similar issues arise in community-based research. Official statements in the British Association of Social Work's *Code of Ethics* cite the presence of a potentially constructive dual relationship between researchers and service users, particularly in cases of participatory social action research. Concerns persist, however, as to whether such relationships violate standards established by institutional review boards (IRBs), especially those involving informed consent; whether they might bias research results; and whether cultural differences between reseachers and subjects are sufficiently considered (Hugman et al., 2011).

Boundary Issues and Cultural Diversity

Although the NASW *Code of Ethics* contains explicit statements about the importance of maintaining professional boundaries and avoiding dual relationships, there is less attention in the literature to how demographic diversity and the cultural context of practice construct different interpretations of the meaning of these concepts. While the *Code of Ethics* clearly prohibits sexual relationships with clients, it is more ambiguous and largely silent about such boundary issues as dual relationships, bartering arrangements, practitioner's self-disclosure, the exchange of gifts, or the use of physical touch (Dutton et al., 2019; Szczygiel, 2019; Barnett, 2017b; Green, 2017). The complexity of the current practice environment also produces a wide range of potential boundary crossings—from minor violations such as sharing household goods with a needy client, to major violations such as having an intimate relationship with a client. Although many social workers may privately "confess" to crossing these boundaries through small, personal gestures, in its present form the *Code* appears to grant few exemptions from its restrictive proscription. Trimberger and Bugenhagen (2015) found that a number of personal and professional factors influence how practitioners interpret ethical guidelines regarding boundary issues. Cultural and class differences among both workers and clients may produce additional confusion around long-standing ethical taboos.

For example, the traditional view of the worker-client relationship regards the acceptance of gifts or personal favors from a client as a boundary violation. In some cultures, however, the lack of reciprocity in a relationship, such as refusing the offer of even the smallest kindness, is rude; it could undermine the trust essential to effective practice. In community practice, social workers forge many relationships in informal, nonprofessional settings, such as social clubs, beauty salons, and religious congregations. As discussed in Chapter 10, the internet has also dramatically altered our relationships with colleagues and opened up the possibility for new boundary issues to appear (Reamer, 2017). For example, what should we do if we become aware of a co-worker's dual relationship?

Widening socioeconomic inequalities create further challenges. If a client does not have sufficient income to cover the cost of a professional service, is it unethical for a social worker to enter a bartering relationship with this person? That is, may a social worker accept payment in kind (a personal service, e.g.) rather than cash or a voucher in exchange for therapy? This type of dilemma is particularly common in rural areas, as discussed later in this chapter. Similar dilemmas may also arise in host institutions, where staff from different professions operate under different ethical codes of conduct and professional norms (Bronstein, 2003).

ETHICAL DILEMMA 9.2   ## A Bartered Arrangement

You work in a nonprofit social service organization in a multiracial, multicultural community that provides a range of counseling and concrete services. One of your clients, the Robinson family, has been seeing you for over a year to address marital and family problems that arose after their teenage son was killed in a drive-by shooting. Mr. Robinson works in construction and belongs to a union that provides good health care benefits. Ms. Robinson is a teacher in a neighborhood pre-K center. They have two other children.

At their last session, Mr. Robinson told you that he was recently laid off due to the coronavirus pandemic and that his health benefits, which had covered the cost of their counseling sessions, will terminate within a month. The Robinsons have little savings. What they have managed to save they plan to use for the college expenses of their remaining children. Mr. Robinson is a skilled carpenter and electrician. He asks if he could do some work on your rowhouse as payment for the sessions until he is able to return to his regular job. Otherwise, the Robinsons will have to terminate their relationship with you.

Questions:
1. Would it be ethical to accept Mr. Robinson's offer of a bartering arrangement in order to enable his family to continue their work with you?
2. Would it be ethical to deny services to the Robinsons because their temporary financial setback precludes their ability to pay for services with cash or their insurance coverage?
3. In this and similar cases, could the use of bartering arrangements be an ethically appropriate way to develop more egalitarian relationships with our clients?

There are few legal guidelines to assist social workers in resolving the dilemma posed in this case. Only a few states address the issue of whether therapists, including social workers, may accept small gifts from clients. Laws do not address and the literature on social work ethics is also inconclusive regarding the ethics of accepting personal invitations from clients or social workers revealing personal information in the course of providing services.

Conversely, altruistic motives may lead social workers to provide various "gifts" to clients who are in financially precarious circumstances. These include both tangible gifts, such as used clothing, to the extension of service hours and the provision of additional benefits beyond those specified by the agency's programs. In such situations, workers should be aware of the effect their gifts have on the dignity and self-worth of the persons receiving the gifts, whether the gifts are compatible with the receivers' culture, and whether the provision of the gift gives the impression that you have promised sustained (indefinite) support in the future (Lewis, 2003a).

Finally, at the core of this ethical challenge there is the problem of definitional ambiguity. Different cultures may have different perspectives, for example, on where the boundary lies between a caring, empathic relationship with another individual and inappropriate intimacy. Even the term *dual relationships* is fraught with confusion and disagreement within the profession. If a client encounters a social worker in a local grocery store or in the waiting room of a dentist office, should the social worker not acknowledge the client's presence? How might the client interpret this "cold shoulder"? If you are a community organizer going door-to-door on a hot summer day to conduct a survey of residents' concerns, would it be rude to refuse a glass of water from someone who admitted you to their home?

The strict proscription on dual relationships also fails to recognize that their deliberate development may enhance the ability of a social worker to establish an effective partnership with a client or constituent and provide support for the worker's legitimacy in an environment characterized by increasing mistrust. Another potential problem produced by a rigid construction of dual relationships is greater tension in a multiservice organization, such as a community center or settlement house, in which clinical social workers engage in therapeutic relationships with the same individuals their community practitioner colleagues involve in social or political action campaigns.

Although there is widespread agreement that sexual relationships between social workers and clients are unethical, there is considerable ambiguity regarding the ethics of nonsexual dual relationships despite their being a frequent cause of client complaints. This dilemma occurs most frequently in programs where former and current clients augment the services provided by professionals (e.g., as peer or community counselors in substance abuse treatment programs), in organizations that stress the importance of reducing the power dynamics between workers and clients, in rural or culturally homogeneous communities, and in agencies that involve "consumer providers" in the delivery of concrete services such as the delivery of groceries to the homebound (Ringstad, 2008).

Two other concerns further complicate this matter. One is how long the proscription against having a personal relationship with a client lasts. Is it indefinite? Freud and Krug (2002b) point out "there is little professional agreement on when a social work relationship is ended" (p. 490). Does the nature of the relationship and the frequency of contact matter? For example, what if any differences exist between dating a former client and seeing a former client from time to time at social gatherings if you or the client has married into each other's family or friendship circle?

There are also clear cultural and generational differences regarding such behaviors as formality of address, forms of appropriate communication, physical touching, and displays of affection.

The *Ethics Code* of the American Psychological Association (2002) establishes a minmal 2-year limit on the prohibition of sexually intimate relationsip with former clients after the termination of therapy. This code also includes specific criteria to assess the risk of former clients being exploited:

1. The amount of time that has passed
2. The nature, duration, and intensity of the therapy
3. The circumstances of termination
4. The client's personal history
5. The client's current mental status
6. The likelihood of adverse consequences on the client
7. Whether the therapist suggested or invited a posttermination relationship in the course of working with the client.

A related issue concerns what if any distinctions there are between different types of clients. Should a former participant in a job training program at your agency be viewed through the same ethical lens as someone who once received psychotherapy in the agency's counseling program? What about neighborhood residents who were active in a local community organizing effort or constituents who testified in an advocacy campaign you directed? As these illustrations reveal, boundary issues in our practice are far more complex than they are often portrayed in professional codes or literature.

Another issue arises due to the increasing concern in the profession about the importance of "self-care." When does meeting our emotional needs or protecting our physical and mental health go too far in interactions with clients or constituents? Is any form of self-disclosure to connect with them a taboo? Given the inadequacy of most social work salaries, where is the line between looking out for our financial security and putting this issue above our client's interests? As discussed in Chapter 8, what behaviors are appropriate in our efforts to "do good" for others? Finally, because of the unique and varied backgrounds of the people with whom we work and the complicated circumstances of their lives, there are inevitably unanticipated consequences of forging virtually any type of helping relationship.

Boundary Issues in the Age of Social Media

Despite these complexities and ambiguities, there remain numerous reasons why attention to the risks of dual relationships is still a critical ethical issue in social work practice. One is a consequence of the ever present power imbalance between workers and clients, and the inherent vulnerability of the latter, regardless of the reasons they initially sought a service or benefit. This power imbalance creates a risk of exploitation if any sort of dual relationship exists, however innocent in its origins and intentions. Even in a cultural environment in which traditional norms of self-disclosure have dramatically changed due largely to social media, boundary issues are still important, particularly in clinical relationships, to protect vulnerable clients from all forms of exploitation, intentional or inadvertent, and to preserve the integrity and trust at the heart of the helping process. Without this trust, no intervention, whether the provision of a tangible benefit or a therapeutic service, can remain effective. This is equally true in macro practice, although the definition of a dual relationship and the rules that govern such relationships are often less clear.

Another issue of increasing concern in the social service field is the legal liability that dual relationships potentially create for social workers and their employing organizations in an increasingly litigious environment (Reamer, 2015a). In addition to the risk of a malpractice suit, there is the equally important danger that a dual relationship could damage the reputation and career prospects of the violator and the reputation of the agency and the profession as a whole (Gricus, 2019). It could also have negative effects on the quality of services an agency provides due to its impact on future clients who may learn of the organization's violations in the past.

The maintenance of appropriate boundaries also complements our commitment to other ethical principles discussed in this book. It reaffirms our ethical obligation to protect the primacy of the client's interest and to avoid potential conflicts that may undermine this objective. Consistent with Kant's "categorical imperative," it proscribes using clients as a means to other ends, such as the satisfaction of our emotional, physical, financial, or ego needs. It is consistent with the *Code*'s ethical imperative to practice with competence, as it helps us develop and sustain an appropriate, nonexploitive, and effective professional role.

Tricky or Ambiguous Issues

As discussed above, numerous "gray areas" inevitably arise in our practice with clients and constituents. For example, what if a client baked some cookies and brought a small bag to a counselling session? Should you refuse it? What does the acceptance or refusal of the cookies imply? How might the client from a culture in which gift giving is a sign of respect and appreciation for authority figures interpret your response?

In a community setting, where you might meet with neighborhood leaders in a local pub, is it appropriate for you to buy one of them a beer on occasion? What if they told you the "next round is on me"? A similar situation might arise when going door-to-door in a neighborhood canvassing activity. If someone lets you in and asks if you would like a cup of coffee or tea, what should you do? (As an MSW student, I learned you always say "yes" in such situations, even if you do not like coffee.) In an organizational setting, is it an ethical violation to buy your secretary a birthday or holiday gift, or to accept one? How would you explain your refusal? How might acceptance of the offer affect your relationship with this individual, particularly if they were of a different culture or gender? Does one's hierarchical or nonhierarchical relationship with a colleague matter in such instances?

Sometimes, a client or constituent may develop a healthy, appropriate affection for a social worker and invite them to a family event such as a wedding or bar mitzvah. If you counselled a couple whose marital problems stemmed in part from difficulties conceiving a child and they finally were able to have a baby, would it be an ethical violation to accept or decline an invitation to the child's naming ceremony or christening? In San Francisco, I consulted with a leading organization in the fight against HIV/AIDS. A significant number of the people involved in the organization ultimately died or lost their long-time partners. Would it have been a boundary transgression to go to their funeral or, in happier times, to a commitment ceremony?

Proponents of applying an ethic of care to our practice would probably answer "no" to these questions. They would argue that an ethic of care involves taking a more nuanced and contextual approach to a worker-client relationship (Hay, 2019). This tension between expressing care and providing expertise is also exemplied in such ethical dilemmas as whether social workers should hug a client, help them pack for a move, or lend them money in an emergency (Dybicz, 2012).

Boundary rules have different implications in our work with individuals from diverse cultural backgrounds, particularly with people whose cultures may regard rigid, traditional professional boundaries as disrespectful, untrustworthy, or cold (O'Neill, 2018). In certain communities, "the ability to enter into a relationship of thirdness (i.e., breaking down the usual worker-client separation) requires ... the social worker ... to soften the self-boundary" (Arnd-Caddigan & Pozzuto, 2009, p. 327). This implies that practitioners need to establish a more flexible relationship with clients, one in which we seek to create a closer emotional connection through a variety of nontraditional means (Crociani-Windland, 2017). Adopting this approach to practice redefines the meaning of boundaries from one of maintaining professional distance to one of establishing more personal contact.

Further complications may emerge when third parties become involved. One example is when a client asks you to help a relative or close friend "just one time" with a specific problem. Another may occur when you become a relative of a client or constituent after your professional relationship begins through no action on your part or that of the client. Would it be unethical to terminate an established counselling relationship with the client that may have taken time to develop or to continue to work with the client in a community organization? The following case puts a slightly different spin on this issue.

ETHICAL DILEMMA 9.3

Boundary Issues and a Conflict of Duties

You work for an organization that provides job training and placement and a variety of related services to new immigrants and refugees. The agency is chronically short of funds and the waiting list to receive assistance is quite long. At a recent social event, a cousin with whom you are very close tells you excitedly that she is engaged to marry a man from West Africa whom she knew while working as a Peace Corps volunteer 5 years ago. They reconnected online through a dating app, have corresponded for nearly a year, and have met several times in the United States. Your cousin knows about your work and asks you, as a favor, if you could assist her fiancé in enrolling in one of the job training programs your agency runs. Although her fiancé has a green card, which makes him eligible for the program, it would require you to use your influence to give his application priority over those who have been on the waiting list for months. You are very fond of your cousin and want to help her, but you feel conflicted. What should you do?

Questions:

1. What is the nature of the ethical dilemma?
2. Who created the dilemma?
3. Where is the locus of responsibility for its resolution?
4. What is the nature, basis, and extent of your ethical obligations? To whom?
5. What are the short- and long-term consequences of your decision?
6. What social work values or ethical frameworks would you use as guides in your decision-making?

Finally, the issue of physical contact with clients or constituents is a subject of increasing concern for numerous reasons. The #MeToo movement has heightened our awareness of the need for clear boundaries in professional relationships, particularly between supervisors and their staff. In a different context, fear of accusations of child abuse has increased anxiety among social workers who work with children in schools or childcare settings. Lastly, cultural and generational differences about touching have led to greater uncertainty about whether even the most minor and well-intentioned gesture is now ethically off-limits. For example, in the current cultural context, is it ever appropriate, let alone physically safe, to hug a weeping colleague or client when they have lost a loved one during the coronavirus pandemic? What about a child who fell and got hurt or a patient who just received a devastating health diagnosis? Could you give a high school student an encouraging pat on the back when the student tells you that they received a much-needed college scholarship? The uncertainties such situations produce has given rise to recent challenges to strict boundary rules, as discussed in the next section.

Challenges to Strict Boundary Rules

In part as a reaction to these ambiguous situations, scholars have raised a number of objections to the profession's imposition of strict boundary proscriptions. One criticism of strict boundary rules is that they maintain the unequal power dynamic between workers and clients by constructing a barrier between them that serves to reinforce professional dominance. Such critics argue that developing a multifaceted, warmer, and more egalitarian personal relationship with clients facilitates the helping process by increasing openness, trust, and closeness.

In addition, blurring traditional boundaries gives clients more power and increases the possibility of recognizing the diverse array of their expertise and strengths. As discussed briefly earlier in this chapter, another criticism is that boundary rules, as currently formulated, do not (or perhaps should not) apply to macro practice settings because of the more egalitarian relationships social workers have (or should have) with our constituents. If you work as an organizer, administrator, or advocate, should you treat your constituents the same way as if they were clients? Would all the established rules about professional boundaries still apply? For example, is dating a community resident who attended a meeting to discuss a possible rent strike equivalent to dating someone you counseled?

Boundary Issues, the Internet, and Social Media

The growing application of digital technology to social work practice and the widespread use of social media, particularly among younger generations, have produced new ethical issues and required us to reexamine the meaning of professional boundaries. Easy access to electronic communication not only jeopardizes social workers' ability to adhere to the principle of confidentiality (as discussed in Chapter 6), it also may give rise to increased boundary-crossing behavior by both workers and clients, potentially of an "antisocial" character. It creates particular boundary concerns for social workers who believe that the disclosure of personal information may be useful in the helping process.

There are numerous ways in which traditional worker-client boundaries may be crossed in the current digital age. These include online, telephone, or video counseling, teletherapy, self-guided web-based interventions, electronic social networks such as Facebook, Instagram, and What's App, e-mail, or texting (Reamer, 2017). Other forms of social media used in our practice include virtual world games, and photo sharing and information management sites. These technological innovations create greater potential for conflicts of interest and dual relationships to emerge.

Unfortunately, standards of practice have not kept pace with rapid technological developments (Boddy & Dominelli, 2017). Recent concerns about the role of Facebook, Google, Instagram, and Twitter in spreading false or misleading information further complicates this issue (Roose, 2020; Voshel & Wesala, 2015). In response, NASW (National Association of Social Workers, 2017) recently published standards on the use of technology in practice for the first time.

The ubiquitous presence of the internet has also dramatically increased the possibility that unintended boundary challenges may arise. A social worker may have an unanticipated virtual encounter with a client or former client in an online support group, chat room, or dating service. It is also possible that a social work could meet a client or constituent while shopping online, participating in a virtual conference or interactive podcast, or playing a group video game. As our interconnected world gets smaller daily, the potential to develop overlapping relationships is more likely to occur and raise difficult unanticipated ethical issues.

For example, is it ever ethically appropriate for a social worker and client to share a group social media site? Is there an enhanced ethical risk in providing services electronically or "meeting" with a client or constituent online outside of scheduled appointments, even for professional reasons? Does a social worker trespass professional boundaries if they search for personal information about a client on the internet in order to clarify some ambiguities in the

FIGURE 9.2. The Use of the Internet in Practice Has Complicated Boundary Issues

client's background? To what extent does a social worker violate ethical obligations if they self-disclose in order to increase their rapport with clients, particularly if clients can obtain personal information about them online, even unintentionally?

Using the Internet for Oneself

A related set of issues involves our personal use of the internet (Reamer, 2015a). This issue has particular salience for younger social workers who have grown up with the internet yet often fail to realize the risks involved in its use. Above all, social workers need to consider the possible consequences of sharing personal information for their professional reputation, their agency's public image, and the well-being of third parties. On a personal level, this concerns not merely the immediate consequences of certain forms of self-disclosure, which may be temporarily embarrassing, but the long-term effects on their career prospects. This may be an unpleasant reality, but we now know that nothing ever disappears forever from the virtual world.

Many social workers still fail to recognize how easily accessible to clients and former clients the information they post on the internet is, and how clients may distort the information's innocent original purposes and undermine the goals of service. As a result, some authors suggest that social workers avoid all communication with clients over social media. This may not be possible, however, in the current digital environment (Groshong & Phillips, 2015), particularly when we have shifted most social services online during the pandemic. Kimball and Kim (2013) propose a somewhat more modest response to the challenge of maintaining virtual boundaries: "Social workers need to be aware of the identities they create and maintain in the realm of social media" (p. 185). In addition, social service organizations and educational institutions need to acknowledge the increasing importance of this issue and establish clear use policies.

Guidelines Regarding Self-Disclosure

The proscriptions against inappropriate self-disclosure, intimate relationships, and friendships with clients have long been central to social work ethics. The NASW *Code of Ethics* clearly states these proscriptions as well as those that may create conflicts of interests, especially of a financial nature (Reamer, 2015b). Kimball and Kim (2013, p. 187) suggest five criteria to guide social workers and students as to what information to share on social networking sites:

1. The type of information to be shared and its potential effects
2. The reasons for sharing this information (i.e., its benefits or intended outcomes)
3. The persons whom you want to see this information and for what reasons
4. The location(s) where you will share this information
5. The guidelines provided by the NASW *Code* or agency policies regarding information sharing

In a similar vein, Reamer (2012) urges social workers to examine this issue from a consequentialist perspective. We should consider what specific needs we intend to address through our self-disclosure and who is the intended beneficiary. He recommends that practitioners seek the advice of peers and supervisors for assistance in this regard.

When determining how much and what type of information to disclose online, it is important to be sensitive to the level of intimacy that is appropriate to the particular circumstances of the client, potential differences in cultural norms, and assessment of what consequences might ensue for the worker-client relationship and the safety of both parties. In addition, a social worker should determine over what period such self-disclosure should take place. Would an initial act of self-disclosure create an expectation of further revelations that might permanently alter the character of the professional relationship?

FOR REFLECTION
Think about how comfortable you are using self-disclosure in your work. What would you be willing to disclose and under what circumstances? What have you disclosed in the past to clients or colleagues? If you could, what information would you withhold now?

Using the Internet in Practice

Despite its ethical risks and the different type of practice skills required, the internet provides certain indisputable benefits for practice in today's context, particularly during the current pandemic. For clients who may be averse to discussing intimate issues in person, it can be a more effective form of practice. For others, who live at a great distance from service providers or have schedules that make it more challenging to attend sessions in person, it can be more efficient. Online counseling can also provide workers with more time to reflect on what they have learned from clients and to prepare better for subsequent sessions.

Many long-standing boundary rules, however, do not reflect the new social and technological realities that shape contemporary practice or their ethical implications. As discussed earlier in this chapter, boundary issues that may arise from the use of the internet to provide services include the risk of contact outside of office hours, the effects of virtual counseling on the nature of the worker-client relationship, and the possibility of both worker and client obtaining information about each other through the web or social media. There is also a risk of violating confidentiality due to the manner in which we now store and transmit information. (See Chapter 6 for a discussion of this issue.)

Despite its oft-cited benefits, the growing use of cybercommunication (ICT) has led to heightened concerns about boundary issues, especially in clinical practice in health, behavioral health, and educational settings, because of its potential risks. It increases the possibility that clients will get "the impression that their relationship [with the social worker] is fluid and not bound by the parameters that historically defined professional-client relationships" (Reamer, 2013b, p. 13, quoted in Fantus and Mishna, 2013, p. 473) and "that clients may have more information about a practitioner than what the practitioner has disclosed" (Fantus & Mishna, p. 473). The spread of ICT may also produce increased opportunity for unanticipated contacts outside the normal service process as discussed above.

How Far Should We Go to Help?

You are a counselor in a street-front program affiliated with a large medical center that provides a range of services to individuals coping with substance abuse and its consequences. One of your clients, Hector L., is a young man who has made considerable progress in the agency's program. He has stopped using heroin, enrolled in a local community college, and been steadily employed part time for the past 6 months. He maintains a good relationship with his girlfriend and the young daughter he fathered. You consider him one of the program's "successes."

The agency has a policy that clients who miss three consecutive individual or group counseling sessions are automatically subject to termination from the program. The agency states this policy clearly before individuals enter the program and reminds them of it on a regular basis. Hector is aware of the policy because two members of his group have been dismissed from the program for failure to attend sessions regularly.

To your surprise and chagrin, Hector has unexpectedly and without explanation missed the last three weekly sessions. You tried to contact him after each missed appointment by email and text, but he has not responded. You are concerned about his well-being and whether he will be able to continue in the program after violating established agency policy.

Questions:

1. Would you be engaging in a boundary violation if you searched for Hector online to determine if he was safe?

2. Would it be a boundary violation if you tried to contact his girlfriend or another member of his family whose phone number you have from Hector's intake interview?

3. If you decided to search for Hector online, what if in the course of the search you find information about him that he had not previously disclosed that, if disclosed, might have disqualified him from the program?

4. If you located Hector and persuaded him to resume attending weekly sessions, would the extra effort you made to keep him in the program constitute a boundary violation and be unfair to the other program participants who are "playing by the rules"?

The ethical issues in this case underscore the importance of having an open discussion with clients about online privacy at the onset of the service relationship. They also challenge us to think about the effects of our emotions on our ability to treat all of our clients in a consistent professional manner.

Ethical Practice in Small, Rural, or Isolated Communities

A third criticism of rigid boundary restrictions applies to practitioners who live and work in small towns, rural areas, or close-knit, often homogeneous communities. Long-standing concerns about the propriety of dual relationships become more complicated when considered in the context of isolated or insular communities (Luse, 2018; Barnett, 2017a). In these communities, there are usually few practitioners and limited resources. Dual relationships are more likely to occur and may be impossible to avoid because of the multiple roles people possess. Certain dual relationships, such as memberships in the same church, may even be necessary or desirable in some circumstances to gain and maintain trust with one's clients (Sanders, 2017). In addition, "in some communities a worker may have little choice but either to deny service to a client or to negotiate the difficulties of a dual relationship" (Halverson & Brownlee, 2010, p. 248). The recent emphasis on greater collaboration and more egalitarian worker-client relationships also raises ethical challenges in this regard (Dominelli, 2017; Saar-Heiman et al., 2017).

To manage the tension between ethical and effective practice, social workers in such communities have to develop a more nuanced view of their relationships with clients and recognize that a dual relationship might even be beneficial in some circumstances because they enhance their understanding of a client's situation (Freud & Krug, 2002b). One way practitioners in these communities address this issue is by distinguishing between the provision of services that are not especially invasive and where clients are least vulnerable and those that potentially place a client or a client's family member at legal, financial, or health risk. They also consider the nature of the dual relationship and the community's possible perception of the relationship (Halverson & Brownlee, 2010). In sum, as these various examples illustrate, in our complex practice environments there are important distinctions between boundary crossings that are clearly unethical and potentially harmful and those that may be impossible to avoid and even helpful.

Implications for Social Work Education

In social work education, there is growing concern that boundary issues will increase as a generation of students raised in an environment in which a great deal of personal information is shared on the internet enters the professional practice community (Reamer, 2019c). A major consequence of this generational transformation is that "it is ... easier than ever for social work students and practitioners to blur the boundaries between personal and professional relationships online" (Voshel & Wesala, 2015, p. 70). For example, students and the clients in their internships may Google each other. While the former may be somewhat constrained by their awareness of ethical guidelines, there are no similar constraints on clients. Students or younger practitioners may also hesitate to deny a client's "friend request" on Facebook. This raises challenges regarding confidentiality and privacy that could have deleterious consequences on the trust foundation of their practice relationship or the student's reputation.

To avoid or minimize such occurrences, it is important for educators to stress the importance of students separating their personal and professional media identities and avoiding the posting of any content on the internet, such as photos of themselves at a party, that they would not feel comfortable sharing with the public at large. This concern extends beyond Facebook, Instagram, and Twitter accounts to personal blogs. One solution social work ethicists propose is the creation of two Facebook pages and profiles—one for professional purposes and one for personal use.

Summary

This chapter discussed the importance of maintaining appropriate professional boundaries and avoiding conflicts of interest in a practice environment of increasing cultural and technological complexity. It examined the purpose of professional boundaries in social work practice and how recent changes in the context of practice have produced certain definitional ambiguities and technical challenges that complicate the application of this ethical principle. It also discussed the various ways in which dual relationships and conflicts of interest may arise and provided guidelines for determining under what circumstances ethical proscriptions should continue to apply.

The next chapter addresses a different set of ethical issues that involve professional relationships—those with colleagues and employers. It also explores an issue that has particular relevance in today's political environment—whistleblowing.

Reflection Exercise I: Why Have Professional Boundaries?

1. What do you think are the main purposes of ethical guidelines regarding boundaries, particularly in an era when individuals disclose a great deal of personal information on social media?
2. To what extent should these guidelines be rigidly enforced or flexible? By whom should they be enforced or monitored?
3. Should we apply these guidelines differently to different vulnerable populations? If so, under what circumstances? How?
4. For how long should these boundary restrictions apply?
5. What constitutes a "client"? Should the rules be identical in all forms of practice?
6. What should we do in the event of "accidental encounters" with clients?
7. What is the responsibility of clients in this regard?

Reflection Exercise II: Creating New Boundary Rules

In small groups, discuss and try to reach consensus on the following issues if you were to revise the NASW *Code of Ethics*:

1. What behaviors regarding boundaries should the *Code of Ethics* absolutely prohibit?
2. What type of dual relationships are permissible? Under what circumstances?
3. What constitutes an inappropriate relationship with a client or constituent?
4. What criteria should we use to determine how flexible boundary rules should be?
5. What guidelines should we set regarding the use of social media for professional or personal reasons?
6. What guidelines should we set regarding future relationships with former clients or constituents?
7. In developing these guidelines, to what extent should we consider cultural differences about the nature of professional relationships?

Credits

Fig. 9.1: Copyright © 2014 Depositphotos/stevanovicigor.
Fig. 9.2: Copyright © 2013 Depositphotos/vook.

Obligations to Third Parties—Colleagues, Employers, Community, Profession, and Society

Introduction

In previous chapters, we discussed the ethical challenges that occur when practitioners must choose between two competing or conflicting "rights" or "wrongs." As the following case illustrates, this chapter addresses another of the most difficult and emotionally wrenching ethical challenges social workers face: those that involve the resolution of conflicts of duty to different parties. Because our practice does not take place in hermetically sealed rooms, in which the only relevant actors are ourselves and our clients or constituents, the interests of third parties—individuals, groups, communities, organizations, and society as a whole—inevitably complicate the process of ethical decision-making. This chapter will focus on such issues as divided professional loyalties—to colleagues, employers, community, and society—and the ever-controversial topic of whistleblowing.

ETHICAL DILEMMA 10.1

The Impaired Colleague
(Based, in part, on a true story)

You are the executive director of a multiservice non-profit agency. One of your senior staff, Mr. P., is close to retirement. As the founding director of the agency, staff and community members hold him in high regard. Recently, however, several staff members have told you, in confidence, that Mr. P. has appeared to be intoxicated at meetings. When you spoke with

Mr. P. about this, he denied ever drinking on the job and angrily stormed out of your office.

A few days later, he apologizes and tells you that he has been under enormous stress lately because a drunk driver killed his grandson while Mr. P. was holding the child in the backseat of his daughter's car. He swears that he has never been intoxicated when working with clients or speaking with community members. Based on reliable evidence, you remain concerned that his performance was impaired. You believe that if you took no action it would set a bad example for other staff, fail to serve the best interests of clients, and jeopardize the agency's reputation with the community.

Questions:

1. What duties conflict in this situation?
2. How would you decide what to do?
3. What ethical principles would you prioritize?
4. How would you apply these principles to other similar cases?

This situation illustrates the importance of ethics as a process, not merely a set of rules. Determining an ethical course of action depends as much, or more, in this situation on how you decide as it does on what principles guide your decision. If you took a deontological approach, the values you chose to prioritize—for example, protecting the well-being of clients—would take precedence over the protection of a respected colleague. A consequentialist approach, on the other hand, would require an assessment of the short- and long-term effects of sanctioning Mr. P. on him (given his emotional state), his clients, other staff, and the organization as a whole. This would be difficult to do, as you could not predict all the possible consequences.

Obligations to Colleagues

As this case illustrates, conflicts of duties do not exist solely in practice with individuals and families. Social workers, particularly those employed by nonprofit organizations, must frequently negotiate the challenges created by the organizational culture and climate, by the stresses produced by externally imposed accountability demands, and by the different roles and relationships that exist among funders, policy makers, colleagues, service recipients, and members of the surrounding community (Banks, 2016; Olson et al., 2016). In policy advocacy and community organizing, there are often conflicts that involve such issues as informed consent, paternalistic decision-making, group or community self-determination, truth telling, and clashes between our duties to constituents and allies and our obligations to the law and to the broader society (Hoefer, 2019b; Segal-Reich et al., 2019). In an environment characterized by fiscal scarcity and sharp political divisions, conflicts also emerge due to recurrent competition among groups for power, resources, attention, status, and credit (Emanuel et al., 2018). Unless you are the rare individual whose work is exclusively in private practice, and you have no contact with other professionals as sources or recipients of referrals, or belong to community networks or professional organizations, collegial relationships form an essential component of your practice. Often these relationships become friendships, which can further complicate our ethical obligations under certain circumstances as the following case illustrates.

ETHICAL DILEMMA 10.2   *Should You Help a Friend?*

You are a social worker assigned to the emergency room of a community hospital that is besieged with individuals who have tested positive for the coronavirus or who have symptoms that indicate they may have contracted Covid-19. You have a warm collegial relationship with the doctors and nurses in the

ER, who often rely on your judgment in a crisis and respect your commitment to ethical principles. The hospital is facing an increasing shortage of critical protective equipment and test kits as well as a decreasing number of available beds, particularly in the intensive care and critical care units. Staff have been advised to restrict testing and admission to the most seriously ill persons.

One day, a close friend calls you and asks for a special favor. Her mother, Ms. R., has been exhibiting some moderate flu-like symptoms and she is very concerned that she may have contracted Covid-19. She asks you to use your influence to get her tested and admitted to the hospital where you work. You are very fond of Ms. R.; she comforted you when your parents died and

is still vital despite her advancing age. Hospital protocol, however, requires the application of strict criteria before administering the test or admitting individuals for the duration of the public health emergency. Although you could probably persuade the resident physicians in the ER to make an exception, Ms. R. does not at present meet those criteria.

Questions:
1. What are the conflicting duties in this situation? To whom do you owe them?
2. What ethical principles and decision-making framework would you apply?
3. To what extent would you apply these principles and this framework in related situations?

The difference between this ethical dilemma and the previous one is not merely that the former involves a duty to a colleague and the latter a duty to a close friend. At least two other factors further complicate the situation. One is the existence of established protocols by the hospital, which you would violate if you granted your friend's request and placed your duty to your friend above that of following rules to which you have already acceded. A second factor is the likelihood that your decision to provide a scarce resource to your friend's mother would affect unknown third parties—other patients—who have greater need. Other factors to consider include the potential effects on your relationship with colleagues and on the willingness of staff to comply with hospital policy if the exception you made became more common.

Obligations to the Community

This situation illustrates that under some circumstances, our ethical duty extends beyond our friends and the individuals with whom we work to include unknown third parties or the community as a whole whom our decisions may affect in unforeseen and unintended ways. The following case demonstrates this type of conflict, in which the imposition of a prior legal obligation further complicates the dilemma (Pringle & Thompson, 2019; Carr & Goosey, 2017).

ETHICAL DILEMMA 10.3   *The Impaired Social Worker*
(Based on a true story)

You are the president of the board of directors of a nonprofit agency, XYZ Crisis Center. Last year, after a lengthy and somewhat contentious search process, the board hired a new CEO, Ms. S., to replace the

organization's well-respected outgoing director. Ms. S. got off to a good start, but about 4 months into her tenure, senior staff began to express serious concerns about her erratic behaviors. These included sending the staff a 40-page, single-spaced memo for them to review two days before a monthly staff meeting. Troubling evidence also emerged that she was attempting to divide the staff and board along racial lines.

Upon returning from a family vacation one evening, you received an urgent call from a senior staff member asking if he and three other senior staff could meet you right away regardless of the hour. In a lengthy post-midnight conversation, they related incidents at which Ms. S.'s behavior revealed additional disturbing qualities. Their revelations produced a challenging situation for you and the board as a whole. The agency's personnel policies stipulated that all new employees have a 6-month probationary period, after which the organization can only terminate them for cause, which made firing an employee more difficult. Ms. S.'s probationary period was nearly over; the board needed to make a quick decision on her tenure as executive director.

After numerous late-night meetings, the board unanimously voted to fire Ms. S. before the end of her probationary period. Shortly thereafter, she sued the agency for wrongful termination. To settle the suit, the board agreed to write a general letter of recommendation for Ms. S. and to pay her some monetary compensation. The settlement also required both parties not to discuss the matter with third parties. The board reluctantly complied with this agreement to close the matter and avoid bad publicity in the media. The settlement, therefore, imposed a legal obligation on the board and you, as its president, not to discuss the matter with anyone.

A year later at a professional conference, you meet a colleague who informs you in a casual conversation that her agency, ABC Services, is considering hiring Ms. S. as its executive director. The colleague indicates that she knows of Ms. S.'s employment history and asks what you think of her. You have serious concerns about the potential consequences if your colleague's organization hires Ms. S., but the legal settlement forbids you from discussing her performance or the reasons she left the agency.

Questions:

1. What are the ethical issues in this case?
2. To whom do you owe a duty? Which duties should take priority?
3. What would you do? On what ethical principles would you base your decision?
4. To what extent would you generalize these reasons to other similar situations?

This situation underscores the challenges involved whether one uses a deontological or a consequentialist approach; it also illustrates how they often intersect. If you select the former approach, you have to decide whether your duty to third parties—the staff and future clients of ABC Services—overrides your legal obligation to which you willingly and knowingly committed. Yet, in developing this hierarchy of duties, you also have to assess the potential consequences of your decision, but this is difficult because of several unknowns. These include whether Ms. S.'s behavior in her new job will be different, whether her behavior—whatever it might be—would damage the clients of ABC Services, and whether your violation of the terms of the settlement agreement will become public and, if so, with what consequences for you and the XYZ Center. You also have to determine if you can make this decision unilaterally, as the other board members signed the settlement agreement and could incur legal liability as well.

Obligations to Allies

Social workers employed by host institutions, such as hospitals or school systems, and community practitioners, particularly those who work in diverse communities and whose practice includes advocacy, often participate in a range of intergroup organizations, from collaborative programs to professional networks and coalitions. Maintaining good relationships with colleagues who are project partners or allies in multiorganizational coalitions is critical for their survival and success. Frequently, these individuals and the groups they represent possess different values and organizational cultures from those of the social work profession. Learning how to negotiate these value and cultural differences is an important practice skill (Diaz-Edelman, 2017; Gerassi et al., 2017; Song, 2016; Misca & Neamtu, 2016). These differences may also produce a conflict of duties as the following case illustrates.

ETHICAL DILEMMA 10.4　　　An Ethical Dilemma of Coalition Building (*Based in part on a true story*)

You are a community organizer who has been attempting for over a year to build a coalition that would advocate for the needs of the long-term unemployed and displaced workers and their families. You want to involve the local chapter of the construction workers' union in this coalition because you believe its participation is critical to the success of your organizing project. After considerable effort, you finally arrange a meeting at the union's headquarters with its leaders, including a number of shop stewards.

After some awkward introductions, several persons in the group make remarks of a racist nature about a coalition partner and potential beneficiaries of the coalition's advocacy efforts. You are clearly uncomfortable with these comments and want to make it clear that you do not share these views. From a strategic perspective, you are reluctant to jeopardize your

tenuous relationship with the union's leaders that might undermine the prospects of building a successful coalition. From an ethical perspective, you believe that failure to speak up would betray your duties to the profession, the other organizations in the coalition, and the people the coalition purports to assist.

Questions:
1. How would you frame the conflict of duties in this situation?
2. What would you do?
3. What are your reasons for your choice of action?
4. On what ethical principles is your decision based?
5. To what extent would you apply these principles to similar practice situations?

One of the things that makes this situation so difficult is the connection between what might be the best strategic decision and the most ethical course of action. From a short-term strategic perspective, it would probably be best to withhold your reaction to the racist comments until you had established a stronger relationship with the union. In the long term, however, failure to point out your concerns could undermine the coalition's success. If you believed that you had a higher duty to your professional values, the interests of third parties (people of color in the coalition), and your personal integrity, then you would call out what you regarded as unacceptable behavior despite its potential consequences for the success of the coalition, its intended beneficiaries, and your future relationship with the union. This would require you to make a quick decision about how to raise this difficult issue at the meeting.

Obligations to Employers

For decades, scholars and activists have pointed out the effects of sweeping political-economic and ideological developments on the nature of public and nonprofit organizations and their treatment of agency staff, service users, and other stakeholders. Scholars have referred to some of these consequences as the "marketization of social policy" or the "marketization of the welfare state" (Harris, 2018; Schram, 2018). Fabricant and Burghardt (2015) described this phenomenon as the "industrialization" of social service work. Soss and colleagues (2011) assessed the effects of what they termed "neoliberal paternalism" on marginalized populations, particularly racial minorities and low-income groups, who are more likely to become involved in the child welfare, criminal justice, and public assistance systems (Hennigan, 2017). These structural transformations have influenced the character of social work at all levels and in all fields of practice (Harlow, 2018; Lawler, 2018). Citing Ferguson (2008), Banks (2011) analyzed the "erosion of practice premised on values of social justice and human dignity" due to increasing managerialism and privatization in the social services field (p. 132). These changes have had a significant effect on the ability of nonprofit social justice organizations to fulfill their original mission and produced new ethical challenges for social workers (Willner, 2019; Thompson & Wadley, 2018).

Particularly after the Great Recession of 2007–2009, the resultant emphasis on fiscal austerity, even in the face of growing socioeconomic inequality, led the United States to adopt social welfare policies that focus on controlling recipients' behavior rather than addressing their well-being (Berrick, 2017). In combination with the resurgent emphasis on personal and organizational accountability, increased financial pressures have created new ethical challenges for social workers, particularly in the nonprofit sector (Baines, 2017). This has often produced a depersonalization of practice that complicates the application of ethical principles in our work with individuals and families, particularly those from vulnerable and excluded groups (Hartley & Lamarche, 2018). Even in the face of public health or economic crises, the language of government policies and media descriptions of people in need frequently rationalize official indifference and promote bureaucratic routine in lieu of individualization (Allcott & Kessler, 2019; Farrell et al., 2016). Persistent resistance to the expansion of unemployment and food stamp benefits to workers who lost their jobs due to the economic consequences of the pandemic is a recent example of this phenomenon.

As a result, social workers in virtually all industrialized nations have become increasingly aware that "conflicts may arise between [our] legal duties, social work values, and organizational requirements" (Preston-Shoot, 2011, p. 177). In response to fiscal austerity and other government policies that violate the profession's fundamental values, social service agencies, especially in the private, for-profit sector, have frequently circumvented their statutory obligations to clients, particularly in fields like child welfare (Kirton, 2018). Unrelenting pressure for fiscal accountability and a lack of clarity about how to resolve differences between legal and ethical obligations have led to less transparency in the operations of large public sector organizations and a consequent weakening of their professed commitment to social justice (Rummery, 2016).

Important differences exist, however, between nonprofit and for-profit organizations in this regard. These differences appear in several key components of their organizational culture, such as their stated mission and goals, their relationship to service users and the public, and their reasons for establishing and maintaining ethical standards. They also influence the organization's conception of a service itself—how it defines a "need" and "helping," and how it evaluates the effectiveness of its response to need (Miller-Stevens et al., 2018; Green, 1999).

For example, both the legal requirements (to maintain their special tax status) and the mission statements of nonprofit agencies reflect their overriding commitment to public service.

Although for-profit organizations may similarly express a commitment to serve their customers, their primary "clients" are their shareholders or owners. In this light, for-profit organizations may regard their programs merely as vehicles to produce and distribute service "commodities" (Lavalette & Ferguson, 2018). For-profit hospitals, nursing homes, and childcare centers are prime examples of this perspective. These distinctions raise thorny ethical questions for contemporary social workers: Is it ethical to make a financial profit from services to vulnerable populations even if the payment for these services comes from a third party, such as the government, a foundation grant, or a private insurance company? Is it ethical or emotionally healthy for social workers to work for a for-profit organization that makes its resource allocation decisions based on self-interest rather than public service? (Miller et al., 2017; Reisch, 1991)

On a positive note, a decade ago Banks (2011) viewed increased interest in ethics within the profession as "part of a progressive movement to ... critique new public management through [an emphasis on] the role of social workers as active moral agents working for social justice" (p. 1). This trend contrasted sharply with the managerial focus on ethics as a tool to regulate the conduct of social workers and their clients. Yet, as Preston-Shoot (2011) discovered, the number of social workers who openly criticize their agencies—for example, as whistleblowers— remains surprisingly low, and the issue of whistleblowing has been controversial within the profession and other fields for decades (Raymond et al., 2017; Ash, 2016; Reamer & Siegel, 1992).

This is not merely an ethical error by individual social workers or a reflection of their unwillingness to take risks. Sometimes it results from a variety of intimidation rituals, including bullying by superiors (Tiitinen, 2020). British scholars refer to this phenomenon as a "corruption of care"; they have identified four effects of this phenomenon. There is increasing evidence of similar developments in the United States. One is a reassertion of the long-standing tendency to stereotype certain client groups, the consequence of which is greater indifference to their needs. In the United States, the treatment of welfare and food stamp recipients, individuals experiencing homelessness or chronic unemployment, and victims of opioid abuse illustrate this trend.

A second trend is toward heightened bureaucratic control and the repression of criticism and dissent within large social service organizations in both the public and nonprofit sectors, sometimes masked by the popular emphasis on "civility." The purging of scientific experts and agency watchdogs (e.g., climate change researchers in the Environmental Protection Agency and inspector generals in major federal departments) by the Trump administration and persistent attacks on experts by its media supporters illustrate this behavior and set the tone for the entire nation. Reports of similar actions in local and state government organizations, including public hospitals, have surfaced recently as well (Hutchinson et al., 2019).

A third trend is the erosion of discretion among practitioners in the interest of fiscal efficiency, risk reduction, and policy conformity. This is a recurrent pattern in the history of U.S. social welfare since at least the end of World War II. A final trend is that frontline staff now bear more responsibility for the maintenance of their organization's ethical standards, a responsibility that administrative leaders formerly shared (Lawrence, 2019; Preston-Shoot, 2011). This places an additional burden on social workers who already feel the pressure of working with expanding caseloads and more multiproblem clients in the context of resource scarcity.

Most current frameworks for ethical decision-making, however, assume a generally benign organizational environment and focus on individual cases rather than the sociopolitical and agency context in which these cases arise. Because this assumption is not always valid, it is important for both clients and staff to possess as much information as possible in order to hold program administrators accountable. As Banks (2008) pointed out, "matters of … ethical judgment and decision-making cannot be divorced from the political and policy contexts in which they take place" (quoted in Preston-Shoot, 2011, p. 180).

Increasingly, social workers, especially those in the public sector, are not autonomous agents; agency policies and procedures, the organizational culture, and legislative mandates frequently circumscribe practitioners' choices (Juujärvi et al., 2020). Critical variables in resolving the ethical challenges these stressors produce are how susceptible the organization is to political pressure, how compatible its mission and goals are with broader social policy goals, and whether the agency has historically complied with or challenged externally imposed policy requirements (Bowman & West, 2018).

It is unfortunate that despite recent revisions, existing professional ethical codes provide insufficient guidance to resolve these vexing dilemmas. Practice guidelines are similarly ambiguous about how to determine when violations of ethical principles have occurred, the nature of organizational or personal accountability, and the distinction between ethical and legal obligations. This absence is particularly acute in circumstances where social workers have to address multiple, often contradictory pressures, and satisfy divided loyalties.

Faced with these conditions, it is understandable why many social workers fear questioning these policies openly and tend to comply—however reluctantly—with them rather than follow professional norms, often with deleterious consequences for clients. By viewing these tensions as the result of external political choices beyond their control rather than as ethical choices, a form of apolitical practice paralysis sets in that makes it more difficult to challenge potentially unprincipled organizational activities or the policies that influence them (Karagkounis, 2019; Reisch & Jani, 2012).

A particularly compelling example of this development involves social workers in the military, who face a unique situation of divided loyalties especially when they serve in a combat zone (Olson, 2018). Although there is superficial similarity between military ethics and social work ethics, sharp differences exist, particularly regarding the concept of social justice. Military codes of conduct emphasize sacrificing individual freedom for the good of the unit, while social work values attempt to balance the preservation of individual autonomy with the protection of the common good.

Other ethical issues in such circumstances include concerns over confidentiality, the ability of soldiers to exercise self-determination, conflicts with military authorities, and appropriate boundaries. These issues are particularly acute in small units (Olson, 2014). Unfortunately, research by Simmons and Rycraft (2010) found that ethical approaches to resolving such dilemmas tend to take a back seat to clinical judgment.

Social work scholars and educators suggest that the solution to such dilemmas for individual social workers lies in synthesizing an ethic of justice and an ethic of care (Hay, 2017; Segal & Wagaman, 2017). To do so effectively, however, social workers will need to combine ethical literacy and legal literacy. The latter involves knowledge of employment or military law (to prevent coercive measures that require practitioners to act contrary to their professional ethics) and familiarity with legislation, administrative regulations, and court decisions that affect policies and services in their agencies (Pringle & Thompson, 2019). Ethical literacy "requires both external supports, such as codes, but also personal reasoning and responsibility for the content and effects of administrative actions" (Preston-Shoot, 2011, p. 188). This suggestion has important implications for the structure of social service organizations and the content of social work education (Braye et al., 2017).

Writing from the perspective of the so-called independent sector (nonprofit or "voluntary" organizations), Sandra Gray (n.d., pp. 3–4) recommends that in order to maintain their ethical integrity, organizations should create established systems that foster personal and collective accountability. These systems would possess the following qualities: disclosure (of vital information to external and internal publics); analysis (monitoring and evaluating the organization's activities on a regular basis); dissemination (helping the public understand ethical issues and communicating the organization's values); and formal sanctions (a willingness of organizations to "blow the whistle" on themselves).

Finally, changes in the practice environment have implications for the academic community. In teaching future practitioners, social work educators need to reinforce the importance of a critical, structural perspective on practice and the fundamental roles social action and political awareness play in all forms of social work, including the role "politics" plays in promoting or resisting organizational change. Teaching conceptual frameworks for ethical decision-making is, therefore, a necessary, but insufficient, pedagogical strategy unless educators supplement these frameworks with skills students can apply when confronted with the ethical dilemmas they will inevitably face in their practice.

In sum, constructing ethical systems within our organizations and communities involves (1) open disclosure of critical information to internal and external publics, (2) ongoing monitoring and evaluation of our organization and the effectiveness of its programs and practices, (3) democratic forms of information dissemination, and (4) formal mechanisms and processes to apply sanctions to employees when necessary. The goals are to build and sustain the public's confidence and trust, which is always fragile; maintain consistent ethical standards; and balance service effectiveness, resource efficiency, and organizational survival. The following case illustrates the challenge of balancing these competing priorities.

ETHICAL DILEMMA 10.5   Should You Accept "Tainted" Money?

You are the assistant director of a financially strapped, multipurpose nonprofit agency that serves predominantly low-income individuals and families. Due to the recent loss of government grants and contracts, the agency faces the real possibility of major staff layoffs and the cutback or elimination of long-standing programs. At today's executive committee meeting, the CEO informs those present that a wealthy businessperson in the community offered to give the organization a multimillion-dollar gift provided that the programs established with these resources bear the name of their family. This donation would relieve the agency's

current fiscal plight and eliminate the need for program reductions and layoffs.

At first, you are elated at the news, but upon learning the identity of the potential donor, your mood changes. The company they own has been sued a number of times by female employees both for wage discrimination based on race and gender and for tolerating a hostile work environment. Charges of sexual harassment have been leveled against several company executives, including the owner. While none of these charges have been proven and the suits against the company are still making their way through the court system, the public is well aware of them because of frequent coverage in the media.

After the meeting, your boss calls you into her office. She noticed your changed facial expression when you heard the identity of the donor and asks your opinion as to whether the agency should accept the gift. She has to let the potential donor know shortly if your organization will accept the gift. Otherwise, they will offer the funds to another agency in the community that has signalled its readiness to accept them.

Questions:
1. What are the ethical issues in this situation? Which duties are in conflict?
2. What would you advise your boss?
3. On what ethical principles and using which ethical decision-making framework would you rely to make your decision?

In the above scenario, what is your higher duty? Is it to the agency, its clients, and your colleagues, who would clearly benefit from this donation? Is it maintaining your professional values of nondiscrimination that you would violate if you recommend that the agency accept the proffered gift? Another factor to consider is whether you have to make a decision at all in this situation. You might also consider the possible consequences if you abstained from expressing an opinion. Would your boss interpret your silence as consent? If she did and accepted the donation, would you be passively violating your ethical principles?

Regarding these issues, Sweifach et al. (2015) point at that "within the workplace, central to the principle of fidelity (one of the six core principles of social work) is the obligation, in good faith, to keep promises made to an employer" (p. 5). In the above situation, what implied promise have you made to your employer? Is it to protect and promote the interests of the agency and the people it serves or to preserve its underlying mission and values?

Another issue to consider is whether fidelity to an employer without limit? What does fidelity mean in the above situation? What is your ethical duty if your employer makes a decision that could potentially harm the agency's clients or constituents, even indirectly? Unfortunately, the NASW *Code of Ethics* is ambiguous on this point. As discussed in Chapter 4, the *Code* makes the client's interest primary in the resolution of ethical dilemmas even as it establishes an ethical obligation to the employing agency. Regarding the latter, it merely states, "Social workers should *generally adhere* to commitments made to employers and employing organizations" (3.09(a), emphasis added). In the above case, however, it is not clear exactly what these commitments are or how extensive they are.

There are situations, therefore, when two equally reasonable and ethically acceptable choices conflict. There are also situations when a course of action might violate our duties to clients and employers, even as it fulfills our ethical imperative to pursue social justice (Strier & Bershtling, 2016). One such situation is participation in a strike (Beckett et al., 2017). In such circumstances, it is important to assess the entire context, including the past and present behavior of management; whether the agency can still meet clients' needs in the event of a strike; and the long-range consequences of settling labor-management issues for staff, clients, the organization, and other nonsocial work colleagues. (See Ethical Dilemma 11.5 in Chapter 11 for a discussion of other ethical issues such conflicts produce.) Educators should help students become familiar with the ethical challenges of such situations should they be forced to make a difficult decision in their internships or future jobs.

Ethical vs. Legal Obligations

Sometimes, as discussed elsewhere in this chapter and throughout the book, a conflict exists between our duty to the law and a duty to our ethical code or fundamental values. Situations in which we feel compelled to enforce an unjust or unfeeling law or policy fall into this category. For example, imagine the ethical dilemmas you might face if you were a social worker during the Jim Crow era in the American South, during Apartheid in South Africa, or under the Nuremburg Laws in Nazi Germany. Although of a less extreme nature, conflicts may also occur when different types of law—civil and criminal—create incompatible obligations (Gewirth, 2001). As the following case illustrates, the existence of such conflicts underscores the importance of understanding the difference between ethical and legal obligations and the consequences of these different obligations for our relationships to the people with whom we work, and to the organizations, communities, and societies in which this work occurs.

ETHICAL DILEMMA 10.6

When Is It Ethical to Violate an Unjust Law?

You are a social worker in a nonprofit family service agency during the recent coronavirus pandemic. The governor of your state has issued an executive order that the state would not provide "nonessential" health care during the current state of emergency in order to preserve scarce resources for those afflicted with Covid-19. He classified abortions under the category of "nonessential" health care. Individuals or organizations who violate this order could be fined, prosecuted, or lose their operating license. National reproductive rights, health care, and civil liberties organizations, as well as NASW, have decried this action. Yet, because your organization receives the bulk of its financial resources from the state, the CEO has advised staff to comply with the order.

One of your clients recently informed you that she desperately wants an abortion. She is a single mother with three children who has lost her job due to the economic shutdown. She can neither afford nor care for another child. You have a friend who is a hospital social worker in a neighboring state that has not implemented similar restrictions on access to abortions. You speak with her about your client without identifying her name. Your friend offers to assist your client obtain a safe, legal abortion, but you would have to drive her across state lines to the clinic where your friend works. Your agency allows staff to transport clients to appointments but only if they use agency vehicles for a purpose that is consistent with agency policies. You confide in a senior colleague about your dilemma. She points out that you could lose your job and the agency could face severe sanctions if your supervisor found out that you assisted your client and used agency resources in violation of state law. You acknowledge the risk but are also aware of your ethical duty to put the client's interest first and respect her right to self-determination.

Questions:
1. How would you frame the different conflicts of duty involved in this situation?
2. What course of action would you take?
3. How would you justify your decision?
4. Would you apply your rationale to other situations in which the law conflicted with your ethical obligations?

In the above case, you have to determine both what values would have priority and assess the effects on your client, third parties, and yourself if you applied these values. Using a consequentialist approach, you have to decide if the benefits your client would obtain would outweigh the

Ethics/Values   Law

FIGURE 10.1. Ethical and Legal Obligations
Both Overlap and Conflict

potential harms that would occur to your agency's clients and staff if it lost state funding. This demonstrates one of the difficulties involved in developing and applying a utilitarian calculus to resolve thorny ethical situations. On the other hand, if you applied a deontological approach, what values would you place at the top of your hierarchy? If protecting a client's well-being and that of her family would take priority over the interests of the organization, would you apply this lexical ordering to all practice situations?

As discussed in previous chapters, there are a number of other practice situations when legal and ethical obligations collide. For example, professional malpractice may occur when a social worker is derelict in the fulfillment of a legal duty (such as reporting an incident of child or sexual abuse) and there is a direct connection between this failure and resultant harm or injury to a client or third party. If such a violation occurs, several types of sanctions may result. These include the filing of a complaint before the state's licensing board or the state chapter of NASW, a civil lawsuit, and, in unusual circumstances, a criminal charge. It is important to note here that different standards of proof apply in each of these possible scenarios and that the accused has different rights, particularly regarding confidentiality (Pringle & Thompson, 2019; Carr & Goosey, 2017; Dickson, 2009).

As discussed in Chapter 6, there are other circumstances, such as when practitioners are obliged to release confidential material, that are more ambiguous. The NASW *Code* (1.07(j)) states that social workers should not release records or obey a subpoena without a client's consent or receipt of a court order. Here it is important to understand the distinction between a subpoena and a court order to testify. We are legally obligated to respond to the latter under all circumstances; there are justifications, permitted by court decisions (cf. *Jaffee v. Redmond*, 1996), when we can ignore a subpoena.

Conflicts between legal and ethical obligations are particularly common in the field of child protection, although most cases of child abuse fall within the area of civil, not criminal, law. A consequence is that that the constitutional rights of criminal defendants are not automatically available to individuals investigated by child welfare authorities. In addition, while both legal and ethical codes have similar goals—to promote acceptable behavior and sanction unacceptable behavior—their goals emerge from different sources and have different enforcement mechanisms. Violations of the law and violations of established codes are not identical; different bodies determine whether a violation has occurred and what sanction is appropriate. Political decentralization and the variety of professional codes of ethics in the United States make these conflicts more difficult to resolve and make ethical violations more difficult to enforce in a consistent manner.

In the United States, for example, all states require the reporting of child abuse and neglect, but they apply mandatory reporting laws differently to individuals from different occupations. In some states, only certain professionals bear this obligation, while in others all persons must report. A further complication arises where states have extended reporting requirements to any underage sexual activity or defined substance abuse by a pregnant woman as reportable child abuse. These situations underscore the "conflict between a legal requirement to report and ethical mandates of client confidentiality and privacy" (Dickson, 2009, p. 270).

Additionally, as Dickson (2009) points out, it is possible that an act "could be either ethical or unethical under the same code of ethics depending upon the ethical standard applied" (p. 267; see also Lipworth & Montgomery, 2018; Reisch, 2014a). For example, the use of coercion to remove a child from the custody of a biological parent under investigation for child abuse can be viewed as acting in the "client's interest" (i.e., in the "best interests of the child"). On the other hand, in some child welfare cases, we could interpret the treatment of the parent as a violation of the broader ethical principles of human dignity and justice.

FIGURE 10.2. The Pressure to Satisfy Ethical and Legal Obligations Often Comes from Different Sources

The NASW *Code*, however, offers only several vague prescriptions for addressing such conflicts. It states:

> When such conflicts [between agency policies or relevant laws or regulations] occur, social workers must make a *responsible effort* to resolve the conflict in a manner that is *consistent with the values, principles, and standards expressed in this Code*. If a *reasonable solution* of the conflict does not appear possible, social workers should seek *proper consultation* before making a decision (emphasis added). (2018)

Given these limited guidelines, schools of social work should provide students with more education in ethical practice and critical thinking, and social service agencies should invest additional resources in ethical consultants and the establishment of collegial assistance programs for impaired social workers to reduce the likelihood that such instances of ethical misconduct will occur. How schools and agencies will do this in a postpandemic era when online practice and education and resource shortages are the norm is currently unclear.

Ethical Obligations to Society

An underlying assumption of a good society (Bellah et al., 1991) is the existence of caring relationships among its members and a cultural belief that values care itself. There are two aspects to this assumption with ethical implications for our practice. One is that those who cannot care for themselves will be cared for in an appropriate and timely manner. Another is that those who do not currently need care can count on this care should they become dependent. These premises are the foundation of modern welfare states, U.S. social policies such as Medicare and Medicaid, and the social work profession itself (Titmuss, 2018). In the United Kingdom, for example, social workers refer to certain forms of practice as "social care;" they have become increasingly concerned about how ethical challenges in this area have become more complex (Hay, 2017; Banks, 2016; Hugman & Carter, 2016; Whittington & Whittington, 2007; Dombeck & Olsan, 2007).

Western notions of care have traditionally distinguished between care provided in the public and private spheres. The public sphere, which largely restricts care to citizens, provides care based on rational, objective, and near-universal standardized criteria. In the private sphere, however, caring recognizes the importance of emotion, subjectivity, and the unique, multifaceted needs of individuals. These premises underlie the feminist ethics of care (Barnes, 2019).

Distinctions between public and private care have become increasingly important in the United States and other Western societies as polarization over issues such as immigration and the allocation of essential health resources and social benefits intensifies. When some societies and their national governments, like the United States, devalue care or retreat from their former commitments to care through privatization, bureaucratization, tightened eligibility requirements or fiscal austerity, as has occurred in recent decades, they reinforce the long-standing gendered nature of care, which has traditionally possessed both lower economic and social worth (Robinson, 2018). The multiple challenges essential workers such as nursing aides and childcare teachers face today during the current pandemic illustrate this problem vividly.

Another important distinction that underlies U.S. social policies throughout its history is between independence and dependence. Through its social constructions, U.S. culture idealizes the former and stigmatizes the latter, whatever its sources, despite the growing recognition that independence and dependence are relative phenomena shaped by socioeconomic conditions, physical location, power relations, and one's place on the life span (Bhandary, 2019; Brake, 2017). This reified distinction also ignores the reality that all individuals are dependent at some time and that the presence of caring is "a need at all stages of human life" (Kwak, 2008, p. 14). Finally, as issues like climate change and global pandemics demonstrate all too clearly, this social construction fails to acknowledge the increasing global interdependence of peoples and communities.

Growing awareness of the consequences of these distinctions highlights the need to divorce the provision of care from the right of people to exercise their capabilities as citizens, and as human beings. In addition, this heightened awareness has the potential to break down

FIGURE 10.3. Choosing Between Legal and Moral Obligations Is Often Difficult

the dichotomy between care recipients and caregivers and the artificial boundary between public and private forms of caregiving. In effect, it makes caring a collective responsibility; it recognizes both the public function of professional caregivers, such as social workers, and the value of private caregivers, particularly women and, increasingly, low-income women of color and immigrant women.

Ethical Research

Both CSWE curricular guidelines (Council on Social Work Education, 2015) and the revised NASW *Code of Ethics* (2018) require practitioners and educators "to promote economic and social justice, advocate for structural and institutional change, and address the needs of marginalized and oppressed populations." Increased stratification in U.S. society along racial, class, and ethnic lines, however, heightens the challenge of fulfilling these ethical imperatives in our day-to-day practice. Although of equal importance, until the past decade the social work literature paid less attention to the challenges involved in conducting ethical research, especially in marginalized communities (Carey, 2019; Barsky, 2019; Krysik, 2018; Bloom, 2010; Dattalo, 2010; Jackson, 2010).

In this regard, past research conducted by the author in low-income housing projects revealed several interrelated themes (Reisch & Rivera, 1999; Reisch et al., 1995). Community-based researchers often face ethical dilemmas because of the conflicting goals of their project's various constituencies. For example, project funders may have different ideas about the direction and purpose of a research study from the community under study. Racial and ethnic differences between the various stakeholders exacerbate these dilemmas. In addition, political issues are always present when conducting research, particularly when the research requires cooperation among government agencies, nonprofit organizations, local businesses, and community groups.

These realities call into question a long-standing assumption among progressive macro social workers that participatory action research is an approach most likely to acquire community support. In fact, such research raises several difficult yet often overlooked ethical questions: To whom should researchers and practitioners who apply the results of their research be accountable? How can they promote democratic research and practice processes when confronted with hostility from all parties? Do "disenfranchised communities have the right not to be researched, no matter ... the potential significance of the [issues under study]?" (Reisch & Rivera, 1999, p. 58)

Although the NASW *Code of Ethics* now places more emphasis on the environmental context of practice and research than in the past, it still assumes an essentially nonadversarial relationship between practitioners, researchers, and the community. The *Code* also ignores the political complexity of practice and research in contemporary urban communities, especially the effects of social movements like Black Lives Matter. In an environment of increasing interracial suspicion and mistrust, as long as community members view social workers and social work researchers as "outsiders," residents will perceive them "as agents of class mediation and social control," however benign their intentions (p. 56).

These caveats become even more important when conducting research in highly vulnerable and distressed communities, such as research after a devastating natural disaster or pandemic, or with people experiencing trauma due to civil violence (Horney et al., 2019; Dittmer & Lorenz,

2018; O'Mathúna, 2018; Hunt et al., 2016). In such circumstances, Ferreira et al. (2015) stress the importance of applying uniform ethical standards because of the complex nature of these situations and the impaired decisional capacity and greater vulnerability of potential participants. They make a number of important recommendations based on their study's findings. One is that researchers should be constantly aware of the lingering effects of post-traumatic stress disorder (PTSD) and use unobtrusive or noninvasive research methods out of sensitivity to the psychological state of community residents. Researchers should also adhere to established government ethical standards, and screen and assess prospective study participants thoroughly to determine their level of vulnerability and the potential risks and benefits of the study. In addition, they should be particularly sensitive to cultural and gender differences among the population under study, make sure to acquire genuine informed consent, maintain strict confidentiality or anonymity, and provide assistance to those being researched (Ferreira et al., 2015, pp. 38–39).

FIGURE 10.4. Whistleblowers Incur Considerable Personal and Professional Risks

Whistleblowing

One of the most visible and controversial forms of expressing caring in a society is calling attention to wrongdoing by individuals or organizations who have the responsibility to deliver care or the authority to determine who receives it. On occasion, decisions about whether to "blow the whistle" create a conflict between our duty to a colleague, client, or employer and our duty to a community or society. The following case is a powerful and painful example of the emotional risks involved in such dilemmas.

ETHICAL DILEMMA 10.7	Blowing the Whistle on a Colleague and Friend *(Based on real events)*

A professional colleague and close friend, Leonard K., is the executive director of a well-established, multi-service community center in a large metropolitan area. You attended each other's wedding, your spouses are very fond of each other, and your families socialize often. Leonard has had a remarkably successful tenure at the center. He expanded the organization's programs in innovative ways, tripled its annual budget, and established an endowment that is now valued at over $100 million. He is highly respected, even loved, in the community the center serves, and the programs he established have received widespread positive media attention. Major political leaders, including the president, have attended the center's events.

One summer evening while visiting Leonard and his family, you admire the expensive artwork in his home and wonder aloud how he could afford it. He confides in you that, from time to time, he used some of the resources obtained through the center's fundraising appeals to purchase them. He rationalized this unilateral decision on the grounds he used his home for fundraising events and that these enhancements made a positive impression on wealthy potential donors.

You spend a sleepless night wondering what to do. Leonard's actions clearly violated the NASW *Code of Ethics* and were possibly illegal. If you do nothing, his behavior may continue and, ultimately, bring discredit to the center. If it came out you knew what he did and failed to report it, you could jeopardize your professional reputation. On the other hand, if you blow the whistle, you will probably destroy Leonard's career, subject him to possible prosecution, ruin his family, undermine the public image of the center and its programs, and betray the confidence of a friend.

Questions:
1. What would you do? On what ethical principles would you base the decision?
2. What framework for ethical decision-making would you use?
3. If you worked for the center Leonard directed, how would your decision-making change?

Think about the following definition of whistleblowing and the extent to which it applies to you in the above situation:

> Whistleblowing is the disclosure by a person, working within an organization, of facts, omissions, practices, or policies by that organization or by their employees that wrong or harm a third party. The objective of the disclosure is to stop the harmful behavior and to prevent such conduct in the future.

> The revelation can be made to superiors within the employing organization or to authorities outside the organization who are in a position to help. (Mansbach & Bachner, 2008, p. 2)

These authorities could include journalists, the police, or a regulatory agency. Mansbach and Bachner point out that there has been little research on the subject of whistleblowing in the social work profession. They suggest this may be for two reasons: there are few reported incidents of social workers as either whistleblowers or the object of whistleblowing, and because the subject is complex. Ironically, their studies found that students with no experience were more likely to blow the whistle than were classmates with more experience (2008, 2009). It is interesting to speculate on the implications of this finding.

Whatever the circumstances, engaging in whistleblowing is a complex and risky endeavor. It involves resolving the conflict between our duty to an employer or colleague and our obligations to society (Hunt, 2017). On occasion, whistleblowing could place our job, reputation, professional relationships, and even our life in jeopardy, particularly if reports of the wrongdoing appear in the media or threaten powerful individuals or institutions (Shaub, 2020; Stanger, 2020; Arnold, 2019; Devine, 2017).

During the past few years, there have been several stark reminders of this risk. Well-known examples are the online death threats directed at the anonymous official who blew the whistle on President Trump's phone call to the Ukrainian president and the grisly murder of the journalist Adnam Khashoggi because of his criticisms of the Saudi government. More recently, Captain Brett Crozier, the captain of the aircraft carrier U.S.S. Theodore Roosevelt, was relieved of his command after he wrote a letter to the Pentagon complaining of the Navy's inaction when dozens of his crew contracted the coronavirus. As of this writing, Ai Fen, one of the whistleblowers who criticized the Chinese government's response to the coronavirus pandemic, has disappeared. President Trump fired Michael Atkinson, the inspector general of the intelligence community, who forwarded the whistleblower's report about the president's phone call to the Ukrainian president to Congress. Several U.S. hospitals have fired unnamed doctors and nurses who called attention to the lack of critical resources during the coronavirus pandemic.

Despite these considerable risks, what would happen if we remained silent in the face of obvious wrongdoing or indifference? If we do not act when we confront clear instances of injustice, corruption, or harm to our clients or constituents, we "may be violating [our] basic professional commitment ... and ... undermining the very *raison d'etre* of the profession." From this perspective, whistleblowing should be viewed as "a special form of advocacy that is necessary to protect the rights" of those with whom we work and society as well (Mansbach & Bachner, 2008, p. 2; Nanda, 2019; Leong, 2017).

FIGURE 10.5. Whistleblowers Often Have Their Motives Questioned by Their Colleagues

Both Bok (1980) and Lewis (2003b) spelled out clear guidelines for whistleblowing situations that are still applicable today. Think about how you would apply these guidelines to the case above. First, the individual must decide whether, all things being equal, speaking out is in the public interest. Second, the individual must decide whether their responsibility to serve the public interest in the particular situation outweighs their responsibility to colleagues and their employer, to their own reputation, and to the safety and livelihood of their families. The individual must also address three sets of questions, which Bok groups under the categories of dissent, breach of loyalty, and accusation.

The first question is "Am I acting in the public interest or out of personal interest?" Answering this question requires a bit of soul searching. Are we taking a virtuous stand because we believe it will enhance our standing in our organization or community, taking out a personal grudge on the alleged wrongdoer, or making a stand to demonstrate our superior virtue?

Second, do the facts warrant this action? Are we certain the violation occurred and was it such a serious matter that we are obligated to "go public"? Some of the charges of inappropriate sexual conduct leveled against prominent politicians, academics, and media celebrities raise these questions.

Third, is there some way to minimize the potential harm to a colleague and the organization whistleblowing could cause? In other words, what is the least harmful and least consequential course of action one could select? To answer this last set of questions, Bok suggests that while whistleblowers should exhaust all existing avenues for change within the organization before sounding the alarm, they can reject this course of action under three conditions. One is when no viable alternative exists to resolve the problem at hand. Another is when there is insufficient time to pursue "regular channels" within the organization before the effects of the wrongdoing occur. Third, in rare situations where the organization is so corrupt there is imminent danger of silencing the whistleblower. (The dramatic films *The Firm* and *Silkwood* are examples of the latter.) Finally, Bok recommends that prior to blowing the whistle, an individual should ask, "Exactly whom am I accusing?" and "Is it fair to accuse this particular person for what may be a systemic problem?"

In sum, the issue of whistleblowing raises an issue on the macro scale analogous to the one established by the *Tarasoff* decision at the micro level of practice: when are we obligated to report "the conduct of another [or] warn those endangered by that conduct?" (Kopels & Kagle, 1993, p. 102). It requires interpreting such concepts as "serious harm," "special relationships," and "reasonable efforts to protect" in the specific context of the situation (p. 103). Many state statutes "grant immunity to therapists who reveal patient confidences in discharging their duty to warn" (p. 109), but what about individuals, like the whistleblower in the tobacco industry, as portrayed in the film, *The Insider*, who revealed confidential organizational information, such as memoranda or e-mail messages, that demonstrated organizational malfeasance or misfeasance? Although social workers have long considered the protection of confidentiality a basic human right, does it apply to organizational conduct as well?

FIGURE 10.6. Whistleblowers Must Be Prepared to Face the Consequences of Their Truth Telling

According to Bok (1980, 1982, Chapter 9) and Lewis (2003b), in such circumstances potential whistleblowers need to consider whether compelling reasons for disclosure exist. This is particularly important when a legal requirement for disclosure does not exist, when such disclosure may be professionally inappropriate or risky (e.g., recent cases involving the cover up of sexual abuse by the Catholic church hierarchy or violations of international law by members of the U.S. armed forces), or when blowing the whistle might conflict with other ethical duties.

Do the same expectations regarding the prediction of potentially harmful consequences to individuals apply to unknown third parties in cases of agency or institutional misconduct? If so, the same standard procedures used in cases like *Tarasoff* should apply to instances of possible whistleblowing: assessment, documentation, and intervention. Are there different standards, however, depending on the celebrity, status, or power of the alleged wrongdoer, such as the president of the United States?

FIGURE 10.7. Whistleblowers Often Have to Decide Where Their Loyalties Lie

Whistleblowing and Truth Telling

Whistleblowing is closely bound to the issue of truth telling. Both reflect the significance of honesty, integrity, and trust as the basis for establishing and maintaining professional relationships and credible roles for social workers in all methods and fields of practice. It is important, however, to differentiate between the purposeful conveyance of false information—for example, misrepresentation of oneself or one's organization—and misstatements or inadvertent error. We also need to be clear about the distinction between acts of commission, such as deliberate lying, and acts of omission, such as withholding information from a group with whom an organizer or advocates works to fulfill other ethical obligations.

Issues to consider in this regard include the magnitude of the deception and the degree of falsehood. For example, does the deception involve a small detail of strategy that does not affect the overall outcome of a proposed intervention? Alternatively, does it involve a major piece of information or decision that changes the relationship among stakeholders?

Other issues include the nature of the issue about which one lies and the person or persons to whom one lies. It is far more serious, for example, to distort data in testimony before a legislative committee considering an important bill than to fail to tell a legislative supporter that you have already discussed a particular issue with her political rival. Although some ethicists would adopt a deontological position—a social worker should never lie under any circumstances—others might take a consequentialist approach that would consider the actual or potential consequences of a particular act of deception.

Finally, one should take into account the unique aspects of the situation. What other options are available? What is the purpose of the lie? Is it a case of "benign deception"—for example, to preserve the funding of a critical program or the reputation of an individual who has committed a minor transgression? Or, is the purpose of the deception to inflict harm on others? (This issue is one aspect of the ethical challenge of means and ends discussed in Chapter 11.)

Criteria to assess such situations include the extent to which the lie protects, enhances, or harms individuals or a community; the likelihood that failure to use the deception will harm these individuals or the community; and the absence of alternative, more legitimate and ethical means of protecting people's well-being. In her classic book on lying, Bok (1999, Chapter 3) argued: "such a principle [of truth telling] need not indicate that all lies should be ruled out ... nor does it even suggest which lies should be prohibited. But it does make at least one immediate limitation on lying: in any situation where a lie is a possible choice, one must first seek truthful alternatives."

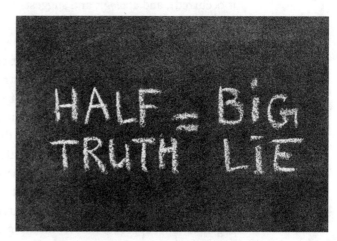

FIGURE 10.8. Whistleblowers Must Be Sure to Tell the Whole Truth

Responding to Ethical Errors in Practice

Given the increasingly complex and often confusing situations in which our practice occurs, it is not only possible, it is understandable and usually forgivable that we will make ethical mistakes, both personally and professionally. Often these mistakes are accidental, the product of excessive caseloads, inflexible deadlines, conflicting demands, physical or mental exhaustion, increased stress, or insufficient or inadequate training. Sometimes, however, we err—perhaps by taking a "shortcut" or misjudging a situation—and fail to follow prevailing ethical standards or best practices. Given the increased emphasis on accountability in our work environments and the long-standing tendency toward litigiousness in U.S. society, we may resist acknowledging such mistakes out of concern over professional sanction or legal liability. In turn, we may withhold critical information, refuse to admit our error, or engage in outright deception to cover it up (Strom-Gottfried, 2019).

While most of our errors are insignificant—where the "no harm, no foul" rule applies—a small number might involve an "injury caused by the provision of care rather than by the client's clinical condition" (Reamer, 2008, p. 62). Few guidelines for dealing with such problems exist, particularly for social workers in macro practice, because there is little research on this topic in general, and because the studies that exist focus almost entirely on work with individuals and families (Strom-Gottfried, 2019). From the author's experience and observation, however, social workers in macro practice also make errors, on occasion egregious errors, but the connection between these errors and evidence of harm to constituents is often more difficult to discern.

As Reamer (2008) asserts, the primary reason to address errors in practice is to fulfill our fiduciary obligations to the people with whom we work and third parties in a manner "that protects and minimizes harm" to them (p. 63) and treats all people with dignity. Doing so is also in our self-interest, as it decreases the likelihood of both malpractice suits and ethics complaints. To minimize the potential punitive consequences of ethical error, Reamer summarizes his recommendations in three words: *acknowledgement* (that an error occurred), *analysis* (of why it occurred), and *apology*, and suggests that this response be communicated with sensitivity, transparency, honesty, and respect.

Another pressing ethical duty that shapes contemporary practice is the obligation to meet minimum standards of competence, particularly when using new forms of intervention in clinical practice or initiating risky change strategies in macro practice. As discussed in previous chapters, among the ethical areas in which errors of competence have occurred with the greatest frequency are client confidentiality, conflicts of interest, informed consent, and boundary issues. The recent prevalence of such errors is a direct consequence of the growing use of digital technology and more demanding professional accountability standards. These changes frequently require us to "walk ... a fine line between valuable innovation that has therapeutic benefits and harmful, possible exploitative treatment of vulnerable clients" (Reamer, 2013a, p. 171).

Common ethical mistakes in these areas can be errors of omission, such as failure to get organizational approval before initiating an intervention, and errors of commission, such as initiating a change strategy without consulting with constituents or coalition allies. More infrequently, clear instances of ethical misconduct occur. Examples of misconduct in clinical practice include "misrepresenting one's credentials and expertise ..., engaging in inappropriate dual relationships with clients ..., and billing for ... services that were not provided" (Reamer, 2013a, p. 170). Illustrations in macro practice include overpromising to a potential funding source about the effects of a proposed program and providing misleading information to policy makers or the media during an advocacy campaign. Instances of such ethical violations are rare, however, and it is even rarer for social workers to face criminal charges (Reamer, 2015c).

Summary

This chapter discussed some of the most challenging ethical dilemmas contemporary social workers face—those that involve conflicts of duty between different parties or between our legal and ethical obligations. These conflicts may involve colleagues, employers, the communities in which we work, and the society of which we are a part. They affect practitioners in all fields and all practice methods, including research. The resolution of these conflicts is not easy, and it often involves personal and professional risk, such as instances where we have to decide whether to blow the whistle on a colleague or an entire organization. Unfortunately, neither the NASW *Code of Ethics* nor the bulk of the professional literature provides clear guidelines that would help us select a course of action in such circumstances. These gaps underscore the need for more rigorous ethical education in our schools of social work, ongoing training even for experienced practitioners, and the availability of ethical consultants in our agencies on an ongoing basis.

The next chapter expands on this material in several ways. It addresses the ethical issues involved in determining the relationship between means and ends in all forms of practice. It also discusses the challenges involved in allocating scarce resources, challenges that are not restricted to agency or program administrators or government policy makers but affect all practitioners on a day-to-day basis. Finally, it examines the global issue of the relationship between the application of our ethical imperative to pursue social justice and the promotion of international human rights, a relationship far more complex than it appears on first glance.

Reflection Exercise I: Creating a Socially Just Organization

Think about an organization in which you currently work, have worked, or in which you would like to work in the future. Working in small groups, discuss how you would address the following questions in constructing or reconstructing this organization.

1. How can the organization create greater equality among service users, staff, and community residents?
2. On a day-to-day basis, what are the features of socially just practice in this organization?
3. How can the organization balance respect for cultural diversity with a consistent programmatic framework and within the law?
4. How would the organization balance culturally competent practice and ethical practice?

Reflection Exercise II: When Would You Violate the Law?

In which of the following situations would you choose to violate the law because you would give priority to your ethical obligations? How would you justify your decision?

1. A 16-year-old female high school student with whom you have been working as a school social worker reveals she has had consensual sex with her 19-year-old boyfriend. According to state law, the state could charge her boyfriend as an adult with statutory rape.
2. You learn that the adolescent son of your client, a disabled public housing tenant, is dealing drugs. The Housing Authority has a policy that tenants (or their family members) who violate drug laws are not eligible to live in public housing. If discovered, your client's entire family would be evicted and barred from other public housing.
3. You work on a crisis hotline. One night, Edward Snowden, whom the federal government wants to expedite to the United States, tells you that the stress of exile causes him to contemplate suicide. The government requires all individuals who have had contact with Snowden to notify federal authorities immediately.
4. You accidentally notice that a colleague at the youth center at which you work has been viewing pornographic websites in his office, including those involving pedophilia.
5. The government bans the provision of services to undocumented immigrants who often seek help at your agency. A family of farmworkers, recently laid off because of an outbreak of the coronavirus in their crew, asks you for assistance in getting food and health care.

Reflection Exercise III: When Would You Blow the Whistle?

In which of the following situations would you be willing to "blow the whistle"? What are the reasons for your decision?

1. You learn that a colleague has been using agency funds for personal travel without receiving approval.
2. You learn that a colleague has been engaged in a consensual sexual relationship with a client.
3. You learn from a reliable source that the newly appointed CEO of your organization falsified their credentials in their application for the position.
4. You work in a "zero-tolerance" organization and you learn that your supervisor has been abusing drugs or alcohol.
5. You learn that the CEO of your organization has hired a company owned by one of the agency's board members to cater its annual fundraising dinner.
6. You find out that your agency has submitted a major proposal to the government that misstates the organization's capacity to deliver the services for which it is seeking funding.

Credits

Fig. 10.2: Copyright © 2015 Depositphotos/bakhtiarzein.
Fig. 10.3: Copyright © 2019 Depositphotos/inueng.
Fig. 10.4: Copyright © 2015 Depositphotos/lightsource.
Fig. 10.5: Copyright © 2015 Depositphotos/prettyvectors.
Fig. 10.6: Copyright © by SportsGuy789 (cc by-sa 4.0) at https://commons.wikimedia.org/wiki/File:Truth_or_Consequences_-_town_sign.jpg.
Fig. 10.7: Copyright © 2019 Depositphotos/lightsource.
Fig. 10.8: Copyright © 2015 Depositphotos/yurizap.

Social Justice and Ethical Practice

Introduction

In my many years of teaching, social work students have told me that the following recurring ethical dilemmas are of greatest concern:

- Fear of compromising their professional principles and personal values if they comply with their duty to employers or must implement policies and laws they consider unjust;
- The impact of their personal values, including their religious beliefs, on the choices they have to make in practice;
- The challenge of being labelled "politically correct" in an environment that often scorns political correctness; and
- Dealing with the ethical conflicts that arise when their professional values conflict with powerful authority figures, particularly when they engage in advocacy or community work.

This list of challenges recalls the book's previous discussion of the sources of ethical dilemmas. To recapitulate, these include:

1. When two ethical principles conflict—that is, when satisfying one of the principles in a particular situation requires you to violate the other;
2. When the reasons to choose a course of ethical action are unclear;
3. When there is insufficient time to make a reasoned, ethical judgment;
4. When one is compelled to choose between equally good or bad options; and
5. When ethical principles conflict with legal or organizational obligations, or powerful community or societal norms.

This chapter will analyze several of the critical ethical challenges that all practitioners encounter—challenges that create fundamental conflicts for our orientation to our work and pose difficult questions regarding the application of basic philosophical approaches to day-to-day practice. To illustrate these conflicts, this chapter will focus on the following issues:

- The meaning of social justice and its implications for social work ethics
- The implications of a human rights perspective for ethical practice

- The challenge of allocating scarce resources at the micro, mezzo, and macro levels
- The relationship of means and ends to ethical practice

To help resolve the issues raised in this chapter, it might be useful to apply a framework first described in Chapter 1 (Reisch & Lowe, 2000). This framework synthesizes ideas derived from other models of ethical problem solving presented in this book and adapts them for dilemmas that arise in both clinical and macro practice situations. The steps in the framework are:

1. Identify the ethical principles applicable to the particular situation
2. Collect the information needed to clarify and analyze the dilemma
3. Identify the values or ethical principles that apply
4. Identify any potential conflicts of interest and those likely to benefit
5. Identify appropriate ethical rules and rank them in order or importance
6. Assess the consequences of applying different ethical rules or ranking these rules differently (p. 26).

In thinking about when and how to apply this framework, note that some practice situations do not require us to resolve them. It is important, therefore, to determine, in advance, who is responsible for their solution, as the following case illustrates.

ETHICAL DILEMMA 11.1   Social Justice and a Conflict of Duties

You are a social worker in a multiservice organization in a semirural, multiracial community. Your agency helps people in the community access critical resources and benefits, such as unemployment insurance, health care, and nutritional and housing assistance. Although a large number of individuals in the community are undocumented agricultural workers, federal and state laws prohibit your organization from providing this population with the vital services they need. These services have become particularly critical during the coronavirus pandemic, as a significant percentage of these workers and their family members have contracted the virus and are now unable to work. As a result, their families face starvation, lack of essential health care, and possible deportation if they seek help.

The head of the local immigrants' rights organization is a former classmate and neighbor. She asks you if you could work with her to find ways to circumvent the laws that bar your organization from using government funds to assist this population. How would you respond?

Questions:
1. What is the nature of the ethical dilemma in this situation?
2. Which duties are in conflict?
3. How would you respond? How would you justify your response to your former classmate?
4. What general principles, if any, would you derive from how you addressed this dilemma?

As this case illustrates, examples of difficult ethical dilemmas "include responsibility for [meeting] clients' basic needs vs. collegiality; allegiance to one's employing agency vs. improvement of services and working conditions; ... and promotion ... of the profession vs. undertaking widely-perceived non-professional [and potentially illegal] activities" (Weisman, 1990, p. 1). In such circumstances, social workers could play an important role in reconciling differences between the parties, achieving a more just outcome, and strengthening the profession's public voice (Ross, 2016). Yet, doing so may involve considerable personal and professional risks.

The situation described in the above hypothetical case is not unprecedented. Even prior to the latest pandemic, manmade and natural disasters affected over 300 million people annually, disproportionately the segments of the population most at-risk (Sweifach et al., 2015). Both types of tragic phenomena require a triggering agent (e.g., a hurricane or a virus) and preexisting vulnerability (e.g., poverty and other precarious conditions). In such situations, ethical dilemmas of greater complexity often arise when practitioners have to choose between two affirmative duties—to determine whether their "commitment to client welfare (beneficence) supersedes conforming to agency rules which are [ostensibly] designed to achieve a *greater good*" (Sweifach et al., 2015, p. 11; italics in original). When faced with conflicting ethical demands, should social workers make tough choices based on a deontological or consequentialist framework? That is, should they prioritize one duty over another under all circumstances (a deontological approach) or should they weigh the potential outcomes of alternate choices? If the former, which duties have priority? If the latter, which consequences should be considered, measured, and weighed against each other, and through what means?

In the above case, two important ethical principles, beneficence and fidelity, conflict. Both values imply an affirmative duty. In different ways, both complement our profession's ethical imperative to pursue social justice, although they define justice differently. Due to a variety of external pressures, during the past two decades many social service organizations faced similar choices and tended to prioritize risk aversion (fidelity) over beneficence to others (Sweifach et al., 2015, p. 11).

These ethical dilemmas appear in different forms in clinical and macro practice. Consequently, we have to apply core social work values to resolve them in different ways. A major difference in this regard stems from the different goals of macro practice (social, political, or institutional change) and clinical practice (individual or family change). In addition, the people with whom macro practitioners work are constituents, not clients. This implies that macro social workers have a different type of interpersonal relationship with the people with whom they work and, consequently, a different set of obligations (Reisch, 2018c).

In macro practice, awareness of the various features of the environment and the importance of partnership and community self-determination are, therefore, more critical. As discussed in Chapter 9, there is also the increased possibility, and perhaps the necessity, of dual relationships developing. Finally, as discussed later in this chapter in the section on means and ends, ethics in macro practice is more often situational and more likely to involve decisions about the role of conflict, including purposive conflict.

Many social workers, however, frequently avoid conflict for a variety of reasons (Haynes & Mickelson, 2010). Based on persistent, system-conserving assumptions about individuals, society, and social change, these include concern that taking a partisan stance in support of clients' interests might jeopardize our professional neutrality and community standing. In recent years, these assumptions have produced a fundamentally apolitical orientation to social work practice that emphasizes scientific "objectivity" through the promotion of "evidence-based practice" over social action (Dominelli, 2019; Lane & Pritzker, 2018b; Briskman, 2017; Hay, 2017; Russell, 2017; Moyo & Courter, 2016). In addition, the trend toward heightened specialization within the social work field leads to viewing the solutions to peoples' problems in "silos" and creates barriers to the development of a systemic perspective that could lead to structural solutions. Finally, ethical dilemmas emerge due to the conflict between our desire to promote people's empowerment and self-determination and incessant pressures to compromise in a contentious political environment.

Social Justice and Ethical Practice

The literature on social justice is vast; space limitations allow for only a brief summary in this chapter of its major arguments and their relationship to ethical practice in social work. (See Reisch & Garvin, 2016, and Finn, 2016, for a fuller discussion of the role of social justice in social work practice.) In their core documents, both national and international professional organizations assert the centrality of social justice. It is one of the six ethical imperatives in the NASW *Code of Ethics* (2018), along with respect for all people, an emphasis on rights as the basis for achieving social justice, and pursuit of the common good. It is also a CSWE accreditation requirement for the curricula of BSW and MSW programs (Council on Social Work Education, 2015), and a key component of the mission statement of the International Federation of Social Workers (2018b). Many social work scholars and practitioners assume that these values are always and inevitably compatible with each other and with the realities of practice in a complex society. The author's research and professional experience, however, indicate that this latter assumption may not always be valid.

Haynes and Mickelson (2010) attributed the gap between the profession's rhetoric and practice realities to the frequent incompatibility of our social justice principles with the values of the "host" organizations in which we work. Throughout social work history, another source of this problem has been the conflict between maintaining an impartial (objective, scientific) posture to enhance social work's occupational status and taking a partisan position to promote social justice and equality for our clients and constituents. Several histories of U.S. social work emphasize this long-standing tension and its consequences (Pritzker & Lane, 2017; Ruth & Marshall, 2017; Reisch & Andrews, 2002; Specht & Courtenay, 1994; Wenocur & Reisch, 1989).

The conceptual frameworks of the social work field also reflect an additional contradiction between our focus on individual dignity and autonomy and our ethical imperative to pursue social justice at the systemic level, particularly for oppressed and marginalized populations (Shdaimah & Strier, 2020). The latter implies the importance of collective responsibility, mutuality in human relations, and a focus on structural change, while the former emphasizes the primacy of satisfying the unique needs and rights of individuals. This dilemma is not merely a byproduct of differences among ambiguous philosophical abstractions; it is a direct consequence of how the profession distributes its material resources, time, and intellectual pursuits, including the focus of its research and scholarship (Valutis et al., 2016). Through a broader lens, this conflict reflects the divisions that emerged in the West between proponents of liberty, equality, and justice during the 200-plus years after French revolutionaries declared these values inseparable (Steiner, 2018).

Since the emergence of the current neoliberal climate, organized social work has implicitly accommodated to its underlying value choices despite maintaining its rhetorical commitment to the goal of a just society (Morley, 2016; Morley & Ablett, 2016; Spolander et al., 2016). This is ironic given the long-standing emphasis within the profession on the importance of the social environment and the indisputable reality that the current economic system affects all areas of human activity from the individual to the global level. The realization of our core ideal of social justice, therefore, requires us to develop a synthetic focus that combines the promotion of individual well-being and concerted efforts to correct the structural causes of people's problems.

For the past half century, numerous social work scholars in both clinical and macro practice have attempted to forge this synthesis (Reisch, 2019d; Finn, 2016; Reisch, 2016a; Reisch & Garvin, 2016; Wakefield, 2016), often relying on the work of the late Harvard philosopher John Rawls (1971, 1999, 2001) and scholars who expanded upon his ideas (Nussbaum, 2013; Sen, 2009). Rawls developed a theory of justice that, in summary, consists of two fundamental principles. First, that in a just society, each individual would be entitled to the maximum amount of liberty, compatible with liberty for all. This principle is consistent with social work values such as self-determination and the primacy of the client's interest. The second principle is that unequal distribution of resources, power, and status may be justified only if this unequal distribution serves to benefit the least advantaged. Core social work documents reflect this principle in the priority they place on the promotion of social justice. The section below on the allocation of scarce resources discusses the practice implications of this second principle.

Rawls's ideas, however, have not gone without criticism, both from libertarians like Robert Nozick (1974) and more sympathetic philosophers such as Amartya Sen (2009) and Martha Nussbaum (2013). Nozick questioned the very basis of Rawls's argument that most inequalities are unfair. He argued that a distinction exists between inequalities that are unfair due to discrimination and those that are merely unfortunate, for example because of the unequal distribution of natural attributes. Sen and Nussbaum, while supportive of Rawls, assert that his conception of justice did not go far enough because it gave insufficient attention to the importance of nonmaterial "goods," the need for just processes to distribute these goods, and the emotionally based role of caring at the individual and societal level.

This latter omission has received increased attention in the social work field during the past several decades, both in the United States and other nations (Hay, 2019; Banks, 2016). The importance of caring expands the idea of social justice and integrates a gendered perspective into contemporary practice frameworks (Jones et al., 2019). As discussed later in this chapter, greater attention to the role of caring in practice is particularly relevant to discussions regarding the allocation of scarce resources at the individual and societal levels. It not only involves decisions about what priorities a society or organization should establish in the distribution of finite material goods. It also raises issues about how much time an individual social worker should give to uncooperative clients or those whose problems show little possibility of resolution when a practitioner's time is limited and the need for self-care becomes increasingly important. As Imre (1989) pointed out over three decades ago, and the coronavirus pandemic illustrates all too painfully, "An overworked, overwhelmed social worker may not be able to care enough. ... Appropriate caring may become impossible unless a society ... provides the necessary resources" (p. 12).

The definition of social justice within the social work field, therefore, varies widely, as it does throughout the world (Grapin & Shriberg, 2020; Olson, et al., 2013; Reisch, 2010a). Some definitions are potentially complementary, while others appear to be mutually exclusive because they are in direct or partial contradiction with each other. These different interpretations or understandings of a fundamental professional value create a great deal of confusion in our efforts to develop consistent practice goals and objectives and measure how effectively we have achieved them. The latter problem is particularly relevant given the profession's emphasis on evidence-based practice, intervention research, and the search for scientific solutions to American society's "Grand Challenges" (American Academy of Social Work and Social Welfare, 2020). As stated above, some of these diverse interpretations of justice lack internal inconsistency; others are difficult to articulate in nonnormative terms or to apply to our practice. A particularly vexing problem in today's increasingly multicultural society is how to resolve definitional conflicts that result from fundamental cultural differences the profession has pledged repeatedly to honor and respect (Weaver, 2016).

If we are to demonstrate heightened sensitivity to the existence of widely diverse views about social justice and their potential implications for practice, we need to recognize the role that social relationships, the distribution of power, and historical traditions have played in producing these differences. Often cultural artifacts, such as art, music, and theatre, express these differences through a combination of rational and emotional elements (Bell, 2017). This underscores the importance of paying closer attention to the "nonscientific" signifiers of a culture's values these artifacts reflect.

Social Work Ethics and Human Rights

Social work has long viewed social justice and human rights as compatible, even synchronous ideals. We have tended, however, to view these values through the lens of individual rights arising from 19th- and 20th-century Western liberalism and efforts to develop universally accepted criteria for justice based on disinterested rationality and contract theory (Lorenz, 2016a; Reisch, 2016b; Wronka, 2016b). The promotion of objective, scientific, evidence-based rationality—the latest product of the positivist tradition in Western social science—complements and reinforces this tendency.

In the present context, social workers need to address a number of critical framing questions before determining whether to integrate a human rights approach into our ethical practice. Two of the most basic questions are what do we mean by "human rights" and what is the philosophical justification for allowing people to make human rights claims?

These vexing issues have particular salience within the macro arena. For example, what are the different categories of rights and how do we translate them into concrete policies and programs? Do these rights have equal weight if they conflict? To whom do these rights apply? Who decides these questions and how? Are human rights and social justice principles always compatible (Clément, 2018; Hibbert, 2017; Reisch, 2014b)? Is a human rights approach compatible with the profession's embrace of multiculturalism (Beauchamp, 2020)? In sum, as Murdach (2011) provocatively asked a decade ago, is social work a human rights profession? Should it be?

Origins and Context of Human Rights Discourse

The concept of universal rights has its secular origins in the 18th-century Enlightenment and the so-called Atlantic revolutions it inspired. By asserting that all people are capable of reason, the philosophers of the Enlightenment, like John Locke and Thomas Jefferson, undermined centuries old hierarchies and prepared the way for rights-based statements in the American Declaration of Independence[1] and the French Declaration of the Rights of Man and of the Citizen.[2] Although revolutionary movements of the 19th and 20th centuries proclaimed similar universal ideals of liberty and equality, it was not until the late 1940s, in the aftermath of World War II, that the newly formed United Nations articulated these ideas in a formal document, the United Nations *Universal Declaration of Human Rights* (1948).

Ife (2012) divides the Declaration into what he terms "three generations of human rights." The first generation consists of negative rights, such as the freedoms listed in the U.S. Constitution's Bill of Rights (its first 10 Amendments) and those expanded upon by the 13th, 14th, 15th, 19th, 24th, and 26th Amendments, the 1964 Civil Rights Act, the 1965 Voting Rights Act, and the 1990 Americans with Disabilities Act. These rights primarily affect people at the individual level.

IMAGE 11.1. Former First Lady Eleanor Roosevelt Played a Leading Role in Drafting the UN Universal Declaration of Human Rights

The second generation of rights, "positive rights," focuses on basic economic and social protections designed to provide an adequate standard of well-being. The proclamation of these rights provided the conceptual foundation for 20th-century welfare state policies. In comparison with the first generation, these rights are social rights.

The third, most recent generation of rights are collective rights, those that promote international cooperation and respect for cultural diversity, values consistent with social work's mission and the current emphasis on multiculturalism. The Declaration also reflects two important underlying assumptions: *all* rights are universal and indivisible from each other.

During the past seven decades, a number of critiques of a human rights approach to policy and practice have emerged. One criticism is that the UN Declaration reflects a Western-centric bias; it focuses primarily on individual rights and political democracy. As a result, rather than promote collective responsibility for their implementation and enforcement, the Declaration places the onus on individuals, often members of subordinated or marginalized groups, to pursue remedies when rights violations occur. Not only is this particularly difficult given vast disparities in economic resources and power, it deflects attention from communities, societies, governments, or private entities, such as multinational corporations, who bear primary responsibility for these violations (Khoury & Whyte, 2019; Scharf & Tyus, 2018).

---

1   "All men [*sic*] are created equal and are endowed with certain inalienable rights."
2   "Men [*sic*] are born and remain free and equal in rights."

Although the second and third generation of rights address this criticism to some extent, the United States has not ratified most of the conventions drafted to amplify and implement their tenets. For example, although the United States ratified the International Covenant on Civil and Political Rights nearly 30 years ago, it still has not ratified the Covenant on Economic, Social, and Political Rights. In addition, the United States has ratified only two of the numerous conventions that expanded on the meaning of these covenants particularly for oppressed populations—the Convention on the Elimination of All Forms of Racial Discrimination and the Convention Against Torture--although the U.S. has frequently violated the latter in Iraq and Afghanistan (Burke-White, 2020; Nacos & Bloch-Elkon, 2018). The United States has also not yet ratified conventions on the rights of children, women, persons with disabilities, and workers (Mapp et al., 2019). In the eyes of some critics, therefore, the Declaration is merely another mechanism that the Global North (developed nations) employs to maintain its cultural hegemony and economic and political dominance over the Global South (developing nations). The persistent challenge of human rights enforcement flows from this fundamental problem.

Social Work Practice and Human Rights

According to Reichert (2007),

> social work ... is the only profession imbued with social justice as its fundamental value and concern. But social justice is a fairness doctrine that provides civil and political leeway in deciding what is just and unjust. Human rights, on the other hand, encompass social justice, but transcend civil and political customs, in consideration of the basic life-sustaining needs of all human beings, without distinction. (p. 4)

Reichert's assertion, which the International Federation of Social Workers (2018a) echoes in its global statement of principles, would appear to place social workers squarely in the camp of other strong proponents of a human rights approach and those who advocate for an ethic of care (Ward & Barnes, 2016).

The appeal of social justice and human rights to social workers rests on the belief that all humans have intrinsic value and the moral imperative that the profession should remove the barriers that lead to dehumanization and the denial of human dignity (Androff, 2016; Libal & Harding, 2015; Mapp, 2014). In the abstract, this implies support for distributive justice, although there is always the risk of ignoring the moral dimensions of our practice when we are inadvertently complicit in dehumanizing a segment of the population (Smith, 2018).

Proponents of human rights also note the distinction between a needs and a rights-based approach to policy and practice. According to the United Nations Development Program, people are entitled to certain rights solely by being a human being. Policies and practices based on a human rights approach, therefore, stem from legal and moral obligations to implement a duty that will permit people to exercise these rights. By contrast, a need is a legitimate aspiration that lacks an association with a governmental or societal obligation to respond to it. It is, therefore, not enforceable. In principle, it could be satisfied through charity or private benevolence rather than state-sponsored action.

Yet, under today's circumstances, it is difficult if not impossible to operationalize human rights principles in ways that do not, in some important ways, reinforce and reproduce the dominant political-economic and social order and affirm prevailing assumptions about universal human needs and the current distribution of power and privilege. In response, some scholars and activists have raised the issue of whether a universal ideal of social justice exists (Reisch, 2010a). Other critics of a human rights approach within social work have questioned whether its underlying universalism conflicts with the profession's ethical premise that individuals and groups have unique needs we have to respond to in distinctive ways (Rees, 2016; Gatenio Gabel, 2016; Katiuzhinsky & Okech, 2014; Reisch, 2014b; Reisch et al., 2012). These persistent challenges underscore the importance of developing an alternative vision of society, community, and our basic institutions in order to realize the aspirations embodied in the UN Declaration. The ongoing effects of the coronavirus pandemic and the protests inspired by recent police violence against African Americans may lead to greater efforts to articulate and implement this alternative vision on the micro and macro levels. It could reflect an approach that Ife (2009) described as "human rights from below."

FOR REFLECTION AND DISCUSSION: THE CONNECTION BETWEEN HUMAN RIGHTS AND SOCIAL JUSTICE

1. Who should have the authority and power to define, implement, and enforce human rights?
2. How can we resolve the conflicts between the goals of universal human rights (Generations 1 and 2) and the preservation of and respect for cultural diversity and cultural autonomy (Generation 3)?
3. What are the ethical implications of a human rights approach for social work practice?
4. If you were on a committee charged with updating the UN Universal Declaration of Human Rights, what additional rights would you include? What rights would you suggest be deleted or revised?
5. If you were on a committee charged with revising the NASW *Code of Ethics* to incorporate a human rights approach, how would you frame this additional content?

Recently, proponents of a human rights approach within U.S. social work have criticized NASW for its failure to mention human rights in the *Code of Ethics* (Mapp et al., 2019). In contrast, the IFSW proclaims the principles of social justice and human rights are part of social work's collective responsibility and the rationale for the existence of the profession. CSWE (2015) includes the presentation of content on both human rights and social justice in its educational policy and accreditation standards. Yet, the stated practice standards of the profession still make no mention of this fundamental concept, although codes in other nations around the world reference human rights.

The failure of NASW to include human rights in its ethical code is somewhat surprising given the role that advocacy on behalf of human rights and leadership in the formation of human rights organizations played during the formative years of the profession. The numerous explanations proposed by Mapp et al. for this failure complement past criticisms of the profession by other scholars (Haynes & Mickelson, 2010; Reisch & Andrews, 2002; Specht & Courtenay, 1994). These criticisms include:

1. A focus on individual problems rather than the creation of a more structurally egalitarian society;
2. An emphasis on human needs rather than rights;
3. A desire to maintain the support of elite sponsors;
4. The linkage of behavioral change to the receipt of social benefits in many social policies;
5. Reluctance to support the redistribution of privilege, power, and resources;
6. The hierarchical model of practice that prevailed for most of U.S social work history; and
7. Persistent dominance of human rights discourse by the legal profession. (Mapp et al., 2019, pp. 261–262)

To correct this omission, Mapp and colleagues propose the integration of the following human rights principles into our practice:

- Human dignity (consistent with self-determination, a strengths- or assets-based model of practice, and the capabilities approach to social justice)
- Nondiscrimination and the reduction of hierarchical structures and relationships
- Meaningful participation in key decisions; transparency; and accountability

This revised focus has potentially radical implications. It would require that we examine the root causes, not merely the symptoms, of people's problems, and would "situate … clients' [and constituents'] concerns within the larger context of their access to their human rights" and the injustices they experience (p. 265). The stark economic and social conditions millions of Americans now endure (Alston, 2018), conditions exacerbated by the inadequate federal response to the coronavirus pandemic (DeParle, 2020a), increase the importance of social workers participating in advocacy coalitions with their clients and communities for the fulfillment of human rights goals and the protection of the fragile social safety net (DeParle, 2020b). This could be an important step toward the infusion of a human rights perspective into ethical social work practice.

Applying Human Rights to Ethical Practice

The UN Declaration lists privacy as a basic human right; social work's emphasis on the importance of confidentiality in practice is a corollary of this right. Yet, according to Gewirth (2001), confidentiality in social work is different from that of other professions like medicine and law, because in the latter professions, clients share their confidences voluntarily. As stated above, human rights claims fall into two broad categories: negative rights, which involve the duty not to interfere with a person's rights, and positive rights, which involve the obligation to enable an individual or group to attain the objective of this right. Gewirth points out that confidentiality contains elements of both. It includes the negative duty "of refraining from divulging [private] information" without prior consent, and "the positive duty to help the client … maintain … autonomy and trust" (p. 485).

This raises the question of whether these obligations are mutual as a rights-based approach implies. In other words, do they create correlative duties on rights holders, in both specific contexts and in general? For example, if a social worker and client engage in online counseling, does the client have a reciprocal duty not to discuss the content of her therapy with Facebook friends?

Ethical issues regarding the application of human rights also exist in macro social work practice. For example, among the fundamental human rights established by international labor law (International Labor Organization [ILO] Convention 98, adopted in 1949) is the right of workers to bargain collectively. In the UN Declaration, "the right to bargain collectively is subsumed under the rights to freedom of association and the right to organize into a trade union (Articles 20 and 23)" (Tarpinian, 2011, p. 1). Although the United States has not ratified this convention, "it is bound by that Convention by virtue of its membership in the ILO" (p. 1).

In addition, as the United States is a signatory to the Declaration, the Supremacy Clause of the Constitution (Article VI, Clause 2) binds state governments to its provisions. Policies designed to eliminate this right, such as the state of New York's Taylor Law that forbids strikes by public employees, Wisconsin's law prohibiting collective bargaining by public sector workers (Madland & Rowell, 2017), and the union-busting "opt out" policies of so-called right to work states, are essentially violations of international law. In principle, the United States is obligated to enforce labor rights by its participation in international trade agreements that prohibit any violation of internationally recognized labor rights. Of course, the government's willingness to enforce this and other rights depends to a considerable extent on who controls the White House, Congress, and the Supreme Court.

The social work profession is not innocent of similar failures. Throughout the history of American social work, there has been controversy over whether it is ethical for social workers to unionize, participate in strikes or other job actions, or support strikes and boycotts organized by other labor organizations and social movements (Reisch, 2015, 2009; Karger, 1988; Fisher, 1987). During conservative political eras, both public and private sector agencies, including universities and schools of social work, fired social workers who were union activists or members and blacklisted them within the profession (Reisch & Andrews, 2002). Increased licensing of social workers to promote the interests of the profession and, ostensibly, the public interest sometimes conflicts with other worthy goals, such as reducing racism within social service organizations, promoting macro social work practice, and supporting public sector social service unions that often represent nonprofessional members (Castex et al., 2019; Plitt Donaldson et al., 2016).

Allocation of Scarce Resources

ETHICAL DILEMMA 11.2   *"The Lottery" (Adapted with liberal changes from Jorge Luis Borges, "The Lottery in Babylon")*

Several thousand years ago in the kingdom of Assyria, His Most Sovereign Majesty, the all-powerful King Nebudchednezzar, was deeply troubled. For seven nights, the same horrible dream had disturbed his sleep: a gigantic earthquake would split his kingdom in half, dividing villages and families, throwing everyone into a desolate void.

The king consulted the high priests of the temple, his most reliable court astrologers, his greatest magicians, and the wisest prophets in the land. He even spoke with his favorite wives about his troubles. Unanimously, they agreed that the dreams were an omen of the impending breakup of his realm—a catastrophe for all—unless he eliminated the sources of the schism: widening economic and social inequality.

The mighty Nebudchednezzar nodded gravely at their advice. He knew in his heart that the words of the priests, the prophets, the magicians, the astrologers, and even his wives were true. Yet, he was no less troubled, for knowing the source of the problem shed no light at all on a possible solution. On the advice of his chief minister and the high priest, the king retired to his chambers for three days of fasting, prayer, and meditation.

For three days and nights, Nebudchednezzar beseeched the gods for an answer to the troubles afflicting his land. Finally, at the end of three days, a tired but elated king called his court together and announced what he believed to be the will of the gods:

"Starting at dawn tomorrow, my soldiers will range over the entire kingdom and do an accounting of all the wealth in the land. While they complete this accounting, my wisest ministers will determine how many of my subjects can live a life of decency on the accumulated wealth of the kingdom. Then, after a week-long festival of games, contests, feasting, dancing, and prayer, we will hold a lottery."

"A lottery?" chorused the courtiers.

"Yes," answered Nebudchednezzar, growing more certain of his decision with each passing moment. "We will place the names of everyone in the realm in a gigantic golden drum. Those whose names are drawn will receive an equal share of the kingdom's wealth. Then, we will live in peace and our land will be saved."

There was a long silence from the court.

"What are you waiting for?" the powerful sovereign shouted. "Captains of the guards—issue the orders to your troops. Ministers, begin your work. Stewards, prepare for the festivities. Everyone take heart. The lottery is the answer to my prayers."

And so, the work began …

Questions:

1. What do you think of the king's solution?
2. On what principles did he base it?
3. What are its implications for the challenge of distributing scarce resources today?
4. What alternative solution would you propose?
5. What are the ethical issues this story raises?

Unlike this allegory, social workers in the real world are regularly involved in the distribution and redistribution of tangible goods, such as cash assistance, employment opportunities, and essential services, and intangible resources, such as status, access, opportunity, and the absence of stigma. Yet, we have long struggled with what values we should use to determine the distributive results we desire. We have primarily used three approaches: utilitarianism, intuitionism, and Rawlsian justice principles.

As Nussbaum (2013) and Sen (2009) point out, justice involves not only equitable outcomes but also process equity. In addition, it involves an understanding of the context in which the distribution of benefits and rights occurs. This has clear implications for our critical analysis of policy and practice issues and for the establishment of advocacy priorities. Although most social workers appear to share, at least in principle, a commitment to downward redistribution, the profession often defines social justice ambiguously and qualifies this definition by several self-interested caveats.

Distributive justice, a key component in resource allocation, applies four criteria: equality, need, compensation, and contribution. Each of these criteria, however, is far more complicated to apply than it initially appears. For example, does the principle of equality refer to equality of opportunity, access, or outcome? Does it refer to equality at an individual or group level? Does it include compensation for past inequalities or take into account the equality of potential future contributions? It is important to note here that while the NASW *Code of Ethics* refers to social justice, it primarily emphasizes individual (not group) needs (not rights), and focuses on equal access rather than equal or equitable outcomes.

FIGURE 11.1. The Competition for Scarce Resources Inevitably Produces Ethical Issues

Dilemmas of Ethical Resource Allocation

Decisions regarding the allocation of scarce resources at the micro, mezzo, and macro levels require the linkage of morality and politics. These decisions confront social workers with different challenges at each of these levels. At the micro level, the challenge involves how to distribute our time and personal resources in the face of constant, complex, and competing client and organizational demands. Issues produced by this challenge include the role of interpersonal and intrapersonal conflict, the need to prevent burnout, and the importance of self-care. It is useful in this regard to keep in mind the following comment from the poet and activist Audre Lorde (2017): "Self-care is not about self-indulgence. It is about self-preservation." The day-to-day challenges health care providers, including social workers, face due to the coronavirus pandemic illustrate this dictum clearly.

REFLECTION EXERCISE: HOW DO YOU ALLOCATE YOUR PERSONAL RESOURCES?

Think about the pressures you have experienced regarding the allocation of your personal resources (e.g., your time, your influence, your access to critical information, your knowledge and skills) in your internship or place of employment. In small groups, discuss:

1. What competing demands did you encounter?
2. What consequences did the stress of these demands have on you personally?
3. How did you address these pressures and resolve these allocation decisions ethically?
4. What factors and ethical principles influenced your decision-making at the time?
5. To what extent would you apply these principles in all circumstances?

Allocating Scarce Resources at the Organizational Level

At the mezzo (organizational) level, agencies make allocation decisions through the design of their programs, the criteria they establish to determine eligibility for services or benefits, the distribution of staff workloads and rewards, and the processes they employ for resource development and budgeting. The growing privatization of social services, increased concerns about organizational accountability, and the persistence of fiscal austerity even in times of global crises such as the coronavirus pandemic have heightened competition for scarce resources in both the public and nonprofit sectors. These developments have produced new ethical challenges for agency administrators, particularly in small grassroots organizations (Pereira, 2020; Paarlberg et al., 2018; Sharp, 2018; Beaton & Hwang, 2017).

The decades-long shift in philanthropic funding patterns—from underwriting general operating costs to sponsorship of programmatic innovations and from long-term to time-limited support—has further compounded these resource development challenges as critics of the "new managerialism" have pointed out (Harlow & Lawler, 2018). It has also produced dramatic changes in the historical relationship between nonprofits and government (Phillips & Blumberg, 2017; Young, 2006; Austin, 2003), between the federal government and the states, and between state and local government (Bender, 2019; Berman, 2019; Welsh et al., 2019). The transformation of the funding environment has not only affected agency staff who are responsible for resource acquisition, it has also created new fiscal challenges for many social service organizations and for how practitioners allocate their most precious resource—their time—on a daily basis.

Different internal and external factors determine how organizations and their staff allocate these finite resources. They consider such distributive criteria as the nature of the need that requires a specific resource. For example, is it a short-term need (e.g., an emergency) or a long-term one (a structural or systemic issue)? (Lipsky & Smith, 1989). Do sufficient resources exist to have a positive effect on this particular need? A related factor is how devoting a scarce resource to this particular need might affect third parties (Beauchamp & Childress, 2019). The rationing of scarce health care resources by hospitals struggling with the effects of the coronavirus provides a vivid illustration of these constant ethical dilemmas (Hamblin, 2020).

Although seldom acknowledged, especially in crises, organizations also take into account certain core philosophical issues. For example, they consider the type of equality they will apply in the distribution of finite resources: equal shares, equal access, or random assignment. Decisions about resource allocation also include interpretations of equity (fairness or justice), factor in compensation for past inequities, and take into account such issues as an individual's or group's past, present, or potential future contributions to society, their ability to pay, their merit (or deservedness), and their ability to take advantage of the service or benefit. Today, hospitals employ similar criteria to determine which patients to admit to the ICU in life-and-death circumstances when there are not enough beds for everyone that needs one.

Even in noncrisis situations, internal organizational politics, ideological differences among staff, personal biases, external pressures, and agency traditions often influence the allocation of scarce resources (Reamer, 2018b; Rana et al., 2017). In times of national emergencies, such as the Covid-19 pandemic, awareness of these factors becomes even more important (Emanuel et al., 2020). From an ethical perspective, it is just as important to analyze how societies, organizations, and individuals resolve this recurrent dilemma as it is to analyze the outcomes of these decisions.

Although the misuse of funds or other types of misconduct by social service agencies is quite rare, the sector is not immune from ethical challenges regarding resource acquisition and allocation. Ethical issues in the area of resource development include the use of for-profit ventures by nonprofit organizations (Child, 2016). Critics charge that the favored tax status of nonprofits gives them an unfair advantage, especially when their business endeavors—such as restaurants—compete directly with their for-profit counterparts (Alm & Teles, 2018). Critics in the social welfare field have also questioned at what point these agencies are still nonprofits in the traditional meaning of the term and ask whether their increased reliance on for-profit ventures risks betraying their original missions and jeopardizing their social legitimacy (Kickul & Lyons, 2020).

In today's increasingly competitive resource development environment, there is also a growing risk that organizations will violate ethical principles or standards of propriety in their pursuit of funds. For example, resource-starved agencies may eliminate programs for marginalized clients because of donors' interest in other causes (Paarlberg & Hwang, 2017). Social service organizations may play on the gratitude of grateful clients to solicit contributions, as many hospitals have done (Collins, Rum, & Sugarman, 2018; Collins et al., 2018).

In earlier research, Moxley and Bueche (2002) identified six other ethical issues that nonprofits may confront today. One is the erosion of their core identity, as new hybrid organizational forms, like the "0-5" agencies in California counties, appear. A second issue is the growing disjuncture between an agency's historic image and the way it now portrays itself to potential donors. A third issue, with possible legal overtones, is the potential risk of using resource development as a tool for cause advocacy rather than to support agency programs as the agency had in the past. This strategy could also compel agencies to prioritize one cause over another, without consulting the opinions of affected third parties.

Another ethical issue, briefly cited above, could occur if an organization takes advantage of the emotional or physical vulnerability of potential donors in the pursuit of financial contributions. This is a particular problem in the health and behavioral health fields. There is the additional possibility that the method used to attract external funding—an organization's "case statement"—could exploit the population the agency hopes to serve and, in so doing, perpetuate long-standing stereotypes that contribute to this group's marginalization. Finally, in competing for scarce resources, organizations may withhold or distort certain information about their operations or the effectiveness of their programs to portray themselves in a more favorable light (pp. 267–272).

FOR REFLECTION AND DISCUSSION: HOW DOES YOUR AGENCY ALLOCATE ITS FINITE RESOURCES?

In small groups, discuss the process by which your agency determines how to allocate its finite resources, particularly in times of fiscal cutbacks, and compare the process used by your organization to the framework outlined below.

1. What internal and external factors influence these decisions?
2. What, if any, conflicts exist between them?

3. How does your agency resolve the conflicts that arise?
4. How does the ultimate distribution of resources in your organization reflect the ranking of these criteria?
5. What ethical framework would you use to determine how to allocate scarce resources?
6. What are the advantages and disadvantages of each possible framework?
7. What do you think about the guidelines listed below? Which ones should have priority?

Based on Rawlsian principles of distributive justice, Reisch and Taylor (1985) proposed the following guidelines for the allocation of scarce resources in noncrisis cutback situations. Organizations might consider applying them when faced with ongoing fiscal austerity.

1. Maintain the programs that primarily benefit the least advantaged.
2. Provide services based on need rather than fiscal efficiency.
3. Adopt a unitary system of service design and delivery to ensure that the least advantaged do not receive services of inferior quality or lesser accessibility.
4. Use the concept of distributive justice to make agency decisions not a utilitarian calculus.
5. Refrain, as much as possible, from cutting programs that primarily affect populations with the least ability (power) to resist or to receive comparable services elsewhere;
6. Affirm the organization's duty to advocate for just policies and programs. (p. 303)

More recently, similar guidelines to address resource issues have emerged during the Covid-19 pandemic (Berlinger et al., 2020; Binkley & Kemp, 2020; Emanuel et al., 2020). Think about the criteria you would use in the following situation.

ETHICAL DILEMMA 11.3   Allocating Scarce Resources
                                        During a Pandemic

You are the chief social worker in the intensive care unit (ICU) of a large research and teaching hospital in a major metropolitan area that is a "hot spot" in the Covid-19 pandemic. You are part of an interprofessional leadership team that includes the chief medical resident, the head of ICU nursing, and the director of the hospital's division of infectious diseases. Due to the federal government's failure to prepare adequately for the crisis, the hospital faces an acute shortage of ventilators and other critical life-saving equipment, including an experimental antiviral drug that clinical trials indicate has the potential to be an effective treatment. The hospital lacks sufficient equipment or dosages of the drug, however, to save the lives of all patients afflicted with the virus.

To help create a standard protocol, the leadership team developed the following exercise to determine how the hospital should prioritize the distribution of its finite resources. It used a sample of seven (7) patients who represent a cross-section of those in the ICU. In this scenario, there are insufficient dosages available to initiate the prescribed treatment regimen for all of them. At best, the ICU can provide four (4) of the patients with the optimal treatment regimen. In all likelihood, however, only three (3) of the patients can receive optimal treatment.

The patients are:

1. John B: He is a 55-year-old married White male with two college-age children. He works as a sales manager for a local office supply company.

His health condition is the most serious of all the patients in the sample because he has previously had a heart attack and has high blood pressure. If he is to receive the necessary treatment regimen, it must begin immediately.

2. Donna H: She is a White single mother, aged 28, who is raising three small children, ages 2–6, with the help of TANF and other social service benefits. She has a high school diploma; prior to the epidemic, she worked part-time in a local beauty salon. She is currently unemployed. Although she smokes, she has no other health conditions.

3. Olivia J: She is a 42-year-old African American public school teacher, who is married to the president of the city council. She has a daughter who is 9 years old. She is generally healthy, although she has a family history of type 2 diabetes.

4. Roger W: He is a distinguished emeritus professor, aged 75, who has received the Nobel Prize in Medicine and continues to be an active researcher. Despite his age, he has no prior medical conditions that would indicate he would not respond positively to the treatment regimen.

5. Terry S: She is a 15-year-old Asian American violin prodigy, who is studying at the local conservatory. Her teachers have referred to her as "the next great violinist."

6. Richard B: He is a 35-year-old man who has been homeless since his discharge from the Army six years ago. Diagnosed as schizophrenic with an addiction to crack cocaine, remarkably he has no other physical ailments.

7. Jennifer B: She is a 50-year-old married White woman whose family has donated over $10 million to the hospital during the past 5 years. Her husband has intimated that the family would make another substantial contribution if she were to receive the experimental drug treatment.

As you have a reputation for good judgment, and have taken continuing education courses in ethics to retain your social work license, the team relies on you in such challenging situations.

Questions:

1. What guidance would you provide the team?
2. What model of ethical decision-making would you apply?
3. What ethical principles would you prioritize?
4. To what extent would you apply a similar framework and similar principles to other decisions regarding the allocation of scarce resources?

Allocating Scarce Resources at the Societal Level

Fulfilling our professional commitment to work for social justice often requires us to make critical decisions at the societal level about the allocation of scarce resources. Sometimes, as in both past and recent pandemics (Warzel, 2020; "Who Shall Live," 1978), these decisions have life and death consequences. For example, U.S. policy in the past has prioritized funding for the research and treatment of certain diseases, such as kidney failure and cancer, over those of other ailments that are equally serious and more widespread. For over a half century, ethicists, health care providers, and policy makers have struggled with the fundamental question of who shall live and who shall die when faced with dire shortages (Rothman, 1992). Usually, policy makers and administrators do not make such decisions primarily on a rational or ethical basis; rather they often rely on political considerations.

The coronavirus pandemic has raised new and more urgent questions about the rationing of health care both during a health crisis and in "normal" times. Hospitals in different states have developed different criteria to determine who shall receive life-saving equipment, reflecting in stark terms what the fragmented U.S. health care system has been doing with less media attention for decades (Steenhuysen, 2020). In the aftermath of the coronavirus pandemic, the nation may finally grasp the implications of recognizing the finite nature of our health care resources and the human effects of allocating these resources so unequally and without forethought regarding the consequences.

The response to the pandemic has also renewed debates over how much our society should spend on health and behavioral health care and other vital services. In addition, we need to consider what type of care we should prioritize (primary/prevention, secondary, or tertiary) and determine what constitutes an equitable allocation of resources—that is, decide who is most deserving of care. Now and in the future, similar issues about the allocation of scarce resources will influence decisions about virtually every area of the nation's frayed and fragmented social safety net.

In making these difficult choices, distributional criteria have included an individual's perceived economic worth (i.e., productivity), social status, age, ability to pay, and past or future contribution. Sometimes we have allocated resources on a "first come, first serve" basis, which implicitly advantages certain privileged individuals and groups. Whatever criteria we employ, a just distribution scheme requires egalitarian participation to ensure a social consensus about whatever outcomes ensue. It is also important to keep in mind that health is not merely a desirable end in itself but also a means to the fulfillment of other personal and societal goals. This leads to the issue—equally applicable to other distributional challenges as well—of what proportion of our resources we should allocate proactively or reactively. Another issue in the years ahead that should be of particular concern to social workers is that whatever distributional criteria we adopt should not produce a restriction of vital resources to the least advantaged as occurred during the recent pandemic (DeParle, 2020b).

At present, however, our society does not make policy decisions about resource allocation on well-articulated principles or through a well-defined consensual process; rather, we often base these decisions on which groups have greater influence over public opinion, the media, and lawmakers. Past examples of this phenomenon include the specific provision for aid to the blind in the 1935 Social Security Act and the federal program for treating kidney disease in Medicare. During the past several decades, the government provided a higher level of funding to HIV/AIDS and breast cancer research than to other diseases (e.g., prostate or cervical cancer) that have similar or greater levels of morbidity.

In the health care field—and we could conceivably define nearly every social issue as a health issue—there will always be an intractable conflict between infinite demand and finite resources. The shortage of ventilators, protective equipment, and testing kits during the recent pandemic reflects this conflict with startling and painful clarity. During the pandemic, debates in Congress and demonstrations at state capitols demanding the lifting of "stay at home" orders have also reflected what Rothman (1992) referred to as "an even broader but no less inescapable conflict between the well-being of the individual ... and social pressures for 'economic efficiency'" (p. 33).

Finally, let us return to the connection between morality and politics. The distribution or redistribution of resources at all levels of society inevitably involves a host of political, economic, cultural, ideological, and situational factors. Policies that separate these decisions from morality inevitably favor the affluent and powerful and impose harsh conditions on the distribution of modest social benefits to the vulnerable.

More than ever, our society needs to recognize that policy decisions that exploit people and that prioritize profit over human need, particularly during a global health crisis, are irresponsible, unethical, and even evil. In a speech that was eerily prescient about the effects of the current pandemic, labor leader Leo Perlis asked 60 years ago, "Is it an act of morality to ask the sick to heal themselves, and the poor to feed themselves?" (1960, p. 6). His appeal to take concerted action still resonates today: "Justice is not served by an above-the-battle ... attitude. [It] is often served ... by taking sides squarely and without equivocation. ... Social justice can be achieved often through the collective morality of social action as well as through the individual morality of personal responsibility" (p. 7).

As the hypothetical case below illustrates, ethical dilemmas regarding resource allocation also occur when stakeholders are required to make proactive policy decisions.

ETHICAL DILEMMA 11.4   ## Distributing Burdens Equitably in Social Policy

There is widespread agreement that the U.S. economy will never fully recover from its current crisis until the coronavirus pandemic is under control, and that this is unlikely to occur until a successful vaccine is developed and widely distributed. As a leading social work ethicist, you are a member of a government commission charged with making recommendations regarding the criteria for distributing the vaccine. The commission must recommend which populations should receive the vaccination first and provide the justification for its recommendations.

After considerable deliberations, the commission identified the following potential priority groups by consensus:

- Doctors, nurses, and other health care workers
- School personnel, including teachers, and child care workers
- Other essential workers, such as grocery store employees, postal workers, police and firefighters, sanitation workers, agricultural workers, and workers in food processing plants
- Communities of color, particularly the African American, Latinx, and Native American communities because they have been particularly hard hit by the pandemic
- Individuals who are vulnerable because of their age (60 or older) or preexisting health condition
- Young children, who may spread the virus despite displaying no noticeable symptoms
- Government officials, including members of the armed forces

- Youth of high school and college age, because they are most likely to engage in behaviors that could spread the virus
- Individuals in regions of the country that have been most compliant with public health regulations, as measured by their ability to bring the virus under control
- A random distribution of the vaccine, determined by lottery

The chair of the commission asked each member to list these groups in their order of priority for receipt of the vaccine.

Questions:

1. How would you prioritize the distribution of the vaccine among these groups?
2. What are your reasons for this priority order?
3. Which ethical approach did you employ to make your decision: deontological or consequentialist? Why did you use the approach you selected?
4. If you used a deontological approach, what hierarchy of values did you employ?
5. If you used a consequentialist approach, which consequences did you consider and how did you weight them?
6. To what extent would you apply the principles that guided your decision to other policy issues?
7. What would be the implications of applying these principles more broadly?

This case demonstrates how, on occasion, ethical decisions need to be made proactively –i.e., prior to the emergence of an ethical dilemma. A possible model for how to address such issues is the role that social workers played during the initial outbreak of the pandemic in Wuhan, China (Petruzzi et al., 2020).

Of Means and Ends

Although all societies have articulated a vision of social justice, people have struggled with the ethical issue of what means are acceptable to achieve this goal since Biblical times. In the Old Testament Book of Exodus, it took 10 plagues, including the killing of Egyptians' first born, before Pharaoh freed the Hebrews. In the Gospel according to Matthew (10:34), Jesus says, "I did not come to bring peace, but a sword." Yet, in Luke 6:29, Jesus is quoted as saying: "If someone strikes you on one cheek, turn to him the other also." Clerical scholars have struggled with the meaning of these events and words for millennia.

During the Renaissance, Niccolo Machiavelli (1532/2015), in his classic treatise, *The Prince*, presented a secular view of means and ends based on what we would now refer to as "realpolitik." He asserted, "In the actions of all men, and especially of princes, where there is no court to appeal to, one looks to the end. So let the prince win and maintain his state: the means will always be judged honorable, and will be praised by everyone" (Chapter 18).

Two hundred fifty years later, Immanuel Kant, in his *Critique of Pure Reason* (1781/1999), presented an alternative perspective. His "categorical imperative" stipulated that all actions that treat persons merely as means to an end are morally wrong. As the quotations below illustrate, philosophers and politicians, revolutionaries and reformers, radicals and reactionaries have debated this issue for the past century. The challenges this issue represents are no less relevant today.

Some writers have expressed an absolute position on one side of the argument or other:

- "The end cannot justify the means, for the simple and obvious reason that the means employed determine the nature of the ends produced." – Aldous Huxley, *Ends and Means* (1937)

IMAGE 11.2. Aldous Huxley

IMAGE 11.3. Ayn Rand

IMAGE 11.4. Malcom X

- "The end does not justify the means. No one's rights can be secured by the violation of the rights of others." – Ayn Rand, *Capitalism: The Unknown Ideal* (1986)
- "By any means necessary." – Malcolm X, Speech at the founding rally of the Organization of Afro-American Unity (1964)

Others have articulated a somewhat more nuanced position:

- "The end justifies the means only when the means used are such as actually bring about the desired and desirable end." – John Dewey, *Intelligence in the Modern World* (1939)
- "If the injustice is part of the necessary friction of the machine of government, let it go, let it go; perchance it will wear smooth, certainly the machinery will wear out. If the injustice has a spring, or a pulley, or a rope, or a crank, exclusively for itself, then perhaps you may consider whether the remedy will not be worse than the evil; but *if it is of such a nature that it requires you to be the agent of injustice, then, I say, break the law.*" – Henry David Thoreau, *On the Duty of Civil Disobedience* (1849, emphasis added)
- "The end may justify the means as long as there is something that justifies the end." – Leon Trotsky, *Their Morals and Ours: The Class Foundations of Moral Practice* (1938)

IMAGE 11.5. John Dewey   **IMAGE 11.6.** Henry David Thoreau   **IMAGE 11.7.** Leon Trotsky

In his classic treatise on community organizing, *Rules for Radicals* (1971), Saul Alinsky presented a cynical view of this age-old issue:

1. One's concern with the ethics of means and ends varies inversely with one's personal interest in the issue.
2. The judgment of the ethics of means is dependent upon the political position of those sitting in judgment.
3. In war, the end justifies almost any means.
4. Judgments (regarding means and ends) must be made in the context of the times in which the action occurred and not from any other chronological vantage point.
5. Concern with ethics increases with the number of means available and vice versa.

IMAGE 11.8. Saul Alinsky Had a Cynical View of the Means vs. Ends Dilemma

6. The less important the end to be desired, the more one can afford to engage in ethical evaluations of means.

7. Generally, success or failure is a mighty determinant of ethics.

8. The morality of a means depends upon whether the means is being employed at a time of imminent defeat or imminent victory.

9. Any effective means is automatically judged by the opposition as being unethical.

10. You do what you can with what you have and clothe it in moral garments (requires assessment of resources, strengths, feasibility, etc.). In community organizing, the major negative in the situation has to be converted into the leading positive.

11. To justify the use of certain means, one's goals must be phrased in general terms of higher purpose (e.g., liberty, equality, fraternity; bread and peace, pursuit of happiness). (pp. 24–27)

FOR REFLECTION AND DISCUSSION: WHAT IS THE RELATIONSHIP BETWEEN MEANS AND ENDS?

Read the above quotations carefully. Think about the background of each of the authors, the context in which they wrote, and the purpose of their statements. Then compare your conclusions in small groups.

1. Which of the above perspectives is closest to your own?
2. For what reasons?
3. What might be the effects of applying this perspective to practice?
4. Which of Alinsky's statements reflects your practice experience?

The temptation to use exploitive means to achieve desired ends exists in both clinical and macro practice. Clinical social workers, for example, may use therapeutic techniques that manipulate clients through coercive or paradoxical interventions. Community organizers may demonize opponents in order to increase solidarity and motivate the groups with whom they work to take concerted action. In pursuit of the bottom line, agency administrators may seek sources of funding by misrepresenting the capacity of their agencies to implement certain programs or services (Friedman, 2018; Nathan & Tempel, 2016). Other means/ends issues that affect both clinical and macro practitioners in both practice and research include the use of deception, the need to balance long-term and short-term gains, and restrictions on the self-determination of individuals and communities (Israel et al., 2017; Hardina, 2004).

In a controversial introduction to their book on community organizing, Rivera and Erlich (1998) argued that a practitioner's demographic and cultural relationship with the community should be a factor in determining both the role they play and the tactics they use. This is why the acquisition of the elusive goal of cultural competence and treating people with respect in all areas of practice is so important. As the experience of the welfare rights movement demonstrates (Sherwin & Piven, 2019; Nadasen, 2012, 2019), "if advocates want their communications and relationships to be effective, they must take into consideration the cultural differences of the parties with whom they interact" (Ezell, 2013, p. 47). Unfortunately, because the NASW *Code of Ethics* does not include anything that could provide guidance to social workers regarding means/ends dilemmas, each of us needs to devise our own consistent framework to resolve these vexing issues.

| ETHICAL DILEMMA 11.5 | What Means Are Ethical to Achieve a Just End? |

You are a social worker in a community hospital in a large metropolitan area. For over a year, you have been working with a coalition of health care providers and consumers around a range of issues that focus on access to health care, quality of care, and consumer sovereignty in the provision of health care. One of the major partners in the coalition is the local Health and Hospital Workers Union. The union, which has successfully organized health care and social workers in nonprofit and private hospitals, managed care companies, and HMOs in the region, is involved in serious and conflict-ridden negotiations over its contract. Among the issues are (a) differential salary levels for new and long-term employees; (b) health and pension benefits; (c) improved working conditions, including the provision of protective equipment; and (d) enhanced quality of care. In addition, the union has pressed for greater influence for workers and consumers in making health policy in the hospital, especially on matters of client care and the distribution of institutional resources. Social workers in your hospital, however, are not unionized; they disagree about the benefits and ethics of unionization.

After weeks of negotiations, the two sides are at an impasse. It appears that the hospital administration is not bargaining in good faith because it doubts the union's ability to sustain an effective strike or job action. They also contend that the unionization of some hospital staff, including social workers, nurses, interns, and residents, violates their professional ethical codes and renders the hospital administration under no moral or legal obligation to engage in collective bargaining.

Last night, union members voted overwhelmingly to strike effective next Monday. The union's representative to the coalition asks you to use your influence to persuade the coalition to endorse the strike and encourage your social work colleagues not to cross any picket line. While you are sympathetic to the union's position, you know that a strike will affect the quality of care for the people you serve and the constituents you represent (at least temporarily). It will also create divisions within the social work department of the hospital and between social workers and the hospital administration, which has previously expressed skepticism about the value of social workers in the provision of health care and threatened to eliminate the department.

Questions:
1. What would you do? What are your reasons for your decision?
2. What is the nature of the ethical dilemma? Who created the dilemma?
3. Where is the locus of responsibility for its resolution?
4. What is the nature, basis, and extent of your ethical obligation? To whom?
5. Would the use of a strike in these circumstances be an ethical means to achieve the desired ends?
6. What are the short- and long-term consequences of your decision for your constituents?
7. What social work values or ethical frameworks help guide you in your decision-making?

Over a half century ago, during a time of social and political ferment somewhat similar to today, Goulet (1969) astutely commented that an ethical dilemma regarding means and ends can only exist if people faced with the dilemma are aware of alternative courses of action. Yet, he argued, even if we try to avoid resolving a sticky means/ends issue, the personal and professional dilemma created by the conflict between desired outcomes and our reluctance to adopt the means that may be required to produce them will still exist. "Ethical purists," Goulet commented acerbically, "want revolution and love simultaneously, but the two are incompatible" (p. 44). To reframe the dilemma to which he referred in terms applicable to the social work profession, we have always sought both social change and social acceptance, and the two may not always be entirely compatible. The attacks on our professional ancestors who fought for social reforms during the 1920s and the McCarthy period illustrate this ongoing tension (Reisch, 2020a; Reisch & Andrews, 2002).

The assessment of what constitutes a "just" or "unjust" means to achieve a just end also assumes a priori knowledge of what justice means in a specific context (Lebacqz, 1987). One solution proposed by proponents of liberation theology in Latin America is to apply the following six criteria:

1. A determination that the legitimate authority that would ordinarily be able to initiate or support a desired change is corrupt and incapable of working toward the common good;
2. All other less controversial means have been exhausted or are totally unrealistic in the current circumstances;
3. The positive effects of the desired change outweigh any anticipated negative consequences;
4. There is a reasonable possibility of success if the controversial means are employed;
5. The means employed are not "intrinsically" evil; and
6. The means used cannot deliberately exacerbate the original problem in order to rationalize their employment. (Cited in Goulet, 1969, p. 45)

Each of these criteria, however, creates its own dilemmas. For example, who will determine whether the first criterion exists and how? How will we take into account the historical factors that shaped the issue? How will we ensure that we conduct a realistic and not an idealistic assessment of the situation? How will we avoid replacing unjust institutions, policies, and procedures with new hierarchies and injustices as has often occurred in the past (Reisch & Garvin, 2016)? Will the means we employ intensify social divisions to such an extent that we cannot heal them? Today, these difficult issues are equally relevant. They complicate the resolution of the complex problems created by increasing socioeconomic inequality, persistent racial injustice, and the existential threats of climate change and the coronavirus pandemic.

The pressure to resolve the means/ends dilemma has increased recently due to growing dissatisfaction with U.S. institutions among Americans of all races, classes, genders, religions, regions, and ideologies. Particularly during times of crisis, distrust of government by both libertarians and progressives intensifies. Although groups like Black Lives Matter, #MeToo, and Occupy, in which social workers have participated and served as allies, have effectively diagnosed many of our society's problems, they have been less successful in proposing feasible solutions or developing realistic means to achieve them. Activists remain divided over whether they should participate in efforts to reform systems they believe are beyond redemption. They fear that any compromise in the attainment of partial victories will be a form of co-optation and leave the status quo intact. They have also not absorbed Sartre's comment that it may be impossible for activists of all political persuasions to keep their hands clean. Deciding whether such ideological or tactical purity is ethical presents us with an ongoing ethical dilemma, as the following case illustrates.

ETHICAL DILEMMA 11.6

Can Unethical Means Produce an Ethical End?

You are in charge of the policy advocacy unit of a statewide organization that advocates for a range of issues affecting the LGBTQI community. A prominent member of the state legislature has introduced a bill that would deny a range of health and behavioral health benefits to lesbian, gay, or transgendered individuals and forbid them from adopting a child or serving as a foster parent. Given the influence of this legislator, the bill has a good chance of passage. The governor has already indicated support for the measure.

A board member of your agency confides to you that he has seen this legislator in several gay bars in the community. The public image that the legislator has cultivated, however, is of a married, church-going man with moral probity. If this information leaked to the media, it could discredit the legislator and help defeat the bill. The board member asks if you will assist him in developing a strategy to make this information public and maximize its potential impact. Time is of the essence as the legislature has scheduled a vote on the measure for next week.

Questions:
1. What are the ethical conflicts in this situation?
2. How would you respond to the board member?
3. What process would you use to make your decision?
4. On what principles would you base your decision?
5. What are the potential consequences of your decision—for you, your agency, its constituents, and other third parties?
6. Which of the above statements regarding means and ends most closely matches your decision?
7. Under what circumstances would you apply this process and these principles to similar cases?

Activists have also struggled for centuries over the issue of whether the use of force or violence, against property or persons, is ever justifiable to achieve a worthy end. This issue emerged again in 2020 as the largely peaceful protests against racial injustice have occasionally led to the destruction of property and the violation of existing laws. The chart below represents the continuum of possible responses to this long-standing dilemma.

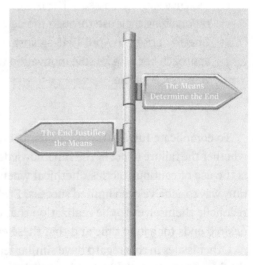

IMAGE 11.9. A Perpetual Dilemma for Social Work Activists

ETHICS AND THE SPECTRUM OF NONVIOLENCE

- Pacifism – The belief that any violence, including war, is unjustifiable under any circumstances, and that people should settle all disputes by peaceful means. American pacifists like Dorothy Day, the founder of the Catholic Workers Movement, and Jane Addams, the co-founder of Hull House, promoted this principle.

- Nonresistance – The practice or principle of not resisting authority, even when those with power exercise their authority in an unjust manner. The tactics used by the modern civil rights movement under the leadership of Dr. Martin Luther King Jr., vividly exemplified by the late Representative John Lewis, reflected this principle.

- *Satyagraha* ("truth force" or "soul force") – A strategy of nonviolent political resistance. Mohandas Gandhi used this strategy against British rule in India.

- Civil disobedience – The refusal to comply with certain laws or orders from authorities, or pay taxes and fines, as a peaceful form of protest against policies or practices one believes are unjust. (See Thoreau quote above for a rationale for this tactic.) Protests used by ACT-UP to increase public attention to the HIV/AIDS crisis or by Black Lives Matter to heighten public awareness of police violence against African Americans are examples of this approach.

- Nonviolent coercion – A strategy that does not change an opponent's mind but renders the opponent incapable of continuing to struggle because the sources of the opponent's power have been taken away without the use of violence. A boycott, such as the Montgomery Bus Boycott, is a good example.

- Nonviolence by necessity – A situation in which there is an immutable distribution of the instruments of violence in a community or society. In such situations, activists have no alternative other than to use nonviolent means to promote their goals. The situation of dissidents in totalitarian or authoritarian societies falls into this category.

- Violence without hatred – The use of violent means out of perceived necessity without rationalizing their use through the demonization of one's opponents. The Warsaw Ghetto uprising in April 1943 against Nazi occupiers is a possible illustration of this approach because its sole motivation was self-defense and other, nonviolent means were not available.

To complicate further the means/end equation, Ezell (2013) raises the searching question whether the failure to act in the full knowledge of existing inequalities is unethical. Conversely, is the use of cautious tactics unethical when it is clear that a more aggressive approach is the only way to achieve even limited success? Ezell points out that advocates and activists must also reconcile themselves to the realization that even the most successful means will not produce desired ends for a long time and that these ends may not be permanent (p. 42).

Other issues in this regard have similar features to the ethical issues discussed elsewhere in this book. In both individual and class advocacy, for example, it is important to obtain informed consent from our clients or constituents before engaging in certain means, assess whether

IMAGE 11.10. Gandhi Was a Proponent of Nonviolent Resistance to Oppression

IMAGE 11.11. Rosa Parks Being Arrested for an Act of Civil Disobedience That Triggered the 1955 Montgomery Bus Boycott

IMAGE 11.12. Jane Addams, a Leading Proponent of Pacifism, Was Awarded the Nobel Peace Prize

IMAGE 11.13. Dorothy Day Was a Pacifist and Social Activist on Behalf of the Poor

these means serve their interests, and determine how much risk they can assume. It is also critical for advocates not to overstate the case (which could result in a loss of credibility), act *for* rather than *with* people (Freire, 1971), and pit vulnerable groups against each other in the competition for attention, resources, or influence.

The complexity of many ethical dilemmas in contemporary practice, therefore, creates two options for social workers regarding means and ends. One is to do nothing, because the situations we confront are incapable of satisfactory resolution, or rationalizing inaction by engaging in what Homan (2016) termed meaningless means/ends arguments. The other is to take action "after making an ethically defensible, less than perfect decision and continue to manage the tension [involved in balancing] the rights and interests of several stakeholders" (Ezell, 2013, p. 49).

Summary

This chapter discussed several challenging ethical conflicts that contemporary national and global developments have intensified. One involves the interpretation of social justice in an increasingly diverse society and multipolar world. Although the NASW *Code of Ethics* and the mission statement of the International Federation of Social Workers proclaim social justice an ethical imperative of the profession, and the Council on Social Work Education requires social work students to learn how to apply the concept to practice, definitions of the term remain fraught with ambiguity. Resolving this ambiguity is not merely a philosophical matter; it has real world implications at every level of practice.

A similar dilemma exists regarding the interpretation of human rights. There is an ongoing debate in the profession over whether the goal of universal human rights is compatible or in conflict with the goal of social justice. Striking differences in this regard exist among various racial and cultural groups both within the United States and throughout the world. The resolution of this issue will have significant consequences for practitioners and policy makers alike.

The chapter also discussed two persistent issues that all social workers experience or will inevitably encounter in their practice. One involves the allocation of scarce resources at the micro, mezzo, and macro levels. In this regard, it is equally important for us to develop a consistent and consensual process for making decisions about the way we distribute finite resources, as it is to evaluate the results of these decisions.

The final ethical issue the chapter covered is the persistent conflict between means and ends. Although many social workers think this issue is only relevant to activists, a similar challenge, albeit on a different scale, exists for practitioners working with individuals, families, and groups. Because the NASW *Code of Ethics* does not provide specific guidelines about the resolution of means/ends issues, it is particularly important for every social worker to develop their own framework to determine the appropriate balance of means and ends in widely varying circumstances. Once again, this demonstrates that ethical practice involves constant critical reflection by each of us, and not merely applying universal prescriptions or proscriptions developed by others.

The final chapter takes a broad overview of the various issues discussed in the book and contemplates what will be the features of ethical social work practice in an uncertain future.

Reflection Exercise I: Reconciling Social Justice, Human Needs, and Human Rights

1. How can we determine what are "common human needs" in an increasingly diverse society? Who should make this determination? Through what means?
2. In what ways are the pursuit of social justice and the promotion of human rights compatible or in conflict in policy and practice?
3. How can a human rights perspective enable an organization to balance its commitment to social justice and multiculturalism?

Reflection Exercise II: Allocating Scarce Organizational Resources

1. What criteria should an organization use to allocate its finite financial resources? How should it establish these criteria? By whom?
2. What criteria should an organization use to allocate the scarce resource of staff time?
3. What criteria would you employ to allocate the scarce resource of your time?

Reflection Exercise III: Determining the Ethics of Means and Ends

1. Which of the following actions would you consider acceptable to achieve a just end:
   - Breaking a law you consider unjust or refusing to pay taxes
   - Committing civil disobedience (e.g., blocking traffic in a demonstration)
   - Destroying the property of opponents
   - Destroying the property of innocent third parties to draw attention to an issue
   - Ruining the reputation of an opponent
   - Lying or withholding critical information
   - Outing a powerful political opponent
   - Committing violence against your "enemies"
   - Committing violence against innocent third parties

2. What principles and decision-making framework did you use to determine your answers?
3. What means/end dilemma have you confronted or witnessed in your practice?
4. How did you address these dilemmas or observe how others addressed them?
5. What principles would you derive from this experience or observation about the way to resolve means/end dilemmas in your future practice?

Credits

Img. 11.1: Copyright © by FDR Presidential Library & Museum (cc by 2.0) at https://commons.wikimedia.org/wiki/File:Eleanor_Roosevelt_UDHR_(27758131387).jpg.

Fig.11.1: Copyright © 2011 Depositphotos/Krisdog.

Img. 11.2: Source: https://commons.wikimedia.org/wiki/File:Aldous_Huxley_psychical_researcher.png.

Img. 11.3: Source: https://commons.wikimedia.org/wiki/File:Ayn_Rand_(1943_Talbot_portrait).jpg.

Img. 11.4: Source: https://commons.wikimedia.org/wiki/File:Malcolm_X_NYWTS_2a_cropped.jpg.

Img. 11.5: Source: https://commons.wikimedia.org/wiki/File:John_Dewey_cph.3a51565.jpg.

Img. 11.6: Source: https://commons.wikimedia.org/wiki/File:Benjamin_D._Maxham_-_Henry_David_Thoreau_-_Restored.jpg.

Img. 11.7: Source: https://commons.wikimedia.org/wiki/File:Leon_Trotsky_(crop).jpg.

Img. 11.8: Copyright © by (cc by-sa 4.0) at https://commons.wikimedia.org/wiki/File:Saul_Alinsky.jpg.

Img. 11.9: Copyright © 2012 Depositphotos/lapinpix2.

Img. 11.10: Source: https://commons.wikimedia.org/wiki/File:Mahatma-Gandhi,_studio,_1931.jpg.

Img. 11.11: Source: https://commons.wikimedia.org/wiki/File:Rosa_Parks_being_fingerprinted_by_Deputy_Sheriff_D.H._Lackey_after_being_arrested_on_February_22,_1956,_during_the_Montgomery_bus_boycott.png.

Img. 11.12: Source: https://commons.wikimedia.org/wiki/File:Famous_Living_Americans_-_Jane_Addams.jpg.

Img. 11.13: Source: https://commons.wikimedia.org/wiki/File:Dorothy_Day_1916.jpg.

Conclusion

Ethical Practice in an Uncertain Future

Introduction

You cannot change any society unless you take responsibility for it, unless you see yourself as belonging to it and taking responsibility for changing it.

Grace Lee Boggs

The world will not be destroyed by those who do evil, but by those who watch them without doing anything.

Albert Einstein

I'm for truth, no matter who tells it. I'm for justice no matter who it's for or against.

Malcolm X

IMAGE 12.1. Grace Lee Boggs   **IMAGE 12.2.** Albert Einstein   **IMAGE 12.3.** Malcolm X

In recent years, my students have reported experiencing the following personal issues in their lives and work:

- Difficulty establishing trust with people from different demographic or cultural backgrounds
- Difficulty understanding and having empathy for world views different from their own
- Separating the pressures of their professional and personal lives

- Recognizing their ignorance and acknowledging their implicit biases
- Maintaining patience and courage in the midst of increasing external stresses

Although the NASW *Code of Ethics* provides many important behavioral guidelines for new social workers to assist them in navigating the difficult ethical terrain of practice, its prescriptive nature does less to assist them in resolving these and other issues, particularly the issues that have emerged in today's anxiety-ridden and unprecedented times.

To complicate matters further, the policies of the Trump administration, both prior to and during the coronavirus pandemic, have exacerbated long-standing ethical challenges for social workers. The combination of fiscal austerity, hostile federal and state laws, and widespread indifference to human suffering and human need challenges the core values of the profession. In virtually every field and method of social work, we confront situations that compel us to behave in ways that conflict with our ethical principles, particularly those that prioritize clients' interests, obligate us to resist organizational policies and procedures that interfere with ethical practice, and require us to pursue social justice. In effect, due to circumstances largely beyond our control, we become complicit in the implementation of discriminatory and unjust behaviors. Under these seemingly impossible conditions, it is not unreasonable for social workers, particularly younger social workers and social work students, to feel that the NASW *Code* is no longer applicable to their work, that it is idealistic, impractical, and in need of substantial revision (Byers & Shapiro, 2019).

This chapter will conclude the book with an exploration of the role of ethics in today's perilous and anxiety-producing environment. It will discuss the ethical challenges we face and some possible responses. It will examine how we might overcome emotions of helplessness and apathy, and practice ethically in an unjust and uncertain context.

ETHICAL DILEMMA 12.1

Ethical Practice During a Pandemic

You are the chief social worker in the intensive care unit (ICU) of a large hospital. The hospital has been overwhelmed with people who have contracted the coronavirus, many of whom are in the ICU and cannot receive visitors even if they are dying. Although it has placed a strain on the hospital's resources, the hospital has also admitted other critically ill patients to the ICU but has subjected them to the same social isolation, even in the final stages of their lives.

A group of influential community leaders, representing both religious and secular organizations, petitioned you to use your influence with the hospital administration to revise this policy and allow terminally ill patients who have not contracted the virus to have visitors. They argue that these patients are not contagious, that the hospital could take reasonable precautions to ensure that visitors would not spread the virus,

and that permitting close relatives to visit their family members would comfort them enormously.

You understand and sympathize with this request but are bound to follow hospital policy. You are also concerned about equity issues if the hospital acceded to the request. From first-hand experience, you know that individuals afflicted with the virus would also benefit from the comfort their families could provide.

Questions:
1. How would respond to this request?
2. On what ethical principles would you base your response?
3. How would you reconcile your response with the concept of social justice (equity)?
4. To what extent would you generalize the principles you used in this situation?

Your response to this dilemma might vary depending on the approach you took. A deontological perspective would require you to determine which values take precedence in this situation. They could be compassion for the dying and their families, protection of family visitors from harm, obeying hospital policy, or treating all people equitably. A consequentialist approach would attempt to measure the relative effects of complying or not complying with the request you received. You would have to balance the emotional benefits for the ICU patients and their loved ones against the potential harm that might occur to them, the erosion of hospital protocols, and the damage to your reputation and interprofessional relationships.

Challenges to Ethical Practice Today

The International Federation of Social Workers (2018a) defines the purpose of ethical practice in the following way:

> Social work is a practice-based profession and an academic discipline that facilitates social change and development, social cohesion, and the empowerment and liberation of people. Principles of social justice, human rights, collective responsibility and respect for diversities are central to social work. Underpinned by theories of social work, social sciences, humanities and indigenous knowledge, social work engages people and structures to address life challenges and enhance wellbeing.

The ethical challenges created by the policies of the Trump administration and its predecessors are not unique. In the past, social workers in the United States and other nations have occasionally been actively or passively complicit in the development and implementation of unjust policies, often of a racist or sexist nature. In the United States, this included support for eugenics during and immediately after the Progressive Era (Gibson, 2015; Kennedy, 2008), cooperation with the internment of Japanese Americans during World War II (Park, 2019), the repression of dissidents during the McCarthy era (Reisch, 2020a), and active monitoring of the sexual behavior of Aid to Families with Dependent Children recipients (Sherwin & Piven, 2019; Lefkovitz, 2011). Outside the United States, some social workers collaborated with racist regimes in Nazi Germany, Spain, and South Africa (Harms-Smith, 2020; Kuhlmann, 2020; Martinez Herrero, 2020; Sunker, 2020; Jarratt & Moorhead, 2011), and with repressive governments in Chile and Argentina (Alabarce, 2020; Munoz Arce, 2020). During the past few years, social workers conducting confidential clinical assessments of undocumented immigrant children might have inadvertently abetted the restrictive immigration policies of the Trump administration, which sought to exploit the information these interviews provide (Jani & Reisch, 2018).

Today, the entrenched divisions in U.S. society in the midst of profound existential crises challenge us to articulate a consistent way to apply our ethical principles to the public policies that address both immediate issues like the coronavirus pandemic and longer-term issues like climate change and socioeconomic inequality. Several factors complicate our efforts to resolve this crisis of values. One is the very complexity of the institutions upon which we rely to address these societal challenges (Nguyen et al., 2017). This complexity obscures accountability and responsibility, as the varied responses of the federal government and state governments to the coronavirus pandemic demonstrated, particularly if media spokespersons, opportunistic political leaders, and disinformation posts on the internet deliberately obfuscate these issues. Even prior to the recent crisis, political discourse in the United States reflected the absence of a consensus regarding what type of society we wanted to create and what alternative means we could use to address the existential threats we face.

The fragmented political structure of the United States further compounds our ability to confront these problems effectively (Béland et al., 2020; Michener, 2018). In our decentralized political system, states and localities compete with each other for public attention and finite resources, as the scramble for protective equipment during the pandemic sharply reveals (Smith et al., 2020). Market-oriented organizations, such as multinational pharmaceutical corporations and insurance giants, have different priorities from their nonprofit counterparts. Even in the midst of a crisis, they often describe identical phenomena, such as the provision of health care, in dramatically different terms.

This fragmentation exists as well within the social welfare arena, in the competition for resources (and students) between schools of social work, fields of practice (e.g., child welfare vs. services to the aged), and identity groups. These divisions impede our efforts to develop a comprehensive vision for the future or even a coordinated response to a pandemic, as some other industrialized societies have done more successfully. A further complication arises from the gap between our capabilities, which inevitably are limited, and our expectations, which are always expanding. The history of the past century demonstrates that we possess more knowledge and greater technical capacity to solve formerly intractable problems, such as those created by a mysterious virus. The presence of these tools creates frustration when we cannot find immediate solutions to public health crises or develop "quick-fix" interventions to issues such as climate change, structural racism, and global socioeconomic inequality.

The pull of divergent loyalties—to clients, colleagues, employers, community, society, and ourselves—further complicates our application of ethical principles. Conversely, the organizations in which we work increasingly have to reconcile their different, often competing, interests, values, and convictions with the compromises required for their survival. This underscores the importance of recognizing how these organizations are each greater than the sum of their parts. Like individuals, families, communities, and societies, their histories, customs, and traditions shape their current goals and the range of available strategies to achieve them.

This recognition has direct implications for our ability to practice ethically. In an interactive and interdependent agency context, the unethical conduct of a single person can destroy the organization's reputation, while the maintenance of ethical standards can enhance its image in the community as a model of responsibility, accountability, and integrity. This underscores the importance of cooperation among colleagues, not only in attaining organizational goals but also in preserving its ethical commitments (Chang, 2016).

This is equally true in the policy-making sphere, where the most vulnerable populations have little voice (Gilens & Page, 2014). The development of responsive policies requires a synthesis of ethical principles and empirical evidence, particularly regarding which issues we prioritize and which data we consider most relevant in shaping difficult choices. Sometimes, an individual who is somewhat removed from (outside of) the policy-making process can see the ethical implications of that process and its potential outcomes more clearly, as the experience of frontline health care workers and first responders reveals both prior to and during the current pandemic (Gellert, 2020; Solnica et al., 2020; Fantus et al., 2017).

Ethical policy-making in the future, therefore, will require three essential features. One is a greater emphasis on shared responsibility for visioning and implementation. This will generate more alternatives and a wider range of potential action. Another is an integrated future-oriented vision, one that our society and polity sadly lack today. A third is a set of strategies that attend to both individual needs and group interests rather than viewing them as locked in eternal, irreconcilable conflict.

Initial steps toward this goal would possess four components. First, they would include a critical, in-depth analysis of how problems and policies affect different social groups differently, based on their race, class, gender, geography, occupation, age, and other attributes. Second, they would involve an assessment of how policy recipients view the effects of policies purportedly designed to assist them. Third, based on these analyses, they would create mechanisms to obtain fresh perspectives on people's needs and the efficacy of existing policy options. Finally, it would then be necessary to determine through our previous experiences and an analysis of alternative policies how they would affect or neglect broader social goals.

FIGURE 12.1. Ethical Practice in the Future Will Be Even More Important than Today

Ethical Practice in the Current Context

Ethical dilemmas exist when we are aware of alternative courses of action even in the unavoidable and uncomfortable circumstances alluded to above. As discussed in other chapters, one possible solution to the dilemmas we confront today may lie in reframing our practice to emphasize an ethic of care (Hay, 2019). This may enable practitioners to strike "a critical and pragmatic balance" (Byers & Shapiro, 2019, p. 176) between service provision and case and class advocacy. It may also reduce the secondary trauma and moral distress social workers increasingly experience due to their participation in unjust practices over which they have little control (Fantus et al., 2017). In preparing students to practice in the current and future environment, social work educators need to pay increased attention to these problems and their possible solutions. At the same time, when discussing practice issues with a clear moral component, they have to find an approach that affirms the profession's core values, emphasizes the important role of science, and avoids shutting down students with different or questioning views (Singh, 1989).

In an astute and comprehensive essay and text, Banks (2011, 2012) points out two contending impulses that have recently produced increased interest in ethics within the social work field. On the one hand, ethical discourse in the profession has expanded to resist conservative trends in social policy and management practice. Banks sees this growth of interest in ethics as part of a strategy to reclaim professional autonomy in unjust and inhumane practice situations; assert the rights of the people with whom we work; reassert the profession's social justice mission; and integrate an ethics of virtue and care into the more rational and rule-bound ethical frameworks that have largely dominated practice.

On the other hand, she identifies an opposing trend that seeks to make social work ethics more compatible with regressive policy developments. Examples of this trend include increased regulatory proscriptions within existing codes, greater emphasis on the responsibilities of social workers and clients rather than systems for problems that arise, and more attention to risk management (Reamer, 2015b). They also reassert a focus on the worker-client dyad rather than the broader social context of people's problems and on the nonpersonal aspects of ethics (Banks, 2011, pp. 10–11). These trends exacerbate the recent "depoliticization" of the profession (Reisch & Jani, 2012).

To counteract these trends, Banks (2011) suggests that social workers adopt "a *situated ethics of social justice. ...* [that] ... takes social justice as its starting point" (p. 12). From this perspective, ethics is not merely a means to resolve "dilemmas and [make] difficult decisions about rights and rational deduction from abstract principles." It sees them "as embedded in everyday practice and in [all facets of] people's everyday lives" (p. 12). The personal values underlying this concept of ethics would include a radical conception of social justice that addresses all forms of oppression, what Banks terms "empathic solidarity," and what Reynolds (1951) and more contemporary empowerment theorists (Stepney, 2019) refer to as mutuality between workers and clients.

In a similar vein, philosophers and ethicists in the health care field, including social work, have recently emphasized the importance of relational autonomy. This concept represents an alternative to the Western liberal idea of what it means to be a free, self-governing agent. It reflects a social, rather than atomistic view of freedom by including individuals who define their basic value commitments in terms of interpersonal relations and mutual dependencies. This redefinition of autonomy has particular relevance for social work practitioners and researchers, especially those who work with or study people with chronic physical or intellectual disabilities or illnesses and those dealing with end-of-life issues (Killackey et al., 2020; Dowling et al., 2019; Durocher et al., 2019; Gómez-Vírseda et al., 2019; Dove et al., 2017). If adopted, it would commit us to assuming collective responsibility to resist unjust policies and practices and require us to integrate moral courage into all dimensions of our practice. Finally, it would require us to become more comfortable working with complexity, contradiction, uncertainty, and ambiguity in our practice (Jani et al., 2016).

Overcoming Apathy and Helplessness

An important part of empowerment practice involves overcoming the feelings of hopelessness and helplessness that produce apathy at the individual and societal level. The overwhelming nature of today's crises, combined with the entrenched power of elites who resist structural transformation, creates widespread psychological inertia and political paralysis. This response, while understandable, is not a new phenomenon. Past traumas on a similar scale produced a widespread shock that generated long-lasting passivity, even when conditions most needed concerted action.

In words that are eerily prophetic, Childers and Ferris (1984) pointed this out over 35 years ago:

> That people have many ways of avoiding dealing with serious problems around them is, of course, nothing new. But what is new and what makes this pervasive apathy hard to understand is that for the first time in history the problems clearly threaten everyone, and quite likely the very existence of life itself, at least in our corner of the universe. (p. 1)

Perhaps the immediacy and existential nature of the present global crises will shatter the apathy that has impeded recent social change efforts. Perhaps they will shatter the persistent belief in American exceptionalism and superiority, our lack of global awareness, and our unwillingness to listen to and learn from the perspectives of other societies and cultures. It is also possible that these crises will cause us to rethink our long-standing preference for individual responsibility over collective responsibility, competition over cooperation, "pragmatism" over idealism, and partisanship over partnership. This rethinking will require a new consciousness, one that recognizes the blurring of the boundaries between personal and societal problems and that overcomes the psychological impediments of fatalism, inadequacy, powerlessness, guilt, fear of the unknown, and resistance and even hostility to change. Such changes will inevitably affect the nature of social work practice, education, and research, and of the meaning of ethical conduct for the profession. Perhaps we will develop a new, transformative professional consensus. Perhaps not.

FIGURE 12.2. Overcoming Apathy and Helplessness Is Critical to the Development of Ethical Practice

It is likely, however, that whatever becomes the "new normal," social workers will continue to differ about what constitutes an ethical dilemma even when confronted with the same practice situation (Silva et al., 2017; Shapiro & Stefkovich, 2016). This is because, as discussed in

Chapter 3, we cannot avoid bringing our personal experiences and values to their resolution. As our history demonstrates, even widely shared societal crises produce different interpretations of their cause and different strategies to address them.

The constant pressure to address these seemingly intractable challenges will continue to be a major contributor to the increased incidents of burnout among social workers. Yet, despite the growing literature on self-care within the profession (Decker et al., 2019; Lewis & King, 2019; Miller et al., 2017), the emphasis continues to be primarily on individual responses to these pressures. This focus implies—not so subtly—that social workers have the primary responsibility for addressing the symptoms of this condition. The proliferation of articles on self-care largely fails to acknowledge the role that external factors, such as resource scarcity, increased caseloads, more complex client problems, and the barely disguised disdain some politicians and media figures express about our clients and our values, play in creating what Lewis (2003d) termed the "battered helper."

One acknowledged source of work-related stress, however, is the increased conflict between organizational demands and professional values. During the past few years, researchers found that regardless of the practice setting, this conflict was a major factor contributing to depression among practitioners. It produced a wide range of symptoms, such as mood instability, hopelessness, hypervigilance, fear, anger, frustration, and feelings of isolation and disconnection from others (Hussein, 2018; Travis et al., 2016; Lizano & Mor Barak, 2015). Similar to the experience of many clients and constituents with whom we work, externally imposed stress also produces internal physiological problems such as fatigue, more frequent illness, and a resurgence of prior health conditions including hypertension and insomnia. Although some social workers have responded to this increased stress in constructive ways—exercising more frequently, eating well, planning vacation breaks, and finding ways to prioritize multiple tasks more efficiently and effectively—for the most part, the increasing complexity and urgency of ethical issues affected them in negative ways. The coronavirus pandemic has exacerbated these recent developments to a considerable extent (National Association of Social Workers, 2020; Quinones, 2020).

In the immediate future, these external stresses will almost certainly intensify, necessitating our development of more constructive short-term and long-term responses to ensure our personal and professional survival, and our ability to help people in desperate situations. This imperative underscores the critical importance of maintaining social supports, becoming more aware of the effects of political realities, engaging in critically reflective practice, and clarifying our underlying values, particularly our commitment to social justice, in order to diminish their damaging effects (Wilson, 2016; Travis et al., 2016).

In the face of the 21st-century equivalent of the "4 Horsemen of the Apocalypse"—a global pandemic, the existential challenge of climate change, the disruptive effects of increasing socioeconomic inequality, and growing threats to democratic governance—we need to clarify our shared aspirations and ideals, and to translate these values into ethical policies and daily practices (Walter-McCabe, 2020). This includes support for a revitalized version of democracy at the micro and macro levels that requires the genuine participation of all members of society (Schneier, 2019).

As Bertha Capen Reynolds (1951) asserted over 70 years ago, this will not be easy to integrate into our practice. Ceaseless ideologically driven attacks by individuals in the media and politics who do not share our values continue to undermine trust in government, nonprofit institutions in general, and science, as they have for decades. It will also not be easy because the problems we face do not lend themselves to simple, quick fixes; their magnitude and complexity understandably create emotions of despair, hopelessness, and fatalism. The solution to what may become spiritual, social, and political inertia lies both within us as individuals and in our collective efforts through the relationships we forge and the organizations through which we work.

What Can We Do?

As Engelhardt (1982b) pointed out four decades ago, in our increasingly diverse society and interdependent world, "the moral certainties of the past have, at least insofar as they can lead easily and directly to public policy, been fragmented into numerous competing moral accounts" (p. 1). In a multicultural nation like the United States, the development and implementation of socially just public policies in the future will require us to choose among conflicting moral claims. This task will be particularly difficult in such controversial areas as the definition of death, reproductive rights, and the allocation of precious resources in the midst of a global pandemic. As discussed in Chapter 3, this requires all individuals, but particularly social workers committed to our "value-based profession," to live on two moral levels in order to respond effectively to the cultural and political conflicts we will inevitably face. One consists of our personal values drawn from our specific religious and cultural convictions and history; the other draws from our public and professional values, based on universal, secular norms.

Engelhardt suggests that the resolution of these persistent cultural and ideological conflicts occurs in one of four ways. One is through the overt or indirect use of some type of overwhelming force, even though its use without a compelling moral justification violates the notion of a moral community. Ongoing efforts by the Trump administration to restrict immigration to the United States and repress protests against systemic racism are powerful examples of this solution, as are recent protests against government regulations regarding social distancing during the pandemic. This approach, if successful, ends the controversy but does not resolve it.

A second method is through education or voluntary conversion to a common set of values. To some extent, dramatic shifts in public attitudes in the United States about marriage equality, end-of-life care, recreational use of marijuana, and excessive and racially disproportionate incarceration for minor crimes fall into this category. A related approach, which underlies the appeal of evidence-based practice, is resolution by sound argument based on scientific findings.

The partisan response to the advice of public health experts during the current pandemic and the persistence of climate change denial, however, provide a cautionary lesson regarding this approach. In the current environment, this caution may be justified because "in the area of morals, at least outside of particular communities of belief ... one needs to know which goods and costs are more important than others ... and under what circumstances. ... Because the choice of such a criterion will itself require a moral criterion" (Engelhardt, 1982, pp. 5–6). That is, we can only make ethical choices in complex situations if we have previously developed in our minds and implemented in our practice a clear set of values and a consistent framework for ethical decision-making. As of this writing, no such consensual framework exists in the United States.

A final method is resolution by negotiation. This approach "recognizes the extent to which the moral world is constructed by a community rather than discovered" (p. 7). For social workers, it underscores the need to view our professional ethics not merely as a set of rules or practice principles, as emphasized in the NASW *Code*, but as a process to resolve persistent controversies and dilemmas. Sadly, such a process requires both a common vocabulary and mutual respect among the participants. In today's environment of alternative facts and hyperpartisanship, this will be particularly challenging to achieve. Yet, it may be the only means to resolve such conflicts and maintain a moral basis for our ultimate decisions. It may also incur the least cost of all the aforementioned approaches and prevent a resort to the use of force (Reisch, 2018b).

ETHICAL DILEMMA 12.2   Maintaining Our Core Values in Challenging Times

You are a social worker in a multiservice agency that is providing counselling online during the slow transition to "normal operations" following the pandemic. You have been active for several years in a variety of coalitions that advocate for the rights of women, immigrants, and the LGBTQI population. In a teletherapy session with one of your clients, you notice she is wearing a MAGA hat and has several large placards resting against the wall behind her. These placards indicate your client's support for antiabortion, anti-immigrant, and antigay policies. They also reveal that she participated in demonstrations that opposed the "social distancing" and business closures imposed by your state's governor to slow the progress of the pandemic.

You understand that the NASW *Code of Ethics* requires social workers to provide services in a nondiscriminatory manner to all people, regardless of

their beliefs, and you have always had a strong commitment to this ethical principle. Your client, however, keeps making increasingly provocative statements and seems to sense your discomfort with the positions she takes on controversial issues. You are unsure how to respond to her provocations and are concerned that your emotions might affect your ability to treat her fairly and provide her with competent services.

Questions:

1. How would you respond to your client's provocations?
2. What would be the rationale for your response?
3. What ethical issues are in conflict in this situation?
4. Which ethical concepts would you prioritize and why?

In the above situation, a deontological approach might be most effective. In determining which values are most important, you would probably prioritize working in the client's interest. This requires you to maintain an effective relationship with her and underscores the need to separate your personal values and emotions from your professional values and commitments.

Conclusion: Ethical Practice in an Unjust and Rapidly Changing Environment

In our complex, rapidly changing environment, the need to expand social work's knowledge base is a necessary, but insufficient, response. Equally important is the development and application of a critical lens to our underlying assumptions about the contexts that shape our practice and the lives of the people with whom we work. This requires us to pay closer attention to the ethical foundations of our practice.

The tools to assist us in this important endeavor already exist in our literature. We can also benefit by examining ideas generated outside the United States, in other Western nations and the developing world. Gandhian thought, for example, could serve as a useful complement to Western ideas about social justice, the meaning of service, the role of truthfulness and moral courage in our practice, the definition of "environment," the goals of social welfare, and even the scale of social service organizations (Prasant, 2016). It might help us expand our practice in the area of environmental justice, as social workers in other nations have already begun to do (Erickson, 2018; Philip & Reisch, 2015).

Reaffirming our commitment to social justice does not require an embrace of either a purely secular or a specifically religious value framework. Although elites have used both religious and secular beliefs for millennia to rationalize persistent injustices, foundational principles of justice exist in all religions and a wide range of secular philosophies (Reisch & Garvin, 2016). As a profession with both religious and secular roots, social work reflects what rabbinical scholars refer to as priestly (nurturing) and prophetic (advocacy/social action) functions. While most social workers embrace the former role more readily—in part because it is more tangible, personally fulfilling, less risky, and more socially acceptable—the latter, more activist function is required to "heal the world" at large (Shlensky, n.d.). From this dual perspective, the goal of social justice would involve work that is both highly visible and unseen; it would seek to improve the lives of people with whom we work and those we will never meet, including our opponents.

This type of ethical, value-driven practice will also require us to narrow the gap between our rhetoric and our behavior—to "walk the walk" and not just "talk the talk." Although our *Code of Ethics* and educational accreditation standards emphasize social justice, most social work practice today stresses adaptation to the neoliberal reality and rationalizes this capitulation through the application of a veneer of cultural sensitivity (National Association of Social Workers, 2018; Council on Social Work Education, 2015). The increasingly apolitical nature of social work practice and the retreat from a universal framework as the basis for policy advocacy have also made it more difficult for social workers to respond to the emergence of right-wing populism or articulate a viable alternative to the individualistically oriented philosophy that still dominates U.S. culture and politics (Reisch, 2019b). Protests against "social distancing" have demonstrated this phenomenon all too clearly.

Social work throughout the world is once again at a crossroads not of its own making. Nevertheless, this critical juncture requires us to make a series of difficult and consequential decisions (Scollan et al., 2019; Mongan, 2018; Reisch, 2018a). To meet the ethical

FIGURE 12.3. Ethical Practice Will Be Shaped by an Uncertain Future

challenges ahead, we will need to pool our collective wisdom with the wisdom our clients, constituents, and colleagues in other fields possess.

In this light, in April 2017, the NASW's Office of Ethical and Professional Review hosted a roundtable discussion to examine the effects of the current environment on social work ethics. Participants discussed the following questions, each of which is more relevant today:

- How can social workers navigate differences in their political opinions with colleagues, clients, constituents, and employees?
- How can we participate in political action while adhering to the *Code of Ethics*?
- How will the Trump Administration's proposed policies affect social work values?
- Is support for these policies a violation of social work ethics?
- In our practice, how can we adhere to the core principles of respect, dignity, and worth of all people, including those with opposing views in the current partisan political climate?
- Finally, how can we adhere to imposed policies that discriminate against the most vulnerable people in society without violating the *Code of Ethics*? (Pace, 2017)

It is our individual and collective responsibility to address these issues in a serious and sustained manner in order to continue to practice ethically in an uncertain and frequently unethical environment (Reisch, 2014a). This book represents a modest effort to stimulate us to initiate this critical process.

Reflection Exercise: Identifying Future Ethical and Value Conflicts

1. Write down three to five ethical and value conflicts that most concern you about your future practice. Note briefly (a) which of these conflicts have concerned you before; (b) which have emerged because of recent developments; and (c) how you have responded, to date, to these conflicts.
2. In small groups, compare the list of conflicts and responses each person compiled.
3. By consensus (i.e., two-thirds or more of the group members agreeing), identify the three conflicts that are of the greatest concern and indicate the reasons for selecting them.
4. Develop a list of possible responses to these conflicts and indicate the pros and cons of each approach and the ethical principles on which you based them.
5. Convene the entire class and have each group summarize their results. Compare and contrast each group's responses. Discuss what they might imply for ethical practice in the future.

Credits

Img. 12.1: Copyright © by Kyle McDonald (cc by 2.0) at https://commons.wikimedia.org/wiki/File:Grace_Lee_Boggs_2012.jpg.
Img. 12.2: Copyright © by (cc by-sa 4.0) at https://commons.wikimedia.org/wiki/File:Albert_Einstein.png.jpg.
Img. 12.3: Source: https://commons.wikimedia.org/wiki/File:Malcolm x.jpg.
Fig. 12.1: Copyright © 2013 Depositphotos/deberarr.
Fig. 12.2a: Copyright © 2017 Depositphotos/gustavofrazao.
Fig. 12.2b: Copyright © 2013 Depositphotos/Bewitchment.
Fig. 12.3: Copyright © 2013 Depositphotos/lightsource.

References

Abramovitz, M. (2018). *Regulating the lives of women: Social welfare policy from colonial times to the present* (3rd ed.). Routledge.

Addams, J. (1895). The settlement as a factor in the labor movement. In J. Addams (Ed.), *Hull House maps and papers* (pp. 183–204). T. Y. Crowell.

Addams, J. (1922). *Peace and bread in time of war.* MacMillan.

Alabarce, M. C. (2020). The long night of the last dictatorship in Argentina. *Social Dialogue, 22,* 21–22.

Alden, S. (2015). Discretion on the frontline: The street level bureaucrat in English statutory homelessness services. *Social Policy and Society, 14*(1), 63–77.

Aldrich, R. (2017). Appraising the Diagnostic and Statistical Manual against recovery philosophies in elderly dementia. *Aotearoa New Zealand Social Work, 21*(1–2), 22–30.

Alexander, R., Jr. (1997). Social workers and privileged communication in the federal legal system. *Social Work, 42*(4), 387–391.

Alinsky, S. D. (1971). *Rules for radicals: A practical primer for realistic radicals.* Vintage Books.

Allcott, H., & Kessler, J. B. (2019). The welfare effects of nudges: A case study of energy use social comparisons. *American Economic Journal: Applied Economics, 11*(1), 236–76.

Alm, J., & Teles, D. (2018). State and federal tax policy toward nonprofit organizations. In *Handbook of Research on Nonprofit Economics and Management.* Edward Elgar.

Alston, P. (2018). *Report of the special rapporteur on extreme poverty and human rights on his mission to the United States of America.* Presented to the 38th session of the Human Rights Council. Geneva, Switzerland.

American Academy of Social Work and Social Welfare. (2020). *Grand challenges for social work.*

American Psychological Association. (2002). *Ethical principles of psychologists and code of conduct.*

Androff, D. (2016). *Practicing rights: Human rights-based approaches to social work practice.* Routledge.

Androff, D. (2018). Practicing human rights in social work: Reflections and rights-based approaches. *Journal of Human Rights and Social Work, 3*(4), 179–182.

Arbeiter, E., & Toros, K. (2017). Participatory discourse: Engagement in the context of child protection assessment practices from the perspectives of child protection workers, parents and children. *Children and Youth Services Review, 74,* 17–27.

Aristotle. (1999). *Nicomachean ethics* (2nd ed.; T. Irwin, Trans.). Hackett.

Arnd-Caddigan, M., & Pozzuto, R. (2009). The virtuous social worker: The role of "thirdness" in ethical decision-making. *Families in Society: The Journal of Contemporary Social Services, 90*(3), 323–328.

Arnold, J. R. (2019). *Whistleblowers, leakers, and their networks: From Snowden to Samizdat.* Rowman & Littlefield.

Ash, A. (2016). *Whistleblowing and ethics in health and social care.* Jessica Kingsley.

Austin, D. M. (1997). The institutional development of social work education. The first 100 years—and beyond. *Journal of Social Work Education, 33*(3), 599–612.

Austin, M. (2003). The changing relationship between nonprofit organizations and public social service agencies in the era of welfare reform. *Nonprofit and Voluntary Sector Quarterly, 32*(1), 97–114.

Auyong, Z. E. G., Smith, S., & Ferguson, C. J. (2018). Girls in gangs: Exploring risk in a British youth context. *Crime and Delinquency, 64*(13), 1698–1717.

Ayalon, L., & Gewirtz-Meydan, A. (2019). Physicians' moral dilemmas in the age of Viagra. *Men and Masculinities.* https://doi.org/10.1177%2F1097184X19886007

Bailey, N. W., & West, D. (2020). Are the COVID19 restrictions really worth the cost? A comparison of estimated mortality in Australia from COVID19 and economic recession. https://arxiv.org/abs/2005.03491

Baines, D. (2017). Resistance in and outside the workplace: Ethical practice and managerialism in the voluntary sector. In M. Carey & L. Green (Eds.), *Practical social work ethics* (pp. 239–256). Routledge.

Band-Winterstein, T. (2018). The elder abuse and neglect phenomenon in the ultra-Orthodox Jewish society: Social workers' perspectives. *International Psychogeriatrics, 30*(9), 1403–1412.

Banks, S. (2006). *Ethics and values in social work* (3rd ed.). Palgrave MacMillan.

Banks, S. (2008). Critical commentary: Social work ethics. *British Journal of Social Work, 38*(6), 1238–1249.

Banks, S. (2011). Ethics in an age of austerity: Social work and the evolving new public management. *Journal of Social Intervention: Theory and Practice, 20*(2), 5–23.

Banks, S. (2012). *Ethics and values in social work* (4th ed.). Macmillan International Higher Education.

Banks, S. (2016). Everyday ethics in professional life: Social work as ethics work. *Ethics and Social Welfare, 10*(1), 35–52.

Barak, M. E. M. (2016). *Managing diversity: Toward a globally inclusive workplace.* Sage Publications.

Barnes, M. (2019). Contesting and transforming care: An introduction to a critical ethics of care. In Rachael Langford (Ed.), *Theorizing feminist ethics of care in early childhood practice: Possibilities and dangers.* (p. 17). Bloomsbury Academic.

Barnes, V. (2012). Social work and advocacy with young people: Rights and care in practice. *British Journal of Social Work, 42,* 1275–1292.

Barnett, J. E. (2017a). Unavoidable incidental contacts and multiple relationships in rural practice. In O. Zur (Ed.), *Multiple relationships in psychotherapy and counseling: Unavoidable, mandatory, and common dual relationships in therapy* (pp. 97–107). Routledge.

Barnett, J. E. (2017b). Fees and financial arrangements in private practice. In S. Walfish, J. E. Barnett, & S. Zimmerman (Eds.), *Handbook of private practice: Keys to success for mental health practitioners.* Oxford University Press.

Barsky, A. (2014, April 1). *Do involuntary clients have a right to self-determination? The New Social Worker.* https://www.socialworker.com/feature-articles/ethics-articles/do-involuntary-clients-have-a-right-to-self-determination%3F/

Barsky, A. (2018). Serious imminent harm to non-identifiable others: Updated exceptions to confidentiality. *Journal of Baccalaureate Social Work, 23*(1), 341–353.

Barsky, A. E. (2017). Social work practice and technology: Ethical issues and policy responses. *Journal of Technology in Human Services, 35*(1), 8–19.

Barsky, A. E. (2019). *Ethics and values in social work: An integrated approach for a comprehensive curriculum.* Oxford University Press.

Barsky, A. E. & Northern, H. (2017). Ethics and values in group work. In C. D. Garvin, L. M. Gutierrez, & M. J. Galinsky (Eds.), *Handbook of Social Work with Groups* (2nd ed., pp. 74–85). Guilford Press.

Barsky, E. (2010). The virtuous social work researcher. *Journal of Social Work Values and Ethics, 7*(1), 1–10.

Bauman, Z. (1993). Postmodernity, or living with ambivalence. In J. Natoli & L. Hutcheon (Eds.), *A post-modern reader* (pp. 9–24). State University of New York Press.

Beaton, E., & Hwang, H. (2017, December). Increasing the size of the pie: The impact of crowding on nonprofit sector resources. *Nonprofit Policy Forum, 8*(3), 211–235. https://doi.org/10.1515/npf-2016-0012

Beauchamp, T. L. (2020). The compatibility of universal morality, particular moralities, and multiculturalism. In W. Teays & A. D. Renteln (Eds.), *Global Bioethics and Human Rights: Contemporary Perspectives.* Rowman & Littlefield.

Beauchamp, T. L., & Childress, J. (2019). *Principles of biomedical ethics* (8th ed.). Oxford University Press.

Beckett, C., Maynard, A., & Jordan, P. (2017). *Values and ethics in social work* (3rd ed.). Sage.

Begun, S., Kattari, S. K., McKay, K., Ramseyer Winter, V., & O'Neill, E. (2017). Exploring US social work students' sexual attitudes and abortion viewpoints. *Journal of Sex Research, 54*(6), 752–763.

Béland, D., Rocco, P., & Waddan, A. (2020). The Affordable Care Act in the states: Fragmented politics, unstable policy. *Journal of Health Politics, Policy and Law, 45*(4), 647–660. https://doi.org/10.1215/03616878-8255565

Bell, L. (Ed.). (2017). *Social justice and the arts.* Routledge.

Bell, L., & Hafford-Letchfield, T. (Eds.) (2015). *Ethics, values and social work practice.* McGraw Hill.

Bellah, R. N., Madsen, R., Sullivan, W. M., Swidler, A., & Tipton, S. M. (1991). *The good society.* Random House.

Bender, L. G. (Ed.). (2019). *Administering the new federalism.* Routledge.

Bent-Goodley, T. B. (2017). Living our core values. *Social Work, 62*(4), 293–295.

Bentham, J. (1907). *An introduction to the principles of morals and legislation.* Clarendon Press. (Original work published 1789)

Bentham, J. (1996). *The collected works of Jeremy Bentham: An introduction to the principles of morals and legislation.* Clarendon Press. (Original work published 1838–1843)

Bereiter, C. (1978). The morality of moral education. *Hastings Center Report, 8*(2), 20–26.

Berlin, I. (1969). *Four essays on liberty.* Oxford University Press.

Berlinger, N., Wynia, M., Powell, T., Hester, D. M., Guidry-Grimes, L. K., Watson, J. C., Bruce, L., Chuang, E. J., Oei, G., Abbott, J., & Jenks, N. P. (2020, March 16). *Ethical framework for health care institutions & guidelines for institutional ethics services responding to the coronavirus pandemic: Managing uncertainty, safeguarding communities, guiding practice.* The Hastings Center. https://www.thehastingscenter.org/ethicalframeworkcovid19/

Berman, D. R. (2019). *Local government and the states: Autonomy, politics, and policy.* Routledge.

Bernacchi, D. L. (2017). Bulimia nervosa: A comprehensive analysis of treatment, policy, and social work ethics. *Social Work, 62*(2), 174–180.

Bernard, C., & Thomas, S. (2016). Risk and safety: A strengths-based perspective in working with black families when there are safeguarding concerns. In C. Williams & M. J. Graham (Eds.), *Social work in a diverse society: Transformative practice with Black and minority ethnic individuals and communities* (pp. 59–74). Policy Press.

Berrick, J. D. (2017). Targeting social welfare in the United States: Personal responsibility, private behavior, and public benefits. In N. Gilbert (Ed.), *Targeting Social Benefits: International Perspectives and Trends* (pp. 129–156). Routledge.

Berringer, K. R. (2019). Reexamining epistemological debates in social work through American pragmatism. *Social Service Review, 93*(4), 608–639.

Bhandary, A. (2019). *Freedom to care: Liberalism, dependency care, and culture.* Routledge.

Bhatia, R. (2020). *Quantitative estimation of Covid-19 related unemployment on suicide and excess mortality in the United States.* medRxiv. https://doi.org/10.1101/2020.05.02.20089086

Bhuyan, R., Bejan, R., & Jeyapal, D. (2017). Social workers' perspectives on social justice in social work education: When mainstreaming social justice masks structural inequalities. *Social Work Education, 36*(4), 373–390.

Biestek, F. P. (1951). The principle of client self-determination. *Social Casework, 32*(9), 369–375.

Binkley, C. E., & Kemp, D. S. (2020). Ethical rationing of personal protective equipment to minimize moral residue during the COVID-19 pandemic. *Journal of the American College of Surgeons, 230*(6), 1111–1113. https://doi.org/10.1016/j.jamcollsurg.2020.03.031

Blau, J. (2019). The political economy of U.S. social policy. In M. Reisch (Ed.), *Social policy and social justice: Meeting the challenges of a diverse society,* 3rd ed. (pp. 111–132). Cognella.

Bloom, M. (2010). Client-centered evaluation ethics for 21st century practitioners. *Journal of Social Work Values and Ethics, 7*(1), 24–31.

Blumenfield, S., & Lowe, J. I. (1987). A template for analyzing ethical dilemmas in discharge planning. *Health and Social Work, 12*(1), 47–56.

Boddy, J., & Dominelli, L. (2017). Social media and social work: The challenges of a new ethical space. *Australian Social Work, 70*(2), 172–184.

Bok, S. (1980). Whistleblowing and professional responsibility. *New York Education Quarterly, 11*(4), 2–10.

Bok, S. (1982). *Secrets: On the ethics of concealment and revelation.* Pantheon Books.

Bok, S. (1999). *Lying: Moral choice in public and private life* (2nd ed.). Pantheon Books.

Börjeson, L. (2018). Trust and betrayal in interorganizational relationships: A systemic functional grammar analysis. *Human Relations, 71*(3), 399–426.

Bowman, J. S., & West, J. P. (2018). *Public service ethics: Individual and institutional responsibilities.* Routledge.

Bows, H., & Penhale, B. (2018). Elder abuse and social work: Research, theory and practice. *British Journal of Social Work, 48*(4), 873–886.

Brady, S., Sawyer, J. M., & Perkins, N. H. (2019). Debunking the myth of the 'radical profession': Analysing and overcoming our professional history to create new pathways and opportunities for social work. *Critical and Radical Social Work, 7*(3), 315–332.

Brake, E. (2017). Fair care: Elder care and distributive justice. *Politics, Philosophy and Economics, 16*(2), 132–151.

Braye, S., Orr, D., & Preston-Shoot, M. (2017). Autonomy and protection in self-neglect work: The ethical complexity of decision-making. *Ethics and Social Welfare, 11*(4), 320–335.

Brekke, J. S., & Anastas, J. W. (Eds.) (2019). *Shaping a science of social work: Professional knowledge and identity.* Oxford University Press.

Briggs, L. (2018). *How all politics became reproductive politics: From welfare reform to foreclosure to Trump* (Vol. 2). University of California Press.

BrintzenhofeSzoc, K., & Gilbert, C. (2017). Social workers have an obligation to all patients regarding confidentiality … however, for some patients, the obligation is greater. *Social Work in Health Care, 56*(9), 779–793.

Briskman, L. (2017). Revitalising radical social work. *Aotearoa New Zealand Social Work, 29*(2), 133–136.

Bronstein, L. (2003). A model of interdisciplinary collaboration. *Social Work, 48*(3), 297–306.

Brownlee, K., LeBlanc, H., Halverson, G., Piché, T., & Brazeau, J. (2019). Exploring self-reflection in dual relationship decision-making. *Journal of Social Work, 19*(5), 629–641.

Brown, E. C. F. (2018). Health reform and theories of cost control. *Journal of Law, Medicine and Ethics, 46*(4), 846–856.

Brown, H. C. (2017). Lesbians and gay men: Social work and discrimination. In B. Lesnik (Ed.), *Countering discrimination in social work* (pp. 89–110). Routledge.

Brown, S. L., Johnson, Z., & Miller, S. E. (2019). Racial microaggressions and black social work students: A call to social work educators for proactive models informed by social justice. *Social Work Education, 38*(5), 618–630.

Burke-White, W. (2020, March 11). *The Trump Administration misplayed the International Criminal Court and Americans may not face justice for crimes in Afghanistan.* Brookings Institution. https://www.brookings.edu/blog/order-from-chaos/2020/03/11/the-trump-administration-misplayed-the-international-criminal-court-and-americans-may-now-face-justice-for-crimes-in-afghanistan/

Bussey, S. R., Jemal, A., & Caliste, S. (2020). Transforming social work's potential in the field: A radical framework. *Social Work Education,* 1–15. https://doi.org/10.1080/02615479.2020.1723536

Butz, A. M. (2016). Theorizing about poverty and paternalism in suburban America: The case of welfare sanctions. *Poverty and Public Policy, 8*(2), 129–140.

Byers, D. S., & Shapiro, J. R. (2019). Renewing the ethics of care for social work under the Trump Administration. *Social Work, 64*(2), 175–178.

Canda, E. R., Furman, L. D., & Canda, H. J. (2019). *Spiritual diversity in social work practice: The heart of helping.* Oxford University Press.

Caras, A., & Sandu, A. (2018, May). The need for ethical committees for the ethical evaluation of social services. In *Proceedings of the XXIII World Congress of Philosophy* (Vol. 5, pp. 11–15).

Carey, M. (2019). The tyranny of ethics? Political challenges and tensions when applying ethical governance to qualitative social work research. *Ethics and Social Welfare, 13*(2), 150–162.

Carlson, M. L., Wittrup, E., Moylan, C. A., & Ortiz, D. V. (2019). A good call? Contextual factors influencing mandated reporting in domestic violence programs. *Journal of Family Violence, 35*, 1–10. https://psycnet.apa.org/doi/10.1007/s10896-019-00101-y

Carr, H., & Goosey, D. (2017). *Law for social workers.* Oxford University Press.

Castex, G., Senreich, E., Phillips, N. K., Miller, C. M., & Mazza, C. (2019). Microaggressions and racial privilege within the social work profession: The social work licensing examinations. *Journal of Ethnic and Cultural Diversity in Social Work, 28*(2), 211–228.

Chandler, J., Ellison, M., Berg, E., & Barry, J. (2017). Reconfiguring professional autonomy? The case of social work in the UK. In B. Blom, L. Evertsson, & M. Perlinski (Eds.), *Social and caring professions in European welfare states* (pp. 69–82). Policy Press.

Chang, C. J. (2016). The factors on elderly employment project outcome: Appropriation of work, job training satisfaction, intra-organizational cooperation. *International Journal of Social Science and Humanity, 6*(1), 14–18.

Chappell, M. (2018). *Protecting Soldiers and Mothers* twenty-five years later: Theda Skocpol's legacy and American welfare state historiography, 1992–2017. *Journal of the Gilded Age and Progressive Era, 17*(3), 546–573. https://doi.org/10.1017/S1537781418000105

Charon, R. (2017). *Narrative in social work practice: The power and possibility of story.* Columbia University Press.

Cheak-Zamora, N. C., Maurer-Batjer, A., Malow, B. A., & Coleman, A. (2019). Self-determination in young adults with autism spectrum disorder. *Autism, 24*(3), 605–616. https://doi.org/10.1177%2F1362361319877329

Chichilnisky, G., Hammond, P. J., & Stern, N. (2020). Fundamental utilitarianism and intergenerational equity with extinction discounting. *Social Choice and Welfare, 54*(2), 397–427.

Child, C. (2016). Tip of the iceberg: The nonprofit underpinnings of for-profit social enterprise. *Nonprofit and Voluntary Sector Quarterly, 45*(2), 217–237.

Childers, B., & Ferris, E. (1984). The individual and the change process in social action. *Peace and Change, 10*(1), 41–52.

Chovanec, M. G. (2017). Increasing client voice within involuntary groups. *Social Work with Groups, 40*(4), 315–329.

Christie, D. L. (2018). Reviews of *Ethics and the elderly: The challenge of long-term care* by S. M. Moses, and *Loving later life: An ethics of aging* by F. de Lange. *Journal of the Society of Christian Ethics, 38*(1), 214–216.

Clark, C. (2012). From rules to encounters: Ethical decision-making as a hermeneutic process. *Journal of Social Work, 12*(2), 115–135.

Clark, T., & Jaffe, D. T. (2018). *Toward a radical therapy: Alternate services for personal and social change* (Vol. 6). Routledge.

Clément, D. (2018). Human rights or social justice? The problem of rights inflation. *International Journal of Human Rights, 22*(2), 155–169.

Clement, G. (2018). *Care, autonomy, and justice: Feminism and the ethic of care.* Routledge.

Clifford, D. (2016). Oppression and professional ethics. *Ethics and Social Welfare, 10*(1), 4–18.

Cohen, S. (2019). The logic of the interaction between beneficence and respect for autonomy. *Medicine, Health Care and Philosophy, 22*(2), 297–304.

Collins, M. E., Rum, S. A., & Sugarman, J. (2018). Navigating the ethical boundaries of grateful patient fundraising. *Journal of the American Medical Association, 320*(10), 975–976.

Collins, M., Rum, S., Wheeler, J., Antman, K., Brem, H., Carrese, J., Glennon, M., Kahn, J., Ohman, E. M., Jagsi, R., Konrath, S., Tovino, S., Wright, S., & Sugarman, J. (2018). Ethical issues and recommendations in grateful patient fundraising and philanthropy. *Academic Medicine, 93*(11), 1631–1637.

Congress, E. P. (2017). What social workers should know about ethics: Understanding and resolving practice dilemmas. *Social Work Ethics, 1*(1), 1909–35.

Cooper, P. J. (2016). *Civil rights in public service.* Taylor & Francis.

Corey, G., Corey, M. S., Muratori, M., Austin, J., & Austin, J. (2016). Multiple relationships and multiple roles in higher education. In O. Zur (Ed.), *Multiple relationships in psychotherapy and counseling: Unavoidable, common, and mandatory dual relations in therapy* (pp. 174–182). Routledge.

Council on Social Work Education (2015). *Educational policy and accreditation standards* (Rev. ed.).

Council on Social Work Education (2019). *Curriculum content in schools of social work.*

Craig, S. L., Iacono, G., Paceley, M. S., Dentato, M. P., & Boyle, K. E. (2017). Intersecting sexual, gender, and professional identities among social work students: The importance of identity integration. *Journal of Social Work Education, 53*(3), 466–479.

Crociani-Windland, L. (2017). Deleuze, art and social work. *Journal of Social Work Practice, 31*(2), 251–262.

Daly, M. (1978). *Gyn/Ecology: The metaethics of radical feminism.* Beacon Press.

Dattalo, P. (2010). Ethical dilemmas in sampling. *Journal of Social Work Values and Ethics, 7*(1), 12–23.

Davson-Galle, P. (2016). *Reason and professional ethics.* Routledge.

De Graaf, G. (2019). What works: The role of confidential integrity advisors and effective whistleblowing. *International Public Management Journal, 22*(2), 213–231.

De la Cruz, C. (2020). The persistent maternalism in labor programs. In A. Ramm & J. Gideon (Eds.), *Motherhood, social policies and women's activism in Latin America* (pp. 245–266). Palgrave Macmillan.

Deck, P. (2016). Law and social work: Reconciling conflicting ethical obligations between two seemingly opposing disciplines to create a collaborative law practice. *Western New England Law Review, 38,* 261.

Decker, J. T., Brown, J. L. C., Ashley, W., & Lipscomb, A. E. (2019). Mindfulness, meditation, and breathing exercises: Reduced anxiety for clients and self-care for social work interns. *Social Work with Groups, 42*(4), 308–322.

DeMartino, E. S., Dudzinski, D. M., Doyle, C. K., Sperry, B. P., Gregory, S. E., Siegler, M., & Kramer, D. B. (2017). Who decides when a patient can't? Statutes on alternate decision makers. *New England Journal of Medicine, 376*(15), 1478–1482.

DeParle, J. (2020a, April 16). A gloomy prediction on how much poverty could rise. *The New York Times.* https://www.nytimes.com/2020/04/16/upshot/coronavirus-prediction-rise-poverty.html

DeParle, J. (2020b, April 2). The safety net got a quick patch. What happens after the coronavirus? *The New York Times.* https://www.nytimes.com/2020/03/31/us/politics/coronavirus-us-benefits.html

Devine T. (2017) Whistleblowing in the United States of America: "Irrefragable proof" and the next generation of U.S. government whistleblower rights. In C. Apaza & Y. Chang (Eds.), *Whistleblowing in the world.* Palgrave Macmillan.

Dews, C. L. B., & Law, C. L. (Eds.) (1995). *This fine place so far from home: Voices of academics from the working class.* Temple University Press.

Diaz, C., & Drewery, S. (2016). A critical assessment of evidence-based policy and practice in social work. *Journal of Evidence-Informed Social Work, 13*(4), 425–431.

Diaz-Edelman, M. (2017). Activist etiquette in the multicultural immigrant rights movement. In R. Braunstein (Ed.), *Religion and progressive activism: New stories about faith and politics* (pp. 138–160).

Dickson, D. T. (2009). When law and ethics collide: Social control in child protective services. *Ethics and Social Welfare, 3*(3), 264–283.

DiFranks, N. N. (2008). Social workers and the NASW *Code of Ethics*: Belief, behavior, disjuncture. *Social Work, 53*(2), 167–176.

Dittmer, C., & Lorenz, D. F. (2018, September). Research in the context of vulnerability and extreme suffering—ethical issues of social science disaster research. *Forum Qualitative Sozialforschung/Forum: Qualitative Social Research, 19*(3).

Doel, M. (2019). Ethics and values in social group work. In S. M. Marson & R. E. McKinney Jr. (Eds.). *The Routledge handbook of social work ethics and values.* Routledge.

Dolgoff, R., Harrington, D., & Loewenberg, F. M. (2012). *Ethical decisions for social work practice* (9th ed.). Brooks/Cole.

Dolinsky, H. R., & Helbig, N. (2015). Risky business: Applying ethical standards to social media use with vulnerable populations. *Advances in Social Work, 16*(1), 55–66.

Dombeck, M., & Olsan, T. (2007). Ethics and the social responsibility of institutions regarding resource allocation in health and social care: A US perspective. In A. Leathard & S. McLaren (Eds.), *Ethics: Contemporary challenges in health and social care* (pp. 169–183). Policy Press.

Dominelli, L. (2017). *Anti-racist social work.* Macmillan International Higher Education.

Dominelli, L. (2019). Green social work, political ecology and environmental justice. In S. A. Webb (Ed.), *The Routledge handbook of critical social work* (pp. 233–243). Routledge.

Donnelly, S., Begley, E., & O'Brien, M. (2019). How are people with dementia involved in care-planning and decision-making? An Irish social work perspective. *Dementia, 18*(7–8), 2985–3003.

Donovan, K., & Regehr, C. (2010). Elder abuse: Clinical, ethical, and legal considerations in social work practice. *Clinical Social Work Journal, 38*(2), 174–182.

Dotolo, D., Lindhorst, T., Kemp, S. P., & Engelberg, R. A. (2018). Expanding conceptualizations of social justice across all levels of social work practice: Recognition theory and its contributions. *Social Service Review, 92*(2), 143–170.

Dotolo, D., Petros, R., & Berridge, C. (2018). A hard pill to swallow: Ethical problems and digital medication. *Social Work, 63*(4), 370–372.

Dove, E. S., Kelly, S. E., Lucivero, F., Machirori, M., Dheensa, S., & Prainsack, B. (2017). Beyond individualism: Is there a place for relational autonomy in clinical practice and research? *Clinical Ethics, 12*(3), 150–165.

Dowling, S., Williams, V., Webb, J., Gall, M., & Worrall, D. (2019). Managing relational autonomy in interactions: People with intellectual disabilities. *Journal of Applied Research in Intellectual Disabilities, 32*(5), 1058–1066.

Doyle, O. Z., Miller, S. E., & Mirza, F. Y. (2009). Ethical decision-making in social work: Exploring personal and professional values. *Journal of Social Work Values and Ethics, 6*(1), 3–33.

Drisko, J. W., & Grady, M. D. (2019). *Evidence-based practice in clinical social work.* Springer.

Duffy, J., & Hayes, D. (2012). Social work students learn about social work values from service users and carers. *Ethics and Social Welfare, 6*(4), 368–385. https://doi.org/10.1080/17496535.2012.654497

Dupper, D. (2017). Strengthening empathy training programs for undergraduate social work students. *Journal of Baccalaureate Social Work, 22*(1), 31–41. https://doi.org/10.18084/1084-7219.22.1.31

Durkheim, E. (1964). *The rules of sociological method* (S. A. Solovay & J. H. Mueller, Trans.). Free Press.

Durkheim, E. (1976). *The elementary forms of religious life* (J. W. Swain, Trans.). Allen & Unwin.

Durocher, E., Kinsella, E. A., Gibson, B. E., Rappolt, S., & Ells, C. (2019). Engaging older adults in discharge planning: Case studies illuminating approaches adopted by family members that promote relational autonomy. *Disability and Rehabilitation, 41*(25), 3005–3015. https://www.tandfonline.com/author/Kinsella%2C+Elizabeth+Anne

Dustin, D. (2016). *The McDonaldization of social work.* Routledge.

Dutton, H., Bullen, P., & Deane, K. L. (2019). "It is OK to let them know you are human too": Mentor self-disclosure in formal youth mentoring relationships. *Journal of Community Psychology, 47*(4), 943–963. https://doi.org/10.1002/jcop.22165

Dworkin, G. (1972). Paternalism. *The Monist, 56*(1), 64–84.

Dworkin, G. (1988). *The theory and practice of moral autonomy.* Cambridge University Press.

Dworkin, R. (1977). *Taking rights seriously.* Gerald Duckworth.

Dybicz, P. (2012). The ethic of care: Recapturing social work's first voice. *Social Work, 57*(3), 271–280.

Edin, K. J., & Shaefer, H. L. (2016). *$2 a day: Living on almost nothing in America.* Houghton Mifflin.

Edwards, B., & Addae, R. (2015). Ethical decision-making models in resolving ethical dilemmas in rural practice: Implications for social work practice and education. *Journal of Social Work Values and Ethics, 12*(1), 88–92.

Eisenstein, Z. (1979). *Capitalist patriarchy and the case for socialist feminism.* Monthly Review Press.

Ekberg, S., Parry, R., Land, V., Ekberg, K., Pino, M., & Antaki, C. (2020). *Communicating with patients and families about difficult matters: A rapid review in the context of the COVID-19 pandemic.* medRxiv. https://doi.org/10.1101/2020.04.27.20078048

Elshtain, J. B. (2002). *Jane Addams and the dream of American democracy: A life.* Basic Books.

Eltaiba, N. (2019). An ethical decision-making model. In S. M. Marson & R. E. McKinney Jr. (Eds.), *The Routledge handbook of social work ethics and values* (pp. 289–296). Routledge.

Emanuel, E. J., Govind Persad, J. D., Upshur, R., Thome, B., Parker, M., Glickman, A., Zhang, C., Boyle, C., Smith, M., & Phillips, J. P. (2020, May 21). Fair allocation of scarce medical resources in the time of Covid-19. *New England Journal of Medicine, 382*(21), 2049–2055. https://doi.org/10.1056/nejmsb2005114

Emanuel, E., Schmidt, H., & Steinmetz, A. (Eds.). (2018). *Rationing and resource allocation in healthcare: Essential readings.* Oxford University Press.

Engel, D. W., & Wolfe, J. S. (2017). Paternalism and the rise of the disability state. *Journal of the National Association of Administrative Law Judiciary, 37*, 355–504.

Engelhardt, H. T., Jr. (1982a). Bioethics in pluralist societies. *Perspectives in Biology and Medicine, 26*(1), 64–78.

Engelhardt, H. T., Jr. (1982b, May 25). Philosophy, health care, and public policy [Paper presentation]. Ethics Seminar, University of Maryland, Baltimore, MD, United States.

Engelhardt, H. T., Jr. (1986). *The foundations of bioethics.* Oxford University Press.

Erickson, C. L. (2018). *Environmental justice as social work practice.* Oxford University Press.

Eriksson, K., & Englander, M. (2017). Empathy in social work. *Journal of Social Work Education, 53*(4), 607–621.

Etzioni, A. (2018a). *Happiness is the wrong metric: A liberal communitarian response to populism.* Springer.

Etzioni, A. (2018b). A communitarian perspective on sustainable communities. In D. Warburton (Ed.), *Community and sustainable development: Participation in the future* (pp. 40–51). Routledge.

Etzioni, A. (2019). *Law and society in a populist age: Balancing individual rights and the common good.* Bristol University Press.

Evans, T., & Hardy, M. (2017). The ethics of practical reasoning—exploring the terrain. *European Journal of Social Work, 20*(6), 947–957.

Ezell, M. (2013). *Advocacy in the human services.* Brooks/Cole.

Fabricant, M.B., & Burghardt, S. (2015). *The welfare state crisis and the transformation of social service work.* Routledge.

Falender, C. A. (2016). Multiple relationships and clinical supervision. In O. Zur (Ed.), *Multiple relationships in psychotherapy and counseling: Unavoidable, common, and mandatory dual relations in therapy.* Routledge.

Faller, K. C. (2017). Interventions for physically and sexually abused children. In L. Davis & T. Mizrahi (Eds.), *Encyclopedia of Social Work.* Oxford University Press.

Fantus, S., & Mishna, F. (2013). The ethical and clinical implications of utilizing cybercommunication in face-to-face therapy. *Smith College Studies in Social Work, 83*(4), 466–480. https://psycnet.apa.org/doi/10.1080/00377317.2013.833049

Fantus, S., Greenberg, R. A., Muskat, B., & Katz, D. (2017). Exploring moral distress for hospital social workers. *British Journal of Social Work, 47*(8), 2273–2290.

Farrell, M., Smith, J., Reardon, L., & Obara, E. (2016, March). *Framing the message: Using behavioral economics to engage TANF recipients* (OPRE Report 2). Office of Planning, Research and Evaluation. https://www.acf.hhs.gov/sites/default/files/opre/bias_la_acf_compliant.pdf

Ferguson, I. (2008). *Reclaiming social work: Challenging neo-liberalism and promoting social justice.* Sage.

Ferguson, I., Ioakimidis, V., & Lavalette, M. (Eds.) (2018). *Global social work in a political context: Radical perspectives.* Policy Press.

Fernandez, M., & Montgomery, D. (2020, May 14). Shops open in Texas, aided by crews with rifles. *The New York Times,* A1, A12.

Ferreira, C. M., & Serpa, S. (2018). Informed consent in social sciences research: Ethical challenges. *International Journal of Social Science Studies, 6*(5), 13–23. https://doi.org/10.11114/ijsss.v6i5.3106

Ferreira, R. J., Buttell, F., & Ferreira, S. B. (2015). Ethical considerations for conducting disaster research with vulnerable populations. *Journal of Social Work Values and Ethics, 12*(1), 29–40.

Ferretto, G. (2018). Revisions to the NASW *Code of Ethics* effective January 2018. University of Maryland.

Finn, J. (2016). *Just practice: A social justice approach to social work* (3rd ed.). Oxford University Press.

Fisher, D. (1987). Problems for social work in a strike situation: Professional, ethical, and value considerations. *Social Work, 32*(3), 252–254. https://doi.org/10.1093/sw/32.3.252

Fitzgerald, R. (Ed.). (2016). *Human needs and politics.* Elsevier.

Fleck-Henderson, A. (1991). Moral reasoning in social work practice. *Social Service Review, 65*(2), 185–202.

Folayan, S. W., Hitchcock, L. I., & Zgoda, K. (2018). Using Twitter in reclaiming macro practice, and affirming our social work roots. *Reflections: Narratives of Professional Helping, 24*(1), 56–64.

Foley, S. (2017). *Intellectual disability and the right to a sexual life: A continuation of the autonomy/paternalism debate.* Routledge.

Fook, J. (2016). Social justice and critical theory. In M. Reisch (Ed.), *The Routledge international handbook of social justice* (pp. 160–172). Routledge.

Foster, C. H. (2017). Anchor babies and welfare queens: An essay on political rhetoric, gendered racism, and marginalization. *Women, Gender, and Families of Color, 5*(1), 50–72.

Foucault, M. (1998). *Essential works of Foucault, 1954–1984, Vol. 2: Aesthetics, method, epistemology* (J. D. Faubion, Trans. and Ed.). New Press.

Fram, M. S., & Miller-Cribbs, J. (2008). Liberal and conservative in social work education: Exploring student experiences. *Social Work Education, 27*(8), 883–897.

Francoeur, R. B., Burke, N., & Wilson, A. M. (2016). The role of social workers in spiritual care to facilitate coping with chronic illness and self-determination in advance care planning. *Social Work in Public Health, 31*(5), 453–466.

Frankel, C. (1969, Spring). Social values and professional values. *Education for Social Work,* 29–35.

Freedberg, S. (1989). Self-Determination: Historical perspectives and effects on current practice. *Social Work, 34*(1), 33–38.

Freeman, D., & Shaler, L. (2016). Introduction: Special issue on religious and spiritually-oriented interventions with veteran and military populations. *Social Work and Christianity, 43*(3), 3.

Freire, P. (1971). *Pedagogy of the oppressed.* Seabury.

Freud, S., & Krug, S. (2002a). Beyond the Code of Ethics, Part I: Complexities of ethical decision making in social work practice. *Families in Society: The Journal of Contemporary Human Services, 83*(5–6), 474–482. https://doi.org/10.1606%2F1044-3894.55

Freud, S., & Krug, S. (2002b). Beyond the Code of Ethics, Part II: Dual relationships revisited. *Families in Society: The Journal of Contemporary Social Services, 83*(5–6), 483–492. https://doi.org/10.1606%2F1044-3894.228

Friedman, D. A. (2018). Bringing candor to charitable solicitations. *Maryland Law Review, 78*(4), 709–765.

Fronek, P., & Kendall, M. B. (2017). The impact of professional boundaries for health professionals' (PBHP) training on knowledge, comfort, experience, and ethical decision-making: A longitudinal randomized controlled trial. *Disability and Rehabilitation, 39*(24), 2522–2529.

Gambrill, E. (2011). Evidence-based practice and the ethics of discretion. *Journal of Social Work, 11*(1), 26–48.

Gambrill, E. (2017). *Social work ethics.* Routledge.

Gambrill, E. (2019). Criticism and its critics: Reply to Holloway and Golightley. *Research on Social Work Practice, 29*(4), 473–474.

Garrett, P. M. (2018). *Social work and social theory: Making connections* (2nd ed.). Policy Press.

Gatenio Gabel, S. (2016). *Rights-based approaches to social policy.* Springer.

Gaylin, W., Glasser, I., Marcus, S., & Rothman, D. (1978). *Doing good: The limits of benevolence.* Pantheon Books.

Gellert, M. D. (2020). Ethical imperatives critical to effective disease control in the coronavirus pandemic: Recognition of global health interdependence as a driver of health and social equity. *Online Journal of Health Ethics, 16*(1), 2–8. http://dx.doi.org/10.18785/ojhe.1601.03

George, M., & Awal, N. A. M. (2019). The best interest principle within Article 3 (1) of the United Nations Convention on the Rights of the Child. *International Journal of Business, Economics and Law, 19,* 30–36.

Gerassi, L., Nichols, A., & Michelson, E. (2017). Lessons learned: Benefits and challenges in interagency coalitions addressing sex trafficking and commercial sexual exploitation. *Journal of Human Trafficking, 3*(4), 285–302.

Gewirth, A. (1978). *Reason and morality.* University of Chicago Press.

Gewirth, A. (2001). Confidentiality in child welfare practice. *Social Service Review, 75*(3), 479–489.

Gibson, M. F. (2015). Intersecting deviance: Social work, difference and the legacy of eugenics. *British Journal of Social Work, 45*(1), 313–330.

Gil, D.G. (2013). *Confronting injustice and oppression: Concepts and strategies for social workers* (Updated ed.). Columbia University Press.

Gilens, M., & Page, B.I. (2014). Testing theories of American politics: Elites, interest groups, and average citizens. *Perspectives on Politics, 12*(3), 564–581.

Gill, H., Cassidy, S. A., Cragg, C., Algate, P., Weijs, C. A., & Finegan, J. E. (2019). Beyond reciprocity: The role of empowerment in understanding felt trust. *European Journal of Work and Organizational Psychology, 28*(6), 845–858.

Gill, M., & Schlund-Vials, C. J. (2016). *Disability, human rights and the limits of humanitarianism.* Routledge.

Gilliam, J. (2015, December). *Using an enhanced e-textbook to facilitate the education and practice of social workers*

[Unpublished doctoral dissertation]. University of Baltimore.

Gilligan, C. (1993). *In a different voice: Psychological theory and women's development.* Harvard University Press.

Gillingham, P. (2018). Evaluation of practice frameworks for social work with children and families: Exploring the challenges. *Journal of Public Child Welfare, 12*(2), 190–203.

Gillon, R. (1986). More on professional ethics. *Journal of Medical Ethics, 12*(4), 59–60.

Gilster, M. E., Kleinschmit, J. L., Cummings, S. P., & Ronnenberg, M. M. (2020). Teaching note—Pick your platform: Social media advocacy skill building. *Journal of Social Work Education, 56*(1), 170–178.

Glassman, R. (2016). *Finding your way through field work.* Sage.

Godwin, S. (2020). Children's capacities and paternalism. *Journal of Ethics.* https://doi.org/10.1007/s10892-020-09327-1

Goldberg, M. (2000). Conflicting principles in multicultural social work. *Families in Society: The Journal of Contemporary Human Services, 81*(1), 12–16.

Goldmeier, J. (1984). Ethical styles and ethical decisions in health settings. *Social Work in Health Care, 10*(1), 45–60.

Gómez-Vírseda, C., de Maeseneer, Y., & Gastmans, C. (2019). Relational autonomy: What does it mean and how is it used in end-of-life care? A systematic review of argument-based ethics literature. *BMC Medical Ethics, 20*(1). https://doi.org/10.1186/s12910-019-0417-3

Gordon, W. (1965). Knowledge and values: Their distinction and relationship in clarifying social work practice. *Social Work, 10*(3), 32–39.

Gorin, S., & Moniz, C. (2019). Health and mental health policy: Past, present, and future. In M. Reisch (Ed.), *Social policy and social justice: Meeting the challenges of a diverse society* (3rd ed., pp. 411–438). Cognella.

Goulet, D. (1969). The troubled conscience of the revolutionary. *Center Magazine,* 43–50.

Graber, A., & O'Brien, M. (2019). The promise of accountable care organizations: "The Code," reimbursement, and an ethical no-win situation for behavior analysts. *Behavior Analysis in Practice, 12*(1), 247–254.

Grange, J. (1974). Social welfare and the science of man: An existential approach. In J. M. Romanyshyn (Ed.), *Social science and social welfare* (pp. 197–210). Council on Social Work Education.

Grapin, S. L., & Shriberg, D. (2020). International perspectives on social justice: Introduction to the special issue. *School Psychology International, 41*(1), 3–12.

Gray, B. (2019). (Bio)ethics in a pluralistic society. *Challenges, 10*(1). https://doi.org/10.3390/challe10010012

Gray, M. (2010). Moral sources and emergent ethical theories in social work. *British Journal of Social Work, 40*(6), 1794–1811. https://doi.org/10.1093/bjsw%2Fbcp104

Gray, S. T. (n.d.). Constructing ethical systems. *Resources on Leadership and Management in the Nonprofit Sector.* Independent Sector, 3–4.

Green, J. W. (1999). *Cultural awareness in the human services: A multi-ethnic approach* (3rd ed.). Allyn & Bacon.

Green, L. (2017). The trouble with touch? New insights and observations on touch for social work and social care. *British Journal of Social Work, 47*(3), 773–792.

Greene, R. R. (2017). Power factors in social work practice. In R. R. Greene & N. P. Kropf (Eds.), *Human behavior theory: A diversity framework* (pp. 251–274). Routledge.

Gricus, M. (2019). "Of all the social workers … I'm the bad one": Impact of disciplinary action on social workers. *Social Work Research, 43*(1), 5–16.

Grise-Owens, E., Owens, L. W., & Miller, J. J. (2016). Recasting licensing in social work: Something more for professionalism. *Journal of Social Work Education, 52*(Suppl.), S126–S133.

Groshong, L., & Phillips, D. (2015). The impact of electronic communication on confidentiality in clinical social work practice. *Clinical Social Work Journal, 43,* 142–150.

Guichon, J., Mohamed, F., Clarke, K., & Mitchell, I. (2016). Autonomy and beneficence in assisted dying in Canada: The eligibility of mature minors. *Alberta Law Review, 54*(3). https://doi.org/10.29173/alr774

Gunnell, D., Appleby, L., Arensman, E., Hawton, K., John, A., Kapur, N., Khan, M., O'Connor, R. C., & Pirkis, J. (2020). Suicide risk and prevention during the COVID-19 pandemic. *Lancet Psychiatry, 7*(6), 468–471. https://doi.org/10.1016/S2215-0366(20)30171-1

Gustavsson, N., & MacEachron, A. (2014). Ethics and schools of social work: A role for the practice community. *Social Work, 59*(4), 355–357.

Guthmann, D., Heines, W., & Kolvitz, M. (2019). One client: Many provider roles—Dual relationships in a counseling setting. *JADARA, 33*(3).

Haber, R., & Deaton, J. D. (2019). Facilitating an experiential group in an educational environment: Managing dual relationships. *International Journal of Group Psychotherapy, 69*(4), 434–458.

Halverson, G., & Brownlee, K. (2010). Managing ethical considerations around dual relationships in small rural and remote Canadian communities. *International Social Work, 53*(2), 247–260.

Halvorsen, T. (2019). Philosophy of social work–a new and advantageous field of training and research. *Journal of Social Work Practice, 33*(1), 55–66.

Hamblin, J. (2020, March 28). The curve is not flat enough. *The Atlantic.* https://www.theatlantic.com/health/archive/2020/03/coronavirus-forcing-american-hospitals-ration-care/609004/

Hancock, T. (2012). Facing structural inequality: Students' orientation to oppression and practice with oppressed groups. *Journal of Social Work Education, 48*(1), 5–25. https://doi.org/10.5175/JSWE.2012.201000078

Hardesty, M. (2015). Epistemological binds and ethical dilemmas in frontline child welfare practice. *Social Service Review, 89*(3), 455–498.

Hardina, D. (2004). Guidelines for ethical practice in community organization. *Social Work, 49*(4), 595–604.

Hardy, T. (2019). Then and now: The history and development of social work ethics. In S. M. Marson & R. E. McKinney Jr. (Eds.). *The Routledge handbook of social work ethics and values*. Routledge.

Harlow, E. (2018). New managerialism and social work: Changing women's work. In E. Harlow & J. Lawler (Eds.), *Management, social work and change* (pp. 73–92). Routledge.

Harlow, E., & Lawler, J. (Eds.). (2018). *Management, social work and change*. Routledge.

Harms-Smith, L. (2020). Horrible histories: Tracing Europe in the South. The case of South Africa. *Social Dialogue, 22,* 6–9.

Harrington, D., & Dolgoff, R. (2008). Hierarchies of ethical principles for ethical decision making in social work. *Ethics and Social Welfare, 2*(2), 183–196. https://doi.org/10.1080/17496530802117680

Harris, B., & Birnbaum, R. (2015). Ethical and legal implications on the use of technology in counselling. *Clinical Social Work Journal, 43,* 133–141.

Harris, M. (2018, March). UK civil society: Changes and challenges in the age of new public governance and the marketized welfare state. *Nonprofit Policy Forum, 8*(4), 351–368).

Hartley, R. P., & Lamarche, C. (2018). Behavioral responses and welfare reform: Evidence from a randomized experiment. *Labour Economics, 54,* 135–151.

Hartman, A. (2019). *A war for the soul of America: A history of the culture wars*. University of Chicago Press.

Hasenfeld, Y. (2010). *Human services as complex organizations* (2nd ed.). Sage.

Hatch, T., Alghafli, Z., Marks, L., Rose, A., Rose, J., Hardy, B., & Lambert, N. (2017). Prayer in Muslim families: A qualitative exploration. *Journal of Religion and Spirituality in Social Work: Social Thought, 36*(1–2), 73–95.

Hay, J. (2017). Two sides of the same coin of a critical care ethics in social work. In B. Pease, A. Vreugdenhil, & S. Stanford (Eds.), *Critical ethics of care in social work: Transforming the politics and practices of caring*. Routledge.

Hay, J. (2019). 'Care is not a dirty word!' Enacting an ethic of care in social work practice. *European Journal of Social Work, 22*(3), 365–375.

Hayes, D. D., & Varley, B. K. (1965). Impact of social work education on students' values. *Social Work, 10*(1), 40–46.

Haynes, K., & Mickelson, J. (2010). *Affecting change: Social workers in the political arena* (7th ed.). Pearson.

Healy, M., & Sofer, E. (2019). Policy advocacy at the federal level. In M. Reisch (Ed.), *Social policy and social justice: Meeting the challenges of a diverse society* (3rd ed., pp. 247–266). Cognella.

Heisler, C. J. (2019). Ethical dilemmas, vulnerable elders, and elder abuse. *Innovation in Aging, 3* (Suppl. 1), S238. https://doi.org/10.1093/geroni/igz038.891

Hennigan, B. (2017). House broken: Homelessness, housing first, and neoliberal poverty governance. *Urban Geography, 38*(9), 1418–1440.

Hessle, S. (2016). *Global social transformation and social action: The role of social workers: Social work-Social development Volume 3*. Routledge.

Hibbert, N. (2017). Human rights and social justice. *Laws, 6*(2). https://doi.org/10.3390/laws6020007

Hills, B. R. (2020). The cat is already out of the bag: Resolving the circuit split over the dangerous patient exception to the psychotherapist–patient privilege. *University of Baltimore Law Review, 49*(2), Art. 3.

Hittinger, J. P. (1989). Philosophy and the quest for ethical foundations: An overview. *Social Thought, 15*(3–4), 18–32.

Hobbes, T. (2016). *Leviathan*. Taylor & Francis. (Original work published 1651)

Hodge, D. (2006). Moving toward a more inclusive educational environment? A multi-sample exploration of religious discrimination as seen through the eyes of students from various faith traditions. *Journal of Social Work Education, 42*(2), 249–267. https://doi.org/10.5175/JSWE.2006.200400455

Hodge, D. R., Bonifas, R. P., & Chou, R. J.-A. (2010). Spirituality and older adults: Ethical guidelines to enhance service provision. *Advances in Social Work, 11*(1), 1–16.

Hoefer, R. (2019a). State and local policy advocacy. In M. Reisch (Ed.), *Social policy and social justice: Meeting the challenges of a diverse society* (3rd ed., pp. 267–290). Cognella.

Hoefer, R. (2019b). *Advocacy practice for social justice*. Oxford University Press.

Holland, T. P., & Kilpatrick, A. C. (1991). Ethical issues in social work: Toward a grounded theory of professional ethics. *Social Work, 36*(2), 138–144.

Homan, M. (2016). *Promoting community change: Making it happen in the real world* (6th ed.). Brooks/Cole.

Hondius, D. (2017). *Blackness in Western Europe: Racial patterns of paternalism and exclusion*. Routledge.

Hopps, J. G. (1987). Valuing others: The bedrock of ethics. *Social Work, 32*(2), 179–180.

Horne, M. (2018). *Values in social work*. Routledge.

Horney, J. A., Rios, J., Cantu, A., Ramsey, S., Montemayor, L., Raun, L., & Miller, A. (2019). Improving Hurricane Harvey disaster research response through academic–practice partnerships. *American Journal of Public Health, 109*(9), 1198–1201.

HuAlmeida, J., McManama, K. H., & O'Brien, K. N. (2017). Social work's ethical responsibility to train MSW students to work with suicidal clients. *Social Work, 62*(2), 181–183.

Hudson, K. D. (2016). With equality and opportunity for all? Emerging scholars define social justice for social work. *British Journal of Social Work, 46*(1), 1–20.

Hugman, R. (2003). Professional values and ethics in social work: Reconsidering post-modernism? *British Journal of Social Work*, *33*(8), 1025–1041.

Hugman, R. (2013). *Culture, values and ethics in social work: Embracing diversity*. Routledge.

Hugman, R. (2016). Power and authority in social work practice: Some ethical issues. In R. Hugman & J. Carter (Eds.), *Rethinking values and ethics in social work* (pp. 64–79). Palgrave Macmillan.

Hugman, R. (2017). Humanitarian aid and social development: A political ethics of care view of international social work practice. In P. Pease, A. Vreugdenhil, & S. Stanford (Eds.), *Critical ethics of care in social work: Transforming the politics and practice of caring* (pp. 116–126). Routledge.

Hugman, R. (2019). Practical justice in social work and social welfare. In P. Aggleton, A. Broom, & J. Moss (Eds.), *Practical justice: Principles, practice and social change*. Routledge.

Hugman, R., & Carter, J. (Eds.) (2016). *Rethinking values and ethics in social work*. Palgrave MacMillan.

Hugman, R., Pittaway, E., & Bartolomei, L. (2011). When 'do no harm' is not enough: The ethics of research with refugees and other vulnerable groups. *British Journal of Social Work*, *41*(7), 1271–1287.

Hunt, G. (2017). The principle of complementarity: Freedom of information, public accountability and whistleblowing. In M. Hunt & R. A. Chapman (Eds.), *Open government in a theoretical and practical context* (pp. 57–68). Routledge.

Hunt, M., Tansey, C. M., Anderson, J., Boulanger, R. F., Eckenwiler, L., Pringle, J., & Schwartz, L. (2016). The challenge of timely, responsive and rigorous ethics review of disaster research: Views of research ethics committee members. *PLOS ONE*, *11*(6), e0157142.

Hussein, S. (2018). Work engagement, burnout and personal accomplishments among social workers: A comparison between those working in children and adults' services in England. *Administration and Policy in Mental Health and Mental Health Services Research*, *45*(6), 911–923.

Hutchinson, E., Balabanova, D., & McKee, M. (2019). We need to talk about corruption in health systems. *International Journal of Health Policy and Management*, *8*(4), 191–194. https://doi.org/10.15171/ijhpm.2018.123

Hyde, C. (2011). What's ethics got to do with it? Using evidence to inform management practice. In M. Roberts-DeGennaro & S. Fogel (Eds.), *Using evidence to inform practice for community and organizational change* (pp. 35–53). Lyceum.

Hyde, C. A. (2012). Ethical dilemmas in human service management: Identifying and resolving the challenges. *Ethics and Social Welfare*, *6*(4), 351–367.

Ife, J. (2009). *Human rights from below: Achieving rights through community development*. Cambridge University Press.

Ife, J. (2012). *Human rights and social work: Towards rights-based practice* (3rd ed.). Cambridge University Press.

Iglehart, A. P., & Becerra, R. M. (2011). *Social services and the ethnic community: History and analysis* (2nd ed.). Waveland Press.

Iles, S. (2020). Prescription restriction: Why birth control must be over-the-counter in the United States. *Michigan Journal of Gender and Law*, *26*(2), 389–422.

Imre, R. (1989, March 5). *Caring about justice: A philosophical inquiry* [Paper presentation]. Symposium of the Study Group for Philosophical Issues in Social Work, Annual Program Meeting of the Council on Social Work Education. Chicago, IL, United States.

Ingmire, J. (2014, April 30). Using a foreign language changes moral decisions. *University of Chicago News*. https://news.uchicago.edu/story/using-foreign-language-changes-moral-decisions?msource=MAG10#sthash.h6dCguwA.dpuf

International Association of Schools of Social Work (2018, July 5). Global social work statement of ethical principles. https://www.iassw-aiets.org/archive/ethics-in-social-work-statement-of-principles/

International Federation of Social Workers (2018a, July 5). *Global social work statement of ethical principles*. https://www.ifsw.org/global-social-work-statement-of-ethical-principles/

International Federation of Social Workers (2018b). *Global definition of social work*. http://ifsw.org/get-involved/global-definition-of-social-work/

International Federation of Social Workers (2019). *Code of ethics* [Edited]. https://www.ifsw.org/?s=Code+of+Ethics

Israel, B. A., Schulz, A. J., Parker, E. A., Becker, A. B., Allen, A. J., Guzman, J. R., & Lichtenstein, R. (2017). Critical issues in developing and following CBPR principles. In N. Wallerstein, B. Duran, J. Oetzel, & M. Minkler (Eds.), *Community-based participatory research for health: Advancing social and health equity* (3rd ed., pp. 31–46). Jossey-Bass.

Izlar, J. (2019). Local–global linkages: Challenges in organizing functional communities for eco-social justice. *Journal of Community Practice*, *27*(3–4), 369–387.

Jackson, K. F. (2010). Ethical considerations in social work research with multiracial individuals. *Journal of Social Work Values and Ethics*, *7*(1), 1–10.

Jaffee v. Redmond, *518 U.S. 1* (1996).

Jaggar, A. M. (2018). *Living with contradictions: Controversies in feminist social ethics*. Routledge.

Jani, J. S. (2010). Mental health, poverty and agency in Managua, Nicaragua: A gendered perspective. *Social Work in Mental Health*, *8*, 356–374.

Jani, J. S., Osteen, P., & Shipe, S. (2016). Cultural competence and social work education: Moving toward assessment of practice behaviors. *Journal of Social Work Education*, *52*(3), 311–324.

Jani, J. S., & Reisch, M. (2011). Common human needs, uncommon solutions: Applying a critical framework to perspectives on human behavior. *Families in Society*, *92*(1), 13–20.

Jani, J. S., & Reisch, M. (2018, September). Assisting the least among us: Social work's historical response to unaccompanied immigrant and refugee youth. *Children and Youth Services Review, 92,* 4–14. https://doi.org/10.1016/j.childyouth.2018.02.025

Jarratt, S., & Moorhead, B. (2011). Social eugenics practices with children in Hitler's Nazi Germany and the role of social work: Lessons for current practice. *Journal of Social Work Values and Ethics, 8*(1), 1–10.

Johnson, W. B., & Johnson, S. J. (2017). Unavoidable and mandated multiple relationships in military settings. In O. Zur (Ed.), *Multiple relationships in psychotherapy and counseling* (pp. 61–72). Routledge.

Johnson, W. B., Leach, M., & Welfel, L. (2018). Ethical considerations for working with military service personnel. In M. M. Leach & E. R. Welfel (Eds.), *The Cambridge handbook of applied psychological ethics* (pp. 3–19). Cambridge University Press.

Joiner, J. M. (2019). Digital ethics in social work education. *Journal of Teaching in Social Work, 39*(4–5), 361–373.

Jones, M., Mlcek, S. H., Healy, J. P., & Bridges, D. (2019). Gender dynamics in social work practice and education: A critical literature review. *Australian Social Work, 72*(1), 62–74.

Jönsson, J. H., & Flem, A. L. (2017, June 27–29). Teaching social work values and ethics in international field training. In *EASSW-UNAFORIS 2017 European Conference–Social Work Education in Europe: Challenging Boundaries, Promoting a Sustainable Future* (pp. 72–92). Paris, France.

Joseph, M. V. (1985). A model for ethical decision making in clinical practice. In C. B. German (Ed.), *Advances in clinical practice* (pp. 207–217). National Association of Social Workers.

Joseph, M. V. (1988). *Developing and teaching models of ethical decision-making* [Lecture]. School of Social Work, Loyola University of Chicago, October 21, 1987.

Joseph, M. V. (1991). Standing for values and ethical action: Teaching social work ethics. *Journal of Teaching in Social Work, 5*(2), 95–109.

Joseph, M. V., & Conrad, A. P. (1983). Teaching social work ethics for contemporary practice: An effectiveness evaluation. *Journal of Education for Social Work, 19*(3), 59–68.

Josephson, M. (2002). *Making ethical decisions.* Josephson Institute.

Judah, E.J. (1979). Values: The uncertain component in social work. *Journal of Education for Social Work, 15*(2), 79–86.

Juhila, K., Ranta, J., Raitakari, S., & Banks, S. (2020). Relational autonomy and service choices in social worker-client conversations in an outpatient clinic for people using drugs. *British Journal of Social Work.* https://doi.org/10.1093/bjsw/bcaa011

Juujärvi, S., Kallunki, E., & Luostari, H. (2020). Ethical decision-making of social welfare workers in the transition of services: The ethics of care and justice perspectives. *Ethics and Social Welfare, 14*(1), 65–83. https://doi.org/10.1080/17496535.2019.1710546

Kane, E. W. (2018). The neoliberal baseline? A community-based exploration of beliefs about poverty and social policy. *Journal of Poverty, 22*(1), 65–87.

Kang, H. K., & Garran, A. M. (2018). Microaggressions in social work classrooms: Strategies for pedagogical intervention. *Journal of Ethnic and Cultural Diversity in Social Work, 27*(1), 4–16.

Kant, I. (1999). Critique of pure reason. In P. Guyer & A. W. Wood (Trans. and Eds.), *The Cambridge edition of the works of Immanuel Kant.* Cambridge University Press. (Original work published 1781)

Kaplan, L. E., Bryan, V., & Sanders, S. (2017). Ethics for helping professionals: Teaching a framework that supports collaborative ethical decision-making [Paper presentation]. Barbara Solomon School of Social Work, Walden University, United States.

Karagkounis, V. (2019). Implications and challenges for social work education in Greece in the time of austerity. *Social Work Education, 38*(3), 330–346.

Karger, J. (1988). *Social workers and labor unions.* Greenwood Press.

Karpman, H., & Miller, J. (2020). Social class and social work in the age of Trump. *Smith College Studies in Social Work, 90*(1–2), 1–17. https://doi.org/10.1080/00377317.2020.1706416

Karvinen-Niinikoski, S., Beddoe, L., Ruch, G., & Tsui, M. S. (2017). Professional supervision and professional autonomy. In B. Blom, L. Evertsson, & M. Perlinski (Eds.), *Social and caring professions in European welfare states* (pp. 53–66). Policy Press.

Katiuzhinsky, A., & Okech, D. (2014). Human rights, cultural practices, and state policies: Implications for global social work practice and policy. *International Journal of Social Welfare, 23*(1), 80–88.

Katz, C. C., Elsaesser, C., Klodnik, V. V., & Khare, A. (2019). Mentoring matters: An innovative approach to infusing mentorship in a social work doctoral program. *Journal of Social Work Education, 55*(2), 306–313.

Keddell, E., & Stanley, T. (2019). Critical debates in child protection: The production of risk in changing times. In S. A. Webb (Ed.), *The Routledge handbook of critical social work* (pp. 412–423). Routledge.

Keith, K. (2020). The ACA at the Supreme Court and beyond: A review of upcoming challenges and developments involving the Affordable Care Act. *Health Affairs, 39*(4), 554–555.

Kelley, F. (1905). *Some ethical gains through legislation.* MacMillan.

Kennedy, A. C. (2008). Eugenics, "degenerate girls," and social workers during the progressive era. *Affilia, 23*(1), 22–37.

Khoury, E. (2019). A response to the notion of avoidable ignorance in critiques of evidence-based practice. *The British Journal of Social Work, 49*(6), 1677–1681.

Khoury, S., & Whyte, D. (2019). Sidelining corporate human rights violations: The failure of the OECD's regulatory consensus. *Journal of Human Rights, 18*(4), 363–381.

Kickul, J., & Lyons, T. S. (2020). *Understanding social entrepreneurship: The relentless pursuit of mission in an ever-changing world*. Routledge.

Killackey, T., Peter, E., Maciver, J., & Mohammed, S. (2020). Advance care planning with chronically ill patients: A relational autonomy approach. *Nursing Ethics, 27*(2), 360–371. https://doi.org/10.1177%2F0969733019848031

Kimball, E., & Kim, J. (2013). Virtual boundaries: Ethical considerations for the use of social media in social work. *Social Work, 58*(2), 185–188.

Kirton, D. (2018). Neoliberalism, 'race' and child welfare. *Critical and Radical Social Work, 6*(3), 311–327. https://doi.org/10.1332/204986018X15388225078517

Knight, L. K. (2005). *Jane Addams and the struggle for democracy*. University of Chicago Press.

Koepsell, D. (2017). *Scientific integrity and research ethics: An approach from the ethos of science*. Springer.

Koggel, C. & Orme, J. (2010). Care ethics: New theories and applications. *Ethics and Social Welfare, 4*(2), 109–114.

Koh, B. D., & Reamer, F. G. (2020). Why moral theories matter: A review of ethics and adoption literature. *Adoption Quarterly*. https://doi.org/10.1080/10926755.2020.1719255

Kopels, S., & Kagle, J. D. (1993). Do social workers have a duty to warn? *Social Service Review, 67*(1), 101–126.

Krugman, P. (2019, July 11). The new plot against Obamacare. *The New York Times*. https://www.nytimes.com/2019/07/11/opinion/obamacare-court.html

Krysik, J. L. (2018). *Research for effective social work practice*. Routledge.

Kuhlmann, C. (2020). Social work in Nazi Germany: Why resistance would have been necessary. *Social Dialogue, 22*, 27–28.

Kukla, A. (2013). *Social constructivism and the philosophy of science*. Routledge.

Kusmaul, N., Bern-Klug, M., & Bonifas, R. (2017). Ethical issues in long-term care: A human rights perspective. *Journal of Human Rights and Social Work, 2*(3), 86–97.

Kwak, M.-Y. (2008, April 21). Caring and justice: Focused on the exploitation of women's labor in South Korea [Unpublished paper]. School of Social Work, University of Michigan, Ann Arbor, MI, United States.

Landi, D. S. (2017). New York psychologists and social workers: Confidentiality and professional malpractice. *Catholic Lawyer, 32*(2), Art. 4.

Lane, S. R., & Pritzker, S. (2018a). *Political social work: Using power to create social change* (pp. 3–21). Springer. https://doi.org/10.1007/978-3-319-68588-5

Lane, S. R., & Pritzker, S. (2018b). *Political social work: Using power to create social change* (pp. 431–460). Springer. https://doi.org/10.1007/978-3-319-68588-5

Lane, S. R., Ostrander, J., & Smith, T. R. (2018). 'Politics is social work with power': Training social workers for elected office. *Social Work Education, 37*(1), 1–16.

Larrabee, M. J. (2016). *An ethic of care: Feminist and interdisciplinary perspectives*. Routledge.

Larsson, S. (2019). Narrative analysis and critical social work. In S. A. Webb (Ed.), *The Routledge handbook of critical social work* (pp. 218–229). Routledge.

LaSala, M. C., & Goldblatt Hyatt, E. D. (2019). A bioethics approach to social work practice with transgender clients. *Journal of Gay and Lesbian Social Services, 31*(4), 501–520.

Lasch-Quinn, E. (1993). *Black neighbors: Race and the limits of reform in the American settlement house movement, 1890–1945*. University of North Carolina Press.

Lavalette, M., & Ferguson, I. (2018). Marx: Alienation, commodity fetishism and the world of contemporary social work. *Critical and Radical Social Work, 6*(2), 197–213.

Lawler, J. (2018). The rise of managerialism in social work. In E. Harlow & J. Lawler (Eds.), *Management, social work and change* (pp. 33–56). Routledge.

Lawrence, J. (2019). A life worth living: The ethical base for social work education and practice. *Australian Social Work, 72*(2), 133–138.

Lazari-Radek, K., & Singer, P. (2017). *Utilitarianism: A very short introduction*. Oxford University Press.

Lebacqz, K. (1987). *Justice in an unjust world*. Augsburg.

Lee, J. A., & Hudson, R. E. (2017). Empowerment approach to social work treatment. In F. J. Turner (Ed.), *Social work treatment: Interlocking theoretical approaches* (6th ed., pp. 142–165). Oxford University Press.

Lefkovitz, A. (2011). Men in the house: Race, welfare, and the regulation of men's sexuality in the United States, 1961–1972. *Journal of the History of Sexuality, 20*(3), 594–614.

Lens, V. (2001). When the personal and the political collide. *Journal of Social Work, 1*(3), 361–363.

Leong, C. (2017). A critical look into the Whistleblower Protection Act 2010. *Policy Ideas, 36*.

Lerner, J. E. (2020). "Social workers can't be Republicans": Engaging conservative students in the classroom. *Journal of Social Work Education, 56*(1), 56–67.

Levy, C. S. (1973). The value base of social work. *Journal of Education for Social Work, 9*(1), 34–42.

Levy, C. S. (1976a). *Social work ethics*. Human Sciences Press.

Levy, C. S. (1976b). Personal versus professional values: The practitioner's dilemma. *Clinical Social Work Journal, 4*, 110–120.

Levy, C. S. (1983). Client self-determination. In A. Rosenblatt & D. Waldfogel (Eds.), *Handbook of Clinical Social Work* (pp. 904–919). Jossey-Bass.

Lewis, H. (1972). Morality and the politics of practice. *Social Casework, 53*(7), 404–417. Reprinted in M. Reisch (Ed.). (2003). *For the common good: Essays of Harold Lewis*. Brunner-Routledge.

Lewis, H. (1980, January 31). The client's interest [Lecture]. Ethics Committee, New York University School of Medicine.

Lewis, H. (1982). *The intellectual base of social work practice: Tools for thought in a helping profession*. Haworth Press.

Lewis, H. (1984a). Ethical assessment. *Social Casework, 65*(4). Reprinted in M. Reisch (Ed.) (2003), *For the common good: Essays of Harold Lewis* (pp. 82–92). Brunner-Routledge.

Lewis, H. (1984b, November). *The problem with the problem-solving paradigm* [Paper presentation]. New York State Conference of Social Work Educators, Albany, NY, United States. Reprinted in M. Reisch (Ed.) (2003), *For the common good: Essays of Harold Lewis* (pp. 39–47). Brunner-Routledge.

Lewis, H. (1987, April). The ethical component in practice. In *Ethical practice in troubled times: Papers, 1955–1985* [Unpublished manuscript]. Reprinted in M. Reisch (Ed.) (2003), *For the common good: Essays of Harold Lewis* (pp. 71–80). Brunner-Routledge.

Lewis, H. (1988, May). Values and ethics in agency practice for a caring and just service [Paper presentation]. Westchester Family and Children's Services. In M. Reisch (Ed.) (2003), *For the common good: Essays of Harold Lewis* (pp. 122–129). Brunner-Routledge.

Lewis, H. (2003a). Ethics and the private nonprofit human service organization. In M. Reisch (Ed.) (2003), *For the common good: Essays of Harold Lewis* (pp. 112–121). Brunner-Routledge.

Lewis, H. (2003b). The whistleblower and the whistleblowing profession. In M. Reisch (Ed.) (2003), *For the common good: Essays of Harold Lewis* (pp. 93–101), Brunner-Routledge.

Lewis, H. (2003c). Teaching ethics through ethical teaching. In M. Reisch (Ed.) (2003), *For the common good: Essays of Harold Lewis* (pp. 102–111). Brunner-Routledge.

Lewis, H. (2003d). The battered helper. In M. Reisch (Ed.) (2003), *For the common good: Essays of Harold Lewis* (pp. 48–53). Haworth Press.

Lewis, M. L., & King, D. M. (2019). Teaching self-care: The utilization of self-care in social work practicum to prevent compassion fatigue, burnout, and vicarious trauma. *Journal of Human Behavior in the Social Environment, 29*(1), 96–106.

Li, J. (2019). A study on the participation of social work in the refinement of social governance. *American Journal of Social Research*.

Libal, K., & Harding, S. (2015). *Human rights-based community practice in the United States*. Springer.

Lindemann, H. (2019). *An invitation to feminist ethics*. Oxford University Press.

Lipsky, M. (2010). *Street-level bureaucracy: Dilemmas of the individual in public services*. Russell Sage Foundation.

Lipsky, M., & Smith, S. (1989). When social problems are treated as emergencies. *Social Service Review, 63*(1), 5–25.

Lipworth, W., & Montgomery, K. (2018). *Making sense of professional conflicts and quandaries*. Routledge.

Lizano, E. L., & Mor Barak, M. E. (2015). Job burnout and affective wellbeing: A longitudinal study of burnout and job satisfaction among public child welfare workers. *Children and Youth Services Review, 55*, 18–28. https://doi.org/10.1016/j.childyouth.2015.05.005

Lloyd, L., & Sullivan, M. P. (2018). Ageing, ethics and social welfare: Contemporary social work and social care practices with older people [Editorial]. *Ethics and Social Welfare, 12*(3), 201–203. https://doi.org/10.1080/17496535.2018.1537545

Lloyd-Hazlett, J., Moyer, M. S., & Sullivan, J. R. (2018). Adolescent risk-taking behaviors: When do student counselors break confidentiality? *Journal of Child and Adolescent Counseling, 4*(2), 178–193.

Locke, J. (1689). *Two treatises on government*. London: C. Brown.

Loewenberg, F., & Dolgoff, R. (1988). *Ethical decisions for social work practice* (3rd ed.). Peacock.

Logan, J., Kershaw, S., Karban, K., Mills, S., Trotter, J., & Sinclair, M. (2017). *Confronting prejudice: Lesbian and gay issues in social work education*. Taylor & Francis.

Logan, S. (2018). *The Black family: Strengths, self-help, and positive change*. Routledge.

Lorde, A. (2017). *A burst of light: And other essays*. Courier Dover.

Lorenz, W. (2016a). The emergence of social justice in the West. In M. Reisch (Ed.), *The Routledge international handbook of social justice* (pp. 14–26). Routledge.

Lorenz, W. (2016b). Is history repeating itself? Reinventing social work's role in ensuring social solidarity under conditions of globalization. In T. Harrikari & T.-L. Rauhala (Eds.), *Social change and social work: The changing societal conditions of social work in time and place* (pp. 15–29). Routledge.

Lorenzetti, L., Halvorsen, J., Dhungel, R., Lorenzetti, D., Oshchepkova, T., Haile, L., & Biscette, K. (2019). Community based mentors and journey guides: A transformative learning approach to social work education. *Social Work Education, 38*(7), 875–893.

Loue, S. (2017). Strengths-based social work: Issues, controversies, and ethical considerations. In A. Sandu & A. Frunza (Eds.), *Ethical issues in social work practice* (pp. 62–81). IGI Global.

Loue, S. (2018). *Legal Issues in Social Work Practice and Research*. Springer.

Løvseth, L. T. (2017). The hidden stressor of child welfare workers: Client confidentiality as a barrier for coping with emotional work demands. *Child and Family Social Work, 22*(2), 923–931.

Lowe, M. (2018). Ethics and the care of the elderly. In B. K. R. Nair (Ed.), *Geriatric Medicine* (pp. 283–293). Springer.

Lu, L., Li, F., Leung, K., Savani, K., & Morris, M. W. (2018). When can culturally diverse teams be more creative?

The role of leaders' benevolent paternalism. *Journal of Organizational Behavior, 39*(4), 402–415.

Lunt, C. (2016). Breaching confidentiality and 'empowerment'? *Ethics and Social Welfare, 10*(1), 75–81. https://psycnet.apa.org/doi/10.1080/17496535.2015.1126902

Lunt, N., Bainbridge, L., & Rippon, S. (2020). Strengths, assets and place—The emergence of local area coordination initiatives in England and Wales. *Journal of Social Work.* https://doi.org/10.1177%2F1468017320918174

Luse, M. M. (2018). Ethical vocational rehabilitation practice and dual relationships in rural settings. In D. A. Harley, N. A. Ysasi, M. L. Bishop, & A. R. Fleming (Eds.), *Disability and vocational rehabilitation in rural settings* (pp. 95–115). Springer.

Machiavelli, N., & Connell, W. J. (Trans. and Ed.) (2015). *The Prince with related documents* (2nd rev. ed.) St. Martin's Press. (Original work published 1532)

Madland, D., & Rowell, A. (2017, November 15). Attacks on public-sector unions harm states: How Act 10 has affected education in Wisconsin. Center for American Progress Action Fund. https://cdn.americanprogress.org/content/uploads/sites/2/2017/11/15074954/ImpactofWisconsinAct10-brief.pdf

Maguire, D. (1978). *The moral choice.* Doubleday.

Mansbach, A., & Bachner, Y.G. (2008). On the readiness of social work students to blow the whistle to protect the client's interests. *Journal of Social Work Values and Ethics, 5*(2), 1–14.

Mansbach. A., & Bachner, Y. (2009). Self-reported likelihood of whistleblowing by social work students. *Social Work Education, 28*(1), 18–28.

Mapp, S., McPherson, J., Androff, D., & Gatenio Gabel, S. (2019). Social work is a human rights profession. *Social Work, 64*(3), 259–269.

Mapp, S. C. (2014). *Human rights and social justice in a global perspective: An introduction to international social work* (2nd ed.). Oxford University Press.

Marc, C., DimÉny, J. M., & Bacter, C. (2019). The social worker-client relationship: Difficulties and solutions. *Bulletin of the Transylvania University of Brasov, Series VII, Social Sciences and Law, 12*(2), 377–386.

Margolin, L. (1997). *Under the cover of kindness: The invention of social work.* University of Virginia Press.

Marson, S. M., & McKinney, R. (2019). Abortion and *The Routledge handbook of social work ethics and values* [Editorial]. *Journal of Social Work Values and Ethics, 16*(1), 1.

Martela, F., & Riekki, T. J. (2018). Autonomy, competence, relatedness, and beneficence: A multicultural comparison of the four pathways to meaningful work. *Frontiers in Psychology, 9*, 1157. https://doi.org/10.3389/fpsyg.2018.01157

Martinez Herrero, M. I. (2020). Facing a dark and unknown chapter in the history of social work in Spain: Social work in times of Franco's eugenics and stolen babies. *Social Dialogue, 22*, 16–18.

Marx, K. (1978). *Theses on Feuerbach* and *The German ideology.* In R. C. Tucker (Ed.), *The Marx-Engels reader* (2nd ed., pp. 143–200). W. W. Norton.

Maryland Courts and Judicial Proceedings. (2012). Limitations, prohibited actions, and immunities—Health and public safety. *Maryland Courts and Judicial Proceedings Code Ann.*, Title 5, Subtitle 6, 5–609. Matthew Bender.

Maryland Family Law Code Ann. (2013). Investigative provisions. Family Law: Adult Protective Services, Title 14, Subtitle 3, *Maryland Family Law Code Ann. 14-302.*

Maslow, A. (1943). A theory of human motivation. *Psychological Review, 50*(4), 370–396.

Mathews, J. (1983, December 17). Judge rejects palsy victim's bid to starve. *Washington Post*, A1.

Mathieu, S. (2016). From the defamilialization to the "demotherization" of care work. *Social Politics: International Studies in Gender, State and Society, 23*(4), 576–591.

Matier, P., & Ross, A. (1991, August 4). Social worker's Catch-22. *San Francisco Examiner.*

Mattison, M. (2018). Informed consent agreements: Standards of care for digital social work practices. *Journal of Social Work Education, 54*(2), 227–238.

Maurer, M., Mangrum, R., Carman, K. L., Ginsburg, M., Gold, M. R., Sofaer, S., Pathek-Sen, E., Richmond, J, & Siegel, J. (2017). Setting boundaries: Public views on limiting patient and physician autonomy in health care decisions. *Journal of Health Politics, Policy and Law, 42*(4), 579–605.

Mayans, I., & Vaca, M. (2018). The paternalistic argument against abortion. *Hypatia, 33*(1), 22–39.

McBeath, B. (2016). Re-envisioning macro social work practice. *Families in Society, 97*(1), 5–14.

McCallion, P., & Ferretti, L. A. (2017). Understanding, supporting and safeguarding self-determination as we age. In M. L. Wehmeyer, K. Shogren, T. D. Little, & S. J. Lopez (Eds.), *Development of self-determination through the lifecourse* (pp. 145–158). Springer.

McGirr, S. A., & Sullivan, C. M. (2017). Critical consciousness raising as an element of empowering practice with survivors of domestic violence. *Journal of Social Service Research, 43*(2), 156–168.

McGuire, J. T. (2018). Raising government children: A history of foster care and the American welfare state by Catherine E. Rymph. *Journal of Southern History, 84*(4), 1046–1047.

McInroy, L. B. (2017). Innovative ethics: Using animated videos when soliciting informed consent of young people for online surveys. *Social Work Research, 41*(2), 121–128.

McKenzie-Mohr, S., & Lafrance, M. N. (2017). Narrative resistance in social work research and practice: Counter storying in the pursuit of social justice. *Qualitative Social Work, 16*(2), 189–205.

McLaughlin, K. (2016). *Empowerment: A critique.* Routledge.

Meenaghan, T. M., Kilty, K. M., Long, D. D., & McNutt, J. G. (2013). *Policy, politics, and ethics: A critical approach* (3rd ed.). Lyceum Books.

Mendes, P. (2019). Top-down paternalism versus bottom-up community development: A case study of compulsory income management programmes in Australia. *International Journal of Community and Social Development, 1*(1), 42–57.

Mersky, J. P., Topitzes, J., & Britz, L. (2019). Promoting evidence-based, trauma-informed social work practice. *Journal of Social Work Education, 55*(4), 645–657.

Metzger, E. (2017). Ethics and intimate sexual activity in long-term care. *AMA Journal of Ethics, 19*(7), 640–648.

Meyfroidt, G., Vlieghe, E., Biston, P., De Decker, K., Wittebole, X., Collin, V., Depuydt, P., Nguyen, D-N., Hermans, G., Jorens, P., Ledoux, D., Taccone, F., & Devisch, I. (2020). *Ethical principles concerning proportionality of critical care during the COVID-19 pandemic: Advice by the Belgian Society of IC medicine.* Hartcentrum Hasselt. https://www.hartcentrumhasselt.be/professioneel/nieuws-professioneel/ethical-principles-concerning-proportionality-of-critical-care-during-the-covid-19-pandemic-advice-by-the-belgian-society-of-ic-medicine

Michener, J. (2018). *Fragmented democracy: Medicaid, federalism, and unequal politics.* Cambridge University Press.

Mill, J. S. (1859). *On liberty.* Cambridge University Press.

Mill, J. S. (1971 ed.). *Utilitarianism.* Bobbs-Merrill. (Original work published 1861)

Miller, J. J., Lianekhammy, J., Pope, N., Lee, J., & Grise-Owens, E. (2017). Self-care among healthcare social workers: An exploratory study. *Social Work in Health Care, 56*(10), 865–883.

Miller, J., & Garran, A. M. (2017). *Racism in the United States: Implications for the helping professions.* Springer.

Miller-Stevens, K., Taylor, J. A., Morris, J. C., & Lanivich, S. E. (2018). Assessing value differences between leaders of two social venture types: Benefit corporations and nonprofit organizations. *VOLUNTAS: International Journal of Voluntary and Nonprofit Organizations, 29*(5), 938–950.

Mills, M. (2017). Dementia and guardianship: Challenges in social work practice. *Australian Social Work, 70*(1), 30–41.

Millstein, K. (2000). Confidentiality in direct social work practice: Inevitable challenges and ethical dilemmas. *Families in Society, 81*(3), 270–282.

Misca, G., & Neamtu, N. (2016). Contemporary challenges in social work practice in multicultural societies. *Social Work Review,* (1), 7–9.

Mongan, P. (2018). At a crossroads: Social work, conscientious objection, and religious liberty laws. *Online Journal of Health Ethics, 14*(1), Art. 8.

Morley, C. (2016). Promoting activism through critical social work education: The impact of global capitalism and neoliberalism on social work and social work education. *Critical and Radical Social Work, 4*(1), 39–57.

Morley, C., & Ablett, P. (2016). A critical social work response to wealth and income inequality. *Social Alternatives, 35*(4), 20–26.

Morley, C., Le, C., & Briskman, L. (2019). The role of critical social work education in improving ethical practice with refugees and asylum seekers. *Social Work Education, 39*(4), 403–416. https://doi.org/10.1080/02615479.2019.1663812

Morris, K., Mason, W., Bywaters, P., Featherstone, B., Daniel, B., Brady, G., Bunting, L., Hooper, J., Mirza, N., Scourfield, J., & Webb, C. (2018). Social work, poverty, and child welfare interventions. *Child and Family Social Work, 23*(3), 364–372.

Morris, R. (1977, September). Caring for vs. caring about people. *Social Work, 22,* 353–359.

Mossialos, E., & Le Grand, J. (Eds.). (2019). *Health care and cost containment in the European Union.* Routledge.

Moxley, D. P., & Bueche, L. (2002). Ethical issues in agency resource development: Implications for social administration. *Families in Society: The Journal of Contemporary Human Services, 83*(3), 265–273.

Moyo, O. N., & Courter, D. (2016). Political consciousness: A perpetual quest in social work. *Journal of Progressive Human Services, 27*(3), 137–142.

Munn-Giddings, C., & Borkman, T. (2017). Reciprocity in peer-led mutual aid groups in the community: Implications for social policy and social work practices. In M. Torronen & C. Munn-Giddings (Eds.), *Reciprocal relationships and well-being* (pp. 57–76). Routledge.

Munoz Arce, G. (2020). Chilean social work and the legacy of the dictatorship. *Social Dialogue, 22,* 13–15.

Murdach, A. D. (2011). Is social work a human rights profession? [Commentary]. *Social Work, 56*(3), 282–283.

Muskens, I. S., Gupta, S., Robertson, F. C., Moojen, W. A., Kolias, A. G., Peul, W. C., & Broekman, M. L. (2019). When time is critical, is informed consent less so? A discussion of patient autonomy in emergency neurosurgery. *World Neurosurgery, 125,* e336-e340.

Nacos, B. L., & Bloch-Elkon, Y. (2018). US media and post-9/11 human rights violations in the name of counter-terrorism. *Human Rights Review, 19*(2), 193–210.

Nadasen, P. (2012). *Rethinking the welfare rights movement.* Routledge.

Nadasen, P. (2019). Response to Sherwin and Piven's "The Radical Feminist Legacy of the National Welfare Rights Organization." *Women's Studies Quarterly, 47*(3), 155–163.

Nanda, G. (2019). The protection and encouragement of whistleblowers in the context of access to justice: A critical analysis of Indian public sector law. *Australian Journal of Asian Law, 19*(2).

Nathan, S. K., & Tempel, E. R. (2016). Philanthropy and fundraising. In D. O. Renz & R. D. Herman (Eds.), *The Jossey-Bass handbook of nonprofit leadership and management* (pp. 488–508). Jossey-Bass.

National Association of Social Workers (2017). *Standards for technology in social work practice.* https://www.socialworkers.org/Practice/Clinical-Social-Work/Technology

National Association of Social Workers (2018). *Code of ethics* (Rev. ed.). https://www.socialworkers.org/About/Ethics/Code-of-Ethics

National Association of Social Workers (2020). Self-care during the coronavirus pandemic. https://www.social-workers.org/Practice/Infectious-Diseases/Coronavirus/Self-Care-During-the-Coronavirus-Pandemic

Naughton, J. (2020, April 18). When Covid-19 has done with us, what will be the new normal? *The Guardian.* https://www.theguardian.com/commentisfree/2020/apr/18/when-covid-19-has-done-with-us-what-will-be-the-new-normal

Nedjat-Haiem, F. R., Carrion, I. V., Gonzalez, K., Ell, K., Thompson, B., & Mishra, S. I. (2017). Exploring health care providers' views about initiating end-of-life care communication. *American Journal of Hospice and Palliative Medicine, 34*(4), 308–317.

Ngene, N. C., Onyia, C. O., & Moodley, J. (2019). Requesting a patient to document her decision for refusal of hospital treatment promotes beneficence. *South African Medical Journal, 109*(1), 9–9.

Nguyen, M. T., Zavoretti, R., & Tronto, J. (2017). Beyond the global care chain: Boundaries, institutions and ethics of care. *Ethics and Social Welfare, 11*(3), 199–212.

Nothdurfter, U., & Lorenz, W. (2010). Beyond the pro and contra of evidence-based practice: Reflections on a recurring dilemma at the core of social work. *Social Work and Society, 8*(1), 46–59.

Nozick, R. (1974). *Anarchy, state, and utopia.* Basic Books.

Nussbaum, M. (2013). *Creating capabilities: The human development approach.* Harvard University Press.

O'Brien, P. J. (2014). Ethics do matter, but where? *Advances in Social Work, 15*(2), 262–277.

O'Mathúna, D. (2018). The dual imperative in disaster research ethics. In R. Iphofen & M. Tolich (Eds.), *The Sage handbook of qualitative research ethics* (pp. 441–454). Sage.

O'Hare, T. (2020). *Evidence-based practices for social workers: An interdisciplinary approach.* Oxford University Press.

Olson, C., Reid, C., Threadgill-Goldson, N., Riffe, H. A., & Ryan, P. A. (2013). Voices from the field: Social workers define and apply social justice. *Journal of Progressive Human Services, 24*(1), 23–42. https://doi.org/10.1080/10428232.2013.740407

Olson, M. D. (2014). Exploring the ethical dilemma of integrating social work values and military social work practice. *Social Work, 59*(2), 183–185.

Olson, M. D. (2018). Exploring military social work from a social justice perspective. *International Social Work, 61*(1), 119–129.

Olson, S., Brown-Rice, K., & Keller, N. (2016). Mental health practitioners' knowledge of colleagues' problems of professional competency. *Journal of Mental Health Counseling, 38*(4), 308–326.

O'Neill, P. (1989). Responsible to whom? Responsible for what? Some ethical issues in community intervention. *American Journal of Community Psychology, 17*(3), 323–341.

O'Neill, S. (2018). *Process facilitation in psychoanalysis, psychotherapy and social work.* Routledge.

Osho, G. S., Joseph, J., Scott, J., & Adams, M. (2016). An investigation of juvenile gang membership and psychopathic behavior: Evidence from multilinear analysis. *International Journal of Social Work, 3*(2), 29–48.

Osteen, P. J. (2011). Motivations, values, and conflict resolution: Students' integration of personal and professional identities. *Journal of Social Work Education, 47*(3), 423–444.

Oxhandler, H. K., & Giardina, T. D. (2017). Social workers' perceived barriers to and sources of support for integrating clients' religion and spirituality in practice. *Social Work, 62*(4), 323–332.

Paarlberg, L. E., & Hwang, H. (2017). The heterogeneity of competitive forces: The impact of competition for resources on United Way fundraising. *Nonprofit and Voluntary Sector Quarterly, 46*(5), 897–921.

Paarlberg, L. E., An, S. H., Nesbit, R., Christensen, R. K., & Bullock, J. (2018). A field too crowded? How measures of market structure shape nonprofit fiscal health. *Nonprofit and Voluntary Sector Quarterly, 47*(3), 453–473.

Pace, P. R. (2017, June). Experts examine social work ethics and political opinion. *NASW News, 62*(6), 1.

Palk, A. C., & Stein, D. J. (2020). Ethical issues in global mental health. *Global Mental Health and Neuroethics,* 265–285. https://doi.org/10.1016/B978-0-12-815063-4.00016-2

Papouli, E. (2019). Aristotle's virtue ethics as a conceptual framework for the study and practice of social work in modern times. *European Journal of Social Work, 22*(6), 921–934.

Park, Y. (2019). *Facilitating injustice: The complicity of social workers in the forced removal and incarceration of Japanese Americans, 1941–1946.* Oxford University Press.

Park, Y., & Kemp S. P. (2006). 'Little alien colonies': Representations of immigrants and their neighbors in social work discourse, 1875–1924. *Social Service Review, 80*(4), 705–734.

Pawar, M., Hugman, R., Alexandra, A., & Anscombe, A. B. (Eds.). (2017). *Empowering social workers: Virtuous practitioners.* Springer.

Payne, M., & Askeland, G. A. (2016). *Globalization and international social work: Postmodern change and challenge.* Routledge.

Pease, B., Vreugdenhil, A., & Stanford, S. (Eds.). (2017). *Critical ethics of care in social work: Transforming the politics and practices of caring.* Routledge.

Pellegrino, E. P. (1989). Can ethics be taught? An essay. *Mount Sinai Journal of Medicine, 56*(6), 490–494.

Pereira, I. (2020, April 2). *Nonprofit organizations ask for stimulus money as resources dry up in coronavirus pandemic.* ABC News. https://abcnews.go.com/Health/nonprofit-organizations-stimulus-money-resources-dry-pandemic/story?id=69925503

Perlis, L. (1960, September 24). *Morality, ethics and social action* [Address]. National Conference of Catholic

Charities, New York, NY, United States. Located in the archives of the University of Pennsylvania School of Social Work.

Petrovich, J. (2012). Culturally competent social work practice with veterans: An overview of the U.S. military. *Journal of Human Behavior in the Social Environment, 22*(7), 863–874. https://doi.org/10.1080/10911359.2012.707927

Petruzzi, L., Milano, N., Zeng, W., & Chen, Q. (2020, April 16). Lessons from Wuhan: The role of social workers during the COVID-19 pandemic. *Social Work Today.* https://www.socialworktoday.com/archive/exc_041620.shtml

Philip, D., & Reisch, M. (2015). Rethinking social work's interpretation of 'environmental justice': From local to global. *Social Work Education, 34*(5), 471–483.

Phillips, S. D., & Blumberg, M. (2017). International trends in government-nonprofit relations: Constancy, change, and contradictions. In E. Boris, C. E. Steuerle, & S. R. Wartell (Eds.), *Nonprofits and government: Collaboration and conflict* (pp. 313–342). Rowman & Littlefield.

Plitt Donaldson, L., Fogel, S. J., Hill, K., Erickson, C., & Ferguson, S. (2016). Attitudes toward advanced licensing for macro social work practice. *Journal of Community Practice, 24*(1), 77–93.

Powers, L. E., Fullerton, A., Schmidt, J., Geenen, S., Oberweiser-Kennedy, M., Dohn, J., Nelson, M., Iavanditti, R., & Blakeslee, J. (2018). Perspectives of youth in foster care on essential ingredients for promoting self-determination and successful transition to adult life: My life model. *Children and Youth Services Review, 86*, 277–286. https://doi.org/10.1016/j.childyouth.2018.02.007

Prasant, J. P. (2016). The Gandhian concept of social justice. In M. Reisch (Ed.), *The Routledge international handbook of social justice* (pp. 39–47). Routledge.

Preston-Shoot, M. (2011). On administrative evil-doing within social work policy and services: Law, ethics, and practice. *European Journal of Social Work, 14*(2), 177–194.

Pringle, N. N., & Thompson, P. J. (2019). *Social work, psychiatry and the law.* Routledge.

Pritzker, S., & Lane, S. R. (2017). Political social work: History, forms, and opportunities for innovation. *Social Work, 62*(1), 80–82.

Prochner, L., & Nawrotzki, K. (2019). The origins of the current era of early childhood care and education. In C. P. Brown, M. B. McMullen, & N. File (Eds.), *The Wiley handbook of early childhood care and education* (pp. 7–28). Wiley-Blackwell.

Prusaczyk, B., Cherney, S. M., Carpenter, C. R., & DuBois, J. M. (2017). Informed consent to research with cognitively impaired adults: Transdisciplinary challenges and opportunities. *Clinical Gerontologist, 40*(1), 63–73.

Pugh, G. L. (2017). A model of comparative ethics education for social workers. *Journal of Social Work Education, 53*(2), 312–326.

Quinones, L. A. (2020, March 13). Social work in a time of pandemic. *The New Social Worker.* https://www.socialworker.com/feature-articles/practice/social-work-in-time-of-pandemic/

Raithby, M., & Willis, P. (2017). 'No sex, please, …': Applying a critical ethics of care perspective to social care provision for older lesbian, gay and bisexual (LGB) adults. In B. Pease, A. Vreugdenhil, & S. Stanford (Eds.), *Critical ethics of care in social work: Transforming the politics and practices of caring* (pp. 148–160). Routledge.

Rajan-Rankin, S. (2016). Paternalism and the paradox of work–life balance: Discourse and practice. *Community, Work and Family, 19*(2), 227–241.

Ramm, A. (2020). Latin America: A fertile ground for maternalism. In A. Ramm & J. Gideon (Eds.), *Motherhood, social policies and women's activism in Latin America* (pp. 13–37). Palgrave Macmillan.

Rana, R. A., Rana, F. Z., & Rana, H. A. (2017). Strategic planning role in nonprofit organizations. *Journal for Studies in Management and Planning, 3*(6), 166–170.

Rasell, M., Join-Lambert, H., Naumiuk, A., Pinto, C., Uggerhoj, L., & Walker, J. (2019). Diversity, dialogue, and identity in designing globally relevant social work education. *Social Work Education, 38*(6), 675–688.

Rawls, J. (1971). *A theory of justice.* Harvard University Press.

Rawls, J. (1999). *A theory of justice* (Rev. ed.). Harvard University Press.

Rawls, J. (2001). *Justice as fairness: A restatement.* Harvard University Press.

Raymond, S., Beddoe, L., & Staniforth, B. (2017). Social workers' experiences with whistleblowing: To speak or not to speak? *Aotearoa New Zealand Social Work, 29*(3). https://doi.org/10.11157/anzswj-vol29iss3id305

Reamer, F. G. (1979). Fundamental ethical issues in social work: An essay review. *Social Service Review, 53*(2), 229–243.

Reamer, F. G. (1980). Ethical content in social work. *Social Casework, 61*(9), 531–540.

Reamer, F. G. (1983a). Ethical dilemmas in social work practice. *Social Work, 28*(1), 31–35.

Reamer, F. G. (1983b). The concept of paternalism in social work. *Social Service Review, 57*(2), 254–271.

Reamer, F. G. (1986, November–December). The use of modern technology in social work: Ethical dilemmas. *Social Work, 31*, 469–472.

Reamer, F. G. (2001). Moral philosophy meets social work: Commentary on Alan Gewirth's "Confidentiality in Child Welfare Practice." *Social Service Review, 75*(3), 490–496.

Reamer, F. G. (2006). Nontraditional and unorthodox interventions in social work: Ethical and legal implications. *Families in Society, 87*(2), 191–197.

Reamer, F. G. (2008). Social workers' management of error: Ethical and risk management issues. *Families in Society, 89*(1), 61–68.

Reamer, F. G. (2012). *Boundary issues and dual relationships in the human services* (2nd ed.). Columbia University Press.

Reamer, F. G. (2013a). Social work in a digital age: Ethical and risk management challenges. *Social Work*, 58(2), 163–172.

Reamer, F. G. (2013b). The digital and electronic revolution in social work: Rethinking the meaning of ethical practice. *Ethics and Social Welfare*, 7(1), 2–19.

Reamer, F. G. (2015a). Clinical social work in a digital environment: Ethical and risk-management challenges. *Clinical Social Work Journal*, 43, 120–132.

Reamer, F. G. (2015b). *Risk management in social work: Preventing professional malpractice, liability, and disciplinary action.* Columbia University Press.

Reamer, F. G. (2015c, September–October). Ethical misconduct and negligence in social work. *Social Work Today*, 15(5), 18–23.

Reamer, F. G. (2017). Evolving ethical standards in the digital age. *Australian Social Work*, 70(2), 148–159.

Reamer, F. G. (2018a). *Social work values and ethics* (5th ed.). Columbia University Press.

Reamer, F. G. (2018b). Ethical issues in integrated health care: Implications for social workers. *Health and Social Work*, 43(2), 118–124.

Reamer, F. G. (2018c). Pursuing social work's mission: The philosophical foundations of social justice. *Journal of Social Work Values and Ethics*, 15(1), 34–42.

Reamer, F. G. (2019a). Boundary issues and dual relationships in social work. In S. M. Marson & R. E. McKinney Jr. (Eds.), *The Routledge handbook of social work ethics and values* (pp. 157–166). Routledge.

Reamer, F. G. (2019b). Essential ethics knowledge in social work. In S. M. Marson & R. E. McKinney Jr. (Eds.), *The Routledge handbook of social work ethics and values.* Routledge.

Reamer, F. G. (2019c). Social work education in a digital world: Technology standards for education and practice. *Journal of Social Work Education*, 55(3), 420–432.

Reamer, F.G., & Siegel, H.D. (1992). Should social workers blow the whistle on incompetent colleagues? In E. Gambrill & R. Pruger (Eds.), *Controversial issues in social work* (pp. 66–73). Allyn & Bacon.

Rees, S. (2016). Justice, culture, and human rights. In M. Reisch (Ed.), *The Routledge international handbook of social justice* (pp. 455–462). Routledge.

Reese, E., Breckenridge-Jackson, I., & McCoy, J. (2017). Maternalist and community politics. In H. J. MaCammon, V. Taylor, J. Reger, & R. L. Einwohner (Eds.), *The Oxford handbook of US women's social movement activism* (pp. 232–253). Oxford University Press.

Reese, E., Marg, L., & McCoy, J. (2018). Social policy in the United States. In S. Shaver (Ed.), *Handbook on gender and social policy.* Edward Elgar.

Reichert, E. (Ed.) (2007). *Challenges in human rights: A social work perspective.* Columbia University Press.

Reimer, E., & Thompson, L. J. (2019). How a relational approach to practice can encourage social work to return to its ethical endeavour. In S. M. Marson & R. E. McKinney Jr. (Eds.), *The Routledge handbook of social work ethics and values.* Routledge.

Reisch, M. (1992). Social workers should not work in for-profit organizations. In R. Pruger & E. Gambrill (Eds.), *Controversial issues in social work* (pp. 27–38). Allyn and Bacon.

Reisch, M. (Ed.) (2003). *For the common good: Essays of Harold Lewis.* Routledge.

Reisch, M. (2007). Constructing a socially just system of social welfare in a multicultural society: The U.S. experience. In *Human rights and social justice: Rethinking social welfare's mission* (pp. 133–161). Korean Academy of Social Welfare.

Reisch, M. (2009). Social workers, unions, and low-wage workers: An historical perspective. *Journal of Community Practice*, 17(1–2), 50–72.

Reisch, M. (2010a). Defining social justice in a socially unjust world. In J. M. Bierkenmaier, A. Cruce, J. Curley, E. Burkemper, R. J. Wilson, & J. J. Stretch (Eds.), *Educating for social justice: Transformative experiential learning* (pp. 11–28). Lyceum Books.

Reisch, M. (2010b). United States social welfare policy and privatization in post-industrial society. In J. L. Powell & J. Hendricks (Eds.), *The welfare state in post-industrial society: A global perspective* (pp. 253–270). Springer.

Reisch, M. (2012). The challenges of health care reform for hospital social work in the U.S. *Social Work in Health Care*, 51(10), 873–893.

Reisch, M. (2013a). Not by the numbers alone: The effects of economic and demographic changes on social policy. In I. Colby, K. Sowers, & C. Dulmus (Eds.), *Social Welfare Policy: A Foundation of Social Work* (pp. 135–163). Wiley.

Reisch, M. (2013b). Social work education and the neoliberal challenge: The U.S. response to increasing global inequality. *Social Work Education*, 32(6), 715–733.

Reisch, M. (2014a). Ethical practice in an unethical environment. In S. Banks (Ed.), *Ethics* (pp. 45–49). Policy Press.

Reisch, M. (2014b). The boundaries of justice: Addressing the conflict between human rights and multiculturalism in social work practice and education. In K. Libal, L. Healy, M. Berthold, & R. Thomas (Eds.), *Advancing human rights in social work education* (pp. 177–195). CSWE Press.

Reisch, M. (2015). *Coalizione o conflitto: Lavoro sociale e classe lavoratrice negli Stati Uniti* (U.S. social work and the working class: Coalition and conflict). *Zapruder*, 37, 40–57.

Reisch, M. (2016a). Social justice. In R. Hugman & J. Carter (Eds.), *Rethinking values and ethics in social work* (pp. 33–48). Palgrave MacMillan.

Reisch, M. (2016b). Social justice and liberalism. In M. Reisch (Ed.), *The Routledge international handbook of social justice* (pp. 132–146). Routledge.

Reisch, M. (2018a). The year 1968: The turning point when U.S. social work failed to turn. *Critical and Radical Social Work*, 6(1), 7–20.

Reisch, M. (2018b, November). The declining significance of evidence: Effective advocacy in an "alternative facts" environment [Paper presentation]. Annual Program Meeting of the Council on Social Work Education, Orlando, FL, United States.

Reisch, M. (2018c). *Macro social work practice: Working for change in a multicultural society.* Cognella.

Reisch, M. (2018d). *Soziale arbeit den USA: Eine ungewisse Zukunft.* (Social work in the U.S.: An uncertain future) In H.-U. Otto, H. Thiersch, R. Treptown, & H. Ziegler (Eds.), *Handbuch soziale arbeit* (6th ed., pp. 1384–1399). Reinhardt.

Reisch, M. (2019a). Critical social work in the U.S.: Challenges and conflicts. In S. Webb (Ed.), *The Routledge handbook of critical social work* (pp. 35–45). Routledge.

Reisch, M. (2019b). Social work under Trump: Experiences from the USA. In K. Dunn & J. Fischer (Eds.), *Stifled progress: Social work and social policy in the era of right populism* (pp. 147–165). Barbara Budrich.

Reisch, M. (2019c). Social movements (Rev.). In C. Franklin (Ed.), *Encyclopedia of social work.* https://oxfordre.com/socialwork/

Reisch, M. (2019d). The interpretation of social justice, equality, and inequality in social work—A view from the U.S. In M. Payne & E. R. Hall (Eds.), *The Routledge handbook of social work theory* (pp. 122–134). Routledge.

Reisch, M. (2020a). The complicity of organized social work with McCarthyism. *Social Dialogue*, 22, 19–21.

Reisch, M. (2020b). Social movements. In D. Bailey & T. Mizrahi (Eds.), *Encyclopedia of macro social work.* Oxford University Press.

Reisch, M. (2020c). Promoting social justice through social work research in an "alternative facts" environment [Keynote address]. Annual Conference of the European Social Work Research Association, Bucharest, Romania.

Reisch, M., & Andrews, J. L. (2002). *The road not taken: A history of radical social work in the United States.* Routledge.

Reisch, M., & Garvin, C. (2016). *Social work and social justice: Concepts, challenges, and strategies.* Oxford University Press.

Reisch, M., & Jani, J.S. (2012). The new politics of social work practice: Understanding context to promote change. *British Journal of Social Work*, 42(6), 1132–1150.

Reisch, M., & Lowe, J. I. (2000). 'Of means and ends' revisited: Teaching ethical community organization in an unethical society. *Journal of Community Practice*, 7(1), 19–38.

Reisch, M., & Rivera, F. (1999). Ethical and racial conflicts in urban-based action research. *Journal of Community Practice*, 6(2), 49–62.

Reisch, M., & Taylor, C. L. (1985). Ethical guidelines for cutback management: A preliminary approach. In S. Slavin (Ed.), *Social administration: The management of the social services: Vol. II. Managing finances, personnel, and information in human services* (2nd ed., pp. 294–307). Haworth Press.

Reisch, M., Ife, J., & Weil, M. (2012). Social justice, human rights, values, and community practice. In M. Weil, M. Reisch, & M. Ohmer (Eds.), *Handbook of community practice* (2nd ed., pp. 73–103). Sage.

Reisch, M., Rivera, F., Flynn, H., Walser, E., & Bradford, C. (1995). *A case study of the Hope VI Project in San Francisco.* U.S. Department of Housing and Urban Development.

Reynolds, B. C. (1951). *Social work and social living.* NASW Press.

Rhodes, M. L. (1985, March–April). Gilligan's theory of moral development as applied to social work. *Social Work*, 30(2), 101–105.

Rhodes, M. L. (1992). Social work challenges: The boundaries of ethics. *Families in Society*, 73(1), 40–47.

Richmond, M. E. (1917). *Social diagnosis.* Russell Sage.

Richmond, M.E. (1922). *What is social casework? An introductory description.* Russell Sage.

Ringstad, R. (2008). The ethics of dual relationships: Beliefs and behaviors of clinical practitioners. *Families in Society: The Journal of Contemporary Social Work*, 89(1), 69–77.

Rivera, F., & Erlich, J. (1998). *Community organizing in a diverse society* (3rd ed.). Allyn & Bacon.

Rivlin, A. (2013). *Implementing the Affordable Care Act: Why is this so complex?* Brookings Institute. http://www.brookings.edu/blogs/up-front/posts/2013/07/08-affordable-care-act-implement-health-rivlin

Robinson, F. (2018). A feminist practical ethics of care. In C. Brown and R. Eckersley (Eds.), *The Oxford handbook of international political theory.* Oxford University Press.

Roe v. Wade, 410 U.S. 113 (1973).

Rollins, W. (2019). Social worker–client relationships: Social worker perspectives. *Australian Social Work*, 1–13. https://doi.org/10.1080/0312407X.2019.1669687

Rooney, R. H., & Mirick, R. G. (Eds.). (2018). *Strategies for work with involuntary clients.* Columbia University Press.

Roose, K. (2020, May 14). Bracing for a vaccine information war. *The New York Times*, B1, B7.

Rosen, T., Lien, C., Stern, M. E., Bloemen, E. M., Mysliwiec, R., McCarthy, T. J., Clark, S., Mulcare, M. R., Ribaudo, D. S., Lachs, M. S., Pillemer, K., & Flomenbaum, N. E. (2017). Emergency medical services perspectives on identifying and reporting victims of elder abuse, neglect, and self-neglect. *Journal of Emergency Medicine*, 53(4), 573–582. https://doi.org/10.1016/j.jemermed.2017.04.021

Ross, A. (2016). The social work voice: How could unions strengthen practice? *Aotearoa New Zealand Social Work*, 26(4), 4–13.

Ross, D. (2019). Practising community and dialogical communities of practice for ecological justice and loving relationships. *Australian Journal of Community Work*, 1, 1–13.

Ross, D. G., & Parks, M. (2018). Mutual respect in an ethic of care: A collaborative essay on power, trust, and stereotyping. *Teaching Ethics*, 18(1), 1–15.

Rothman, D. J. (1992, March 5). Rationing life. *New York Review of Books*, 32–37.

Royse, D., Dhooper, S. S., & Rompf, E. L. (2016). *Field instruction: A guide for social work students*. Waveland Press.

Rummery, K. (2016). Equalities: The impact of welfare reform and austerity by gender, disability and age. In H. Bochel & M. Powell (Eds.), *The coalition government and social policy: Restructuring the welfare state* (pp. 309–346). Policy Press.

Russell, A. (2017). Competent solidarity: The alternative for professional social work. *Aotearoa New Zealand Social Work*, 29(2), 137–144. https://doi.org/10.11157/anzswj-vol29iss2id406

Ruth, B. J., & Marshall, J. W. (2017). A history of social work in public health. *American Journal of Public Health*, 107(Suppl. 3), S236–S242. https://dx.doi.org/10.2105%2FAJPH.2017.304005

Saar-Heiman, Y., Lavie-Ajayi, M., & Krumer-Nevo, M. (2017). Poverty-aware social work practice: Service users' perspectives. *Child and Family Social Work*, 22(2), 1054–1063.

Sadowski-Smith, C. (2018). *The new immigrant whiteness: Race, neoliberalism, and post-Soviet migration to the United States* (Vol. 10). New York University Press.

Sage, M., Anthony, B., & Hitchcock, L. I. (2019). Navigating social and digital media for ethical and professional social work practice. In S. M. Marson & R. E. McKinney Jr. (Eds.), *The Routledge handbook of social work ethics and values*. Routledge.

Salamon, L. M. (1993). The marketization of welfare: Changing nonprofit and for-profit roles in the American welfare state. *Social Service Review*, 67(1), 16–39.

Salazar, A. M., Noell, B., Cole, J. J., Haggerty, K. P., & Roe, S. (2018). Incorporating self-determination into substance abuse prevention programming for youth transitioning from foster care to adulthood. *Child and Family Social Work*, 23(2), 281–288.

Saldov, M., and Kakai, H. (2016). The ethics of medical decision-making with Japanese-American elders in Hawaii: Signing informed consent documents without understanding them. In S. M. Cummings & C. Galambos (Eds.), *Diversity and Aging in the Social Environment* (pp. 131–172). Routledge.

Salvatore, S. (2017). The formalization of cultural psychology. Reasons and functions. *Integrative Psychological and Behavioral Science*, 51(1), 1–13.

Sandel, M. (2010). *Justice: What's the right thing to do?* Farrar, Straus, & Giroux.

Sandel, M. (2013). *What money can't buy: The moral limits of markets*. Farrar, Straus, & Giroux.

Sanders, R. K. (2017). Multiple relationships in faith communities. In O. Zur (Ed.), *Multiple relationships in psychotherapy and counseling: Unavoidable, common,* *and mandatory dual relations in therapy* (pp. 108–117). Routledge.

Sanders, S., & Hoffman, K. (2010). Ethics education in social work: Comparing outcomes of graduate social work students. *Journal of Social Work Education*, 46(1), 7–22. https://doi.org/10.5175/JSWE.2010.200800112

Scharf, M. P., & Tyus, B. (2018). Corporations on trial for human rights violations [Forward]. *Case Western Reserve Journal of International Law*, 50(1).

Schneier, E. (2019). *Putting people back in politics: The revival of American democracy* (2nd ed.). AuthorHouse.

Schrag, D., Hershman, D. L., & Basch, E. (2020). Oncology practice during the COVID-19 pandemic. *JAMA*. https://doi.org/10.1001/jama.2020.6236

Schram, S. F. (2018). Neoliberalizing the welfare state: Marketizing social policy/disciplining clients. In D. Cahill, M. Cooper, M. Konings, & D. Primrose (Eds.), *The Sage handbook of neoliberalism* (pp. 308–322). Sage.

Schriver, J.M. (1990, March). The gentrification of social work: Philosophical implications and value issues [Unpublished paper presentation]. 1990 Annual Program Meeting of the Council on Social Work Education, Reno, NV, United States.

Scollan, A., Farini, F., & McNeill, E. (2019). Irish social work at the crossroads: Cultural and organisational boundaries between professional practices and the voices of the children. *Journal Socialno delo/Journal of Social Work*.

Seattle, B. (2011). "Paternalistic" v. "self-organizing" communities [Unpublished paper].

Seervai, S. (2020, March 6). *Coronavirus reveals flaws in the U.S. healthcare system*. Commonwealth Fund. https://www.commonwealthfund.org/publications/podcast/2020/mar/coronavirus-reveals-flaws-us-health-system

Segal, E. A., & Wagaman, M. A. (2017). Social empathy as a framework for teaching social justice. *Journal of Social Work Education*, 53(2), 201–211.

Segal-Reich, M., Doron, I., & Mor, S. (2019). Ethical issues in advocacy by nonprofit organizations: The case of legal consultation and representation of older clients in Israel. *Journal of International Aging Law and Policy*, 10, 1–44.

Sen, A. (2009). *The idea of justice*. Harvard University Press.

Sennett, R. (1981). Paternalism, an authority of false love. In *Authority* (pp. 50–83). Norton.

Sexton, M. (2012). Assessing capacity to make decisions about long-term care needs: Ethical perspectives and practical challenges in hospital social work. *Ethics and Social Welfare*, 6(4), 411–417. https://doi.org/10.1080/17496535.2012.735817

Shannon, S. K. (2017). Punishment, religion, and the shrinking welfare state for the very poor in the United States, 1970–2010. *Socius*, 3. https://doi.org/10.1177%2F2378023117742259

Shapiro, J. P., & Stefkovich, J. A. (2016). *Ethical leadership and decision making in education: Applying theoretical perspectives to complex dilemmas*. Routledge.

Sharp, Z. (2018). Existential angst and identity rethink: The complexities of competition for the nonprofit. *Nonprofit and Voluntary Sector Quarterly, 47*(4), 767–788.

Shaub, W. M., Jr. (2020, February 7). Trump's quest for revenge could mean the end of whistleblowing. *Washington Post.* https://www.washingtonpost.com/outlook/trumps-quest-for-revenge-could-mean-the-end-of-whistleblowing/2020/02/07/a576b860-4918-11ea-9164-d3154ad8a5cd_story.html

Shaw, J. (2018). Introducing post-secular social work: Towards a post-liberal ethics of care. *British Journal of Social Work, 48*(2), 412–429.

Shdaimah, C., & Strier, R. (2020). Ethical conflicts in social work practice: Challenges and opportunities. *Ethics and Social Welfare, 14*(1), 1–5. https://doi.org/10.1080/17496535.2020.1718848

Shdaimah, C.S., & McGarry, B. (2018). Social workers' use of moral entrepreneurship to enact professional ethics in the field: Case studies from the social justice profession. *British Journal of Social Work, 48*(1), 21–36.

Shenoy, A., & Appel, J. M. (2017). Safeguarding confidentiality in electronic health records. *Cambridge Quarterly of Healthcare Ethics, 26*(2), 337–341.

Sheridan, M. J. (2010, May). Ethical issues in the use of prayer in social work: Implications for professional practice and education. *Families in Society, 91*(2), 112–120.

Sherwin, W., & Piven, F. F. (2019). The radical feminist legacy of the National Welfare Rights Organization. *Women's Studies Quarterly, 47*(3), 135–153.

Shlensky, E. L. (n.d.). Wholeness and holiness: Social justice as a vital component of religious living. *New Menorah, 5,* 11–12.

Shore, J. H., Yellowlees, P., Caudill, R., Johnston, B., Turvey, C., Mishkind, M., Krupinski, E., Myers, K., Shore, P., Kaftarian, E., & Hilty, D. (2018). Best practices in videoconferencing-based telemental health April 2018. *Telemedicine and e-Health, 24*(11), 827–832.

Sieghart, P. (1985). Professions as the conscience of society. *Journal of Medical Ethics, 11,* 117–122.

Silas, C.J. (n.d.). Perspectives. *Ethics Journal.*

Silva, E., Till, A., & Adshead, G. (2017). Ethical dilemmas in psychiatry: When teams disagree. *BJPsych Advances, 23*(4), 231–239.

Simmons, C. A., Shapiro, V. B., Accomazzo, S., & Manthey, T. J. (2016). Strengths-based social work: A meta-theory to guide social work research and practice. In N. Coady & P. Lehmann (Eds.), *Theoretical perspectives for direct social work practice* (3rd ed., pp. 131–154). Springer.

Simmons, C. A., & Rycraft, J. R. (2010). Ethical challenges for military social workers serving in a combat zone. *Social Work, 55*(1), 9–18.

Simon, B. L. (1994). *The empowerment tradition in American social work: A history.* Columbia University Press.

Singh, B. R. (1989). Neutrality and commitment in teaching moral and social issues in a multicultural society. *Educational Review, 40*(3), 227–242.

Singh, G., & Cowden, S. (2017). Is cultural sensitivity always a good thing? Arguments for a universalist social work. In M. Carey & L. Green (Eds.), *Practical social work ethics: Complex dilemmas within applied social care* (pp. 75–94). Routledge.

Skipper, A., Moore, T. J., & Marks, L. (2018). "The prayers of others helped": Intercessory prayer as a source of coping and resilience in Christian African American families. *Journal of Religion and Spirituality in Social Work: Social Thought, 37*(4), 373–394.

Sklar, K. K. (1990). Who funded Hull House? In L. McCarthy (Ed.): *Lady bountiful revisited* (pp. 94–115). Rutgers University Press.

Sklar, K. K. (1995). *Florence Kelley and the nation's work: The rise of women's political culture, 1830–1900.* Yale University Press.

Slater, E. L. (2020). Private practice social workers' commitment to social justice. *Clinical Social Work Journal,* 1–9.

Smith, D. L. (2018). Manufacturing monsters: Dehumanization and public policy. In D. Boonin (Ed.), *The Palgrave handbook of philosophy and public policy* (pp. 263–275). Palgrave Macmillan.

Smith, M. (2020). Recognising strategy and tactics in constructing and working with involuntary social work clients. *Australian Social Work, 73,* 321–333. https://doi.org/10.1080/0312407X.2020.1717562

Smith, M. J., Thompson, A., & Upshur, R. E. (2019). Public health as social justice? A qualitative study of public health policy-makers' perspectives. *Social Justice Research, 32*(3), 384–402.

Smith, M. R., Villenueve, M., & Santana, R. (2020, April 4). Competition for supplies sharpening as coronavirus pandemic worsens. *Boston Globe.* https://www.bostonglobe.com/2020/04/04/nation/competition-supplies-sharpening-coronavirus-pandemic-worsens/

Smith, S. (2012). Personalisation in social work. *Ethics and Social Welfare, 6*(4), 419–421. https://doi.org/10.1080/17496535.2012.735819

Smith, S. J., & Davis, A. J. (1980, August). Ethical dilemmas: Conflicts among rights, duties, and obligations. *American Journal of Nursing, 80*(8), 1463–1466.

Solnica, A., Barski, L., & Jotkowitz, A. (2020). Allocation of scarce resources during the COVID-19 pandemic: A Jewish ethical perspective. *Journal of Medical Ethics, 46*(7). https://doi.org/10.1136/medethics-2020-106242

Song, K. H. (2016). *Multicultural and international approaches in social work practice: An intercultural perspective.* Rowman & Littlefield.

Soss, J., Ford, R. C., & Schram, S. F. (2011). *Disciplining the poor: Neoliberal paternalism and the persistent power of race.* University of Chicago Press.

Specht, H., & Courtenay, M. (1994). *Unfaithful angels: How social work abandoned its mission.* Free Press.

Spolander, G., Engelbrecht, L., & Pullen Sansfaçon, A. (2016). Social work and macro-economic neoliberalism:

Beyond the social justice rhetoric. *European Journal of Social Work*, 19(5), 634–649.

Stanger, A. (2020). *Whistleblowers: Honesty in America from Washington to Trump*. Yale University Press.

Steenhuysen, J. (2020, March 30). *U.S. panel outlines how doctors should ration care in a pandemic*. Reuters. https://www.reuters.com/article/us-health-coronavirus-usa-care/u-s-panel-outlines-how-doctors-should-ration-care-in-a-pandemic-idUSKBN21I03C

Steiner, H. (2018). On the conflict between liberty and equality. In D. Schmidtz & C. E. Pavel (eds.), *The Oxford handbook of freedom* (pp. 76–89). Oxford University Press.

Stepney, P. (2019). Empowerment ideas in social work. In M. Payne & E. R. Hall (Eds.), *The Routledge handbook of social work theory* (pp. 331–339). Routledge.

Stern, M. J., & Axinn, J. (2017). *Social welfare: A history of the American response to need* (8th ed.). Pearson.

Stoltzfus Jost, T. (2017). The morality of health care reform: Liberal and conservative views and the space between them. *Hastings Center Report*, 47(6), 9–13.

Strickland, J. C., & Stoops, W. W. (2018). Evaluating autonomy, beneficence, and justice with substance-using populations: Implications for clinical research participation. *Psychology of Addictive Behaviors*, 32(5), 552–563. https://psycnet.apa.org/doi/10.1037/adb0000378

Strier, R., & Bershtling, O. (2016). Professional resistance in social work: Counterpractice assemblages. *Social Work*, 61(2), 111–118.

Strom-Gottfried, K. (2016). *Straight talk about professional ethics* (2nd ed.). Oxford University Press.

Strom-Gottfried, K. (2019). Ethical action in challenging times. In S. M. Marson & R. E. McKinney Jr. (Eds.), *The Routledge handbook of social work ethics and values*. Routledge.

Sun, A. Y., & Wasser, T. (2017). Confidentiality and privilege. In T. Wasser (Ed.), *Psychiatry and the Law* (pp. 21–33). Springer.

Sunker, H. (2020). Social work and social care under National Socialism. *Social Dialogue*, 22, 25–26.

Sutton, A., & Carlson, C. (2019). Advocating for self-determination, arriving at safety. In S. M. Marson & R. E. McKinney Jr. (Eds.), *The Routledge handbook of social work ethics and values*. Routledge.

Sweifach, J. S., Linzer, N., & LaPorte, H. H. (2015). Beneficence vs. fidelity: Serving social work clients in the aftermath of catastrophic events. *Journal of Social Work Values and Ethics*, 12(1), 3–12.

Szczygiel, P. (2019). Navigating student self-disclosure through a relational lens: Examples of increased self-awareness from a social work classroom. *Clinical Social Work Journal*, 1–8.

Tarasoff v. Regents of the University of California, 13 *Cal. 3d* 177, 118 *Cal. Rptr.* 129, 529 P. 2d 553 (1974).

Tarasoff v. Regents of the University of California, 17 *Cal. 3d* 425, 131 *Cal. Rptr.* 14, 551 P. 2d 334 (1976).

Tarpinian, G. (2011, March 7). Bargaining rights are human rights. *HuffPost*. https://www.huffpost.com/entry/bargaining-rights-are-hum_b_831957

Taylor, N., Fraser, H., Signal, T., & Prentice, K. (2014). Social work, animal-assisted therapies and ethical considerations: A programme example from Central Queensland, Australia. *British Journal of Social Work*, 46(1), 135–152. https://doi.org/10.1093/bjsw/bcu115

Teaster, P. B., & Anetzberger, G. (2019). The intersection of ethics and vulnerable elders. *Innovation in Aging, 3* (Suppl. 1), S238–239.

Theobald, J., Gardner, F., & Long, N. (2017). Teaching critical reflection in social work field education. *Journal of Social Work Education*, 53(2), 300–311.

Thomas, D.C. (1978, December). Training in medical ethics: An ethics workup. *Forum in Medicine*, 1(9), 33–36.

Thompson v. County of Alameda, 27 *Cal. 3d* 741, 167 *Cal. Rptr.* 70, 614 P. 2d 728, 735 (Sup. Ct.) (1980).

Thompson, H. B., & Thompson, H. O. (1981). *Ethics in nursing*. MacMillan.

Thompson, L. J., & Wadley, D. A. (2018). Countering globalisation and managerialism: Relationist ethics in social work. *International Social Work*, 61(5), 706–723.

Thyer, B. A. (2010). Social justice: A conservative perspective. *Journal of Comparative Social Welfare*, 26(2–3), 261–274.

Tice, C. J., Long, D. D., & Cox, L. E. (2019). *Macro social work practice: Advocacy in action*. Sage.

Tiitinen, L. (2020). The power of silence: Silencing as a method of preventing whistleblowing. *European Journal of Social Work*, 23(1), 68––.

Timms, N. (2018). *Social work values: An enquiry*. Routledge.

Titmuss, R. (2018). *The gift relationship: From human blood to social policy*. Policy Press.

Tobach, E. (n.d.). *Personal is political is personal is political* [Unpublished paper]. American Museum of Natural History.

Toft, J., & Calhoun, M. (2020). The unexamined identity: Students' conservative ideology, perspectives of poverty, and implications for practice. *Journal of Social Work Education*, 56(1), 1–17.

Towle, C. (1945). *Common human needs*. U.S. Department of Health, Education, and Welfare.

Towle, C. (1957). *Common human needs* (Rev. ed.). National Association of Social Workers.

Travis, D. J., Lizano, E. L., & Mor Barak, M. E. (2016). 'I'm so stressed!': A longitudinal model of stress, burnout and engagement among social workers in child welfare settings. *British Journal of Social Work*, 46(4), 1076–1095.

Trimberger, G., & Bugenhagen, M.J. (2015). A new look at an old issue: A constructive-development approach to professional boundaries. *Journal of Social Work Values and Ethics*, 12(1), 13–28.

Trnka, R., Kuška, M., Tavel, P., & Kuběna, A. A. (2019). Social work leaders' authenticity positively influences their dispositions toward ethical decision-making.

European Journal of Social Work. https://doi.org/10.1080/13 691457.2019.1608513

Turan, N., İpekçi, B., & Yılmaz, M. Y. (2019). Self-determination and psychological adaptation in forcibly displaced people. *New England Journal of Public Policy, 31*(2), Art. 11.

Ugurluoglu, O., Aldogan, E. U., Turgut, M., & Ozatkan, Y. (2018). The effect of paternalistic leadership on job performance and intention to leave the job. *Journal of Health Management, 20*(1), 46–55.

Unguru, E. (2018). The limits of confidentiality and of the right to privacy: A bioethical approach to social work. In A. Sandu & A. Frunza (Eds.), *Ethical issues in social work practice* (pp. 155–173). IGI Global.

United Nations (1948). *Universal declaration of human rights.* https://www.un.org/en/universal-declaration-human-rights/index.html

Úriz, M. J., Idareta, F., Viscarret, J. J., & Ballestero, A. (2017). Methodologies for ethical decision making in social work. *Ljetopis socijalnog rada. 24*(1), 33–54. https://hrcak.srce.hr/index.php?show=clanak&id_clanak_jezik=273185

Valutis, S. (2012). Professional socialization and social work values: Who are we teaching? *Social Work Education, 31*(8), 1046–1057. https://doi.org/10.1080/02615479.2011.610785

Valutis, S., & Rubin, D. (2016). Value conflicts in social work: Categories and correlates. *Journal of Social Work Values and Ethics, 13*(1). 11–24.

Van Breda, A. D. (2018). A critical review of resilience theory and its relevance for social work. *Social Work, 54*(1), 1–18. https://doi.org/10.15270/54-1-611

Varghese, R. (2020). Intergroup dialogue: Frequencies of social justice. *Social Work with Groups, 43*(1–2), 109–113.

Vecchione, A. (2012, September 26). Debating the ethical implications of the Affordable Care Act. *NJSpotlight.* http://www.njspotlight.com/stories/12/09/26/ethical-implications-of-the-affordable-care-act/

Visse, M., Widdershoven, G. A., & Abma, T. A. (2012). Moral learning in an integrated social and healthcare service network. *Health Care Analysis, 20*(3), 281–296.

Voshel, E. H., & Wesala, A. (2015). Social media and social work ethics: Determining best practices in an ambiguous reality. *Journal of Social Work Values and Ethics, 12*(1), 67–76.

Wahler, E. (2012). Identifying and challenging social work students' biases. *Social Work Education, 31*(8), 1058–1070. https://doi.org/10.1080/02615479.2011.616585

Wakefield, J. C. (2016). Psychological justice: Distributive justice and psychiatric treatment of the non-disordered. In M. Reisch (Ed.), *The Routledge international handbook of social justice* (pp. 353–384). Routledge.

Wald, L. (1915). *The house on Henry Street.* Henry Holt.

Walker, P., & Tumilty, E. (2019). Developing ethical frameworks in animal-assisted social service delivery in Aotearoa, New Zealand. *British Journal of Social Work, 49*(1), 163–182.

Wallace, C. L., Thielman, K. J., Cimino, A. N., & Adams Rueda, H. L. (2017). Ethics at the end of life: A teaching tool. *Journal of Social Work Education, 53*(2), 327–338.

Walter-McCabe, H. (2020). Coronavirus pandemic calls for an immediate social work response. *Social Work in Health Care, 35*(3), 69–72.

Walton, M. T. (2018). Administrative discharges in addiction treatment: Bringing practice in line with ethics and evidence. *Social Work, 63*(1), 85–88.

Wand, A. P. F., Zhong, B. L., Chiu, H. F. K., Draper, B., & De Leo, D. (2020). Covid-19: The implications for suicide in older adults. *International Psychogeriatrics.* https://doi.org/10.1017%2FS1041610220000770

Ward, A. S., & Ward, T. (2016). The complexities of dual relationships in forensic and correctional practice: Safety vs. care. In O. Zur (Ed.), *Multiple relationships in psychotherapy and counseling* (pp. 84–93). Routledge.

Ward, L., & Barnes, M. (2016). Transforming practice with older people through an ethic of care. *British Journal of Social Work, 46*(4), 906–922.

Warner, J. (2015). *The emotional politics of social work and child protection.* Policy Press.

Warzel, C. (2020, May 5). Open states, lots of guns. America is paying a heavy price for freedom. *The New York Times.* https://www.nytimes.com/2020/05/05/opinion/coronavirus-deaths.html

Weaver, H. (2016). Indigenous struggles for justice. In M. Reisch (Ed.), *The Routledge international handbook of social justice* (pp. 111–122). Routledge.

Wehmeyer, M. L., & Shogren, K. A. (2016). Self-determination and choice. In N. Singh (Ed.), *Handbook of evidence-based practices in intellectual and developmental disabilities* (pp. 561–584). Springer.

Weil, J. G. (2020). Constructing maternalism from paternalism: The case of state milk programs. In A. Ramm & J. Gideon (Eds.), *Motherhood, social policies and women's activism in Latin America* (pp. 69–95). Palgrave Macmillan.

Weinberg, M. (2010). The social construction of social work ethics: Politicizing and broadening the lens. *Journal of Progressive Human Services, 21*(1), 32–44. https://doi.org/10.1080/10428231003781774

Weinberg, M. (2016). *Paradoxes in social work: Mitigating ethical trespass.* Routledge.

Weisman, D. (1990, March). Strikes in field placements: Ethical dilemmas for social work students and faculty. Unpublished paper presented at the Annual Program Meeting of the Council on Social Work Education. Reno, NV, United States.

Welsh, D., Anastasio, J., Fulton, S., & Quast, S. (2019). Rethinking the federal-state relationship. *Environmental Law Reporter News and Analysis, 49*, 10619–10630.

Weng, S. S., & Gray, L. (2020). Racial microaggressions within social work: Perceptions of providers. *Journal of Social Work Practice, 34*(1), 67–80.

Wenocur, S., & Reisch, M. (1989). *From charity to enterprise: The development of American social work in a market economy*. University of Illinois Press.

Wheeler, A. M., & Bertram, B. (2019). *The counselor and the law: A guide to legal and ethical practice*. Wiley.

White, L. (2017). How autonomy can legitimate beneficial coercion. In J. Gather, T. Henking, A. Nossek, & J. Vollmann (Eds.), *Beneficial coercion in psychiatry?* (pp. 85–99). Brill.

Whittington, C., & Whittington, M. (2007). Ethics and social care: Political, organizational and interagency dimensions. In A. Leathard & S. McLaren (Eds.), *Ethics: Contemporary challenges in health and social care* (pp. 83–96). Cassell.

"Who shall live and who shall die?" (1978, May 6) [Editorial]. *The New York Times*, A22.

Wilkins, D. (2012). Ethical dilemmas in social work practice with disabled people: Young adults with autism. *Ethics and Social Welfare*, 6(1), 97–105.

Will, G. F. (2007, October 14). Code of coercion. *The Washington Post*. https://www.washingtonpost.com/wp-dyn/content/article/2007/10/12/AR2007101202151.html

Willis. N. G., & Molina, V. (2019). Self-care and the social worker: Taking our place in the *Code*. *Social Work*, 64(1), 83–84.

Willner, L. (2019). Organizational legitimacy and managerialism within social justice nonprofit organizations: An interest divergence analysis. *Administrative Theory and Praxis*, 41(3), 225–244.

Wilson, F. (2016). Identifying, preventing, and addressing job burnout and vicarious burnout for social work professionals. *Journal of Evidence-Informed Social Work*, 13(5), 479–483.

Wilson, S. J. (1980). *Confidentiality in social work: Issues and principles*. Simon & Schuster.

Winskel, H., & Bhatt, D. (2019). The role of culture and language in moral decision-making. *Culture and Brain*. https://doi.org/10.1007/s40167-019-00085-y

Wise, S. S. (1909). The conference sermon: Charity vs. justice. In A. Johnson (Ed.), *Proceedings of the National Conference of Charities and Corrections* (Vol. 36, pp. 20–29). Fort Wayne Publishing.

Witkin, S. L., & Irving, A. (2016). Post-modern perspectives on social justice. In M. Reisch (Ed.), *The Routledge international handbook of social justice* (pp. 188–201). Routledge.

Witt, H., Hyatt, E. G., Franklin, C., & Younes, M. N. (2019). Self-determination and abortion access. In S. M. Marson & R. E. McKinney Jr. (Eds.), *The Routledge handbook of social work ethics and values*. Routledge.

Wolfer, T. A., Hodge, D. R., & Steele, J. (2018). Rethinking client self-determination in social work: A Christian perspective as a philosophical foundation for client choice. *Social Work and Christianity*, 45(2), 3–32.

Wong, G., & Ng, B. C. (2018). Moral judgement in early bilinguals: Language dominance influences responses to moral dilemmas. *Frontiers in Psychology*, 9. https://doi.org/10.3389/fpsyg.2018.01070

Woodard, C. (2017). *American character: A history of the epic struggle between individual liberty and the common good*. Penguin.

Woodcock, R. (2011). Ethical standards in the NASW *Code of Ethics*: The explicit legal model, and beyond. *Families in Society*, 92(1), 21–27.

Wooten, N. R. (2015). Military social work: Opportunities and challenges for social work education. *Journal of Social Work Education*, 51(Suppl. 1), S6–S25.

Wronka, J. (2016a). *Human rights and social justice: Social action and service for the helping and health professions*. Sage.

Wronka, J. (2016b). Human rights as pillars of social justice. In M. Reisch (Ed.), *The Routledge international handbook of social justice* (pp. 216–226). Routledge.

Yan, M. C. (2016). Multiple positionality and intersectionality: Towards a dialogical social work approach. In A. Al-Krenawi, J. R. Graham, & N. Habibov (Eds.), *Diversity and Social Work in Canada* (pp. 114–138). Oxford University Press.

Yingling, M. E. (2016). The mother state and her weaker children: Social work and the institutionalization of the "feebleminded." *Affilia*, 31(4), 504–519.

Young, D. R. (2006). Complementary, supplementary, or adversarial? Nonprofit-government relations. In E. T. Boris & C. E. Steuerle (Eds.), *Nonprofits and government: Collaboration and conflict* (pp. 37–80). Urban Institute.

Young, J. A., McLeod, D. A., & Brady, S. R. (2018). The ethics challenge: 21st century social work education, social media, and digital literacies. *Journal of Social Work Values and Ethics*, 15(1), 13–22.

Younggren, J., & Gottlieb, M. (2016). Mandated multiple relationships and ethical decision making. In O. Zur (Ed.), *Multiple relationships in psychotherapy and counseling: Unavoidable, common, and mandatory dual relations in therapy* (pp. 42–56). Routledge.

Zhou, X., Snoswell, C. L., Harding, L. E., Bambling, M., Edirippulige, S., Bai, X., & Smith, A. C. (2020). The role of telehealth in reducing the mental health burden from COVID-19. *Telemedicine and e-Health*, 26(4), 377–379.

Zizek, S. (2018). Lacan between cultural studies and cognitivism. In J. Glynos & Y. Stavrakakis (Eds.), *Lacan and Science* (pp. 291–320). Routledge.

Zúñiga, X., Lopez, G., & Ford, K. A. (Eds.). (2016). *Intergroup dialogue: Engaging difference, social identities and social justice*. Routledge.

Zur, O. (2017). Introduction: The multiple relationships spectrum. In O. Zur (Ed.), *Multiple relationships in psychotherapy and counselling: Unavoidable, common, and mandatory dual relations in therapy*. Routledge.

Index

www.ingramcontent.com/pod-product-compliance
Lightning Source LLC
LaVergne TN
LVHW061131060425
807852LV00006B/503